Jean-Luc Godard is one of the two or three most significant filmmakers of the contemporary era. An extraordinarily inventive and challenging filmmaker, his series of movies in the 1960s remain some of the richest works in the history of cinema.

There's no one else quite like Godard. Where the flood of movies globally now runs into many thousands, Godard's works stand out as original, acerbic, romantic, ironic, humorous and explorative.
This book includes chapters on all of Godard's output.

❊

'Everyone is searching. Everyone is in between'.

Jean-Luc Godard

MEDIA, FEMINISM, CULTURAL STUDIES

The Sacred Cinema of Andrei Tarkovsky
by Jeremy Mark Robinson

Liv Tyler
by Thomas A. Christie

Stepping Forward: Essays, Lectures and Interviews
by Wolfgang Iser

Wild Zones: Pornography, Art and Feminism
by Kelly Ives

'Cosmo Woman': The World of Women's Magazines
by Oliver Whitehorne

The Cinema of Richard Linklater
by Thomas A. Christie

Walerian Borowczyk
by Jeremy Mark Robinson

Andrea Dworkin
by Jeremy Mark Robinson

Cixous, Irigaray, Kristeva: The Jouissance of French Feminism
by Kelly Ives

Sex in Art: Pornography and Pleasure in Painting and Sculpture
by Cassidy Hughes

*The Erotic Object: Sexuality in Sculpture
From Prehistory to the Present Day*
by Susan Quinnell

Women in Pop Music
by Helen Challis

Detonation Britain: Nuclear War in the UK
by Jeremy Mark Robinson

Julia Kristeva: Art, Love, Melancholy, Philosophy, Semiotics
by Kelly Ives

Luce Irigaray: Lips, Kissing, and the Politics of Sexual Difference
by Kelly Ives

Helene Cixous I Love You: The Jouissance *of Writing*
by Kelly Ives

JEAN-LUC GODARD

JEAN-LUC GODARD

THE PASSION OF CINEMA /

LA PASSION DU CINÉMA

VOLUME 2: 1968 ONWARDS

Jeremy Mark Robinson

CRESCENT MOON

First published 2009. Second edition 2024.
© Jeremy Mark Robinson 2009/ 2024.

Set in Rotis Serif, 10 on 14pt.
Designed by Radiance Graphics.

The right of Jeremy Mark Robinson to be identified as the author of this book has been asserted generally in accordance with sections 77 and 78 of the Copyright, Designs and Patents Act 1988.

All rights reserved. No part of this book may be reprinted or reproduced, stored in a retrieval system, or transmitted, in any form or by any means, electronic, mechanical, photocopying, recording or otherwise, without permission from the publisher.

British Library Cataloguing in Publication data available for this title.

ISBN-13 9781861712981
ISBN-13 9781861713315

Crescent Moon Publishing
P.O. Box 1312
Maidstone, Kent
ME14 5XU, Great Britain
www.crmoon.com

CONTENTS

Acknowledgements ✦ *10*
Abbreviations ✦ *12*

PART ONE: JEAN-LUC GODARD

1   Introduction: Godard Cinema / Godard Cinéma ✦ *18*

PART TWO: CINÉMA/CINEMA

16 The Political Films of 1968-1973 ✦ *39*
17 *Un Film Comme les Autres/ A Film Like the Others* ✦ *52*
18 *British Sounds/ See You At Mao* ✦ *60*
19 *Pravda/ Pravda* ✦ *67*
20 *Vent d'Est / Wind From the East* ✦ *75*
21 *Luttes en Italie/ Struggle In Italy* ✦ *90*
22 *Vladimir et Rosa/ Vladimir and Rosa* ✦ *100*
23 *Tout Va Bien / All's Well* ✦ *112*
24 *Sauve Qui Peut (La Vie) / Slow Motion* ✦ *125*
25 *Passion / Passion* ✦ *142*
26 *Prénom: Carmen / First Name Carmen* ✦ *168*
27 *Je Vous Salue, Marie / Hail Mary* ✦ *183*
28 *Détective / Detective* ✦ *215*
29 *King Lear / King Lear* ✦ *222*
30 *Histoire(s) du Cinéma / Stor/ies of Cinema* ✦ *231*
31 *Nouvelle Vague/ New Wave* ✦ *251*
32 *Hélas Pour Moi / Woe Is Me* ✦ *257*
33 *JLG/ JLG / JLG/ JLG* ✦ *269*
34 *Éloge de l'Amour / In Praise of Love* ✦ *274*
35 *Notre Musique / Our Music* ✦ *296*
36 *Film Socialisme / Socialism* ✦ *306*
37 *Adieu au Langage / Goodbye To Language* ✦ *319*
38 Other Films Directed By Jean-Luc Godard ✦ *342*

APPENDICES ✦ *360*
    Film Availability ✦ *361*
    Godardisms ✦ *362*
    The Best of Godard ✦ *363*
    Ingredients For a Godard Movie ✦ *365*
    Fans On the Films of Jean-Luc Godard ✦ *367*
Filmography ✦ *371*
Bibliography ✦ *374*

ACKNOWLEDGEMENTS

Thanks to Colin MacCabe, Chris Fassnidge and Danny Rivers.

To the authors and publishers quoted.
To the copyright holders of the illustrations.
Gaumont. New Yorker Films. Jerry Ohlinger Archives. Cinema Parallel. Collection la Bibliothéque du Film. Argos Films.

Every effort has been made to contact copyright owners of the illustrations. No copyright infringement is intended. We welcome enquiries about any copyright issues for future editions of this book.

ABBREVIATIONS

G   *Godard On Godard*, ed. T. Milne, 1986
M   *Godard, Images, Sound, Politics*, C. MacCabe, 1980
Mac   *Godard*, C. MacCabe, 2003
B   *Everything Is Cinema*, R. Brody, 2008

'This life is either nothing, or it has to be everything'.

Jean-Luc Godard

Roland Quilici©

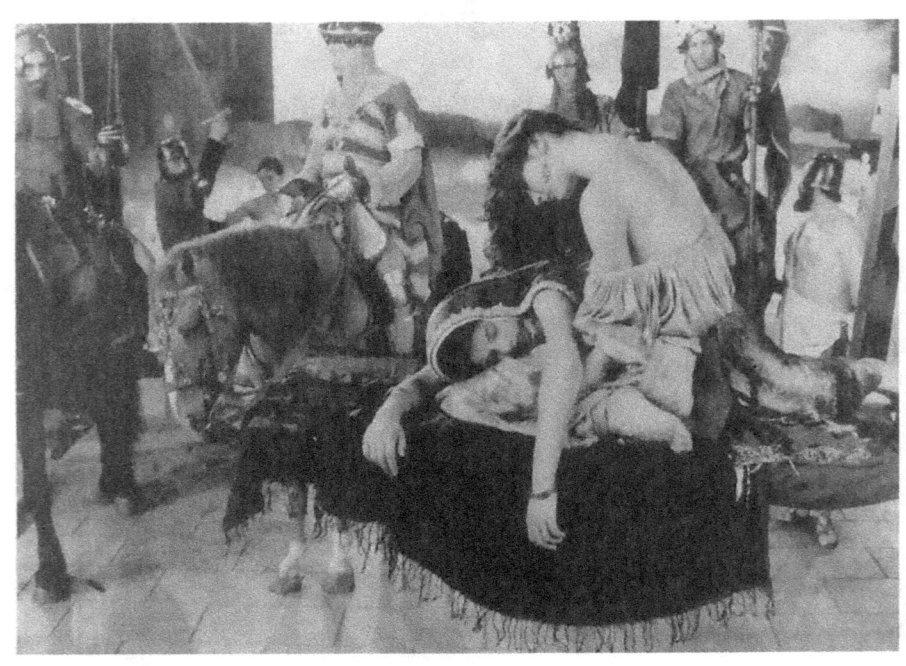

PART ONE

JEAN-LUC GODARD

Cette obscure clarté qui tombe des étoiles.
(This dark brightness that falls from the stars.)

Pierre Corneille, *Le Cid*

I

INTRODUCTION

GODARD CINEMA / GODARD CINÉMA

Everything can be put into a film. Everything should be put into a film.

Jean-Luc Godard (G, 239)

An original, a one-off, a genius – there's no one else quite like Jean-Luc Godard. You could take a few frames from one of his films and know they were by the Maître and nobody else. Where the flood of movies globally now runs into many thousands, and most are interchangeable, or barely make any impression at all, Godard's works stand out as individual, acerbic, romantic, ironic, humorous and explorative.

Watching Jean-Luc Godard's films again after a gap can be astonishing. He remains one of the most inventive and challenging of filmmakers. His series of films in the 1960s (sixteen features!) are still some of the richest works in the history of cinema – a run of movies with few parallels.

I first saw Jean-Luc Godard's films, appropriately enough, at film school in the early 1980s, where our tutor Chris Fassnidge showed us 16mm prints of *Breathless*, *Weekend* (on April 8, 1983) and *Masculin/Féminin* (June 1, 1983), among others. These films make an immediate impact as the work of one of the most distinctive voices in all of film.

Later, I went to double bills of God-Art's movies at the repertory cinemas in London. I remember seeing *Slow Motion* and *Prénom Carmen* in Bloomsbury with Sergio (a guy from São Paolo) and his girlfriend, Sarah Webb, a friend of my sister's (Sarah had much better French than me, having working in Switzerland as an *au pair*. I remember she laughed a lot more at Godard's films than the British audience in the cinema – there seemed to be more jokes and humour in the film than carried through to the subtitles, or to the po-faced British audience). Godard 'seems so serious, but you always had great fun', recalled actress Anna Karina.

For me, Jean-Luc Godard is one of the two or three most significant filmmakers of the period 1960-2010. The others would be Ingmar Bergman and Akira Kurosawa. Go and look at Orson Welles, and *Citizen Kane* in particular, is advice sometimes handed out to film students. Similarly, you can tell people who want to know about contemporary cinema: just go and look at Godard's films. He does *everything*. And then some. Don't bother with whoever is touted as the latest trendy filmmaker (Quentin Tarantino, Luc Besson, Robert

Rodriguez, Christopher Nolan, Kevin Smith, Steven Soderbergh, etc), just go to Godard. Godard has several movies in the top movie lists among critics: *Contempt, Vivre Sa Vie, Pierrot le Fou*[1] and *Breathless*.

While for some film critics watching a Jean-Luc Godard film can be a painful experience – because it's a foreign (i.e., non-American, non-English) film, or because it's an art film (and a European art film), or because it's a *Godard* film (Godard has plenty of detractors) – for me it's hugely enjoyable. Watching a Godard film isn't like doing 'homework',[2] as taking on 'foreign' or subtitled films can be for many. Let's face it, given the choice between watching a big, loud action-adventure film like *Star Wars* or *James Bond* or a soft-centred romantic comedy like *You Got Mail* or *What Women Want,* and watching a Godard film, many audiences will go for Hollywood every time.

I don't agree: a Jean-Luc Godard film like *Pierrot le Fou* or *A Woman Is a Woman* or *Masculin/ Féminin* or *Hail Mary* is very enjoyable: there's constant invention, a lot of humour, and even if you don't 'get it' all, there are beautiful and amazing people like Anna Karina or Jean-Pierre Léaud or Myriem Roussel to watch.

The rapid pace, as Pauline Kael noted (in *Going Steady*), Jean-Luc Godard's restlessness, irritates some viewers (1971, 92), but it's another aspect that's very enjoyable (and helps his movies to stay fresh and not appear dated). By comparison, so many contemporary, Western movies are s-o-o-o-o s-l-o-w. I agree with Orson Welles:[3] do we need to see a shot which shows a character walking right to the end of the road? (no! – Some of us have got lives to lead!). This is one of the chief appeals of Hong Kong action cinema and Japanese *anime*: they are *very fast*.

Jean-Luc Godard assumes that his audience can follow his movies, can understand the cultural and historical references, and enjoys the Americanized, cartoony devices he employs (P. Kael, 92-93). But for the viewers who want a serious, European sensibility, that too can irritate.

So, watching a Godard-helmed movie, you might look for a story. No, there isn't really one. So then you might look for characters. Umm, not really – fragments of characterization, possibly. OK, so you search for themes. Yes – but presented in such a casual, jigsaw (or wilfully obscure) manner, you'll have to work to put the pieces together.

---

1 *Pierrot le Fou* is no. 43 in *Sight & Sound*'s 2012 poll of top movies among critics. *Pierrot le Fou* 'feels like the audacity of a new artistic vision', as David Thomson put it (2012, 380).
2 But Godard's work can seem demanding: Godard makes the audience part of the collaboration: 'Godard makes his audiences work, and demands their full attention and participation at all times,' pointed out Wheeler Dixon (51).
3 Welles was thinking of Michelangelo Antonioni.

D'accord, you could look for performances. Some, but disconnected with (and in) each other – you get 30 seconds of an interesting performance, but then 4m 15s of not much. So then you hunt out ideas, say, or philosophy, or other bits of cleverness (like quotations/ allusions/ *hommages,* etc).

No wonder, then, that some people, including 100s of highly respected critics, many celebrated filmmakers, and thousands of fans, find Godard's movies as director/ writer boring, stupid, patronizing, narrow-minded, pretentious, ugly, chauvinist, anti-semitic, obscure, and difficult. (Sometimes Godard's films don't make it easy for the viewer in other ways: the repeated cuts to a black screen, the repetition of takes, the captions, the brutal chopping up of music, the alarming use of sound, and so on).

Maybe Godard's films should include a summary of the plot like the crawl in *Star Wars*: a few short paragraphs to tell the punters the plot.

Certainly Jean-Luc Godard's films have polarized critics, and tended to create intense reactions, for and against. But there's no ignoring Godard: he's a giant. Among Godard's supporters among critics were Susan Sontag,[4] Richard Roud, Andrew Sarris, Pauline Kael,[5] Vincent Canby, Colin MacCabe, and David Sterritt. (More on Godard's cultural impact below).

Some of Jean-Luc Godard's films have been received badly by critics, and have had bad screenings. The screening of *Le Gai Savoir* in Berlin was 'disastrous', and the audience walked out; when *Un Film comme les autres* was shown at the Lincoln Center in Gotham more than 900 people left, leaving less than 100 to watch the second reel. (And Godard's films have been released out of sequence in the U.S.A., which hasn't helped.[6] It took a while for North[7] America to go Godardian: *Breathless* was shown in 1961, *Vivre Sa Vie* in 1963, but by 1965, the pictures *A Woman Is a Woman, Contempt, A Married Woman, Band of Outsiders* and *Alphaville* had not been released. *La Chinoise* was a hit, however, in the U.S.A.; it opened in Gotham onq April 3, 1968).

---

4 For Sontag, Godard was 'one of the great culture heroes of our time' (*Styles of Radical Will*, Farrar, Straus & Giroux, New York, 1966, 150).
5 Pauline Kael attributed the influence of her writings about Godard to being hired on the *New Yorker*, because they had attracted the attention of the editor, William Shawn. However, Kael didn't get *Slow Motion*, and was among some other American critics who found Godard's later work increasingly difficult.
6 According to Jonathan Rosenbaum, the films have been released in this sequence: 1, 4, 6, 3, 8, 2, 9, 7, 10, 11, 12, 5, 14, 13, 15, 17, 16 (1992).
7 Using the term *North* America, which I do all the time now, is Godardian – in *Éloge de L'Amour*, a character complains that 'America' has no name or history. Do you mean South America? Brazil? Canada? What is 'America'?

J.-L. Godard's films are also difficult to market – not only do they not fit into a particular niche or genre (even when they are genre films, such as thrillers), they can't be summed up in a few words. They are anti-high concept. They have unusual stories, and subjects, and don't always feature recognizable stars.

I don't think *absolutely everything* Jean-Luc Godard has produced (or said) has been a work of genius. Watching Godard's output in the cold light of film criticism[8] reveals some failures: *Slow Motion*, for instance, which some critics greatly admire, is very flawed, *Detective* and *The Soldiers* are patchy, the agit-prop late 1960s/ early 1970s films are very hard-going (and sometimes close to unwatchable), and *King Lear* can appear so bad you wish that Godard had never made it.

It's extraordinary (but not all that surprising) that God-Art, I mean Godard, doesn't rate himself very highly as an *auteur*.

> John Cassavetes, who was more or less my age – now he was a great director. I can't imagine myself as his equal in cinema. For me he represents a certain cinema that's way up above. (2000)

And Jean-Luc Godard told Andrew Sarris in 1994 that he didn't think he'd

> succeeded in making any really good films. There are moments, scenes, whole movements that sing. It has all added up to a cinema of sorts, even though I'm still learning my art. (1994)

Jean-Luc Godard was acutely aware of his own status as a filmmaker in the film community; he knew that he was worshipped by some people. Godard said that some folk, especially men,

> are too overwhelmed by the name... in any relationship with me they [the public] have too much respect and too much admiration, which is ruinous. You can't have a normal relationship, you're constantly being put in an elevated position. (M, 76)[9]

Jean-Luc Godard's films are so recognizable, so familiar, it can seem not only that they are part of your life, as familiar films are of course, but that you have participated in them in some way. Some critics have felt that they *could* have made this or that Godard film, so they *did* make the film. Godard's pictures do seem to enter the bloodstream, the unconscious, the dream life. Except, of course, that *very* few

---
[8] Which can be very, very cold!
[9] Godard is being too modest again: this is someone who's made 45 major film and video pieces (15 of which are masterpieces), and who appears – and will appear – in any history of the first 100 years of cinema.

people could have made those films. There are only a handful of filmmakers on the planet at any one time who would be capable of such brilliance.

*

I have concentrated on the well-known Jean-Luc Godard films for the most part, partly because they are most readily available, partly because they are among the more approachable works, partly because they are among the more enjoyable, and partly because it's difficult to find many items that Godard has produced (so I have left out films/ video/ TV that have not been easily available at the time of writing, such as *Germany Year 90* and *For Ever Mozart*).

Jean-Luc Godard has a truly astonishing output in film, TV, video, visual art, writing, and so on. Apart from the famous feature films, there are a large number of television and video projects. And many of those are hard to track down and obtain (part of the reason is that only a small percentage of films and TV from any particular country gets released or shown outside that territory). Also, some of the TV/ video works are poor quality copies of already low res video (much of it was made for broadcast on French television, and has never been broadcast outside of France).

In Britain, for instance, you just don't have Godard's films and TV and video output being broadcast regularly (actually, even the well-known features are shown only rarely. When was the last time you saw a Godard film on a major television network, not a niche cable/ satellite channel?). To consider Godard's TV work alone, or his video work alone, would require another book.

I reckon the number of people who have seen absolutely everything that Jean-Luc Godard had produced is very small - across the whole globe, and including la France. Filmmakers like Donald Cammell or Andrei Tarkovsky are much easier to take in. You can watch Tarkovsky's seven feature films, the two shorts and the documentary *A Time To Travel*, and that's the whole *œuvre*. But with Godard, as with other prolific filmmakers like Yasujiro Ozu and Ingmar Bergman, there's a huge amount of material to consider. Godard simply never stops. As his biographer put it, one of the remarkable features of Godard's career is that he never ever stops making films'.[10]

---

10 Colin MacCabe, in Mac, 242.

MOVIES AS DIRECTOR.

The following is a select list of the main features and TV work of Jean-Luc Godard as film and TV director – ignoring short films, notes for films, segments in anthologies, documentaries and others:

Breathless (1960), a.k.a. *À Bout de souffle*
The Little Soldier (1960/ 63), a.k.a. *Le Petit Soldat*
A Woman Is a Woman (1961), a.k.a. *Une femme est une femme*
Vivre sa Vie (1962), a.k.a. *My Life to Live*
Contempt (1963), a.k.a. *Le Mépris*
The Soldiers (1963), a.k.a. *Les Carabiniers*
Band of Outsiders (1964), a.k.a. *Bande à part*
A Married Woman (1964), a.k.a. *Une femme mariée*
Pierrot le Fou (1965), a.k.a. *Crazy Pete*
Alphaville, une étrange aventure de Lemmy Caution (1965), a.k.a.
    Alphaville: A Strange Adventure of Lemmy Caution
Made in U.S.A. (1966)
Masculin féminin: 15 faits précis (1966), a.k.a. *Masculine, Feminine*
2 ou 3 choses que je sais d'elle (1967), a.k.a. *Two of Three Things I
    Know About Her*
Weekend (1967), a.k.a. *Le Week-end*
La Chinoise, ou Plutôt à la Chinoise (1967), a.k.a. *La Chinoise Or, More
    Actually, After the Fashion of the Chinese*
One Plus One (1968), a.k.a. *Sympathy For the Devil*
Un film comme les autres (1968), a.k.a. *A Film Like Any Other*
Joy of Learning (1969), a.k.a. *Le gai savoir*
Le vent d'est (1970), a.k.a. *The Wind From the East*
British Sounds (1970), a.k.a. *See You at Mao*
Pravda (1970)
Vladimir et Rosa (1970), a.k.a. *Vladimir and Rosa*
Struggle in Italy (1971), a.k.a. *Lotte in Italia*
Tout va bien (1972), a.k.a. *All's Well*
Numéro deux (1975), a.k.a. *Number Two*
Ici et ailleurs (1976), a.k.a. *Here and Elsewhere*
France/ tour/ detour/ deux/ enfants (1977), a.k.a. *France/ Tour/ Detour/
    Two Children*
Comment ça va? (1978), a.k.a. *How's It Going?*
Scénario de 'Sauve qui peut la vie' (1980), a.k.a. *Scenario For Sauve Qui
    Peut La Vie*
Slow Motion (1980), a.k.a. *Sauve qui peut (la vie)*
Passion (1982)
First Name: Carmen (1983), a.k.a. *Prénom Carmen*
Détective (1985), a.k.a. *Detective*
Hail Mary (1985), a.k.a. *Je vous salue, Marie*
Soft and Hard (1986), a.k.a. *A Soft Conversation Between Two Friends
    On a Hard Subject*
Grandeur et décadence d'un petit commerce de cinéma (1986), a.k.a.
    Grandeur and Decadence (part of *Série noire* TV series)
Keep Your Right Up (1987), a.k.a. *Soigne ta droite*
King Lear (1987)
Le rapport Darty (1989), a.k.a. *The Darty Report*
Nouvelle vague (1990), a.k.a. *New Wave*
Germany Year 90 Nine Zero (1991), a.k.a. *Allemagne 90 neuf zéro*
Hélas pour moi (1993), a.k.a. *Woe Is Me*

Les enfants jouent à la Russie (1993), a.k.a. *The Children Plan Russian*
Je vous salue, Sarajevo (1993), a.k.a. *Hail, Sarajevo*
JLG/ JLG – autoportrait de décembre (1995), a.k.a. *JLG By JLG*
For Ever Mozart (1996)
Histoire(s) du cinéma (1998), a.k.a. *Histor(ies) of Cinema*
De l'origine du XXIe siècle (2000), a.k.a. *Origins of the 21st Century*
In Praise of Love (2001), a.k.a. *Éloge de l'amour*
Liberty and Homeland (2002), a.k.a. *Liberté et patrie*
Moments choisis des histoire(s) du cinéma (2004), a.k.a. *Chosen Moments of Histoire(s) of Cinema*
Notre musique (2004), a.k.a. *Our Music*
Vrai faux passeport (2006), a.k.a. *The True False Passport*
Socialism (2010), a.k.a. *Film socialisme*
Adieu au Langage (2014), a.k.a. *Goodbye To Language*
Bridges of Sarajevo (2014), a.k.a. *Les Ponts de Sarajevo*
The Image Book (2018), a.k.a. *Le Livre d'Image*

Even missing out many other pieces, this is a totally remarkable body of work.[11]

Maybe Colin MacCabe is right to say that if Jean-Luc Godard had embraced narrative, he might have been among the greatest filmmakers of narrative cinema. But I still think he is, although it's as a film essayist that Godard is the undisputed master (Mac, 322).[12] Godard has admitted that he just can't make normal films: 'I wish I could make a normal picture, normally, but with me, I don't know why, it's not possible' (ibid). Of course, we wouldn't have Godard make films any way other than however he wants to make them.

✻

It's tempting to get into the manifold ways in which Jean-Luc Godard has influenced contemporary cinema. As an editor, for instance, Godard has influenced Bernardo Bertolucci, Rainer Werner Fassbinder,[13] Pier Paolo Pasolini, Wim Wenders, Arthur Penn, Robert Altman, Oliver Stone, Martin Scorsese and Quentin Tarantino.[14] François Truffaut quoted Professor Chiarini: 'There is the cinema *pre*-Godard and *post*-Godard'. Certainly no filmmaker on Earth is Godard's equal as an editor (despite some strong competition – Tsui Hark, for example).

I think it's probably easiest to name some of the artists who've cited Jean-Luc Godard as an influence: Oliver Stone, Martin Scorsese,

---

[11] About his high productivity, Godard said jokily that was competing with Christian Jacques and Claude Chabrol.
[12] 'I cannot see how anyone can regard him now as other than one of the most important directors and the crucial visionary for an age in which film has yielded to video and worse', remarked David Thomson (1994).
[13] Rainer Fassbinder said what he learnt from Godard 'was a way of reacting quickly to the cinema in terms of my own reality' (in D. Georgakas, 187).
[14] D. Fairservice, 2001, 315. Brian De Palma said he was 'very much influenced by Godard's *Masculin/ Féminin*' when he made *Greetings* (1968). 'Godard s a terrific influence, of course', De Palma remarked (J. Gelmis, 61).

Bernardo Bertolucci, Rainer Werner Fassbinder, Donald Cammell, Pier Paolo Pasolini, Wim Wenders, Francis Coppola, Peter Greenaway, and Robert Altman.[15] All of the *cinéma du look* filmmakers (Luc Besson, Jean-Jacques Beineix and Léos Carax, who appeared in Godard's *King Lear*).[16] Godard also influenced later Ingmar Bergman and Luis Buñuel, Miklós Jancsó, Danièle Huillet, Richard Lester, Ken Russell, Derek Jarman, Jean-Marie Straub, and Latin American political filmmakers.[17]

Chinese filmmaker Wong Kar-Wai (*In the Mood For Love, Chungking Express, Ashes of Time*) is clearly influenced by Jean-Luc Godard. Wong's cinema has the freshness and self-confidence of early Godard: there's a sense of urgency, of energy, of shooting in real places with one or two actors, in urban centres which are full of life. Wong shares other aspects with Godard: the headlong, Eisensteinian montage; the kinetic, handheld camerawork; the impatience with traditional storytelling; the young characters; the use of genres (such as crime and *film noir*); and heterosexual romance. Parts of *Chungking Express* (1994), for instance, recall *Breathless, My Life To Live* and *Le Petit Soldat*: the young couple in the modern city. In the films of Wong and Godard there's a sense of contemporary culture, of the technological, urban environment, of street markets, bars, cafés, brothels, seedy hotels, and bohemian apartments, of life lived at a frenetic pace.

Alain Tanner and John Berger were big admirers of Godard, and they followed his work 'with great interest'. For Berger, Godard was 'the great film critic of our time', but he produced films instead of written works; 'he makes films which are criticism of film' (in D. Georgakas, 301).

Jean-Luc Godard's influence can be spotted in literally hundreds of places in global cinema, although many of the filmmakers who've been influenced by him reach a far bigger audience than Godard's own films. Godard's influence is all over pop music movies like *A Hard Day's Night, Help!, Performance, Catch Us If You Can, Easy Rider,* etc. *JFK* and *Natural Born Killers* are very Godardian films (director Oliver

---

15 David Thomson said that Godard taught him 'so many things', such as 'to be parsimonious with beauty', the importance of montage and collage, that cinema needs ethnologists (novelists, dancers, painters, even critics), not only filmmakers, and how the computer 'now poses such a threat to the validity of life itself' (1994).

16 Godard is one of Léos Carax's key influences. In *Mauvais Sang*, the Godardian influence can be seen in the depiction of young lovers, a favourite Godardian topic, especially in his early 1960s films (but also in later works, such as *Hail Mary*), and in the colour scheme of *Mauvais Sang* (red and grey/ black, which recalls Godard's use of red, blue and yellow in *Le Mépris*).

17 According to Robert Kolker, 1983, 191.

Stone is a huge fan), but how would audiences respond if, instead of *Natural Born Killers* or *The Doors*, *Weekend* or *Breathless* were shown in their local cinema? Truth is, when it comes to absorbing Godard's priceless lessons in making cinema, most of the well-known post-Godardian practitioners have couched their Godardisms within conventional narratives, something that Godard himself has always refused to do.

Pier Paolo Pasolini remarked that Bernardo Bertolucci's 'real master is Godard' (1969, 138). Bertolucci is a passionate Godardian, but his films have been much more mainstream and conventional than Godard's. Bertolucci has used Godard in numerous ways, including obvious ones like the casting of Jean-Pierre Léaud in *Last Tango In Paris* as a New Wave director. For Bertolucci, Godard, like himself, has always made the same film.

> I am making always just one film. The filmmakers I love have made only one film. Godard started with *Breathless* and continued with the same film that proceeds along with his life. It's one film... It's the same film and it walks along with him. To make film is a way of life. (J. Gelmis, 170-1)

Bertolucci was ever Godardian, despite his ambivalence towards Godard, especially Godard's political turn of the late 1960s (P. Kolker, 1985, 215).

So many filmmakers have tried to put some Jean-Luc Godard on the screen: Pier Paolo Pasolini, Francis Coppola, George Lucas,[18] Oliver Stone, Martin Scorsese, Luc Besson, Jean-Jacques Beineix, Bernardo Bertolucci, Terence Malick, Donald Cammell, Abel Ferrara, Rainer Werner Fassbinder, Wim Wenders, Peter Greenaway, and Robert Altman. But not even cinema giants like Coppola or Pasolini have managed it as successfully as the Maestro himself. As they say, Godard is still the Man.

And Pauline Kael is right that Jean-Luc Godard beats every other filmmaker at their own game: he gets there first, he's faster than anyone else,[19] and filmmakers who take up his ideas and approaches come across as mannerist (1971, 173). He is impossible to follow.

---

[18] As well as Akira Kurosawa, George Lucas admired Jean-Luc Godard, as did Francis Coppola and numerous other filmmakers in the 1960s. The influence of Godard's incredible films is direct on films such as *THX-1138* and *American Graffiti*, and Lucas's early shorts. *Alphaville* certainly influenced *THX-1138*.

Godard visited the University of Southern California in the late 1960s (at the invitation of Charles Lippincott), where George Lucas was studying cinema. 'I *loved* the style of Godard's films. The graphics, this sense of humor, the way he portrayed the world - he was very cinematic', enthused Lucas.

[19] As David Thomson commented, 'Godard was too brilliant, too rapid: he saw a new way of doing film that is still beyond the generality of directors, and audiences' (1995, 292).

because he's burned up the ground. He invents his innovative techniques to deal with his material, and you can't follow that, you can't become 'Godardian'. He also possesses the uncanny ability to predict future trends, so he also appears to be in advance of everybody else.

In short, there's only one Jean-Luc Godard.

It's significant, I think, that Jean-Luc Godard has said that he thinks of himself as a *French* filmmaker, rather than an *international* filmmaker, that he has been making films primarily for the French audience (though perhaps not only the French in France),[20] rather than for an international audience. It's an important distinction, except that Godard has become a name well-known outside France, of course. We say 'global' now, instead of 'international'.

Visiting the Pompidou Centre in Paris during Christmas, 2008, I found a marvellous collection of Jean-Luc Godard's films, including his 1970s movies with Anne-Marie Miéville. More and more I think that Godard encapsulates better than most Paris and France and French life and French culture and French cinema from the 1960s to the 2000s. He gets everything into his films. *Everything.* His cinema *is* French cinema, as no other French filmmaker is. He is *so* French, and so amusing, and so much fun.

Jean-Luc Godard's films of the 1960s, before European and international co-production became commonplace in film production (really from the late 1970s for Godard), were films made in France for a French audience. That's one reason why they were low budget films – because they had to make most of their money back in France. Some of Godard's contemporaries, of course, went to Hollywood or tended to mount big, European co-productions. Godard could've been a director-for-hire and never stopped working (and he would've been the greatest hired hand of recent times). Godard, however, has always enjoyed his relative independence – the more film producers that are involved, or the more money there is, the less control the filmmaker has. In the 1960s, Godard said that his movies were financed by advances against future sales by distributors, and they had a say in the production (G, 210). Gaumont has been a valuable source of support Godard. He was their Resident Genius.

As Pauline Kael noted, Jean-Luc Godard 'makes it all seems so effortless – just one movie after another', movies which could be made

---
20 The French Republic has a population of 58 million (in 1997), and a land mass of 210,026 square miles.

because they were low budget, because Godard was 'so skilful and so incredibly disciplined', and could find an audience within France to sustain them (1969, 19). That gave Godard an independence almost unknown among his contemporaries. He could seem to do what he wanted. It was certainly a rare position.

Jean-Luc Godard's is a supremely well-read, well-informed and intellectual cinema (reflecting the man himself). It is not uncommon to find references to writers and thinkers such as Goethe, Hölderlin, Hegel, Proust, Joyce, Rimbaud, Freud, Marx, Mao and Brecht in his films. Brechtian 'epic theatre' is clearly an influence on Godard's cinema, with its separation and foregrounding of the elements of the medium, its alienation effects, its self-reflexivity.[21] The Soviet filmmaker Dziga Vertov, who came to name the group of filmmakers Godard formed in the late 1960s with Jean-Pierre Gorin and company, is another influence, with his notions of *kino-glaz* ('cinema-eye') and theory of *kino-pravda* ('cinema-truth'), and, importantly for Godard, the emphasis, as with Sergei Eisenstein, on montage. Politically, Mao Zedong made an impact on Godard (this is the politics of the Mao of the *Little Red Book*, and the Great Proletarian Cultural Revolution of 1966).

Godard is certainly one of the great interviewees in all of film history. Not only can he talk about cinema at length, referencing 100s of films and filmmakers (including citing many he knew personally),[22] he can also discuss philosophy, politics, science, sculpture, painting, theatre, you name it.

It's hard to think of any filmmaker, producer, studio executive or critic who could take on Godard in a debate and win.

A long interview with Godard, produced in 2010, is remarkable and highly recommended: he may be in his 80s, but he can still talk wittily about cinema, including his own films (and he's still sucking on a giant cigar).

---

21 The distancing or estrangement effect of Bertholt Brecht was called the *Verfremdungseffekt*. The goal was to make the audience always aware of the mechanisms of the play and staging: to allow the spectator to criticize constructively from a social point of view', as Brecht put it. (Quoted in *Brecht On Theatre*, ed. J. Willett, Methuen, London, 1964, 125).
22 'Godard has the entire history of cinema in his head... he is a walking reference library of the cinema', remarked Wheeler Dixon (183).

ACCESS TO GODARD

You'd think, wouldn't you, that the key works by one of the great filmmakers in the history of cinema would be readily available? Not at all with Jean-Luc Godard's films. Ironically, it's Hollywood and the Americans (of the North) who are more concerned with archiving and preservation than the film-mad French.

James Quandt has written of the difficulty of putting together a Jean-Luc Godard film retrospective. Godard's works are in a 'state of near unattainability', and the rights to many pieces are uncertain or disputed (this occurs with so many movies). While the 1960s films (comprising an incredible *sixteen* feature-length movies, plus many shorter films), have become classics, they are often shown in poor conditions, and the Dziga Vertov Group films are virtually unobtainable (go into your local home entertainment store and try to find *Vent d'Est* or *Pravda*. No, not a chance).

And the later works are difficult to find, too, including the one production everyone agrees is a total masterpiece, *Histoire(s) du Cinéma*. If this piece is one of the great works of our time, as every critic attests, it should be easily available. Unfortunately, that isn't the case, as I've found writing this book (it was released on DVD in 2008).

It doesn't help either that some of the items in the Jean-Luc Godard filmography don't actually exist, or are apocryphal, and some have been withdrawn by the companies that commissioned them. [23]

A filmmaker such as Werner Herzog has made many of his films available, with some absolutely wonderful DVD audio commentaries by the director. It would be truly amazing to have Jean-Luc Godard release his films with commentaries – and to have additional commentaries by, say, Anna Karina or Raoul Coutard. (But there are many filmmakers who could have produced audio commentaries on their work but didn't or chose not to: Ingmar Bergman, Woody Allen, Walerian Borowczyk and Steven Spielberg).

As to books, there are many about Godard, but the two must-haves are: Colin MacCabe's 2003 biography, and Richard Brody's 2008 study. [24]

---

[23] You can see some of Godard's films and interviews on the excellent UbuWeb site (ubu.com), and also YouTube (youtube.com). Places such as the Centre Pompidou in Paris have excellent archives.

[24] I would also recommend: R. Bellour & M. Bandy, eds, *Jean-Luc Godard*, W.W. Dixon, *The Films of Jean-Luc Godard*, B.F. Kawin, *Mindscreen: Bergman, Godard and First-Person Film*, P. Kolker, *The Altering Eye: Contemporary International Cinema*, R. Roud, *Jean-Luc Godard*, K. Silverman & H. Farocki, *Speaking About Godard*, and D. Sterritt, *The Films of Jean-Luc Godard*.

Websites about Jean-Luc Godard on the internet come and go, but some of the good ones include:

The Godard Experience: www.carlton.edu
The British Film Institute: www.bfi.org.uk
Senses of Cinema: www.sensesofcinema.com
Film-Philosophy: www.film-philosophy.com
www.geocities.com/Hollywood/Cinema/4355

In the Pompidou Centre in Paris you can study an archive of films, including many by Godard. This is a still from a typical video piece by Godard and Anne-Marie Miéville, *Jean-Luc* (1976).

Jean-Luc Godard absolutely in his element: at work in his studio, surrounded by machines, vision mixing images from *Passion* – and pontificating on cinema, the white screen, art, history, and the image – in the documentary/ essay *Scenario For Passion* (1982).

PART TWO

CINÉMA/ CINEMA

16

THE POLITICAL FILMS OF 1968-1973

1967-1973 was the period when Jean-Luc Godard developed a series of political films, some of which were produced by the Dziga Vertov Group with Jean-Pierre Gorin and others (during this period, he was married to Anne Wiazemsky, who appears in several of the films). The political pictures of the period tend now to be seen as Dziga Vertov Group works, but actually the Dziga Vertov Group – and Gorin – only worked on a proportion of them. According to Gorin, the group only really coalesced around the time of *Struggle In Italy* (by which time Godard had already produced several political pieces. Also, towards the end, it was really only Godard and Gorin. The name Dziga Vertov was made up by Russian filmmaker Denis Kaufman. It means 'spinning top').

The core members of the political period between 1968 and 1973 were le Maître and Gorin; Armand Marco and Jean-Henri Roger joined in 1969. Jean-Pierre Gorin was born in Paris on Apl 17, 1943. He met Godard in 1966, later advising on the script of *La Chinoise* and *La Gai Savoir*. Following the political films and Dziga Vertov Group period, which ended around 1973, Gorin taught at the University of California. He produced several film essays, such as *Poto and Cabengo* (1980), *Routine Pleasures* (1986), *My Crazy Life* (1992) and *Letter To Peter* (1992).

In the Dziga Vertov Group films, collective decision-making was the order of the day – making films by lengthy group meetings. And equal collaborations (needless to say, this didn't always work in practice. Godard was opposed to directing like a dictator, but that's how it often worked out). There was also a move away from auteurism, to embrace the 'death of the author' of Roland Barthes and Structuralism. But that of course clashed on many levels with the *Cahiers du Cinéma* philosophy of enshrining directors.[1]

Well-known political filmmakers of the era included Costa-Gavras, Chantal Akerman, Nagisa Oshima, Pier Paolo Pasolini, Miklos Jancso, Francesco Rosi, Marin Karmitz and Chris Marker. Groups and collectives of political filmmakers included S.L.O.N. Group and M.K. Productions (France), Fugitive Cinema (Belgium), Band of 6 (Greece), Kartemquin (Chicago), Cinema Action and Women's Film Group (London), New Film (Sweden), Militant Cinema Collective and Feminist Film Collective (Italy), Women's Film Collective (Australia), and Workshop (Denmark).

The political film period of 1968 to 1973 and the Dziga Vertov

---

[1] The political films of 1968-1973 and the Dziga Vertov Group projects explore aspects of bourgeois militant practice and theory, but never really address the issue of authorship – that these films come from bourgeois militants, and from a bourgeois militant culture.

Group produced movies that included: *Wind From the East, Lutte In Italia, British Sounds, A Film Like the Others, Until Victory* (*Palestine Will Win*), *Vladimir and Rosa, Pravda, Tout Va Bien* and *Letter To Jane*. Some were unfinished, and some were not broadcast as planned, or released. The Dziga Vertov Group and the 1968-1973 political films were shot on Eastmancolor 16mm, with apparently everything being decided by the group, and everyone being paid equally. The money came from TV channels in Europe, with Jean-Luc Godard typically being commissioned to direct a documentary about a political topic.[2] Short *Ciné-tracts* were also produced (they were 2m 50s long, the length of a reel of 16m,m film). The *Ciné-tracts,* sold for 50 Francs, were shown at universities.

Godard also visited Gotham (in Nov, 1968) to make a movie with D.A. Pennebaker and Richard Leacock: *One American Movie* (Jefferson Airplane, Tom Luddy, Rip Torn, Tom Hayden, LeRoi Jones and Eldridge Cleaver appeared). The collaboration foundered, but Leacock and Pennebaker released a version of the footage in 1971 (as *One Parallel Movie*).

For the TV stations, these were niche items, to be broadcast way outside of prime time. But they were also prestige products (with a name director). Accused of dumbing down and churning out trash, TV channels could point to works like the Dziga Vertov Group films, and claim that they were upholding the broadcasting codes of being educational, inclusive and informative.

☆

The political context of the 1968-1973 films is crucial: these works are aggressively interrogating the ideology and societies of their era. We could launch into an analysis of the politics and the ideology of the period, but noting down some key participants helps to define the time. So, here are some of the leaders continually referenced in Godard's political films:

Soviet leaders
Nikitya Khrushchev   1953-1964
Leonid Brezhnev   1964-1982

U.S. Presidents
John F. Kennedy   1961-1963   Democrat
Lyndon B. Johnson   1963-1969   Democrat

---

[2] Among the financers were Italy's R.A.I., O.R.T.F., and London Weekend Television.

Richard Nixon	1969-1974	Republican

French Presidents

Charles de Gaulle	1959-1969	Union for the New Republic
Georges Pompidou	1969-1974	Union of Democrats for the Republic

The form of Marxism and Leninism in the movies is kind of updated to the 1960s, but Marxism as a political model is of the 19th century, and Leninism of the 1920s. For some, the form of politics was already out of date by the 1960s (the Dziga Vertov Group approach focussed on the factory system,[3] *par example*, which was a 19th century model).

The political outlook of the 1968-1973 Godard films and the Dziga Vertov Group films boils down in the main to simple oppositions, such as:

Right-wing = bad	Left-wing = good
Imperialism = bad	Socialism = good
Bourgeoisie = bad	Working class = good
Amerika = very bad	China/ Russia = very good
Hollywoood = bad	Militant cinema = good

Meanwhile, the political model is simplified to oppositions (because these are movies):

Left   Right

Or to the linear political model:

Left   Centre   Right

So the ideoloigical arguments in the political films seldom go beyond that – to, say, the circular model:

        Authoritarian

Left   Centre   Right

---
[3] There are refs. to the Simca car factory in *La Chinoise*, for instance, and the meat factory in *Tout Va Bien*.

Democratic

Meanwhile, two people are employed as inspirations or reference points: they appear in photos, in quotations, and the voiceover actors are called Vladimir and Rosa:

Vladimir Lenin   1870-1924
Rosa Luxemburg   1871-1919

And two others:

Che Guevara   1928-1967
Mao Zedong   1893-1976

The 1968-73 political works and the Dziga Vertov Group projects are fascinating if you admire Godard, and want to see as much of the Maestro's work as possible. But, really, only *Tout Va Bien* is essential viewing – and *La Chinoise* (though that isn't really part of the Dziga Vertov Group movies – only later did some of the political films become included under the Dziga Vertov Group banner).

It's hard to recommend most of the Dziga Vertov Group films and most of the 1968-1973 political films: there are some compelling moments (such as the tracking shot in the assembly line of a factory in *British Sounds*, and the montage of newsreel footage of Parisian riots[4] in *A Film Like the Others*), but some of the works are definitely hard-going even for dedicated admirers. I guess if you had to pick one work of the Dziga Vertov Group in particular, that represents the works, apart from *All's Well* and *The Chinoise*, it would probably have to be *Wind From the East*.

You could regard the 1968-1973 political movies as Godard's version of *The Idiot's Guide To Maoism* or *Rioting Made Easy*.

Godard called for 'blackboard films' ('films tableaux noirs'): so we're back in school with our teacher, Monsieur Godard (he's the only *sensei* in the M.P.A. (Militant Private Academy) who's allowed to smoke in the classroom). Sit down, be quiet, get our your notebooks, and we'll being the first lesson in the course *Marxism For Beginners*.

'Unwatchable' is the response of some film critics. James Monaco described the Dziga Vertov Group films as 'a series of difficult,

---
[4] Godard had filmed the riots in the Latin Quarter in May, 1968.

tentative, experimental cinematic essays' (1977b, 323). Jean-Pierre Gorin dubbed them 'Unidentified Visual Objects', U.V.O.s. They can be tough going. Both Gorin and Godard later acknowledged that their collaboration had been valuable. 'I gave him hope when he didn't have any,' Gorin said of Godard, and Godard acknowledged that working with Gorin had helped him to keep going (Mac, 237).

It's curious that *La Chinoise* was a hit in the U.S.A., and yet the Dziga Vertov Group and many of the political 1968-1973 films were seen by practically nobody – curious because they cover so much of the same material: young people and left-wing politics, young people getting together to explore political issues, in particular a group undertaking analyses of how political theory relates to social life, what a political revolution might actually mean in practical terms, and how the young generation could tackle issues such as the class struggle, self-criticism, Marxism, Maoism and Communism. But *La Chinoise* is far superior to any of the other Dziga Vertov Group works (it's obvious why).

The response to some of the political films was terrible – at the Lincoln Center in Gotham on Dec 29, 1968, when *A Film Like the Others* was screened, nearly all of the audience walked out (leaving under a hundred people); the audience also abandoned *Le Gai Savoir* when it was shown in 1969 at the New York Film Festival; and *Le Gai Savoir* had a disastrous screening at the Berlin Film Festival.

It was Dziga Vertov (1896-1954) not Sergei Eisenstein for Godard and his comrades for a variety of reasons. From Vertov (best-known for the remarkable *Man With a Movie Camera*, 1929, a film school favourite), Godard assimilated the idea of the camera and cinema as a scientific tool for exploring reality; an emphasis on montage; cinema as a laboratory for experiments with sound and image; a distrust of conventional narrative and scripts; and 'interval' theory, the gaps, movements and transitions between shots.[5]

They are not documentaries. They are experiments – part-essay, part-rant, part-provocation. They employ *some* elements of documentary filmmaking – such as interviews with people related to the main theme or subject; they film some acts and locations asssociated with the theme; and they occasionally use recreations or dramatizations. But for the rest, it is experimentation, knitted together largely by two invisible factors: 1. voices (and sounds), and 2. editing.

Sound was a vital part of the 1968-1973 political films and the

---

[5] M. Witt, in M. Temple, 2000, 36-37.

Dziga Vertov Group films, for several reasons (one being economic: it was simply cheaper to mess about with sound, involving two or three people in the editing suite, than shooting with a crew).6 The late 60s/early 70s films were more like experiments with sounds and images than straight documentaries.7 Jean-Luc Godard had of course been headed that way anyway: he began the 1960s with films composed in the classical manner (with modernist additions), but ended the decade embracing modernism, a disjunction of sound and image. (Conventional sound was rejected on ideological grounds: it meant the dominant system, which the Dziga Vertov Group was opposed to.)

So you could argue that the 1968-1973 political films might be better suited to being radio shows. Godard and co. can do everything that they want to do in the audio format (and they often don't find decent or suitable images to go with their sounds). Sound is cheaper to disseminate, too (you hand out audio cassettes to punters at political rallies, or send open reel tapes to radio stations).

Rostrum camera material is everywhere in the political films and the Dziga Vertov Group films (or, rather, filming material pinned to a wall or handwritten on a piece of paper). It's a cheapo way of padding out the movies with captions and mantras, newspapers and photography, that're repeated many times. Sometimes the captions reduce the ideological rants to simple assertions:

strike	strike	strike	strike	strike
workers	workers	workers	workers	workers
union	union	union	union	union
struggle	struggle	struggle	struggle	struggle
politics	politics	politics	politics	politics
bourgeois	bourgeois	bourgeois	bourgeois	bourgeois

Several of the captions in the '68 to '72 political films seem to come from Godard regressing to being a ten years-old boy on a rainy afternoon, playing with his coloured felt tip pens. So he writes the months of the year in black ink with October written in red ink. So he repeats the word 'blue' in blue ink and the word 'red' in red ink. It's kinda cute.

☆

One of the biggest problems with the 1968-1973 political films and

---

6 Part of the project of the political films was to make something even with very limited means and budgets, to prove that films could be made without huge resources.
7 Godard acknowledged that some of his experiments went wrong. They were bound to, he said – that was in the nature of being an experimenter.

the Dziga Vertov Group films was finding an audience. In the idealism of the time, and with so much political unrest and revolutionary ferment bubbling away in the People's Republic of France, in Europe and in the U.S.A., it seemed the movies *should* find an audience; they *deserved* to. It didn't help that the films that Godard, Gorin and co. made were not broadcast by the TV stations that commissioned them, and few audiences got to see them (and they didn't make much money). Hence the decision to produce *Tout Va Bien*, with big name stars Jane Fonda and Yves Montand.

Making a 'militant' or 'radical' or 'Marxist' movie is one thing; getting people to see it is something else. Here's where the concept of anti-Hollywood, anti-bourgeois, Marxist/ Maoist/ militant/ radical/ socialist/ left-wing cinema runs into numerous problems. One is exhibition and distribution, where the 1968-1973 political films and the Dziga Vertov Group releases foundered. (Most distribution and exhibition networks, as young or new filmmakers soon find out, are controlled by big companies with a thoroughly capitalist agenda).

In 1970, for ex, the big films at the global box office were *Love Story, Airport, M.A.S.H., Patton, Woodstock,* and *Joe.* Faced with the choice between booking *Love Story* or *Wind From the East*, most theatre owners would plump for the Robert Evans-produced movie. A crowd pleaser. A tear-jerker. Similarly, if punters had the choice of a cheesy, all-star disaster movie like *Airport* or *British Sounds*, most would choose *Airport*. (The film industry was suffering one of its worst recessions in 1969-1970, when some pundits thought that Hollywood as it was would cease to exist).

An anti-capitalist/ anti-bourgeois/ anti-Hollywood movie could not morally take advantage of the rampant capitalism and shameless exploitation of conventional distribution and exhibition networks, nor of conventional publicity and advertizing (advertizing was fascism, according to J.L.G.).

In order to reach an audience, then, anti-Hollywood cinema would need to develop alternative means of distribution. The films were backed by money from television stations, and not intended to be released theatrically in the conventional manner (altho' some were). Apart from television, there were other distribution possibilities in 1970 – cinema clubs, independent theatres (or chains), the college/ university circuit, etc (Gorin and Godard undertook some tours of American universities – in Feb, 1968 and in 1970).[8] It's no surprise

---

[8] Godard and Gorin took to the road to present the political films and talk about them to groups (it was exhausting and exhilarating, Gorin recalled).

that the television companies which financed the 1968-1973 political films and the Dziga Vertov Group films opted not to broadcast them.

The production of *All's Well* (*Tout Va Bien*) was thus an admission that the political movie project had failed – at least in terms of finding an audience. Or in developing a non-bourgeois, non-capitalist, non-Western, non-Hollywood form of filmmaking in terms of production, and in terms of content. *All's Well* is a return to the bourgeois/ Hollywood/ capitalist form of film production, with big stars, a story, characters, a narrative structure, publicity, prints and advertizing, release in theatres and all. The story and the themes of *All's Well* derived from the 1968-1973 political films and the Dziga Vertov Group works – strikes, workers, factories, left-wing politics, etc – but the approach was largely jettisoned.

☆

Among the topics that Godard's 1968-1973 political films and the Dziga Vertov Group films tackled were Palestine and Middle East politics in *Jusqu'à la victoire*, Chicago radicals in *Vladimir and Rosa*, revolut-ionary politics in *Vent d'Est*, contemporary British politics and culture in *British Sounds*, and culture and labour in Czechoslovakia in *Pravda*.

For Richard Brody, the movies of the Dziga Vertov Group period do not bear up to scrutiny in the same way that J.-L. Godard's early output does: the films are 'petrified by ideology, by doctrine, suggest hardly a glimmer of the brilliance and the vital energy that went into them' (B, 519). They are films of *process*, of ideas, but some are difficult to sit through. *British Sounds* was a project that took a lot of Godard's time and energy, but the final images 'range from neutral to vacant' in this 'absurd and failed project' which, Brody suggested, 'has the stiff and self-punishing feel of a cinematic hair shirt' (B, 345). But the period was important for Godard, not least as recuperation.

Elio Petri remarked (in 1972) that Godard's political films were interesting but too intellectual and elitist: 'when you appeal to an elite, you fall into the trap of intellectualism'. Thus, for Petri, as revolutionary cinema, Godard's 'efforts were useless. I don't believe one can make a revolution with cinema' (in D. Georgakas, 60).

Thompson and Bordwell sum up the Dziga Vertov Group films in *Film Art*: 'Impossible to consume as entertainment or as engaged documentary, the films carry the modernist project to an abrasive extreme' (522).

Some critics found Godard's Dziga Vertov Group films too

simplistic, too naïve, and too inconsiderate of the audience. As Joan Mellen put it in *Cinéaste*: 'Godard reveals singular contempt for his audience whom he believes he can politicize through the brow-beating of a steady drone of pseudo-Marxist cliché'.[9] The films 'were made for an audience that didn't exist at the time,' commented Colin MacCabe, 'and it is hard to imagine them finding a real one now. Their politics seems grotesque, if not offensive' (Mac, 237).

However, the 1968-1973 political films did receive some critical attention – they are a cinema of ideas, after all, stuffed with captions, one-liners, political rhetoric, and the sort of concepts that can be put into words, and some critics and *cinéastes* enjoy discussing ideas. So you can read film essays about film essays.

The 1968-1973 political films are very earnest and fairly humourless. Why? Why does the exploration of political and ideological concepts always have to be so serious?

As they are so earnest, so desperate to take their topics seriously, the 1968-1973 political films (and the Dziga Vertov Group works in particular) are prime targets for parodies. I'd love to see the Zucker-Abrahams-Zucker team (*The Naked Gun*, *Airplane!*, etc) have a go at the Dziga Vertov Group films. Only they wouldn't bother, because nobody has seen them, and a primary rule of spoofing is that the audience has to know the original.

The 1968-1973 political films and the Dziga Vertov Group films were constructed from short scenes (and some longer rants), just like many of Jean-Luc Godard's movies. Some of the scenes were little bits of business (someone shutting a door, say), but the key factor was: they were repeated. And repeated.

Structurally, these little bits were simply put together by the editing, one after another: the editors were the orchestral conductors of these works. The parts could be arranged in any order: devices like plot development, rising action, dividing films into acts, and all of the æsthetic structures deriving from literature and theatre, were not employed. The films simply started, and then they stopped. There was no Grand Beginning, and no Grand Ending or Finale. Semblances of structure were suggested by the repeated use of title cards or diagrams. But not really. Some films (such as *Struggle In Italy*) were divided into topics (Family, Society, Baked Beans, Ducks, etc).

1968 was a pivotal year for Jean-Luc Godard in other ways – in his professional relationships, leaving behind (some of) his old film

---

9 *Cinéaste*, 4, 3, Winter, 1970.

crews and collaborators, for instance, or the extensive travelling Godard undertook: 'I had to take a break and I left Paris,' Godard explained, 'I went to Cuba, to Canada, to the States, trying to make pictures. I knew the pictures were not successful, but it sort of broke the routine' (Mac, 213).[10] Later, Godard looked back on his ideological years and they seemed to be lost years, in which he stopped living a regular life, didn't go to the movies, didn't read.

But more than a few in the cinema scene in French Republic and elsewhere viewed Jean-Pierre Gorin with distrust: for them, Jean-Luc Godard was being lured away from his true vocation as one of the leading lights of world cinema into cul-de-sacs of extreme ideological projects.

Meanwhile, Anne Wiazemsky saw the influence of Jean-Pierre Gorin as very negative on her relationship with Godard: 'all of my problems with Jean-Luc date from his arrival', Wiazemsky asserted in 2003. They would have had a 'classic actress-director relationship', Wiazemsky maintained, 'if it hadn't been for politics, Gorin, yes' (B, 358). One wonders what Godard might've produced with Wiazemsky if Gorin hadn't been on the scene during this period of re-building in Godard's life. Of course, Wiazemsky does appear in *Tout Va Bien, Struggle In Italy, Vladimir and Rosa* and *Wind From the East*.

The 1968-1973 era political films and the Dziga Vertov Group projects were examined in retrospect in *Here and Elsewhere* (1976), made by Jean-Luc Godard and Anne-Marie Miéville; but it would be fascinating to hear Anne Wiazemsky's view of those years and projects.

The Dziga Vertov Group films in particular are filmed records of the Annual Marxist-Leninist Debating Club – sometimes they have picnics, sometimes they're in cruddy colleges, or in Godard's Paris pad. Anyway, the point is, discussion is central to the concept: a good proportion of the D.-V.-G. movies is simply one debate after another, with captions, off-screen voices and newsreel or images of nude women added occasionally.

The revolutionary politics explored in the 1968-1973 film projects talked about Maoism, Marxism, Communism and socialist ideology and politics, but declined to address the issue of artists working in Communist nations. Filmmakers have been censored, had films suppressed or withheld, projects cancelled, and were even imprisoned (such as Sergei Paradjanov, a world-class film director if ever there

---

10 But that's the problem with travelling: wherever you go, *you are still you*. Godard in Cuba is still Godard.

was one – Paradjanov was making his truly astonishing films at this time, too – *The Colour of Pomegranates* and *Shadows of Our Forgotten Ancestors*). During the Communist era, filmmakers in the Soviet Union, the People's Republic of China and Eastern Bloc countries had restrictions on the subjects they could explore, and were encouraged to address socialist realist topics (as well as Paradjanov, many filmmakers suffered from political suppression, including Andrei Tarkovsky, Andrzej Wajda, and Jafar Panahi).

☆

J.-L. Godard's 68-73 political films such as *Wind From the East* (known in Cuba as *Marxism For Hippies*) are careful to defend Mao Zedong and Joseph Stalin against attacks from bourgeois politicos who have accused their regimes of committing atrocities. According to *Wind From the East*, Mao and Stalin never put a foot wrong, never authorized repression, coercion, aggression or violence of any kind, not even a single punishment against any human (or hamster).[11] No, Mao and Stalin were saintly, kindly rulers, who gave their chiefs of staff handmade candy on their birthdays,[12] and new-born kittens along with their Christmas bonus.

According to *Wind From the East* and the D.V.G. films, Chairman Mao was a gentle, peace-loving philosopher who tended a Zen Buddhist garden designed with quaint, minimal simplicity in Peking. He issued orders to his underlings using Chinese calligraphy (he'd taken a 50-year vow of silence during the founding of the People's Republic of China in 1949), and he looked like Yoda from *Star Wars*. Everybody loved him.

Joseph Stalin was not a loathed, feared and terrifying ruler of a rotten-to-the-core government which led a superpower. No, no: according to *Wind From the East*, Stalin was a sweet, old uncle ('Uncle Joe', they called him), who doted on his family, and spent most of his waking hours sorting through his beloved collection of antique music boxes in his garden shed.

Wind From the East insists that 50 million victims did *not* die in poverty and starvation in the Soviet Union, or were terrorized by the K.G.B.,[13] or were sent away to the Gulags – that was all a naughty lie put about by the Amerikan Imperialists. In reality, as history has shown, those 50 million souls were given all sorts of wonderful choices – a free trip to the holiday camps in Siberia (where the All You Can Eat

---

11 Chickens, alas, were fair game. Very edible with noodles and chow mein.
12 Chairman Mao's intricate icing on his homemade cakes was something to behold (in red, of course).
13 K.G.B. stands for Kind, Gentle Bureaucrats.

Buffet was a hit), and even the once-in-a-lifetime opportunity to make militant, Marxist movies on Sunday afternoons in the country! (weather permitting).

According to *Wind From the East* and the D. Vertov Group films, the Soviet Union's government had a spotless record of human rights, without the slightest hint of corruption; it never imprisoned anybody for political or ideological reasons (honest it didn't); and of course, my dear, dear comrade, it only wanted the very best for its beloved citizens, who were completely free morally, ethically, politically, socially and ideologically to do, print, create and believe what they liked.

Thus, *Wind From the East* launches a pre-emptive nuclear strike against all of those Imperialist, Capitalist Pigs in the Western world who keep pointing out that the Communist regimes of the People's Republic of China and the Soviet Union (and the Eastern Bloc) from the 1920s to the Fall of the Berlin Wall) were not Paradises on Earth. They *were paradise*. They most definitely *were* Paradises for all who were lucky enough to live there.

☆

17

UN FILM COMME LES AUTRES

A FILM LIKE THE OTHERS

*A Film Like the Others*₁₄ (*Un Film Comme les Autres,* 1968) was one of the early political Love-Ins from Godard (this is 1968, *camarades*, a year after the Summer of Love - 1967 - but it's still Love and Peace For All in Sixty-Eight!), in this laugh riot with an average of six big belly laughs per minute (*six*! - not even Bob Hope or Jerry Lewis achieved that level!).

This movie is *really* funny - it's one of the funniest movies you'll ever see.

No, not really.

Not at all, actually.

It's not the Summer of Love.

It never *was* the Summer of Love.₁₅

It's 1968, it's soon after the tumultuous, you-had-to-be-there events of May, 1968, when Paris and then the whole of the People's Republic of France erupted in rev-o-lu-tion.

Or something.

With *A Film Like the Others* (also known as *The Marxist Guide To Tax Evasion - Film Director's Edition*), the politicized Godard was just warming up: he hadn't reached the wacky heights of *Wind From the East* yet, but he was getting there. Just think, ladies and gentlemen - after *A Film Like the Others* you've got *Wind From the East* to look forward to! Followed by - get this! - *Struggle In Italia, British Sounds, Palestine Will Win, Vladimir and Rosa, Pravda* and *Letter To Jane.* (*A Film Like the Others* was a Godard film, however, financed by the man himself; it was not a Godard-Gorin collaboration. But it set the template in every important aspect for the subsequent Godard-and-Gorin collaborations. It reminds us that much of the content and the approach of the political films came from Godard, not Gorin).

❧

Oi, comrade! we're going to sit in the fields and debate Marxism, are you in? We're gonna make a movie with Godard! Yeah, <u>him</u>! *(Free packs of Gitanes included!). Now you're up for it? OK!*

As in later Dziga Vertov Group films, part of *A Film Like the Others* features seven or so young(ish) people sitting about on the grass and conversing (at Flins, near the Renault car factory). The open-air format for the Annual Marxist-Leninist Debating Club Picnic would be revived in *Wind From the East* and other Godard-Gorin films. (Presumably, Godard (and later with Gorin) selected open-air spots because they were (1) free [*all locations should be free! Permits should*

---
14 Or *A Film Like All the Others.*
15 The Summer of Love is a bourgeois, imperialist lie!

never be required to film anywhere on Earth! It's our Planet, too!], (2) didn't need any lighting [*lamps, trucks and cables are bourgeois!*], (3) were relatively devoid of disturbances [*cops are not welcome on Marxist-Leninist film sets*], and (4) were quiet enough for a discussion to be recorded (compared to the noisy cafés favoured by Godard's movies).

From the outset, *A Film Like the Others* slyly alienates the audience in the familiar, Brechtian manner of late Sixties Godard: with, for instance, very lengthy shots of the back of a person sitting in a field and part of the body of another person, while the voices we hear are (presumably but not necessarily) of someone else in the group discussion (not the two people we see). And there are other voices on the soundtrack, too, spouting the familiar Marxist/ Leninist/ left-wing ideology. The people are white and seem to be French; there's only one female. (For a long time we don't see their faces. Sometimes in documentaries that's because the participants wish to remain anonymous, or because the filmmakers want us to listen and not be distracted by identities. Or maybe it's an æsthetic choice: these are just anybody, not particular people.)

The third element in *A Film Like the Others* is slinkier and less in-your-face than the debate in a field or the newsreel footage: the voiceover. Multiple voices are heard, but two predominate: a man and a woman, performing the familiar double act of a Godardian rant.

The narration has been written after the filming, and often it's allowed to overwhelm the group discussion (sometimes cutting into it rudely). In fact, it's striking how Godard's political films use voiceovers: if the on-screen discussions are flagging or veering off into what are deemed uninteresting areas, the voiceovers cut in with more pertinent material. So if someone's talking about topics the filmmakers don't go for, they simply replace the voices with their own verbiage. It's a kind of live dubbing, but instead of accurately syncing the voices up with the actors on screen, the narration just says what it wants to say.

The *very* long debate featuring young people in *A Movie Like Every Other Movie You've Seen* runs on and on: we aren't shown faces, or close-ups, or reaction shots, and we're not introduced to any of them in a conventional manner. No names. No identity. Maybe the camera pans a little (but not too much). We peer thru grass and bushes. Who are these people? Some are apparently students,[16] but they don't want to be recognized as students, because in 1968 students, according

---

[16] Very few of the students or participants in the Dziga Vertov films are non-white.

to this film, were scorned as bourgeois and privileged (actually, they were from Nanterre University). One guy claims he's always worked for a living (two of the participants worked in the nearby Renault plant); the only woman in the group apologetically and guiltily admits that she is a student (her views come from a different ideological place from the rest of the group, and she often has to talk loudly and firmly to get her views across).

The unmistakable hoarse, lipsy tones of Jean-Luc Godard himself are heard, but he, too, isn't seen (is he even there? Is he standing near the camera, throwing out questions, as he often did? (The debaters do seem to be responding to him). Or are his comments added later, in the dubbing studio, as with so much of *A Film Like the Others*). Godard's questions are wry and off-centre, as usual.

Not much of this group debate is clarified at a personal level, because it's the speeches that count, what the youths are debating: strikes, general strikes, unions, the Renault car factory, industrial action, how workers slave for bosses, the exploitation of the labour force, and how intellectuals and students relate to these fractious topics.

There are other elements in this first section of *A Film Like the Others*, however: newsreel footage (mostly in b/w) of civil unrest on the streets of Paris and other cities. Like the voices heard off-screen, the newsreel footage is cut into the sunlit debate (it was recorded by a film collective). There's no faking now, this is the real deal: the imagery of riots. of mass demonstrations, of angry take-overs of factories, of burning cars, of tear gas and smoke, of protestors lobbing rocks at the cops, and of people running for safety from water cannons retain their raw power (even tho' the quality of the camerawork is appalling – why could nobody hold a camera in the 1960s?). So that when we cut back to a small group of people talking in the sunlight in grassy Flins, it reveals just how dull much of *A Film Like Any Other Political Film* is (you have two works here that could be split apart – one a montage of newsreel footage, the other the group debate. I suppose it is mildly interesting that the events of May, 1968 in Paris, as seen in the newsreel footage, are set within a debate about them some time later).

❧

A Film Like the Others tests the determination and endurance of any radical, left-wing, Marxist-Leninist revolutionary firebrand. including a super-cool political anarchist like myself. *A Film Like the Others* is one hour and forty-five minutes long. That's the same length as an average movie like *Raiders of the Lost Ark* or a *James Bond* flick.

But for a political debate it seems interminable.

Just when you thought the bunch of youths sitting in the grass had surely – *by the Gods!* – said everything they want to say, and everything that *could* be said, and everything that *will ever* be said about strikes and unions and students and class struggles, they start up again (or they never stop – every time we cut back to them, they are prattling on and on).

ა

We can see, can't we, ladies and gents, that this film has been *edited*. We can see that someone has sat at a Movieola and cut this baby.[17] We can see that the footage of the group debate has had newsreel footage cut into it, and newspaper photos, and posters, and several voices have been added to it.

But it runs on for too long, it repeats points (several times) that have already made, and it dissipates its impact by out-staying its welcome. So it *isn't* 'edited', as in trimmed into a satisfactory state, it's filled with repetitions and padding (like, actually, many of Godard's movies).

Thus, *A Film Like the Others* becomes what it tries hard *not* to be: a boring lecture. We've all sat through them. We've all listened to dull lectures. And we've all sat in group discussions in cafés or college bars where one or two people (and it's always the *same* darn one or two people) dominate the debate. We have listened to them going on and on, providing one example after another to illustrate this or that ideological point. Sure, they're smart and well-read and all, but enough already!

For those who dislike the cinema of Jean-Luc Godard, the political films of the late 1960s and after are exactly like that: lectures which soon become boring delivered by a very clever, highly educated but ultimately domineering and obsessive tyrant.

You might stand up and begin your opposition to the Ciné-Genius's harangue with a 'but –', or a 'wait a minute –', but you won't get any further than that. Godard silences all. Not when the Master is on a roll. And even when what he's on clearly *isn't* a roll, when he's obviously not on an express train of cinematic energy, you still can't stop him!

With the Dziga Vertov Group films, your job is simple:

Shut up and listen.

And after you've seen a Dziga Vertov Group film, your job is

---

17 Probably in Godard's apartment.

simple:
> *Change your life/*
> *start a strike/*
> *organize a political cell/*
> *bomb a newspaper/*
> *intimidate the bourgeoisie/*
> *overthrow the government/*
> *travel to a new planet and colonize it with Marxists and cinéastes,*

etc.

❧

The debates in A Film Like the Others waffle and wiffle on for what seems like centuries. Even after 20 minutes there's no let-up.

Then 30 minutes.

Then 40 minutes.

You can be reincarnated through several lifetimes (once as a Marxist firebrand in 1930s Spain, once as the Executioner guillotining Marie Antoinette in 1793, etc), and come back here, and *still* the kids are talking about strikes and class struggles and how to take political action. (You won't believe this, but the debate rages (or dribbles) on and on until the very final minutes of A Film Like the Others – a whole one hour and forty-five minutes!).

Thus, *If Only All Other Films Were Like This* is only *in part* a radical film from Jean-Luc Godard, with its intercutting of newsreel footage of May, 1968 in Paris with offscreen voices outlining key events in the history of left-wing/ Marxist political life, and class struggle, and political activism.

But much of the time, A Film Like the Others is *actually* a group debate featuring seven or so youngish people (who seem to be French, or living in France, and some are possibly students). Thus, *A Film Like the Others* resembles a television debate, one of those 'worthy', 'serious' programmes that public service TV channels put on regularly (to show that they are following the government-imposed guidelines on what should be broadcast. Yes, television is State-controlled – or it's the mouthpiece of any government. The Dziga Vertov Groups films remind us of that, but some of us have never forgotten it).

Usually, debates of this kind are staged in a TV studio in Paris or wherever (Godard has participated in many). Someone will be leading the discussion. Sometimes the format includes a live audience, with questions, etc.

True, the TV debate format is wryly subverted by the political films of 1968-1973 – with voices-off competing with the direct sound, with the camera pointedly *not* including close-ups and reaction shots, and allowing the ten-minute roll of 16mm celluloid to focus on bits of bodies seen from awkward angles (no one else has filmed people's backs so often). But it's still basically a television discussion intercut with amazing newsreel footage of May, 1968.

And, like so many television round table shows, this baby keeps repeating the same material, the same points-of-view, the same political whinges. Let's face it, folks, if you keep the same group of contributors in a TV studio (or on a patch of grass near Paris) on screen for more than ten or so minutes, they start repeating themselves. You have to be as incredible a talker as, say, Orson Welles (or Jean-Luc Godard himself), to maintain the energy and the interest beyond, say, 20 minutes. (That's partly why TV shows are based around questions-and-answers, to keep the flow of chat going, and to guide it in certain directions. There *are* people who can talk for lengthy periods without needing prompts or questions, but television *doesn't want that*, either! Television doesn't want to give an individual an unlimited and unplanned (i.e., unagreed) and unrehearsed platform).

This isn't a TV chat show, with an interviewer feeding questions (decided beforehand) to an interviewee so that the celebrity can trot out their favourite stories. And it's not a political interview, where a politico continually avoids questions and keep repeating what he really wants to say, regardless of whatever the stern, serious interviewer asks (politicians, as we know, are slippery customers, and bend any question round to what they want to say).

No: *A Film Like the Others* is essentially a television debate format but without complying to the standard schedules of TV (30 minutes, 45 minutes or 60 minutes tops for a round table discussion). Rather, *A Film Like the Others* flounders past the usual time slots (just as Godard's fiction movies do). Where you might expect a summing up, or the introduction of a new element, *A Film Like the Others* chunters on.

Another issue, related to the seemingly unstoppable political gasbagging, is that these youngsters are – how to put it politely? – not as engaging as their equivalents among professional performers of the period (Terence Stamp, say, or James Fox, or Anna Karina, or Jean-Paul Belmondo, and of course Jean-Pierre Léaud). The adorable Léaud, bless him, could make this kind of radical, left-wing whingeing compelling (as he does in *La Chinoise*). Léaud could be comical, and goofy, and irritating – but *the same political points would have been made.*

The domineering, 'I know better than you' attitude emerges in the group debate in *A Film Like the Others* – one guy (such as the older, beardy guy) treats the others like they are know-nothings: the younger, idealist guy splutters in response that *he* knows best. The young woman tries to compete with the guys, but her opinions are rather small-minded (she's only concerned, it seems, with how the things affect students). And on and on it goes.

ò▲

Towards the end of this *extremely* long film, the group discussion among the youths in the sunny, Flinsian fields of 1958 is still going strong. However, like many round table confabs, it is always the same people talking (how often have we joined discussions or Q. and A.s which are advertised as 'open to all', only to find the same two or three people dominating the proceedings?). Here, only three people have managed to endure: the older, bearded guy, the younger, idealistic guy, and the young woman. The others are listening and playing with grass stalks (and sawing off their legs to alleviate their boredom).

As the debate continues in *A Pill Like the Others*, it gets narrower and narrower, until all that the youths are talking about is workers vs. students, and factories vs. universities. As if these are the only areas of human activity anywhere on the planet (or anywhere in la France).

The end comes with a final newsreel selection, culminating in a shot which pans around the protestors on the street, and a silly image of the camera wavering 'tween the word 'blue' and the word 'rouge' (that's the only option here: blue or red, right-wing or Gauchist).

ò▲

Seen as a whole, there is far less in *A Film Like the Others* to enjoy, in general, as cinema, as an experience, as data sliding past our eyes and ears, compared to some of the other Dziggy Stardust films. Even mostly rubbishy films like *Wind From the East* or *Struggle In Italy* have more moments which lift us out of the muddy, murky trenches of the Marxist-Leninist World War Three.

18

BRITISH SOUNDS

SEE YOU AT MAO

British Sounds (a.k.a. *See You At Mao,* 1969) was directed by Godard,[18] written by Godard and Jean-Henri Roger and prod. by Kenith Trodd and Ivan Teitelbaum for Kestrel Productions. DP: Charles Stewart, editing: Elizabeth Kozmian, sound: Fred Sharp. It was filmed in Feb, 1969. 52 mins.

Godard may've bitched about British cinema in his film criticism, but he made one significant movie in Albion which's still viewed today: *One Plus One* (largely due to the presence of the genuinely legendary Rolling Stones). *British Sounds* was the second 'British' film produced by the Maestro in England. Filming began in Feb, 1969.

British Sounds was commissioned by London Weekend Television, the regional commercial television station for the capital (1963-2002, when it was replaced by I.T.V. (Independent Television) London), along with Thames Television (1968-1992, when it was replaced by Carlton Television). Once London Weekend Television saw what the French Genius and his team had produced, they refused to broadcast it. What a surprise! (And two years later, the TV station criticized *British Sounds* on its talk show *Aquarius*).

Because in *British Sounds*, Jean-Luc Godard and company are being gleefully, childishly (and intelligently) provocative. They know which panic buttons to press, they know how to annoy audiences, they know what images and what statements will angrify people (broadcasters, producers, TV critics and TV audiences). There is plenty in *British Sounds* to wind up viewers, TV producers and their bosses in the TV centre on London's South Bank: the multiple offscreen voices, the ridiculously over-the-top statements from the British establishment, the repeated attacks on the bourgeoisie and capitalist societies, the shots of a naked woman drifting about (plus a two-minute shot of said woman's naked torso), while the voiceovers contemplate feminism and women's rights, etc.

Like the other 1968-1973 political films and the Dziga Vertov Group films, *British Sounds* is a rant – an ideological, political rant which romanticizes the workers and left-wing politics like Mao/ism and Marx/ism, and despises the bosses and the bourgeoisie and of course the social system – capitalism – which benefits the Haves and scorns the Have-nots. Much of the film's voiceover is condensed down to slogans (*solitary pleasure and fascism,* for example. Similarly with the scribbled captions: *Hitler and Hollywood,* for instance, or the months of the year written in black ink with October in red ink).

---

[18] Some say it was co-helmed by Godard and Roger.

Like the other 1968-1973 political films and the Dziga Vertov Group films, *A Fistful of Mao* contains the full compliment of Godardisms – the double voiceovers (male and female, a man and a boy, a woman and a boy), the very lengthy shots, the self-conscious camerawork, the grabbed shots of people at work on the streets, the pithy-political captions, the pseudo-documentary approach, and the enshrinement of Marxist-Leninist politics and ideology.

It's all here in *British Sounds* – segments about the class struggle, about struggling on two fronts, about encouraging a political revolution which would overthrow the dominant ideology of capitalism, anti-Amerikanisms, and the idealized hope for turning a social system on its head, so that the workers would be in the ascendant and the bourgeoisie would be reduced to peeling potatoes in a dingy basement (or, if you're in a *Weekend*-style rage, set on fire).

◆

British Sounds opens with a classical Godardian shot, which is definitely the finest segment of the film:[19] a very lengthy tracking shot along the assembly lines of a car factory (filmed at Cowley at the British Motor Car factory in Oxfordshire). Like the similar shot in *Tout Va Bien* along the rows of cashiers and shoppers in a hypermarket, this shot says it all. There's no need for the voiceover which contextualizes the images in a pro-Marxist, anti-bourgeois philosophy. The image says everything (as with the supermarket scene in *Tout Va Bien*).

It's something to do with the way that Godard and the team set up the shot, with the way that they film the workers putting together the shiny, new cars[20] that consumers buy in their millions, with the way that the shot operates within the context of the film.

British Sounds could've selected more degrading, filthier jobs (cleaning public toilets, for instance), but this shot performs the role of evoking the robotic, dehumanizing of mass labour, where people are reduced to acting as a cog in a giant machine.

Yes, this is what people are doing everyday, day in, day out. It's part of Godard's view of labour in a capitalist social system as slavery or prostitution. As the narration puts it, the workers are not invested in the final product (new cars), but in earning money to live; the voiceover asserts that labourers are sacrificing their lives in order to survive; and they have no say in the system of production they are part of, where the whole enterprise is controlled and run by the bourgeois bosses. (The round table discussion in Dagenham brings out some of

---

[19] At least the best comes first – after it, you can slip out the exit marked 'Workers'.
[20] M.G. cars in tame, conservative Racing Green colours and flashy Phallic Red colours.

these issues, of ownership and having a stake in a business; one guy points out that the workers can't afford to buy the cars they are putting together in the factory).

Like some of the other 1968-1973 political films and the Dziga Vertov Group films, *British Sounds* is several films in one package. The images are only one of the levels here – the voiceovers add at least two more levels. The voiceovers often feature two people – a classic Godardian device, which Godard has employed more effectively (and more often) than anybody else. (Godard used the ploy throughout his career – in later films such as *Socialism*, voices are panned to the left and the right of the stereo spectrum). Some of the voice pairings in *British Sounds* have an adult coaxing a child to repeat their ideological rants and their potted histories [21] – a great touch, which somehow makes the rants and the history lessons even more disburbing (that is, when a child speaks of political injustice and coercion).

Among the topics discussed in the many narrations in *British Sounds* are trade union movements; the Tolpuddle Martyrs; Oliver Cromwell; the Levellers; the British Government's suppression of the working class; feminism and women's rights; condemnations of capitalism and the bourgeoisie; political revolution, and so on.

The captions in *British Sounds* are cheapo – written by the Maestro in his familar script on pieces of paper (rather than the printed, optically-achieved captions of the feature films). The handcrafted captions help to give the Dziga Vertov Group output its homemade feel (charming for some, scrappy for others. Anyway, you'd better get used to it – Godard is a filmmaker dedicated to putting his own handwriting in film after film).

The 16 millimetre footage is horrible in places, as in all of the other Dzviga Vertov Group films (nobody as talented as Raoul Coutard was operating the camera, which is a pity). The filmmakers refuse to employ anything as bourgeois as a movie lamp, so the lighting is often flat and just flaky.

An intriguing sequence captures a bunch of car factory workers (from the Dagenham plant, which had recently seen some political unrest) as they discuss the politics of labour, capitalism vs. socialism, unions, the recent British 'socialist' government, etc. This scene allows the British factory workers to voice their own feelings, rather than have the filmmakers impose their ideology on them.

---

21 References to the Levellers, for instance.

This may be the most valuable episode in the Dziga Vertov Group works, where we hear employees voicing their gripes with the factory-based system. And it seems more authentic than the gatherings of students and one or two workers in the French political films.

Unfortunately, it's spoilt by the camera performing whip-pans between the participants. So instead of the usual round table conflab, we are looking at a bunch of guys, with the camera only occasionally settling on the one who's speaking. The silly, self-conscious camera movement is countered, however, by the sound, which captures the people in the room clearly (so at least, this time, the viewer can follow the flow of the conversation). But of course more voiceovers were added.

Like the other Dziga Vertov Group and late 1960s political works, *British Sounds* has a charming, amateur texture at its best (when the mix of ideological ranting and documentary imagery fuses). Tho' at its worst it comes across as a shoddy, amateur piece (such as the endless images of road crews fixing the highways and byways of England, which are padding. Here, *British Sounds* stumbles when it tries to film people at work, one of Godard's key aims in this period).

◆

The weakest section of *British Sounds* comes near the end, with some youths (who were students at Essex University) playing at being radicals and revolutionaries. They are depicted painting posters and trying (very feebly) to alter the lyrics of songs by the Beatles to reflect trendy Maoist, revolutionary politics (they come across as hippies sitting around with an acoustic guitar in their funky, 1960s clothing, and they're about as radical as a used teabag).

If you want to use the Beatles, once again John Lennon had already done it all in his song 'Revolution' – which the students attempt to rewrite. They also have a go at 'Honey Pie' and 'Hell Goodbye'. (Had London Weekend Television broadcast *British Sounds* they would've needed to clear the rights to the songs we hear by the Beatles, including 'Revolution', 'Hello Goodbye' and 'Honey Pie'. It's likely that the Beatles would have been happy to be part of a Godard movie – Paul McCartney particularly – he was by far the most *avant garde* and experimental of the Beatles).

The near-incoherent, decidely unremarkable conversations of the Essex Uni. students are occasionally superceded by more voiceover from Brits pinpointing significant events in the history of British trade unions, general strikes and workers' movements. (If the discussions on-screen dip below a certain level of interest, the film simply fades them down and puts on a voiceover, a device employed in all of the Dziga Vertov Group pieces).

There's an upper-class twit in a suit and tie at a desk satiriziing a news presenter[22] declaiming about long-haired, work-shy oiks and Indian foreigners who live in squalor and should be deported or killed. Another element of *British Sounds* that would offend the head honchos at London Weekend Television was the full nudity. The shots of a naked woman (of course she's young and slender – Godard very seldom films large or older women – except in *Passion*, when recreating famous paintings) wandering around a house (coming right after the opening salvo of factory workers), and then standing there while the camera captures a very prolonged view of the Centre of the Cosmos (the naked pubis and torso), were not only completely gratuitous (and beside the point – any point!), they were also guaranteed to scandalize radical feminist viewers in a section of the film which supposedly voiced pro-feminist politics. The feminist discourse appeared in the voiceover (femninist writer Shiela Rowbotham collaborated on this section). The views expressed in the female voiceover are classic, second wave feminism, an assertion of women's rights to be on equal terms with men in contemporary, British society.

Once again, Jean-Luc Godard happily outrages his audience: by this time, in 1969, he was a Super-Class-A Genius at surprising and confronting viewers (Godard specialized in cinematic confrontation). And by this time, after so many feature films, it was getting harder to surprise and disturb audiences, as he knew well (but *Weekend* has a good go at it).

◆

British Sounds is a kind of of portrait of contemporary Britain which continued the visual approach of *One Plus One*, which followed Anne Wiazemsky painting slogans around London. Vignettes in *British Sounds* feature workers in a park, on roads, on building sites, and street scenes of London and elsewhere. The muddy, poor quality footage helps to make parts of England look squalid and drearily suburban. This is not the England of myth and legend, or of artists and writers, but a shabby nation still recovering from World War Two.

But Jean-Luc Godard has a fondness for filming out-of-the-way

---

22 This has the feel of a *Monty Python* or Spike Milligan skit (tho' nowhere near as accomplished). But even in jest the Pythons or Milligan wouldn't have been able to get away with some of the vitriol ladled out here.

locales, spots that no one else would bother to film, little corners where nothing is happening.

What's striking in contemplating Godard's two British films is how little the country has changed in 50 years. It's still tatty and mediocre, still hopelessly provincial and miserable... yet it's still the greatest country in the world, and London is still the most wonderful city of all cities (and, in the West, more people visit London than any other city – including, yes, Los Angeles, Roma, Berlin, Madrid, Rio, Paris or even Noo Yoik).

19

PRAVDA

PRAVDA

And so to *Pravda* (1970), filmed in Czechoslovakia in 1969, and dir., ed. and wr. by Jean-Luc Godard, Paul Burron and Jean-Henri Roger. Claude Nedjar produced for Centre Européen Cinéma-Radio-Television. Vera Chytilova and Godard were in the cast. Eastmancolor 16mm. Screened: May 21,1970 (New York). 58 mins.

Some recent events in Czechoslovakia's history which are part of the context of the *Pravda* film include:

1939   Germany took control of the nation.
1945   Russia moves into Czechoslovakia.
1948   A coup is staged by the Communists.
1968   The Prague Spring is suppressed by the Russian military.

(The Prague Spring, overseen by Alexander Dubeck (leader of the Czechoslovak Communist Party), lasted from January to August).

The U.S.S.R., Nikita Khrushchev, Marx, Mao, Lenin, Engels and others are continually referenced. (Yet *Pravda* omits plenty of the recent history of Czechoslovakia, such as the formation of the Czechoslovakia Republic after WWI, in 1918, and the Nazi invasion in 1939).

◆

The structure of *Pravda* comprised filming in contemporary Czechoslovakia (including Bratislava and Praha) combined with voiceovers. As usual with the other political films of Godard of the period, it's the voiceover that knits the whole thing together, that provides the contextual framework, and that makes numerous political points. You could regard *Pravda* as a voiceover illustrated with images, rather than a narration commenting on images. (Once again, the voiceover isn't a single voice explaining everything, as in the usual TV documentary. Instead, it's two voices (male and female), engaged in a dialogue. Yes, it's Vladimir and Rosa once again).

Pravda looks as if Godard gathered two or three cohorts to visit Czechoslovakia and make a documentary about it. They flew in with their 16mm cameras (sounds and voices could be added later), hired a car or two at Prague Ruzyne International Airport, and began driving around and filming whatever took their fancy.

As usual in the political films, Uncle Godard and company concentrated on scenes of people at work, often grabbed from afar (and perhaps without permission): women in a field, labourers outside a factory, and one of the Godardian stand-bys, road-mending crews.

Among the many images and scenes featured in *Pravda* are:
- people at work in factories;
- guys mending roads;
- a farm labourer on a farm;
- women working in the fields;
- images of fields, of farms;
- two people working at a haystack;
- an architect working in an office;
- a blast furnace;
- a classroom of students at a college;
- university students in Prague in a discussion;
- students outside their Prague university;
- an interview with workers in a factory;
- streetcars (lots of streetcars!);
- the colour red (of those streetcars);
- the car rented by the filmmakers at the airport (of course it's red);[23]
- big cars (the upper class) and small cars (the working class);
- waspish comments on Skoda cars;
- soldiers marching;
- military folk filmed secretly, from cars;
- propaganda posters and art;
- hotels;
- TV shows – news;
- television sets re-filmed;
- political rallies (in newsreels);
- a cinema[24] seen from outside;
- photos of films screened in said cinema;
- the covers of boxes of Airfix model kits;
- magazine articles and ads (some with Godard's writing over them);
- a red rose in a puddle;
- red wine being poured into a glass;
- pornographic photographs;
- a crowded tea dance;
- youths playing soccer in a local park;
- street signs and graffiti;
- advertizing hoardings and logos at night.

Godard returned to the same sorts of images when he filmed in

---
[23] But it's not a Maserati, alas.
[24] Kino Orlik.

Sarajevo 36 years later for *Our Music* (2004) – the streetcars again, the signage again.[25]

Pravda carefully avoids the famous sights of Czechoslovakia and Prague. No tourist spots, no Charles Bridge or St Vitus Cathedral or Old Town Square, no castles and ski resorts, no beautiful forests and mountains. Rather, *Pravda* focusses on regular, suburban streets, on factories, on parks. It's everyday Eastern Europe, where real people live and work.

Pravda is filmed in a seemingly socialist or Communist nation, but this time Godard and company are sceptical and critical. Czechoslovakia is not portrayed as a Marxian Paradise. It is compared with the West (and France in particular), but it's not seen as a Socialist Utopia. If you listened to the youths debating politics in Dziga Vertov Group films such as *A Film Like the Others,* you'd imagine that a visit to a Communist country would be a dream trip. What could be more exciting than seeing how Marxist, socialist political theory works in practice, in a real community?

But no. *Pravda* sees similar social differences between the bosses and the workers to those in the French Republic, and exposes the flaws in putting Communist theory into practice.

Pravda is not a State-sponsored work: it's the sort of warts-and-all portrait that Communist authorities wouldn't like to see shown in the West.

Pravda features the usual Godardian pops at Americana – *Playboy* pin-ups, U.S rental firms (Hertz, Avis), and the American military. (None of Godard's political films miss out attacking the U.S.A.).

A red rose held up to the camera and later looking sad and forlorn in a puddle is a symbolic motif in *Pravda* (can the movie get away with such an overtly sentimental device?). Indeed, the colour is rhymed many times in cars, streetcars, walls, blood, clothing, wine, etc (red's also deployed throughout Godard's 1960s movies).

There's a long account featuring Vladimir Lenin, blacksmiths, plows, peasants and the land, evoking notions of labour, collectivism, ownership, and Communism. Rosa, the female voice, speaks rapidly, urging the audience to action – to fight Imperialism, the authorities, the class system, etc.

For whom? against whom? is a recurring question in the voiceover, along with the usual encouragements to resist oppression, to

---

25 The score includes workers' songs and folk songs (and some are in French, not Czech).

fight the system, to be critical, to continue the class struggle, etc.

The most powerful shot in *Pravda* is of a guy working at a giant machine (a lathe?) in a metalworks factory. The beginning of the shot has handwritten captions intercut with it. But then the shot continues – the narration has died away, the captions are left aside, there's no music, but the man keeps working.

The shot says it all about the tedium and numbing repetition of work, the mindlessness of work, the dehumanization of work, the exploitation of work. It also captures the troubled relationship between humans and technology, how people are slaves to machines (rather than vice versa).

Jean-Luc Godard was certainly brilliant when it came to filming people working. And these scenes are often the most striking of all of the material in the political films of the 1968 to 1973 period. Godard often remarked that you don't see people working in movies, so he rectified that.

The 1970 film closes with workers leaving a factory after a day's work – accompanied by a rousing workers' song, this scene forms a sentimental tribute to labourers everywhere. The red rose pops up again. And the final image of *Pravda* is of a small, red flag attached to the front of a truck trundling thru the countryside, filmed from a car driving alongside (it's reminiscent of the flags attached to the camera crane at the end of *One Plus One*).

RIPLEY'S HOME VIDEO

mai 68
mai art x

UN FILM COMME LES AUTRES

un film di Jean-Luc Godard

Un film comme les autres | 1968 | Francia

LA BEAUTÈ SERA CONVULSIVE

20

VENT D'EST

WIND FROM THE EAST

Wind From the East (*Vent d'Est*, 1970) was:

A disgruntled, irritated film.

A self-conscious, defiant, wilfully eccentric rant.

A litany of personal and political disappointments which have been disguised by an off-screen, puritannical political lecture, which has only partially digested Marx, Mao and Lenin, which is accompanied by captions, quotations from Lenin, Eisenstein, Vertov, Althusser *et al*, plus insert images of Stalin, Mao *et al*, and illustrated with irrelevant, repetitious bits of boring actorly business (Actor A wanders over there, *avec* a rifle; Actors B and C lie in the grass; Actor D does something else equally nothingy).

Here be the credits for *Wind From the East*: co.-wr. by Godard, Jean-Pierre Gorin, Sergio Bazzini, Gianni Barcelloni, and Daniel Cohn-Bendit ('Danny the Red'), and co-dir. by Godard, Gorin and Gérard Martin. DP: Mario Vulpiani, editing: Gorin and Godard, sound: Carlo Diotalleri and Antonio Ventura. The cast: Gian Maria Volonté, Anne Wiazemsky, Christiana Tullio-Altan, Allan Midgette,[1] Vanessa Redgrave, Glauber Rocha, Palo Pozzesi, José Varela and Götz George. Released: Aug 19, 1970. 95 mins.

Cineriz put up some of the money (Cineriz had been founded by Federico Fellini and Angelo Rizzoli in the early 1960s, initially to back Fellini's projects).[2] Money also came from Polifilm (Rome), Film Kunst and C.C.C. Studios (Berlin), and Georges du Beauregard.

The initial idea was for a 'Left-Wing Spaghetti Western' to be filmed by Jean-Luc Godard. The concept sounds great – and it's the best thing about *Wind From the East* (known in the People's Republic of China as *Cooking With Chairman Mao* – available on VCDs in the backstreets of Beijing).

Gian Volonté was familiar from the Spaghetti Westerns (you'll recognize him from gun fights with Clint Eastwood in the *Fistful of Dollars* series). Volonté harboured passionate left-wing politics.

Anne Wiazemsky is the other well-known face in *Wind From the East* (tho' at the time – 1970 – only to those who'd seen her appearances in the films of Godard and Robert Bresson and one or two others. She was only 23). With her long, swishy, gypsy dresses, Wiazemsky looks like a Haight-Ashbury flower child,[3] and about as non-revolutionary and non-militant as possible (altho' she's called

---

[1] An Andy Warhol impersonator.
[2] When Federico Fellini established the Cineriz company with Angelo Rizzoli in the 1960s, with the aim of taking on other projects as well as Fellini's own, it soon became apparent that Fellini wasn't that bothered. He liked to immerse himself in his own productions.
[3] She even has a flower in her hair and a white, cotton dress.

Miss Althusser, and is sort of supposed to be one of the radicals/activists).

The filmmakers gathered in the countryside outside Roma (interiors were filmed at De Paoli Studios in Rome, and exteriors at Elios Studios). But the production rapidly became messy. The shooting wound on for three months (*far* too long for Godard, as we know), during Spring, 1969. Godard considered ankling (it's amazing that he stayed that long). Much of the film was re-shot in and around Paris (consequently, some of the cast didn't appear in the re-filmed version).

There was a substantial budget for *Blow-Out From the East* – rumoured to be $220,000. That can't be accurate – *Weekend*'s budget was $250,000, for instance (a much bigger movie in every way). If there really was $220,000 in the coffers, it was likely spent on other things, like cigarettes or purple flared pants. (The budget was big enough, however, for some of the film collective to decamp to the Eternal City, where the production was going to be made. In the end, much of the Italian footage was scrapped, and the film was re-staged back in France. Rumours developed of the money paid to the crew (handed out each week by Uncle Godard himself) finding its way into buying a Ferrari, or paying off debts to the Mafia, or for running guns to Israel. Not really. Whatever).

Like the other 1968-1973 political films from the Maestro and his chums, *Wind From the East* attracted some interest from critics – it's a film essay that's perfect for discussing in film essays (such as Peter Wollen: "Godard and Counter Cinema: *Vent d'est*", Julia Lesage: "Godard-Gorin's *Wind from the East*: Looking at a film politically", and Jacques Derrida: "How I Learned To Love *Vent d'est*").

The 1968-1973 agitprop films raise the question: can a successful film director subsume themselves in a filmmaking co-operative, and be just one of the gang? No – not when they are a superstar *auteur* who has genuinely invented and re-invented cinema (which nobody else in the collective/s had achieved – not then and not since. Let's face it, fellow *cinéastes,* we are only thinking of maybe possibly one day contemplating these movies because God-Art was involved).

But the notion of the *auteur,* the film director as Herr Dicktator, is rejected – because they are bosses, like the bosses who run car factories – in favour of the collective, where all pigs (ooops, I mean all dogs) are equal (why does *Animal Farm* come to mind here?).[4]

Wind From the East draws attention to its manufacture, and how

---
4 *Animal Farm* – now there's a novel that's perfect for late 1960s Godard!

the collective of filmmakers worked: decisions were made by the group (Down With the Boss! Kill Herr Direktor!); film conventions like proper sound and editing were rejected (too mainstream, too bourgeois); the films were made cheaply, with small crews, on 16 millimetre; and in the end it's about (the) process (very 1960s – linking the films with Process/ Systems/ Serial Art, where artworks were based on simple processes or principles).

Wind From the East does come across in parts (the parts which exhibit Jean-Luc Godard's input) as if the Maestro was worrying over his committment to political issues, and how to produce political cinema. Yet we also know that Godard insisted many times (at the time and later), that he was a *superficial* follower or believer in Maoist and Marxist politics. He loved to wind people up. He loved to take the opposing theoretical position (no matter what it was), just for the hell of it – and because that's how he's put together as a person. (You think that Godard is extremely left-wing and Maoist-Marxist-Leninist, but then he'll deliberately annoy everybody with jokes about Adolf Hitler or fascism).

J.-L. Godard asserted that he had never read *Das Kapital* or Karl Marx's other trash novels about jet-setting, coke-addled supermodels. Godard used Marx 'only as a provocation, mixing Mao and Coca-Cola and so forth'. Godard said it was a 'political romanticism': 'I loved Mao as I loved Goethe'. Yet many intellectuals and critics (including some who should've known better), bought it wholesale (at the time *and* since). They really did find the racist, right-wing skit in *British Sounds* disturbing. They really did think (or some of them seemed to think) that this very bourgeois, Swiss-French film director (son of a doctor, from a thoroughly bourgeois background), had become a Left-Wing Rebel Artiste, the Che Guervara of Political Cinema.

⁂

Did Jean-Pierre Gorin lead Jean-Luc Godard astray, into collective filmmaking and over-zealous ideological rants? Anne Wiazemsky, the chief female presence in *Wind From the East*, thought so. For Wiazemsky, it all started to go wrong for her and Godard when he became involved with Gorin and the co-operative approach to filmmaking. (In some scenes, Wiazemsky does not look happy to be there). [5]

Many of the meetings of the political film collective in this late Sixties era took place at Jean-Luc Godard's Paris apartment, where he

---

5 Possibly in the scenes directed by Gorin.

lived with Anne Wiazemsky; some of the group stayed over or lived there. Maybe those meetings and discussions got a little uncomfortable for Wiazemsky.

However, Jean-Pierre Gorin only joined the production of *Wind From the East* late in the shooting; his contribution, rather, was to the editing and the sound. But after *Wind From the Crease*, in films such as *Muggles In Italy*, Gorin's input was considerable.

&

The left-wing politics in *Wind From the East* is Marxist and Leninist – in line with lifestyle magazines such as *Marxist Marie-Claire* and *Leninist Elle* (J.-P. Gorin worked for the *Cahiers Marxistes-Leninistes* magazine).

Wind From the East is also a teaching aid, a guide for militant filmmakers, Godard 'n' Gorin's *Handbook of Radical Cinema*. There are numerous exhortations to the audience (and to the filmmakers themselves – this is Godard's encouragement to himself and to like-minded souls).

Wind From the East begs you to start making militant/ radical/ left-wing films. *Wind From the Lease* reminds you:
- It's OK to rebel.
- Don't be abstract. Be clear.
- Read the Marxist and Leninist texts.
- Be socialist (but not a bourgeois socialist).
- Avoid 'Ollywooood, the West, capitalists, bosses, Swiss cheese.
- Go on strike. Cause trouble. Throw bombs. Terrorize.

Visually, *Wind From the Fleas* is a patchwork of Godardisms, poked and prodded into some kind of simulcrum of life by the process of film editing (cut back to a shot of Stalin, cut to a caption, cut to a shot of the crew sitting about, cut to a shot of Mao, cut to a shot of a tree)… Without the editing chopping up this mess of images (i.e., thankfully shortening the shots), *Wind From the East* would be unbearable. (This is one of many Godard productions which was largely created in post-production).

This time, in *Wind From the East*, the attempts at dramatization were decidedly lukewarm at best, and came across in the main as silly home movies. A bunch of filmmakers (scarily looking like hippies and as bourgeois and non-radical as you can imagine), go into the countryside in Summer to film some actors doing nothing in particular. Oh, all right, they *are* some activities or attempts at some such – they graffiti slogans on walls ('U' or 'UNION' in red paint), they run down a hill (no, this isn't *Jules et Jim*), they climb thru a barbed wire fence and pin a piece of paper on it containing the phrase: 'WHERE'S MY MONEY?' (no, no, it's 'UNION' again), and they... oh, *who cares*?!

Maybe the weedy efforts at dramatizations in *Wind From the East* (also known in Nebraska as *How To Start a Revolution – On 20 Dollars a Day*) are what emerge from the fIilm co-operative approach, the let's-all-be-equal decision process. In which case, the committee failed many times: images of people walking in fields and trees such as these are hollow. There's simply nothing here. (J.-L. Godard would later call such shots 'empty').

◆

Wind From the East opens with a single shot of two people lying on the ground for four minutes – as if the movie has already given up and collapsed from over-indulgence due to ideological ranting even before it's begun. And so by 8 minutes into *Wind From the East* (i.e., a *long* time in movie terms), we've thrilled and gasped at only *four shots* – another angle of the couple on the grass, and two fantastically empty shots of a guy (Volonté) with a rifle walking on a wall (instead of stopping the camera, the guy repeats the action, so we get several takes of absolutely nothing). Will the movie get better than this? *Hmmm*. Don't be on that. (As an opening sequence, it's among the lamest in *das kino*).

Over these scenes several voices off-screen evoke strikes, factories, workers and bosses; the chief voice (female) anchors the movie within a Marxist-Leninist rhetoric; other voices include unionists and the union delegate, in relation to a strike. The narration of the *Windy East* movie thus dramatizes a recent strike (and it sounds more compelling than the images we're shown).

Wind From the East admits to all that it hasn't found or developed the images to visualize or dramatize whatever the film purports to be about. A more honest (or more accurate) approach would be to ditch the stupid scenes of actors wandering about in fields and trees completely.

These scenes look like someone is doing a pastiche of Jean-Luc Godard's form of cinema but without any punchlines or jokes or even a solid point-of-view. The material is so feeble, we wouldn't be discussing it today if we didn't know that Godard was linked to it (without Godard's name, this 1970 film would be dumped in the pile marked 'Might Watch Later' (knowing damn well we'd never watch it later), and never see the light of day again).

The voiceover in *Wind From the East* urges us to:

Think. Read. Look. Wait.

And I would add:

Itch. Yawn. Sleep.

The voiceover castigates you, me, everybody – complaining that you/ me/ all of us aren't making the right sort of movie, that we/ you/ us haven't understood the class struggle or Marxism or revolution properly. This is Godard and Gorin criticizing themselves.

Ingmar Bergman found Godard a 'fucking bore' – that was in relation to the wonderful movie *Masculin Féminin*. Lordy knows what the Big Berg-Man would've made of *Wind From the Priest*! (Bergman can't have seen it – very few people have).

The images of young and middle-aged people sitting about in the sunshine somewhere in the country while a debate rages on the soundtrack are wilfully clumsy (these seem to be filmed during the meetings in the morning where the group decided What To Do). The political arguments we hear are not linked to the images we see. Better to simply use black leader, and have the screen go dark (it's cheaper). [6]

The black leader and the red leader in Godard's films make themselves known in force in the 68-73 politicized films. The movies' voiceovers sometimes refer to the use of the leader, fumbling around with analyses without coming clean about the chief reason: *padding*.

So the group discussion is filmed, but it's all *faked*: all of the voices we hear on the soundtrack are *not* spoken by the figures we see on the screen. We might see people looking as if they are sitting on the grass (and smoking cigs like chimneys), but we don't hear their speech, we hear other voices. And we also hear the female narrator, who's talking about something else entirely (strikes and such). The movie thus imposes a single voice of authority on top of what was supposed to be a democratic group discussion. (The cutting also fakes the notion of the democratic discussion by bringing in images of Chairman Mao and Josef Stalin and the captions).

There's another group discussion scene towards the end of the movie (you can see Godard sitting on the grass with the youths). But it's sabotaged by being cut into uselessly tiny portions, has a different voiceover plastered over it, and then visual noise is superimposed on it (or maybe the footage was wrecked in the lab, but the filmmakers had to use it anyway to make up the running time).

---

6 This occurs later on.

Wait a second – maybe the fooling around by these bourgeois hippies in *Wind From the East* is actually meant to be a Western? The diatribe in the voiceover suggests so: it makes the link between the West and one of Hollywood's famous film genres, the cowboy movie. Get it? The West and the Western. (Let's forget for the mo' that Godard absolutely adores many Westerns, and regarded directors like Anthony Mann and Howard Hawks as gods).

So the horse, the rifle, the Capitalist, the Yankee, and the 'Native American' guy are kind of sort of maybe supposed to be evocations of elements of cowboy flicks?[7] OK. But why spend so much of the movie with a lame send-up/ political satire of a film genre which is detested for what it represents – bourgeois cinema *à la* Hollywood (or "Ollywooood' as it's pronounced in French by the off-screen voice). These scenes are the remnants of the 'left-wing Spaghetti Western' concept, filmed in Italy.

We get the point from five minutes of satire/ spoof/ parody – there's no need for more'n that. The more screen time that *Wind From the Cheat* spends laying into its loathed forms of imperialist cinema means *less* time for putting forward the kind of cinema the filmmakers would like to see. (Sure, it makes sense to clear out the Old before setting up the New (like super-villains in action movies who want to destroy the world), but we already know what the Old is).

Why spend so much time sending up bourgeois, 'Ollywooood cinema? It's a waste of effort: tell us what you really want to film, instead. Or better yet, *show* us. Anybody can send up cowboy flicks.[8] (Besides, 'Ollywooood and cowboy pictures are too easy targets for radical/ political/ activist filmmakers. An attack on such targets is like shooting fish in a barrel.)

One wonders if a cowboy movie was selected as the subject of parody in *Wind From the East* because there had been a brief rivival of Westerns around this time: in 1969, the top-grossing movie globally was *Butch Cassidy and the Sundance Kid* ($97.7 million gross in the U.S. of A.), while *True Grit* had also been a hit. (And maybe the bizarre religious/ hippy Western *El Topo* (1970), directed by Alejandro Jodorowsky, which started the craze for midnight movies, is another reference point, plus *The Wild Bunch* and some of the bleaker Spaghetti Westerns).

---

7 Or maybe a Spaghetti Western.
8 Besides, to be really picky, Spaghetti Western are *European* pastiches of North American film forms. The target should be John Wayne movies, not Sergio Leone movies.

The truth is, *Wind From the East* and the other 68-73 political films and the Dziga Vertov Group films happily *attack* Hollywood, or institutions, or political systems, or bourgeois ideologies, but they have *nothing of their own* to put in their place, nothing to replace them with, nothing for us to focus on.

Yes, we understand the bile and hatred for the Western world, for capitalism, for 'Ollywooood, for bosses, for repression, for the ruling classes. *We're with you, comrade!* But what is going to replace it? Where is the utopian project which outlines a new art, a new cinema, a new politics, a new world, a new life? Where is the flood of thrilling ideas for new forms of existence, new political systems? Are we just going to watch people attacking something without suggesting what might work instead? Anyone can destroy stuff – humans are brilliant at it (it's something they find very easy to do, something they learn how to do very young).

Rainer Werner Fassbinder had a get-out clause: he wouldn't cook up a utopia for you, instead, his view of formulating a utopia was to leave it to the viewer's imagination:

> I don't want to formulate this utopia for you because if I do, it ceases to exist as a utopia. It's an idea and that can be struggled for. (in D. Georgakas, 183)

A bourgeois woman reads aloud from Marcel Proust while people wielding a hammer and sickle attack her – it's the embodiment of 'death to the bourgeoisie' issue. (<u>Don't yawn – stay awake! Think! Read! Be self-critical!</u>).

A table of books set up in a field is the stage for several weedy skits in *Puff of a Breeze From the Orient*. Anne Wiazemsky holds forth (reading from a tract). The Capitalist holds forth (reading from a book). A guy plays a recorder incredibly badly.[9] People heckle from behind the camera (it might be the crew (we hear the Maestro), or it might be a passing busload of drunk, Japanese tourists looking for the Eiffel Tower).

Near the end of *Wind From the East*, close-ups of how to make bombs or weapons were included – a provocation to political activism. These scenes were added later, as were many of the skits).

There's lots of red in *Wind From the East* – it's splashed over actors during scenes (even over Anne Wiazemsky – as at the end of *One Plus One*), evoking political repression, and the screen is tinted red

---

[9] Reminding us that unless the plastic recorder, staple of music lessons in schools, is played properly, it always sounds horrible.

(it makes a change from black).

By the mid-1960s, the films of Jean-Luc Godard included repeated takes of the same action. Oh, it wasn't padding, you understand, because all of Godard's movies fell short of the expected 80-90 mins for a feature film. *Mais non*, it was a brilliant deconstruction of bourgeois, imperialist cinema. *Wind From the East* performs the feat several times (Godard's films only did it once or twice). So we have several takes of a guy (Mr Soldier) on a horse leading a guy (the 'Native American') on a rope; and more shots of the guy on the horse leading the guy on a rope; and several takes of the Yankee strangling Miss Althusser (while someone (likely Godard) off-camera throws red paint over her), etc.

An hour into the 1970 movie, and the shrill woman[10] on the soundtrack is *still* prattling on about strikes and factories and workers and bosses. Eh? Weren't those points (*worthy, to be sure, my donkey-jacketed comrade*) already made by the twelfth minute of the movie? Why are the *same messages* being delivered in the narration 50 minutes later? In case those of us remaining in the audience forgot? We didn't forget! We're right here, watching the fucking movie! (Or is it, like the repeated inserts of 'Comrade Stalin' earlier, more padding?).

Wind From the East isn't all images of young radicals gathered for their Annual Marxist-Leninist Picnic in Rome or the Bois de Boulogne: there *are* images of Other Things: a Parisian street. Workers outside a car factory. The River Seine. Farm labourers. (And immediately, the stern voiceover slaps the film's fingers: you train a camera on people at work and think you're a radical filmmaker?).

☆

Much of *Wind From the Tease* is actually a harrangue like a radio broadcast – not national radio, but college radio, amateur, student radio beamed out over the campus with only eleven people tuning in (and that's only after they've been leafleted on their way to the Student Union bar). Yes – we are preaching to the *converted*, my duffel-coated comrades. It doesn't introduce ideas about revolutionary politics, and about revolution and ideology, or contextualize them, or relate them to other political concepts; it assumes that the audience is already there, with them, manning the imaginary barricades of this imaginary debate.

In case you don't have a brain, and have forgotten something that was intoned on the soundtrack, *Wind From the East* repeats itself:

---

10 She never identifies herself.

Bourgeois = bad	Left-wing = good
'Ollywoood = bad	Militant cinema = good
Nixon & Johnson = bad	Stalin & Mao = good
America = very bad	China = very good
Cheese after 8 p.m. = bad	Cheese on toast before 2 p.m. = good

These simplistic oppositions resemble a list of likes and dislikes of 'what's new' or 'what's cool' in lifestyle magazines.[11] These are regular features, when journos are out of ideas: a list of current cool fashion, say, or current tastes. The Dziga Vertov Group films and 68>73 politi-films are Godard's versions of lists – with the 'dislikes' far outnumbering the 'likes'. Big G.'s political works assert what they *don't* like all the time: the bourgeoisie, bosses, factories, Amerika, capitalism, fake tans, pencil skirts, John Wayne, the colour blue, slow drivers, old men who wear baseball caps, people who don't ever pick up the tab at lunch, and filmmakers who won't shut up.

Don't worry if you've forgotten what the voiceover just said, it'll be repeated ten minutes down the line, in the next pseudo-quasi-meta-para scene. That old voiceover keeps coming up with juicy nuggets from the Class Struggle. Like:

It's right to rebel.[12]
Think about the civil war between labour and capital.
Death to the bourgeoisie.

One thing is very obvious looking at *Wind From the Feast*: this is *not* all Godard-Godard-Godard. For a start, it was co-written with Jean-Pierre Gorin, Sergeio Bazzini and Daniel Cohn-Bendit, and it was co-dir. by Godard, Gorin and Gérard Martin. Many scenes are clearly not directed by Godard (we can tell by the use of the camera, the camera angles (and even the choice of lenses), the blocking of the actors, the movement within the frame – Godard has a very distinctive cinematographic style, and *Wind From the East* was not all overseen by the Maestro). Some of the editing and the sound editing of voices off was also not by Godard. (However, Gorin, recovering from an accident, only joined the production towards the end of the schedule. So maybe it was more Godard and Martin).

☆

---

11 Hey, what a surprise, my beauties, black is 'in' this month again! Like wearing black ever went out of fashion in Paris, Milan, Tokyo or New York!
12 Damn straight 'it's right to rebel'! It's the most sacred act of being human.

And it's humourless.[13]

Wind From the Beast is hard-going, even for dedicated Godard worshippers like us. I mean, even his most passionate admirers have found the Maoist-Marxist works of post-May, 1968 difficult.

(But then, *Wind From the East* doesn't make things easy for the viewer! It opens with a four-minute shot of two people lying on the ground! Is this a spoof of Andy Warhol[14] and his films of people sleeping or doing nothing? Is it a satirical commentary on political activism? (i.e., *non*-activity?). Is it two people embarking on their own political revolution, their fervent class struggle and self-criticism, by doing nothing and resting? Are these people conducting their own strike – a strike from themselves? or a strike against life itself?).

☆

The meat[15] of *Wind From the East* is found in the voiceover: *Wind From the East* presents a collage of (1) rants, (2) several voices off, and (3) found sounds (including extracts from news footage). It's in the off-screen, invisible element of sound that *Wind From the East* delivers its true subject – which is politics in general, ideology in general, and Communist/ left-wing/ socialist politics in particular, and cinema/ media/ representation in particular. (That is, *Wind From the East* was largely created after pre-production and after filming, in post-production).

The 1970 film assumes a good deal – for example, that the audience is already well-informed of the social-political context of the topics it's raising. You do know all about Stalinism in the 1930s, don't you? Of course you do. You know about Sergei Eisenstein's unmade film projects in the '30s? Of course. You know the key dates of revolution (1789, 1871, 1937, 1968)? Yes, you do. You know about the political allegiances of long-gone journals such as the *Humanist*, don't you? *Bien sûr.*

Wind From the Wheeze comes across like a personal film project of a small group of filmmakers (Ye Olde Collective or Co-operative or Workshoppe – very 1970), who have bravely and nobly produced a film. But it's created primarily (maybe solely) for themselves. (Well, they do say that you have to please yourself first as an artist, otherwise you can't expect to thrill anybody else. Unfortunately, it didn't work here).

The impassioned ranting in the voiceover of *Wind From the East*

---

13 Even though Godard in *Vent d'est* is certainly at his jokiest and most playful.
14 And you thought *Chelsea Girls* (1966) was challenging to endure for even 15 minutes.
15 It's not prime steak, of course, but, for the hippies in the audience, a veggie substitute.

evokes all of the usual motifs of socialist/ left-wing political activism:

Strikes	Workers	Unions
Bosses	Capitalists	Governments

The assumptions that *Wind From the East* makes of its audience is that they (we) are all in agreement that:

Communism = heap good	Capitalism = heap bad.
Left-wing = good	Right-wing = bad.
Stalin & Mao = good	Nixon & Johnson = bad.
Militant cinema = good	Hollywood = bad.

In the gimmicky parlance of the voiceover, Nixon-Paramount is pitted against Brezhnev-Mosfilm (that bit is definitely written by Godard). The narration also points out that they're pretty much the same, a Nixon-Paramount-Brezhnev-Mosfilm conglomerate. And, *tch*, they're bourgeois anyway.

☆

Jean-Luc G. and company had done it all before – in *Weekend, One Plus One* and *La Chinoise, par example* (the latter also starred Anne Wiazemsky, like *Wind From the East*). All of the points delivered in *Wind From the Cheese* in that angry but awkward manner, about Communism under Lenin, under Stalin, under Mao • about how Stalinism, Leninism and Maoism relate to the present day • about political filmmaking (here dubbed 'militant filmmaking') • about how very bourgeois and repressive 'Ollywoood cinema is • about the significance of Sergei Eisenstein and Dziga Vertov to today's cinematic practice • about what students, young people, and activists should be doing in contemporary society in the political arena...... *all* of these issues had already been raised and debated in movies such as *One Plus One, La Chinoise* and *Weekend* (and, many would agree, much more successfully. Or, at least, much funnier).

You want an anti-bourgeois film? *Weekend* is that – and *Weekend* is not a polite, well-mannered anti-bourgeois, anti-decadent film, it's violently angry.

But the fictional structure of the feature-length movies helmed by Jean-Luc Godard prior to the politicized pieces of post-1968 doesn't negate or weaken any of the ideological/ political material delivered within stories. On the contrary, the fiction films are far more accomplished at making the same points. (For the political films and for the Dziga Vertov Group project, fiction was deemed bourgeois, imperialist – documentary or 'realism' was the thing).

Well, you could argue (if you could be bothered) that *Wind From the Ease* is a kind of like a look back at 1968, and at Godard's involvement in political cinema, and revolutionary politics, and at the impact of the civil unrest of 1968 two years down the line.

But *Wind From the Freeze* has not dated well, and seems too niche, too self-enclosed, too snobbish about its political, ideological approach. It doesn't invite you in – hell, it doesn't really want you to watch it at all (why? Because you're *too bourgeois*! Because audiences are *bourgeois*! Because the very notion of films playing to audiences is *bourgeois*![16] Because if you've paid for a ticket or for a DVD disc, you are *bourgeois*! And if you're watching this on a television set you bought, you are *bourgeois*!).

John Lennon (not Lenin) did all of this in a three-minute pop song, 'Revolution' (first recorded by the Beatles at the end of May, 1968). Yes – *Wind From the East* has already said all it has to say by – what? – ten minutes into the piece? 20 minutes? After that, it's repetition all the way.

That's common in a lecture in a theatre. We've all sat thru lectures – in colleges, universities, art museums, cinemas, etc – where the speaker has only one thing to say. Maybe two, tops. But they spend 45 minutes, or 75 minutes, repeating it, and providing variations on it.

The best lectures are entertaining *as well as* informative/ provocative/ knowledgable. The worst lectures think it's enough to simply deliver information, like a machine, from mouth to ear, from mind to mind.

It's a sin to be given an audience of 200 people and then to bore them.

☆

I don't buy this movie.[17]

I also reckon that *Wind From the Keys* was a mere footnote to material and issues that Godard and company had presented far more significantly and skilfully elsewhere. *Wind From the East* is like an amateur, Sunday afternoon painter's version of what a political film might be: *grab a camera! call your friends! bring your air guns! jump in the VW camper! let's go and make a movie!* (Or maybe it's the Godardian/ Marxist/ Activist equivalent of a Hollywood musical movie

---

16 Even Eisenstein is *bourgeois*!
17 But I *did* buy this movie! Or the DVD, at least.

like *The Band Wagon* or *Summer Stock*, where Fred Astaire or Gene Kelly or Mickey Rooney can lead a bunch of rosy-cheeked, red-checked-shirt-wearing, eager youngsters: *hey kids, let's put on a show!* And they all pile into the barn to do just that).

Hollywood cinema is the sublimest expression of the Great American Dream, right? (Along with pop music, cars, Coca Cola, etc). So what is *Wind From the East* and the political 1968-1973 films? The Great Marxist Revolution?

Not hardly.

21

LUTTES EN ITALIE

STRUGGLE IN ITALY

Luttes en Italie (*Lotte en Italia/ Struggle In Italy*,[18] 1971) was another of Zen Master Godard's politicized, post-1968 all-action, all-star spectacles. A blockbuster epic filmed on four continents with a cast of thousands, *Struggle In Italy* told the story of the rise and fall of the Roman Empire from its origins in the mists of time to the height of the Caesars and the subsequent invasion by Barbarians, Vandals and Goths – but from the point-of-view of a slave girl called Lottie (who, incredibly, was a Marxist activist two thousand years before that pretentious pose became fashionable among white, bourgeois intellectuals in late 1960s Paris).

You remember *Spartacus* (1960), of course? – a famously left-leaning film starring Kirk Douglas – the team behind it (including the blacklisted writer, the star/ producer and the director) espoused left-wing political views (and not too long after the witch-hunts of the early 1950s). Well, *Struggle In Italy* built on the example of *Spartacus*: yes, my red-flag-waving, wannabe working-class comrades, you *could* make a giant movie in the Hollywood system which delivered action, romance, comedy, spectacle and thrills *and* clear and provocative left-wing politics.

The credits for *Struggle In Italy*: dir. and ed. by Dziga Vertov Group, Godard and Gorin; and prod. by Cosmoseion for R.A.I. TV. The cast: Cristina Tullio-Altan, Anne Wiazemsky, Paolo Pozzesi and Jerome Hinstin. Godard said that Gorin was responsible for much of the film. Most of it was filmed in Godard's Paris apartment, with the odd trip to the *tabac* for a newspaper and packet of cigarettes. (Godard did the same in his later works, which included scenes filmed in his digs, or out of his office window, or on the street just outside. Why bother to trek to distant locales when you can do it all from your home? Godard is brilliant (and bold) enough to be able to pull that off. *Detective,* for example, was set enitrely in a swanky Paris hotel. The budget for these Dziggy Fartoff films didn't stretch to that. And anyway, hotels were too imperialist, comrade, too nationalist and bourgeois for that).

Scenes From the Class Struggle In Italy was centred around a young woman (Paola Taviani, played by Cristina Tullio-Altan); [19] her political activity formed the loose structure of *Struggle In Italy*, but the film was the usual left-wing rant disguised as a pseudo-*avant garde* film which hoped to be a call to arms. (So it's a remake of *La Chinoise*

---
18 The title comes from a supremely bourgeois film, one of Godard's very favourites: *Voyage In Italy* (one of the Top 100 Best Films on many critics' lists. (I haven't been able to get through even half of it).
19 She was in *Wind From the East*.

– a girl and politics).

These are films of ideas, of processes, of the relationship between the filmmakers and the audience – they are not finished, glossy products. *Struggle In Italy* was not intended, either, to be released in theatres alongside *Billy Jack, Fiddler On the Roof, Carnal Knowledge* or *Diamonds Are Forever* (the top-grossing movies of 1971). *Struggle In Italy* was commissioned by German television (where it was shown on February 27, 1971).

☆

This is just miserable.

Struggle In Italy (known in Cuba as *Everything You Never Really Wanted To Know About Marxism*) has no reality, no juice, no *oomph*, no nothing. *Struggle In Italy* is so tough-going, it makes you long for Godard-directed garbage like *King Lear* (1987)! Everybody is free to make mistakes, sure, but nobody watching the dailies of this movie could've imagined that it would make for compelling viewing.

Richard Brody suggested that *British Sounds* 'has the stiff and self-punishing feel of a cinematic hair shirt' (B, 345). Yes, watching the 1968-1973 political films, it does feel as if you've been kidnapped in the night, bundled into a truck (with a smelly sack over your head and your hands bound), driven into the mountains, and told to sit on the freezing ground and wait.[20] After an hour, the hood is roughly removed, you blink, you look round: *oh shit*! – you're one of 300 people making up the audience of an open-air cinema and what's on the screen? *Sunrise? The Magnificent Ambersons? The Seven Samurai? Airplane? Star Wars?* Nope: it's *Struggle In Italy*!

☆

The main character/ figure/ lifeform in *Struggle In Italy* is Paola Taviani (named after one of the Taviani film director brothers, b. 1931). Perhaps Cristina Tullio-Altan was cast for her very ordinariness, a regular Italian woman. But Tullio-Altan doesn't make this film any easier to get through. (So it wasn't, alas, Anne Wiazemsky or Juliet Berto.[21] Maybe Wiazemsky was deemed too glamorous for this part – she had already essayed the same sort of role in *La Chinoise*. And the film wanted an Italian actress).

Lotte en Italia doesn't mean *Lottie In Italy* in English – this isn't a sequel to *Roman Holiday*, charting the adventures of a cute starlet in the Land of Passion and Opera!

---

20 Remember, you must: Wait. Think. Read. Practice. Wait.
21 Anne Wiazemsky, bless her, appears in the role of a saleswoman in a clothing store (!), helping our young activist try on clothes (and speaking in Italian, too).

Hell, no. *Lotte/ Lutte* means *struggle*, folks. Struggle (I repeat this because the film repeats essential items, too – because the film repeats essential things, too).

In a typical piece of Godardian eccentricity, Cristina Tullio-Altan speaks in Italian but is translated by a female voiceover into French. Television prefers this kind of dubbing, instead of subtitles (TV typically uses live dubbing for news interviews), but it always comes across as clunky, and, in the ethical terms of the approach of Godard's political films of 68-73, it's ideologically dubious. Yet we know that Godard preferred dubbing for his own movies, which he thought weas more honest than subtitles)

Struggle In Italy is sort of divided into sections: 'Society', 'Identity', 'Family', 'Sex', 'Shopping', 'Plumbing', etc. But the way that these topics are evoked is rather patchy – 'Family' doesn't particularly evoke the family of the young woman Taviani, but suggests parental figures with off-screen voices[22] (and a close-up of soup being eaten).[23] The parents berate the girl for continuing to live at home, exploiting them.

Struggle In Italy is itself an artefact that questions itself: who is this film for? Who is this film against? Self-criticism is a key practice in the Dziga Vertov Group comedy epics.

I watched *Struggle In Italy* immediately after *Wind From the East*: it's the same movie! No, OK, not exactly – but it's the same left-wing diatribe! It's the same political-ideological-social rant from a left-leaning perspective – the only difference is that the bunch of dopey hippies in the countryside have been replaced by a very boring young woman in an apartment.

Watching the two films gives you the scary, depressing notion that this group of politicized filmmakers actually had only a few things to say. Or they repeated the same things many times. (And they padded out their meagre works with black leader or red leader or they recycled the footage).

This is political, ideological claustrophobia. It feels like being trapped, it's torture in the form of being force-fed rhetoric.

You want to laugh but that has been outlawed.

You want to cry but that has been outlawed.

You want to leave the room but that has been outlawed.

You want to dematerialize to another dimension of space and time

---

[22] Talk about low budget! Where's Dad? Oh, he's an off-screen voice!
[23] The fancy bowl and the formal-ish dinner suggests Taviani's bourgeois background. See, this film *is* thought out!

but that has been outlawed.

☆

Sound was one of the preoccupations of the political films of the post-1968 era and the Dziga Vertov Group works (handily, it was also one of the cheapest components – a voiceover is much cheaper than 25 nights for 30 crew at even a modestly budgeted hotel). The 1968-1973 political films are, literally, sounds and images, pieces which draw attention to their construction as sounds and images. James Monaco noted that for Godard, sound 'suffers under the tyranny of image; there should be an equal relationship between the two' (1977b, 324). Maybe – but Godard got this own back by including black or red leader, thus negating the image with a sledgehammer. Or he recycled the images, anæthetizing the viewer.

At a budgetary level, some of the 68-to-73 politics films impress with their clever use of off-screen voices and sounds to suggest things that they don't have the $$$$ or the FFFFF to show. A police officer (or some such) asking to see the papers of the young woman Taviani in *Bungles In Italy* is merely an off-screen voice and the hand/ arm of a crew member (no need for even a police uniform). Ditto with the store owner who orders a shop assistant back to work, or even parents (Daddy can just be an off-screen voice). One guy – Paolo Pozzesi – plays those off-screen embodiments of patriarchy (cops, fathers, bosses).

Altho' the film is entitled *Struggle In Italy*, it might've been filmed anywhere in the Solar System[24] (most of the scenes are interiors). There are shots of Italy which might come from a film library, or maybe someone was sent to Italia with a 16mm camera to grab some exterior shots. (But there is no feeling whatsoever that this is Italy, no contextualization, and there's nothing particularly Italian about the movie). In fact, most of it was filmed in Godard's pad in Paree.

Struggle In Italy ignores contextualization by, say, looking at the Partito Comunista Italiano,[25] or conducting interviews with left-wing activists. If you take *Struggle In Italy* at face value, the only person pursuing Communist politics in Italy is this one woman, Taviani (and one cohort).

Like other Dziga Vertov Group films, *Struggle In Italy* admits shamelessly that it does *not* have enough material to stretch to an hour of running time. The black leader already appears within minutes of the start (sometimes it's red), so that the screen goes dark for a few

---

[24] Pluto and Neptune have reasonable rates for visiting film productions.
[25] There's a shot of a building with an Italian Communist Party sign outside.

seconds, while nothing is said, nothing is heard, and nothing is seen (in other sections, the voiceover and the dialogue continues over the black leader). In addition, the movie's title card - an ugly, handwritten note on white paper (costing 20 centimes) - is repeated. (Towards the close of the 1971 movie, the red leader lasts for eons - enough time to stage a two-hour, sit-down strike at Pirelli, grab a coffee in your favourite café afterwards, be interviewed for the R.A.I. news at six, and get back to the movie in time for more red leader).

And then there's the vexed issue of repetition (of repetition... of repetition). Pretty much all television documentaries repeat material, often when they hope to make a point. OK. We let that slide. But *Struggle In Italy* takes the concept of repetition to ridiculous lengths:

A shot of someone closing a door.
A shot of the young woman Taviani writing at a table.
A shot of said woman eating soup.
A shot of a factory exterior.

In an outrageous move, the third part of the *Snuggles In Italy* film ('the third part of the film', 'the third part of the film', 'the third part of the film')[26] repeats many of the shots of the first section of the film, but justifies that in the voiceover, because now Ms Taviani is analyzing how she was presented earlier, how the topics were explored. (Yes, it's Maoist/ Marxist self-criticism taken to the limit: part two critiques part one, and part three critiques parts one and two. Handily, the auto-critique format allows filmmakers to recycle what they've already presented).

But the critiques are, it has to be said, meagre, unconvincing and obvious: • meagre because they don't have much to say, • unconvincing because the arguments they make are not justified by the images (an image of a factory does *not* illustrate the link between bourgeois ideology and revolutionary militant action!), and • obvious because all of the points being made are woefully simplistic.

And of course there's a voiceover, to make sense of this mess (or to try to make sense of the mess). In typically eccentric Godardian style, it's spoken in Italian (by a guy), then translated into French (by a woman - but in a hesitant, awkward manner). Later, Taviani's Italian is translated into French. Repetition infects the narration like a deadly virus, *comme ça*:

Reflections.

---

26 Are these repetitions annoying you as much as me?

Reflections.
Reflections.
Reflections.

Practice. Practice.
Practice. Theory. Practice.

The class struggle.
The class struggle.

The third part of the film.
The third part of the film.
The third part of the film.

Oooh là là! it looks like a Gertrude Stein poem when you print it like that! I wish! Stein's famous 'Lifting Belly' poem, this ain't.

You will want to shoot the voiceover itself – plus the stupid French woman reading it out – and the idiot Italian man.

By the way, the phrase 'the third part of the film' is repeated *nine times* – just in case you total nutjobs in the audience didn't hear it the first time (didn't hear it the first time).

If you thought watching the Dziga Vertov Group films was like going back to a crummy school, you are right (you are right):

Come on, pay attention! Quieten down! *Shhh!* Listen! This is your education we're dealing with here! Listen! Think! Sit up straight! Take notes! What did I just say? I said, <u>TAKE</u> <u>NOTES</u>! Write down what I'm saying! Your red pen has run out, Comrade Fritz? Here, use mine!

By the way, you bourgeois morons, we will be having a test on the political ideas outlined in the film at the end of the session. Anybody who gets less than 10/10 will be taken outside and shot. Failure is not an option! Now <u>*shut up* *and listen*</u>!

Buggles In Italy is Gorin and Godard at their school teacherest worst (or, if you're a masochist, their teasingly best). When the Master-Of-All-Cinema talks, <u>you</u> <u>listen</u>, if you value your life.

☆

The politicized films take the form of political leaflets handed out to your co-workers at a factory. Alas, the films last a *lot* longer than the time it takes to glance at a leaflet and toss it away.[27]

This is certainly one reason why the 1968-1973 political films

---

[27] Happily, we see one of the workers in the textiles factory doing just that.

found it difficult to find an audience, or were rejected by audiences. Any decent political-ideological-sociological filmmaker could make their points in a much shorter time, or at least in a much more compelling fashion.

The Dziga Vertov Group films and the 1968-1973 political works refuse to sweeten the deal, to candy dust their messages, to embellish the contract between the artwork and the audience. So there are no car chases, no gun fights, no girls in bikinis, and no explosions.

You get the political messages straight, and repeated, too, as if we're at college, taking notes in a lecture, and the teacher repeats the key phrases for us: class struggle... Marxist critique... workers on strike... (Indeed, *Strangle In Italy* shows us what we should be doing: sitting at a table and writing notes; and later, handing out leaflets in a factory, which is what Taviani does).

Theory and practice. Theory in *Straggle In Italy* means reading lots of stodgy political tracts, and regurgitating them to camera against a wall[28] (often by reading aloud from them). Practice means writing out quotes from said treatises and cobbling together leaflets to hand out to co-workers in factories. And self-critique means going over the whole shebang and analyzing it (which means, in the tradition of all French film, talking about it).

☆

Sections of *Struggle In Italy* (known in Wisconsin as *Cooking Cabbage the Marxist Way*) are offensively simplistic – like the nods to a quasi-second wave feminism expressed in the form of stereotypical evocations of the young couple in the film making love in the afternoon. How this exploration of the class struggle in Italy brings in a romantic couple is really clunky and chauvinist. (Similarly, works such as *British Sounds* bungle the womanist/ feminist issue).

There's a suggestion in *Luggage In Italy* that romance and love are bourgeois and indulgent, and that proper left-wing militants and activists wouldn't waste time lovemaking – there's too much studying and leafleting to be done. In the view of the Dziga Vertov Group and Godard in his 1968-1973 political films, sex and love are best left to others (you'll feel guilty afterwards anyway, like a Catholic sinner, and we can't have that, because religion is also bourgeois). Anway, Marxists and Leninists don't procreate (it's the wrong kind of production!): instead, babies are hatched on an assembly line at the Fiat factory in Turin (but there's a Chinese Communist Party-imposed

---

[28] Lacking sets, the film simply puts actors against a wall.

quota – only one child per household).29

☆

So in the third part of the film ('the third part of the film', 'the third part of the film', 'the third part of the film', 'the third part of the film', 'the third part of the film', 'the third part of the film', 'the third part of the film', 'the third part of the film', 'the third part of the film'– nine times, remember?), *Struggle In Italy* reviews the first and second sections. It's the summing up section of a lecture which is always intolerably boring, *because we've just heard the lecture*! We don't need it to be summarized!

But this is Godard 'n' Gorin in their stern, teacherly mode: you <u>will</u> sit quietly and <u>listen</u> to the summing up (and <u>keep</u> taking notes). The summary is important, you see, sickle-wielding comrades, because of the test that will follow the film (Question 1: Who made the film? Question: What is the film about? Question 3: Who is the film for and against?).

One aspect of *Struggle In Italy* is intriguing: the focus on editing in the third part of the movie ('the third part of the film', 'the third part of the film', 'the third part of the film'). The voiceover explains how shots of the young woman (taken from 'the first part of the film', 'the first part of the film', 'the first part of the film') are now intercut with shots of production (i.e., a factory) on either side. It's one of the instances where Godard/ Gorin contemplate the manufacture of cinema in the form of montage. It's clumsy, and certainly not the finest example of analyzing how cinema works in Godard's *œuvre*, but it does lift *Struggle In Italy* above being another left-wing rant.

☆

It's too long.

It's a familiar complaint that has been made about millions of films. Television demands products built around time slots of 30 minutes and 60 minutes. If there isn't enough news that day, a news show will still have to stretch the material to fit a half-hour slot. I reckon that on slow news days, when nothing is happening, TV news shows should broadcast black screens – exactly as Godard's 1968-1973 political films do. Or admit that there isn't enough news to broadcast, and shorten the news show appropriately (or allow other shows to take over the time slot. So on a boring news day, the six o'clock news would run for three minutes, with 27 minutes of black. Or three minutes of news followed by 27 minutes of commercials).

---

29 And you better hope it's male.

The television industry won't agree to that. A half-hour news show has to be half-an-hour. With the 1968-1973 political works, the pressure of stretching material to 60 minutes was too great: *Noodles In Italy* demonstrates this vividly. You can see that the film editors (Godard and Gorin) sat at the K.E.M. in the editing suite (set up, no doubt, in Godard's front room), and kept reaching for more black leader and more red leader, and spliced it into the film as it was being cut. And the editors snipped off another three feet of the long roll of the title card of *Struggle In Italy* and cut that into the movie too (the 68-73 politicized works are very much celluloid films, cut with scissors and razors, they're not digital, not using computers).[30] Then the editors kept adding and adding – more padding and repetitions and black leader – until they got close to the target of the all-important sixty minutes. (Each 1968 to 1973 political film certainly hits the skids in their final sections. But that's also true of many Godard movies).

☆

Question: Why didn't Jean-Luc Godard use his considerable influence in film circles and invite Pier Paolo Pasolini to appear in *Struggle In Italy*? A movie from a left-wing perspective exploring the class struggle in modern-day Italia (and with references to the Italian Communist Party) is right up Pasolini's street. Godard had contributed a short film to *RoGoPaG* (1963), which featured Pasolini's satirical skit *Curd Cheese*. And for sure the firebrand filmmaker would be an infinitely more compelling presence than anything we see in *Struggle In Italy*. (At the time – 1970-71 – Pasolini was at work on his African *Oresteia* documentary (*Appunti per un'Orestiade Africana*) and shooting *The Decameron*, plus short works such as *Appunti per un romanzo dell'immondizia* and *Le Mura di Sana'a*).

Maybe Pier Palo Pasolini could've been brought in for the Discussion With a Philosopher section which Godard inserted in several of his 1960s films (usually in the final act, where the philosopher chats with the main character). We might've seen Pasolini and Godard debating on-screen, a truly mind-boggling idea.

---

30 And not yet the video experiments that Godard undertook in the Seventies.

22

VLADIMIR ET ROSA

VLADIMIR AND ROSA

INTRO.

Vladimir and Rosa (Grove Press Evergreen Films/ Telepool,[31] 1971) was in part another political rant (in the guise of an essay/ documentary about the Chicago Eight and other right-on topics) • in part another lecture about political theory and practice • in part a whinge about contemporary society in the Capitalist Republic of France • in part another disquisition on the media and representation • and in part a home movie in which Godard and Gorin horse around with their friends in Godard's Paris apartment. *Vladimir and Rosa* raises the issue of putting political views and ideas into a practical form (theory and practice, theory and practice, as the narration waspishly informs us).

When you look at the 1968-1973 political movie output of G. 'n' G., you can't help wondering: what the hell was the Gangster Genius of French Cinema playing at? Why was a hyper-intelligent filmmaker like Godard, who had *already* re-invented cinema several times in films such as *Vivre Sa Vie* and *Breathless*, doing with these amateurish film projects? Surely not to explore other ways of discussing all of the topics (politics included) that his movies had already covered? Surely not to re-invent forms of filmmaking? Surely not to argue and analyze ideology and politics, including left-wing forms, in such a juvenile manner?

The cinema of Jean-Luc Godard was far in advance of this group of filmmakers – indeed, far in advance of pretty much every other filmmaker on the Planet. Was it the lure or the pleasure of getting involved with some younger filmmakers, to explore the same things again, but with fresh faces and new talent? (It sure wasn't the lure of money – these projects were produced on tiny budgets, and the Maestro financed some of them himself).

If you thought *Wind From the East* was hard-going, wait until you see *Blowing Bubbles In Italy* or *Vladimir and Rosie Get Laid*.

૨ઢ

THE CAST.

Everybody in *Vladimir and Rosa* looks ugly – even glamorous figures like Anne Wiazemsky and Juliet Berto (the cinematography is truly horrible – it was filmed on 16 millimetre Kodak scraps left in the trash behind the film processing labs at Joinville, which the filmmakers scavenged after dark). Absolutely, definitely *no* make-up artists were hired for this production (make-up is too capitalist! No actor or actress

---
31 The backing was from New York and Munich.

should partake of Max Factor, it's bourgeois! Only 'Ollywooood uses make-up – not militant-political guerilla filmmakers).

Many in the cast of *Vladimir and Rosa* were culled from the Godard Circus of the 1960s. Often, however, they are called on to pose in flat *tableaux*, which conspicuously lack the zing of similar scenes in, say, *Weekend* or *Masculine/Feminine*. (The cast is squandered in *Vladimir and Rosa*).

In the 1968-1973 political films of Monsieur Godard, it's considered too bourgeois to have performers learning their lines, so dialogue is read from scraps of paper (resulting in some very ropey performances). Eh? How about a Bertholt Brecht play? Is every Brecht play performed with the actors holding scripts as they walk about the stage? No.

Vladimir and Rosa has a shoddy, stingy look that undermines its mission (it seems to relish in its low budget status – it's cool (no, it's militantly radical) to look rubbish! it's cool to look as bad as *The Blair Witch Project* 30 years ahead of time). To compensate for its lack of visual punch, the soundtrack is busy with information, from multiple voiceovers, sudden eruptions of pop music, and sound effects.

THE CHICAGO EIGHT.

The events of the Chicago Eight (later the Chicago Seven) have been made into documentaries, plays, radio plays, and films (including contemporary accounts). If you want a straight documentary account of the Chicago Eight, there are several possibilities available. *Vladimir and Rosa* is, as you'd expect from a filmmaker as unusual and wilfully eccentric as Jean-Luc Godard, not a typical documentary. It takes up the issue of the Chicago Eight as a pretext for exploring other issues, such as revolutionary politics, seen from a left-wing perspective.

Thus, aspects of the Chicago Eight events are referred to, and even jokily dramatized (in a thoroughly cheapo manner, such as the trial, where a crummy room stands in for a courthouse), but much of *Vladimir and Rosa* is about other things (i.e., what the Two G.s really wanted to explore, which was *their* form of revolutionary politics).

That is of course one of Godard's chief approaches to cinema and television: give him a subject, or hire him to make a documentary about a topic, and (*if* he agrees to do it) the project might start out close to the contracted subject. But pretty soon it'll be what Godard wanted to make anyway.

Another ideological tension in *Vladimir and Rosa* is that the

Chicago Eight issue is in part an *Amerikan* story, a narrative of resistance and revolt within the North Amerikan social system. Godard, Gorin and the Dziga Vertov Group had already explored the French and the European aspects of the events of 1968 and political activism in films such as *Wind From the East* (and Godard had examined some of the political events which led to 1968 in films such as *One Plus One*, *Weekend* and *La Chinoise*). Turning their gaze on North Amerikan society in *Vladimir and Rosa* inevitably raised the problematic issue of the political stance of the 1968-1973 political film projects and the Dziga Vertov Group film projects, which were at times virulently anti-Amerikan. To be Amerikan was intolerable, according to the Dziga Vertov Group.

THE GODARD AND GORIN SHOW.

Vladimir and Rosa was another laugh riot from the comedy team of Godard and Gorin – and in this film, they appear on-screen, wryly commenting on the movie as it unfolds. But the Two G.s are no Martin and Lewis, no Hope and Crosby, no Groucho and Chico, no Laurel and Hardy.

A photograph of the Marx Brothers in *Vlady and Rosy* reminds us who the Great Marx is in film history. If only Groucho had been called on to crack wise in *Vladimir and Rosa* (he already has the cigar permanently attached to his maw – and Groucho can act better with a cigar than either Godard or Gorin).

The only people laughing among the cast, the crew and the audience are the directors, Godard and Gorin. (The laugh-out-loud political diatribes of Gorin and Godard continue in the voiceovers, too, with commentaries that escalate to yelling matches.)

Jean-Luc Godard's turn in *Vladimir and Rosa* sees him putting on one of his stupid voices (as does Jean-Pierre Gorin), which he did from time to time in his cameos. It doesn't really work, and neither does the staging of the would-be humorous banter in the middle of a tennis court (Godard was a keen tennis player). Two teams of doubles bat balls back and forth while Gorin 'n' Godard walk on the tennis court beside the net, pontificating into microphones and a portable tape recorder. In the voiceover, Godard uses a different, equally stupid accent.

Why didn't Jean-Luc Godard hire someone to do an impression of him? (which every comedian in France could do). Or a Godard lookalike? Why didn't he have Anne Wiazemsky or Juliet Berto impersonate him? (Godard in drag?). Or why didn't he cast someone who is genuinely funny, like Raymond Devos in *Pierrot le Fou*? (The title – *Vladimir and Rosa* – refers to Vladimir Lenin (not Lennon) and Rosa Luxembourg. They are played by Godard and Gorin. So the film is a kind of double act, the comedy duo of the Dziga Vertov Group).

◆

As it continues, *Vladimir and Rosa* comes across as an indulgent home movie for an audience of two – Godard and Gorin (just like any home movie of, say, a family picnic in Provence, is only of interest to the family). It's not a film about politics, or about a legal trial in the U.S.A. which concerned politics and political activism, or about the class struggle, or about Marxist-Leninist-Maoist ideology. No, *Vladimir and Rosa* is a film in which the Two G.s indulge themselves in adolescent capers which sort of relate to political inquiry.

In one skit, both Gorin and Godard have cigars in their mouths as they evoke nations (France, Israel, Germany, the U.S.A.) and *seig heil* and threaten with batons. During a break in the trial, they fool around with footballs and a chair (oh my, that chair! It's red! Whoopie! A red chair! Hey, kids, let's see another shot of that fucking chair! And another! It's a chair! It's red! A chair, chair, chair!).

❧

THE SKITS,

And so to the sketches... *Vladimir and Rosa* contains would-be humorous ingredients,[32] but it starts with a stern, moralizing lecture, reminding us that we're back at school, and are we taking notes?, and are we listening carefully? In case some of us *aren't* listening closely, the teacherly narration repeats itself (theory and practice, theory and practice, coffee and cigarettes, coffee and cigarettes). If a movie could stretch out a wooden ruler from the movie screen and rap us on the knuckles, it would. (This is not how to start a movie with some witty, comical ingredients).

The off-putting opening scene in *Vladimir and Rosa* (focussing on two photographs of Comrade Vladimir Lenin at his most Communist-ish and working-class-ish, complete with mandatory proletarian cap) sets up the film as an irritable, irritated object.

One of the skits in the *Vlad an' Rosy Show* tackles feminism and women's liberation (from previous outings from the Dziga Vertov Group and Godard's political 68-73 films, we know this won't be good). This is a clunky episode where second wave feminist philosophy

---

32 *Vladimir and Rosa* attempted to use humour to tackle political issues, but it was rather shabbily delivered.

has been inadequately digested by the film, and regurgitated in a series of clichés.

The episode centres on Anne Wiazemsky, hard at work in her militant-hippy apartment screenprinting Tee shirts with right-on images. Yves Afonso plays her boyfriend who's struggling (class-struggling, I should say) to understand the modern woman's form of gender politics (Afonso is a superb example of a loutish, crude Frenchman who's attempting to be reborn as a sensitive New Man. The idea that a radical, politically-active feminist (and played by the dainty, prim princess-like Wiazemsky) would date such a Neanderthal oik isn't addressed).

As in much of the rest of the 1968-1973 political films, Anne Wiazemsky appears grumpy and dissatisfied, flicking back her lovely, amber locks to print some more Tee shirts, while Yves Afonso loons about, reading from feminists' texts. (Is she secretly thinking, *I wish my husband had never that fool Gorin, and can't these smelly, would-be revolutionary idiots get out of my apartment?*).

Jean-Luc Godard would return to this territory many times subsequently (and more successfully), using the battle of the sexes in a heterosexual relationship as the setting for disquisitions on gender politics.

Being provocative comes naturally to Jean-Luc Godard – he just can't help himself. If he stumbles into a situation where authority or rules can be subverted or satirized, he does it. *Vladimir and Rosa* features many prods and teases from the French-Swiss ruffian genius – like characters seig heiling, like using images from porn magazines and having suggestive phrases scrawled over them (so we see 'revolution', 'fascism', 'enculer' and 'merde merde' written over a (picture of a) woman's naked ass).

A lengthy riff on race relations in the U.S.A. is focussed on the figure of Bobby X. (Frankie Dymon), seen in court during the trial with his hands cuffed and a pistol held to his head (and he's in prison earlier). As in films such as *Masculin Féminin* and *One Plus One*, Godard's method of portraying race issues is bold and hysterical (some would say regressive and objectionable).

❧

REPETITIONS.

As with the other 1968-1973 political films, *Vladimir and Rosa* doesn't develop the images and/ or scenes it needs to match its aims, its political deconstruction (or even its voiceover). The telltale black leader appears early on, and continues throughout the piece. (Black leader – it's just rolls of black plastic – is cheaper than raw film stock!). The black leader bulks out the movie. And then we have white leader. And cuts between black leader and white leader. Only Godard would have the guts to create a scene from white and black screens – and use the voiceover to talk about race relations. Only Godard would have the guts to draw attention to the black screen in the voiceover: *coming up next, folks, another section of black leader!* (Could Godard make an entire movie from black leader? Yes. In fact, Godard and Gorin produced *Letter To Jane* using one photograph). *Vladimir and Rosa*, like the other 1968-1973 political films, would work as well (or better) as a radio show.

Incredibly, the filmmakers draw attention to the black screen *again*, later in the 1971 film – this time to further excuse it or explain it. So now, according to the so-droll voiceover from Herr Direcktor, the screen is black because: (1) Columbia Broadcasting System and Gaumont would not permit the filmmakers to include certain images; (2) the filmmakers could not think of shots to fit the material (such as to demonstrate what bourgeois and imperialist cinema is).

What rubbish! That Godard would be put off by copyright threats from companies like C.B.S. is ridiculous (look at *Stor/ies of Cinema*! He includes material from all over the place); or that Godard couldn't develop a way of representing bourgeois cinema (he could insert images from his own *Contempt*! *Le Mépris* is a movie about a disintegrating marriage! And about making a film – talk about bourgeois!).

At one point, Godard even suggests that the black leader is included to dramatize the absence of Bobby X. (following his disappearance from the trail). And he links the black screen with black people in race relations.

Note to Godard: don't show this movie in Brooklyn or Inglewood!

Repetitions occur throughout *Vladimir and Rosa*, too – another admission that the 1971 production doesn't have sufficient material. Shots are repeated, and phrases in the voiceover are repeated (cheese and pickle, cheese and pickle, cheese and pickle • where's my coffee? where's my coffee? where's my coffee? • did you buy my cigarettes? did you buy my cigarettes? did you buy my cigarettes?). If you don't like (don't like) repetition (repetition), don't watch (don't watch) *Vladimir and Rosa* (*Vladimir and Rosa*).

ða

In the last section of *Vlad an' Rosa*, the filmmakers have given up: there are so many repetitions of shots we've already seen it goes beyond a joke. *Vladimir and Rosa* looks like a film where the editors ordered up ten reprints of the same takes, so they could cut the same junk into the movie over and over. (Another shot of the jury; another shot of a TV screen; another shot of the apopleptic judge; another shot of that red chair; another slice of black leader).

Vladimir and Rosa includes, for example, surefire shots which demonstrate that a filmmaker is totally out of ideas: shots of a tape recorder. And later, the same shot (or the same tape recorder but on a TV monitor). And shots of a flatbed editing machine. Well, folks, if that's all you can think of to show in a movie, the enterprise is creatively bankrupt.

❧

EVENTUALLY, EVEN THIS FILM ENDS.

Like all of the other political film projects of the late 60s and early 70s epoch, *Vladimir and Rosa* has made all of the points it wants to make early on, using the rest of the film to repeat them with variations (or, to hell with variations, to repeat them straight. To repeat them straight. To repeat them straight. And to excuse that repetition by calling it Marxist/ Maoist self-analysis. And to excuse that repetition by calling it Marxist/ Maoist self-analysis. And to excuse that repetition by calling it Marxist/ Maoist self-analysis.)

Well, if Godard can (if Godard can) make a film (make a film) by repeating shit (by repeating shit), then maybe I (then maybe I) can write a book (can write a book) by repeating shit (by repeating shit).

The repetitions[33] (meaning, the repetitions – that is, in French, the repetitions – and in English, the repetitions) of the already unappealing material helps to render *Vladimir and Rosa* hard-going. There simply isn't enough content in *Vladimir and Rosa* for a feature-length work. The reptitions (plus that stupid black screen) turn *Vladimir and Rosa* into the very thing it is denouncing: it's like *work*, it's like being on the factory floor, doing those demeaning jobs for Renault or Mercedes or Ford.

Vladimir and Rosa is keen to deride mindless, repetitious work in factories which exploit the workers – *yeah! we're with you, comrade! fight the power! strike! strike!* – but watching this movie is itself drudgery!

---

33 It's like the joke in *A Night At the Opera* by the Marx Brothers – 'the party of the first part shall be known as the party of the first part'. As Groucho and Chico run thru this marvellous send-up of cretinous contracts and legalese, they tear up the sections of the contract they don't-a like. Maybe we should-a do that with this film.

Lastly, the Palestinian trip produced an abandoned film project, *Palestine Will Win* (a.k.a. *Until Victory*, 1970). Gorin and Godard had visited Palestine in Feb, 1970, to work with the political organization Al Fatah. The ideological approach of *Palestine Will Win* comprised the familiar Godardian political rebellion once again – Palestine versus Israel (and, by extension, Amerika). So it was another cinematic rant against Imperialism, against the West, and against Amerika.

The project was about two-thirds complete before it was shelved. The footage was re-edited by Godard and Miéville in 1974, as *Here and Elsewhere* (*Ici et Ailleurs*).

Le Vent d'est

Jean-Luc Godard
(Gruppo Dziga Vertov)

VENTO DELL'EST

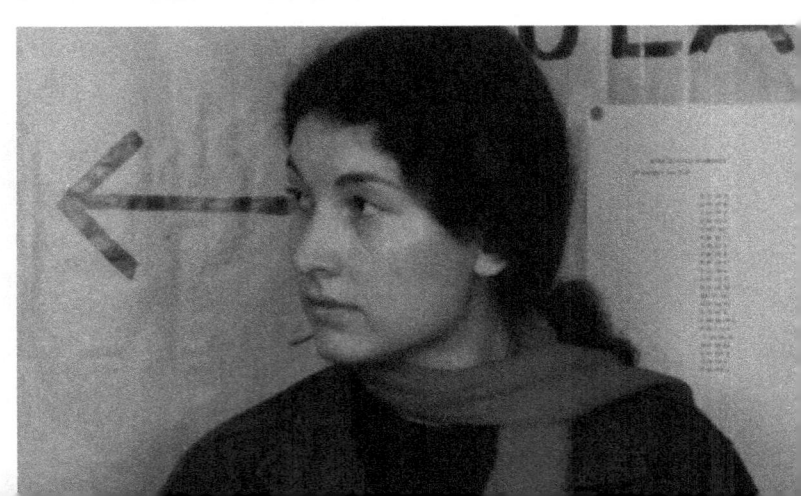

VLADIMIR ET ROSA

A FILM BY JEAN-LUC GODARD AND JEAN-PIERRE GORIN

23

TOUT VA BIEN

ALL'S WELL

The wickedness of the world is so great you have to run your legs off to avoid having them stolen from under you.

Bertholt Brecht, *The Threepenny Opera*

Tout Va Bien (*All's Well* a.k.a. *Just Great*, 1972) was an attempt at making a feature film version of the 1968 to 1973 political films and the Dziga Vertov Group projects which would get seen by actual, real, living audiences.1 Hence the casting of two big stars of the era, Jane Fonda and Yves Montand. Unfortunately, the film wasn't a success economically or critically,2 and was a difficult shoot.

Jean-Pierre Rassam produced for Anouchka Films/ Vieco Films/ Empire Films; Alain Coiffier was assoc. prod.; Jean-Luc Godard and Jean-Pierre Gorin wrote and directed; Jacques Dugied, Olivier Girard and Jean-Luc Dugied designed the sets; music was by Eric Charden, Thomas Rivat and Paul Beuscher, Isabelle Pons was A.D., Antoine Bonfanti and Bernard Ortion did the sound, and Kenout Peltier and Claudine Merlin edited the film. The DPs were Armand Marco, Yves Agostini and Edouard Burgess (filmed on Eastmancolor stock in 1.66 ratio).

In the cast were Vittorio Caprioli, Elizabeth Chauvin, Castel Casti, Éric Chartier, Louis Bugette, Yves Gabrielli, Pierre Oudrey, Jean Pignol, Anne Wiazemsky, Didier Gaudron, Hugette Mieville and Cristiana Tullio-Altan (some of the actors had appeared in the previous Dziga Vertov Group films). Principal photography ran from Dec. 1971 to Jan, 1972. Released: 1972.4.28 (in La France). 95 mins.

You can see the thinking behind *All's Well:* to produce a more audience-friendly feature-length version of the political/ Dziga Vertov Group films, and whole political experiment and ideological explorations of the past five years. So, your story stages a strike – an event that creates a dramatic structure (the beginnings of the strike, the conflicting views of it, the escalation of political activity, and the return to work). A strike is a pretext for discussing all of the left-wing notions you fancy - the relation between workers and bosses, the role of capitalism in contemporary society, the relation between labour and living, how capitalism structures contemporary society, identity, psychology, etc, how socialist principles operate in a real, practical situation, and how the class struggle is unfolding in the wake of the civil and political debates of May, 1968.

Then you plonk two well-known stars into the middle of it. The initial scenario is simple: they get caught up in the strike. Doesn't matter how – they will be the audience's observer figures for what the film *really* wants to discuss: not the romantic relationship of the

---
1 Initially *Tout Va Bien* was set up with the Xerox Corporation, and then with Paramount (B, 359).
2 The budget was just over $1 million. The Paris cinema run was short.

couple, but the situation of the workers at the factory.

★

Jean-Luc Godard was ill at the time of making *Tout Va Bien*, recovering from his near-fatal motorcycle accident in June, 1971 (he was a passenger on the bike with Christine Marsollier). Godard was in a coma for nearly a month (some said a week); he suffered mamy internal injuries, a fractured skull and a broken pelvis. He was in and out of hospital for months afterwards. Jean-Pierre Gorin said he wrote most of the dialogue, and much of the structure, but Godard was on set all of the time. (*All's Well* is thus not 'a Jean-Luc Godard film' like many of his previous outings; not only was it a co-conceived and co-directed piece, Godard was also at a low point, recovering from being in a coma. Even so, *All's Well* is made in the shadow of Godard, so to speak, under the spell of Godard, and in a thoroughly Godardian manner).

There was tension on the set between the two Annes in Godard's life: Anne Wiazemsky and Anne-Marie Miéville, the Wife and the Future Girlfriend of the Director – Godard wanted Wiazemsky to appear in three parts in *Tout Va Bien* (presumably as one of the strikers,3 and perhaps as one of the victims of the May, 1968 scenes), but Gorin and Miéville weren't keen; and when Wiazemsky suggested that she do the on-set photography, Miéville insisted that *she* could do it (B, 361). In the end, Wiazemsky appeared in the Carrefour hypermarket sequence (by the far the best in the movie, and the crowning achievement of the political films of the 1968-1973 era).

All's Well was a meditation on what May, 1968 meant, its influence, how to incorporate its impact into contemporary life; it was also a history of France between 1968 and 1972 (the opening captions flash up 'May, 1968' and 'May, 1972'); and like the other Dziga Vertov Group films, *All's Well* explored left-wing ideology and politics, and topics such as strikes, workers, bosses, capitalism, consumerism, the class struggle, Marxism, Leninism, and the dreaded, loathed and demonized bourgeoisie.

The first half of the 1972 film concentrated on a workers' strike at a factory, in which the boss (Vittorio Capprioli)4 and two visitors (Fonda and Montand) are held hostage by the strikers. (The film orchestrated three social forces, according to Godard – the management

---

3 Notice that among the strikers in the factory there is a woman who resembles Wiazamesky, complete with the trademark very long brown hair.
4 A Brechtian actor and film director.

and the factory boss, the Communist Party, and the left-wing).

The factory boss is a buffoon – of course – which automatically shifts our sympathies to the downtrodden workers (the manager is another of the little, Italian prima donnas that Godard likes to satirize – usually they're film producers of the Carlo Ponti/ Dino de Laurentiis type).

Prior to the strike (where the 'story' starts), *All's Well* set up the world of the narrative in a familiar Godardian fashion: take a man and a woman, a city, the working class, the bourgeoisie, the workers, a factory, and proceed to make a film. The prologue, narrated by a man and a woman heard later on but never seen (the usual unidentified Voices Off of the 1968-1973 political films), consisted of the filmmaking process being examined in a self-conscious, Brechtian manner (for Gorin, *All's Well* was a film of Brechtian realism, not bourgeois realism. Bertholt Brecht remarked that 'realism doesn't consist in reproducing reality, but in showing how things *really* are'. This was one of Godard's favourite Brecht quotes).

Only a Jean-Luc Godard film would begin with the film director signing bank cheques in close-up for each of the departments and services a modern film requires: opticals, laboratories, crew, insurance, etc. Has any other film ever shown the director signing the cheques that pay for everything in a film? Completely outrageous, and totally Godard.

The star images of Jane Fonda and Yves Montand were discussed (films must have stars to obtain financing, runs the movie's commentary), as were other aspects of contemporary entertainment cinema (such as having a story, romantic interest, the 'Him' and the 'Her' of many Godard movies, etc. That's the addition of commercial cinema, a love story, with stars, because a film just about strikes and workers and left-wing politics wouldn't reach the intended audience. The picture acknowledges the necessity of banal elements such as a love story but really doesn't want to be bothered with them. We see vignettes which illustrate the voiceover). Fonda disagreed about some of the movie's politics, and required some convincing to do it.

The prologue of *All's Well* is also an apology to the sections of the film's audience (the young militants) who were expecting a truly left-wing, politically incisive movie: *All's Well* apologizes that it has to use movie stars to raise money and attract an audience.

All's Well is thus yet another of Jean-Luc Godard's many films about films, films about how films are made – and with a romantic couple at the centre. (Godard had already delivered this theme in *Contempt* and others, and would go on to rehash the scenario in pictures such as *Passion*, one of his most elegant and convincing versions of the theme. Making a movie plus a love affair – cinema and love – that's enough to keep Godard going for centuries of filmmaking).

All's Well was meant to be a 'love story', but also a break-up (of course – a happy, affectionate couple wouldn't work in this picture. So it's yet another of Godard's stories of a relationship in crisis). It was about the relationship between the lovers,[5] but also between themselves and production, how they're defined by their work, and the lovers and the social realm. (Romantic love and labour is another of Godard's recurring themes, which he would return to many times after 1972).

Fonda and Montand appear in the exposition prologue of *All's Well*; we see brief vignettes of them at work (Montand watching rushes of a Remington shaving ad in a screening room,[6] echoing the famous scene in *Contempt,* and Fonda as a foreign correspondent doing a V.O. for the American Broadcasting System at a mic in a recording studio), but they are only on the fringes of the strike sequence; so that most of the first thirty minutes of *All's Well* comprises political monologues and scenes of irate workers. The approach seems designed to alienate a general audience (beyond Brechtian alienation effects), to be anti-entertainment or 'anti-bourgoise'.

All's Well's prologue includes a fleeting scene of Jane Fonda and Yves Montand walking together – the dialogue is self-consciously ultra-banal (along the lines of 'what do you love about me?'). Of course 'He' mentions 'Her' body, mouth, ass, etc. The duologue is a reprise of several moments in Godard's previous work, including of course *Contempt* (the 1963 movie is referenced several times in *All's Well*; it seems to slyly dig at having to hire famous stars, just as *Contempt* seemed to rebel against using stars like Brigitte Bardot, by subverting the way that a conventional movie would film said star).

The strike in *All's Well* was staged on a giant, cutaway set of two floors of the factory's administration building (the Chief Executive Offier's office, the outer administration office, and so on, with neon signs added), covered in slow, lateral tracking shots. It was an *hommage* to the films of Jerry Lewis (*The Ladies' Man*, 1961) – Godard

---
5 Instead of showing the sexual side of the relationship, the film offers photographs (Susan holds up a photo of a penis). This might be influenced by *Persona* (*Persona*'s main titles featured an erection).

6 This sequence is distinctly Godardian, with its images of a men's shaver commercial where a guy tests different razors by rubbing his cheek on a woman's naked *cul.* A reference to women's asses also occurs in the banal dialogue introducing the couple.

was a big Lewis fan (Lewis is regarded as a titan for French *cinéastes*). As in *Weekend*, members of the cast performed lengthy monologues to camera (several are reading from idiot boards,⁷ or holding the script; Godard can get away with that).

By the end of the first half of *All's Well*, then, the viewer had been exposed to a rigorous exploration of left-wing politics and strike action, investigated in great detail in the monologues. Socialism, Marxism, Communism and other left-wing ideologies were analyzed in a generally solemn, semi-documentary fashion.

The factory was a Salumi sausage factory: the workers sport white coats with blood stains on the front (unsubtle commentary on exploitation – and the usual symbolic links between meat/ food, survival, killing and eating, pigs and capitalists, etc). There are images of people at work which Jean-Luc Godard favours, and once again an emphasis on the dehumanizing nature of manual labour, on labour as slavery. There's plenty of Godardian to-ing and fro-ing in the cutaway set as the strike continues (with many scenes of angry pushing and shoving, as people try to cross the lines).

We see/ hear several monologues to-camera in the strike section of *All's Well* – from the C.E.O., the shop steward, the workers, etc. Immediately you are struck by a notably different acting style – a much more conventional performance style, a traditional, theatrical manner – which doesn't fit with the rest of Godard's political cinema of the period at all. It presents a different kind of awkward behaviour, self-conscious in a different way. (Vittorio Capprioli's turn as the C.E.O. is completely out of place in *Tout Va Bien*).

More Godardian are the stylized cutaways to other members of the strike force, who're listening to the monologues (echoing the approach of *Weekend*, where one guy talked, but it was off-screen – we watched a different guy in close-up), and arranged in *tableaux*.

The problem with *Tout Va Bien* in its depiction of the strike is that it *is* bourgeois, despite its efforts to be non-bourgeois and pro-Brechtian: it's too straight, too conventional – well, 'conventional', that is, after we've seen what Godard can do in cinema in the previous fourteen years! *All's Well* is too literal, too immature, too much like what a bunch of students *think* political cinema or political theatre might be.

I've seen *All's Well* several times, but watching it after going through nearly all of Godard's work up to 1972, and every single

---

7 Even a professional actor like Yves Montand does it (during his monologue).

feature film, in chronological order, *All's Well* seems a mere footnote, a re-hash of material that Godard had already filmed better elsewhere. Instead of trying to make a version of the 1968-1973 political works and the Dziga Vertov Group films that would appeal to a wider audience, Godard and Gorin could've made the Dziga Vertov Group/political films more appealing in the first place! (*All's Well* is a missed opportunity; its potential is not fulfilled; and the material is squandered and frittered away).

◆

In the second half, *Tout Va Bien* opened out, and followed Yves Montand's Jacques and Jane Fonda's Susan in their daily lives – arguing at home, Susan recording news reports for A.B.S. (American Broadcasting System)[8] and Jacques (named 'Cineaste') shooting an ultra-banal TV commercial for Dim Tights in a film studio (with dancing girls).

Yves Montand's character Jacques, as he explains in a long to-camera speech (in a break during the filming of the television ad), in response to off-camera questions (Jean-Pierre Gorin said it was Montand's best performance on film), was once a *Nouvelle Vague* director, but is now firmly embedded in the capitalist system by making TV ads (a bitter swipe at some of Godard's contemporaries – Godard dubbed advertizing fascism.[9] Hmmm, until the Master himself, the fervent former Maoist-Maxist, later directed TV commercials. And the Dziga Vertov Group had also produced a commercial – which was never shown, of course).

Some critics thought the speech was improvised. Eh? Don't they listen? It's not only clearly scripted, it's stuffed with Godardisms (refs. to Brecht, to the New Wave, to fellow French film directors, to May, 1968, etc). Actors *do not* make up their own dialogue in a Jean-Luc Godard movie!

All's Well played with Jane Fonda's star image as a political activist but also as a glamorous, Hollywood actress – *Barbarella, Klute,, Barefoot In the Park, The Chase, They Shoot Horses, Don't They?,* etc (Fonda was well-known for her outspoken critique of Imperialist Amerika, in which she exploited her fame as a platform for protesting against the Vietnam War; she was dubbed 'Hanoi Jane').

As well as Jane Fonda working at the American Broadcasting System service in Paris and Yves Montand in his film studio, the

---

8 The film plays with multiple languages, as in *Contempt*, with Susan speaking in English and being translated into French. In her to-camera monologue, Susan speaks in American and a female voice translates in voiceover.
9 Such as François Truffaut, who had sold out, according to Godard.

second half of *All's Well* also recreated some of the events of May, 1968 (specifically, the protests which turned ugly, involving riot police storming students).

The staging of these scenes was a little shoddy, reducing incendiary material to an amateur level (compare them with the footage of the real riots included in *A Film Like the Others*). Yet there are more extras, and more ingredients to these scenes than in many Godard films. Looking closer at how these scenes were mounted, they look like they were directed by Gorin or someone else, not the Maestro. Besides, Godard seldom includes fleshed-out flashbacks like this in any of his films. A Godard movie that raised the issue of the events of May, 1968 in France (or any historical event) would do so within dialogue, or at most with photographs (or with the newsreel in *A Film Like the Others*). For example, in *The Little Soldier*, the hero Bruno Forestier tells a long story about the French Resistance. Godard could've illustrated the story with an acted-out flashback, but he didn't, and he hardly ever does.

And, in another Godardian bid for padding out the running time, *All's Well* cleverly recycled material we'd already seen (couched under the guise of discussions of the strike at the sausage factory – which had *already* used the some shots twice).10 Plus, the 1968 recreations used the same shots twice. And more recycling occurred during the domestic spat. And, in a somewhat desperate effort to find something for Jane Fonda to do, the film features a lengthy take or two of her, while we hear dialogue and/ or scenes off-screen (sometimes she turns to look at the camera). Well, I guess that's one way of featuring your (expensive) star– leave the camera on her while Voices Off tell the story or deliver the message. Then you sort justify to yourself that the star is featured in the movie.

A mid-film section of *All's Well* explored the working conditions of the sausage factory, with scenes of delivering animal carcasses, preparing meat, packaging it, etc. The voiceover added explanations of what we're seeing. Godard has been fond of filming people at work throughout his career (even when it's not part of a burning ideological rant).

These scenes were inserted around the halfway point, when the bourgeois couple were released, the strike was over, and the workers went back to work. *All's Well* was keen to detail the working

---

10 Part of this is justified as Marxist self-criticism.

conditions at the factory – the number of breaks the workers had, for example, and the strict adherence to working hours. (In a crude send-up of this issue, the manager is desperate for the restroom, but the workers fill up the bathrooms or send him the wrong way. And while he's busting for relief, they inform him of the breaks they are allowed on the factory floor).

Along the way, *All's Well* featured the customary Godardian settings (a factory, a gas station, an enormous building site, roadsides), and the familiar Godardian techniques (live sound, sudden silences, multiple voices off, music suddenly stopping and starting, etc.).

◆

The domestic scenes in *All's Well*, of 'Him' and 'Her', don't convince, are indifferently staged and performed, and aren't particularly interesting (there isn't much chemistry between Jane Fonda and Yves Montand – they don't convince as lovers). The film as political-ideological text doesn't want or need the pandering to stardom (casting stars), isn't interested in them, can't be bothered to write a decent erotic-psychological narrative for them, and winds up their 'story' or relationship with a sad, inconsequential meeting in a café. Jean-Luc Godard, for one, had been here many times before; and yet, as he admits, he kept coming back to stories or scenes of 'Her' and 'Him' many times after 1972 and *Tout Va Bien*.

The weary, bickering acting style of the relationship scenes in *All's Well* is too easy, and too much like what actors think that they should be doing in a Godard movie. This increasingly became the default performance style in a Godard movie (you see it in *Passion*, in *Slow Motion*, in *First Name: Carmen* and the later films). Or is it the influence of Anne-Marie Miélville?

We have Susan's bitter complaints about how Jacques views their relationship (played largely on close-ups of Jane Fonda); we have Susan finding recording her material frustrating; and we have Susan voicing quasi-feminist views (which would crop up many times in later Godard movies).

The domestic/ psychological/ quasi-romantic subplot of 'Him' and 'Her' in *All's Well* isn't integrated satisfyingly into the movie (the voiceover kind of admits that). *All's Well* stages a strike, recreations of May, 1968, discussions of left-wing/ socialist/ communist politics and ideology, and deconstructions of capitalism – and yet it wants to put a relationship-falling-apart subplot in there! With two film stars! (You can see how the script could be re-structured: you put the scenes of the relationship falling apart *before* the strike, so that when we visit the factory, we already know 'Him' and 'Her'. But then it becomes *their* story, how *they* react to the strike at the factory. It has more dramatic impact for the workers who're striking that we meet them along with the two film stars).

◆

Godard and Gorin saved the best 'til last in *All's Well*: it's a masterpiece sequence shot, a work of genius, one of the greatest shots in recent cinema, hitting social, economic, ideological, psychological, cultural and cinematic targets with absolute self-assurance and skill. If the rest of Godard's political films of 1968 to 1973 and the Dziga Vertov Group films were at this level, we would have one of the greatest series of political works in all cinema.

It's a wonderful scene staged in a Carrefour hypermarket, covered in a single 9.5 minute take. The camera drifts back and forth laterally behind a row of customers, cashiers and check-outs; Jane Fonda wanders up and down (the camera follows her for much of the shot), making notes and speaking a waspish commentary in voiceover (partly reacting to the events); the camera passes a man loudly recruiting for the French branch of the Communist Party, selling subscriptions and Communist Party books at a knock-down price (F 4.75, down from F 5.50!). He reads out passages from the book.[11] It's a great piece of comedy, carefully staged, ending in a Buster Keaton *melée*, as student protesters rush in, closely followed by the riot police.

Anne Wiazemsky leads the young radicals subverting capitalism's operation of consumption, burstng in from the back of the store; at first the militant youths hurry over to the Communist Party guy, and soon argue with him (thus, they might be Gauchists, but they don't align themselves automatically with Communism, or French Communism). Wiazemsky is incensed that the Communist Party book seller is unable to answer a question posed by one of her crew. This leads to a loud argument.

Anne Wiazmensky is foremost among those crying, 'it's free!' and 'help yourself!', and giving out goods to shoppers. The activists encourage customers to take their shopping carts from the check-outs towards the exit without paying. Food is thrown about. The range of reactions runs from people not sure what to do, some are bemused when the militants start to fling things off the shelves into their

---

11 Anne Wiazemsky and her chums argue with the Communist Party guy. Wiazemsky demands that the guy explains what he's talking about. He sees them as trouble-makers (which they are),

shopping carts, to others who head straight for the exits. The police enter the fray towards the end of the sequence, and attack some activists. It's glorious.

All of the critique of consumer capitalism is contained in the images of the camera drifting past endless check-outs and the consumers with their shopping carts of goods. The cash registers chime non-stop. Nothing more is required: the shot says it all. The mindless consumerism of capitalism and its endless bounty of consumer goods and the banality of it all and the moronic stupor of the people buying stuff and yet more stuff, has never been done better. (Susan remarks that the supermarket is just like a factory).[12] It's also extraordinary that even fifty years later supermarkets look *exactly the same*! The row of check-outs, the shelves of goods, the store layout, the interaction of the customers – it's all still the same!

This shot sums up all of Western consumerism in a single, brilliant image – more than the trashy films of Andy Warhol, or the polemical attacks on consumerism by Pier Paolo Pasolini (in *Salò, or 120 Days in Sodom*), or any number of radical, left-wing outings. (Even without the additional, performance art-style bits of business, the shot is dazzling, partly due to context within a film examining left-wing politics and ideology.)

But *Tout Va Bien* is a politicized piece of cinema, and the additions of the guy zealously selling Communism, or the descent into chaos, as the protestors clash with the police, with the consumers caught up in the middle, add narrative elements to the sequence, dramatizing the pro-leftist ideology.

But Godard and Gorin's tight formal control of this set-piece is also what makes it really work. There's something about the lateral tracking shot device here that gives the sequence its magical tension and comedy, the way that it contains at first the regimented lines of check-outs, cashiers, cash tills and consumers, and then the chaotic battle between police and protestors. That it's a sequence shot is vital: the scene could be covered in the conventional manner (breaking it down into short shots), but the long take gives the scene such energy and tension. While *All's Well* was apparently directed largely by Gorin, shots like this are totally Godard (it's full of numerous Godardian touches). If only all of the 1968-1973 political films and the Dziga Vertov Group works had been as good as this.

◆

---

12 True – but Godard relates lots of organizations and buildings to factories.

Go to any industrialized part of the world and you'll soon find the environment which the filmmakers selected for the ending of *All's Well*: shabby waste ground, abandoned industrial buildings, and those in-between zones on the edge of every town on the planet.

All's Well might've ended more satisfyingly with the Carrefour supermarket shot, but it opted for a coda: a summing-up of the film (using the male and female narrators from the prologue), indications of the continuation of the class struggle in La France, and snippets from earlier scenes (including soundbites).

All of this played over another lengthy tracking shot (this one seemingly taken from a slow-moving train. Oh no! A train! Wait – not *that* sort of train? Don't tell me that a modern, capitalist society leads to the cattle trucks!).

Meanwhile, the 'He' and 'She' theme, featuring Fonda and Montand, reached a non-conclusion, as they meet in a café, with nothing much to say.

LETTER TO JANE

You didn't contribute enough donations to the Communist Party, did you? You didn't hand out those Marxist-Leninist leaflets as you promised, did you? You didn't class-struggle enough, did you? You didn't instigate mayhem and strikes at your workplace, did you? This film (52 very long minutes) will remind you again what you have to do.

The companion piece to *All's Well* was *Letter To Jane*, a vitriolic assault on Jane Fonda, comprising a commentary over a still image of Fonda in Vietnam during the Vietnam War which appeared in *L'Express*, taken by Joseph Kraft (as well as a slideshow from *The Grapes of Wrath*, *All's Well*, *Klute*, *The Magnificent Ambersons*, and others, including Vladimir Lenin and Mao Zedong, of course).

Was *Letter To Jane* serious? A joke? For some it would be a nasty and childish trick to play on the star of your latest film. According to Jean-Pierre Gorin, it wasn't a 'letter' to a film star (change the title, then!), but a disquisition on photography, on the media image, on how images relates to politics and to texts.

Letter To Jane is a lecture, or a rant, or a series of questions, in the manner of the Dziga Vertov Group films (remember those? – where the films insisted: keeping asking questions, keeping struggling, keep supplying us with cigarettes, etc).

Godard and Gorin take turns to read out aloud the sacred text they've prepared. If you've seen the Dziga Vertov Group films already, you won't find anything new here. If you don't know the political movies, this will seem a strange form of presentation – two men reading from an essay while we look at a picture of a film star, or at still frames taken from the movie in question, *Tout Va Bien* (and one or two other photos). Thus, *Letter To Jane* is hard-going, just like the Dziga Vertov Group works.

So it's hairshirt time, it's get on your knees on the cold, stone floor of your monk's cell time, it's ten hours in solitary confinement time.

The two G.s circle around the concept of the photograph of Jane Fonda many times: they return to it, they can't leave it alone. They change their mode of address – instead of talking to the audience, they send part of their diatribe towards Jane Fonda herself. (They also hope that she will respond. Did she? I very much doubt it!).

For variety in this over-long political rant, the filmmakers re-frame the photo several times; they also lamely add lots of black leader, the go-to padding for the political films of 1968-1973. (*What do we do now, Jean-Luc? Oh, cut in some more black leader, and I'll repeat a phrase, I'll repeat a phrase*).

◆

Letter To Jane is a continuation of the political films of the 1968-1973 period for Jean-Luc Godard and Jean-Pierre Gorin. And it also resembles a college essay for a politics course. Gorin went to university, but Godard didn't – is this film and the other political films of 68-73 a kind of stand-in or replacement for Godard's lost university years? Maybe this is a (guilt-ridden) equivalent for his post-graduate studies in *Left-Wing Ideology*? It's his course of 12 adult education classes in *Marxism And Maoism the Easy Way* (Wednesday nights, 19.00-21.00)?

Certainly, sections of *Letter To Jane* resemble the too-earnest scribblings of a keen but misguided politics student, the fruit of hours dedicated to intense political discussions in a Left Bank café (they can only afford one cup of coffee, so they nurse it for hours), in between visits to the cinema and ogling girls.

24

SAUVE QUI PEUT (LA VIE)

SLOW MOTION / EVERY MAN FOR HIMSELF

Sauve Qui Peut (La Vie) (1980), another film with alternative titles (a.k.a. *Slow Motion*, a.k.a. *Every Man For Himself*),13 was one of those European co-productions with a hundred companies apparently contributing their two *sous* of finance: Sara Films/ MK2/ Saga Productions/ Sonimage/ C.N.C./ Z.D.F./ S.S.R./ O.R.F. Alain Sarde, Jean-Luc Godard and Marin Karmitz were the producers. Released: Oct 15, 1980. 87 mins.

It was *not* written by Jean-Luc Godard, but by Anne-Marie Miéville and Jean-Claude Carrière (the Maestro is credited as 'composer': 'composé par Godard'). That's a vital point: Godard wrote and directed many of his films, but not all of them. The influence of Anne-Marie Miéville should never be under-estimated on Godard's later work. So *Slow Motion* is a Godard-and-Miéville film (Godard acknowledged that Miéville was 'at least 50% of this film', and that she had been a prime mover in encouraging him to return to cinema).14 As well as co-writing it, Miéville is also credited as co-editing it. But the movie is still known as a Godard movie – because he tends to overshadow everyone else on any production, even big film stars.

Romain Goupil was another vital member of the team, including working on the script, location scouting, art direction and as assistant director. Yes, and photography was by William Lubtchansky,15 Renato Berta and Jean-Bernard Menoud, with sound by Luc Yersin and Oscar Stellavox, music by Gabriel Yared, editing by Godard and Miéville, and Jacques Maumont oversaw the sound mixing.

The cast included Paul Dutronc, Nathalie Baye, Roland Amstutz, Isabelle Huppert, Cécile Tanner, Anna Baldaccini, Roger Jendly, Monique Barscha, Michel Cassagne, Paule Muret, Marie-Luce Felber and Erik Desfosses, with a pseudo-cameo from Marguerite Duras.

This is the first significant movie from the Godard and Miéville team which presents many elements that would appear over the next decades in their collaborations: Switzerland and France (centring on Lake Geneva); very bourgeois characters (with very bourgeois settings and very bourgeois lives – this is the affluent French-Swiss borderland); older characters (gone are the angry, energetic teens of the Sixties); *very* hostile interactions (particularly among romantic couples); more explicit sexual material (though not always shown – it's

---
13 The film was given alternative titles, Godard explained, because he wanted titles that would be both commercial and classical. Godard always wants to have it both ways. In English, the title ought to be 'Save Your Ass', Godard reckoned
14 Quoted in C. Pajaczkowska, in S. Hayward, 1990. And Mac, 403.
15 Lubtchansky worked again with the Maestro on *Nouvelle Vague*, but it wasn't a happy experience: 'it was the same hell', Lubtchansky complained in 2001 (B, 525).

often suggested, or presented in dialogue); and a more static, underplayed approach to blocking, camerawork and performance.

This is a mean-spirited movie, with a shitty, even life-hating attitude – it's a movie which really doesn't like people at all. Nobody's anything approaching balanced or content, and everybody seethes with issues (some of them can't hide them, either, such as Paul). The youthful idealism of the 1960s has completely vanished: we are now into crabbed, grouchy middle-age.

It is also one of the first movies where the bitterness and self-loathing in the Godardian artistic project is exposed for all to see, and is not tempered by notions such as youth or beauty or idealism or creativity. This is a very angry movie – but the rage seems to have nowhere to go – a feeling we find in many of Godard's movies from here onwards. In the 1960s films, such as *Weekend* and *Pierrot le Fou*, the anger seemed to have more focus, something of a purpose, or it could isolate its targets with wit and flash. From *Slow Motion* onwards, the bile that Godard seems to be feel towards everything just splurges messily over the films and the characters.

Thus, instead of being regarded as a Grand Return To Form for the Rebel Angel of the French New Wave, and the Inauguration of a New Group of Theatrically-Released Movies, as the general trend of journalism saw *Slow Motion*, it's more like an ending, an admission of defeat.

This is also one of the first appearances of the fragmented, eccentric narrative style that Godard and Miéville developed: incomplete evocations of stories and characters which sometimes come across as awkward, or undecided. As if the films couldn't quite determine what they wanted to do, or who they were made for (or maybe they were trying to deal with too many conflicting demands). The fiery, endlessly inventive attitude of the 1960s films, unique in all cinema, has evaporated in the cool, grey-blue, Swiss atmosphere. The mountains, the Lake, the clear air, the fancy houses, it's all so relaxing... let's have another cup of coffee, light another cigarette (or cigar), and... maybe... we might switch on the camera and film something... but maybe we won't...

Jean-Luc Godard was in a tense, nervous state during pre-production of *Sauve Qui Peut*, and wept at some of the meetings (that's not a good sign when you're preparing a production). He suffered losses of confidence and was undecided about technical aspects, such as whether to shoot on video or film, or even what he wanted to shoot at all. Camera tests and video were made.[16] Eventually, Godard decreed it would be shot on film (after giving the crew the chance to vote – they opted for video. As Godard recalled, the film people wanted to film on video, and vice versa).

Notice, also, the gap of eight years, from 1972 to 1980, in feature film releases from Godard: and also in this study (the 1970s pieces for TV and video are difficult to see or obtain; partly for that reason I haven't included them. It's a pity, because there is plenty of material there to see – including *Here and Elsewhere, How's It Going?* and *Number Two*).

◆

For me, *Slow Motion* is a lesser piece in the Jean-Luc Godard *œuvre*: it's a film essay couched in terms of a film narrative or film drama which makes points Jean-Luc Godard and Anne-Marie Miéville had made better elsewhere. In this retread through the power relations between romantic couples and between groups of people in a late capitalist society (plus a relationship falling to bits), the film seems unsure of what it really wants to be. In short, the elements don't gel (and aren't that compelling on their own). The video notes for the film (*Scénario vidéo de Sauve qui peut (la vie)*), included in the DVD release, are in a way more satisfying than the film itself (Godard explains at length his æsthetic choices in *Slow Motion*, and demonstrates devices such as video superimpositions and freeze frames. Having Godard explain, in voiceover, how he planned to make *Slow Motion* was more to the point than the film itself).

It doesn't help *Savue Qui Peut (La Vie)* that the characters aren't particularly appealing or interesting (and that the film itself seems ambiguous about them: are they interesting? are they worth following?): Paul Godard is just a pain in the ass, Denise Rimbaud is neurotic/ unhappy (but in a rather bland way), and Isabelle Huppert is one of the least intriguing of female characters in Godard's cinema. (Huppert is a lacklustre performer here: she appeared in *Heaven's Gate*, a wonderful movie, made around the time of *Slow Motion*, but putting Huppert in *Heaven's Gate* had to be one of the worst casting decisions in recent times.[17] Of course, it was another target for critics to gripe about when *Heaven's Gate* flopped at the box office).[18]

---

16 Godard was much concerned, to the point of obsession, with getting the look of *Slow Motion* exactly right. He wanted the natural light look, again, and had his DPs use special 'super speed' lenses (by Zeiss), which could shoot in low light.
17 Godard had visited Huppert during the making of *Heaven's Gate*, where he told her he wanted her role 'to be the face of suffering'.
18 United Artists didn't want Isabelle Huppert for *Heaven's Gate* at all, but Michael Cimino insisted. U.A. were right, though.

In *Slow Motion*, characters double up, mirror each other, as Godard and Miéville explore their favourite concerns. The lead character (Jacques Dutronc) is a TV producer, Paul Godard, an eternally unhappy, alienated, middle-aged, white European, worrying about everything (while at the same time not caring in the slightest about anything – or anyone), estranged from his wife Paulette (Renato Berta), with a confused personal life, and on-off affairs with several women (and always wanting the one he hasn't got).

Paul G. also spends time musing with a buddy at a sports field about having sexual relations with his 11 year-old daughter Cécile[19] (in the politically correct atmosphere of later decades – or any era – these scenes, of the two men discussing taking their daughters in the ass, are fantasies of incest and paedophilia). This is a guy who roughly throws his birthday presents at his daughter (no gift wrapping here!), jokes blackly about wanting to see her tits, and even, by the chauvinist standards of Godard's cinema, is a major, deeply unpleasant prick. (The discussions of men sodomizing their children are delivered in the sour, cynical manner you find in much of Godard's later work. And the camera dwells on Cécile in close-up, innocently playing with her friends, which makes it all the more objectionable. Although I've emphasized that Miéville and Carrière scripted this movie, I can't imagine they came up with this un-P.C. riff about incestuous, under-age sex).

There's yet another play upon the director himself – his name's Godard, he wears glasses and has a cigar glued to his mouth (and he wears Godard's own clothes[20]). And the settings're in Godard Central – Nyons in Switzerland. It's Godard being provocative again – maybe he'd heard the question so many times about whether his characters were based on himself, he decided to send the notion up.

The other two leads in *Slow Motion* are Denise Rimbaud (Nathalie Baye), a TV journalist who's extricating herself from a troubled relationship with Paul Godard,[21] whom she works with professionally,[22] and the prostitute Isabelle (Isabelle Huppert), whose story runs alongside that of Denise and Paul. There are five sections to *Slow Motion*, with each section concentrating on a particular character.

The trajectories of the characters intersect – Paul hires Isabelle for a night, for example, and Isabelle rents the apartment that Denise has

---

19 Cécile was played by filmmaker Alain Tanner's 12 year-old daughter.
20 Presumably washed first.
21 There's another ex-boyfriend, Piaget (Michel Cassagne), who works at the printer's.
22 Both Baye and Dutronc knew they were playing characters drawn on Godard and Anne-Marie Miéville. As with Michel Piccoli in *Contempt*, Dutronc also wore some of Godard's own clothes.

advertized (which Paul wants to hang onto). In the video notes, Godard speaks about the characters in literary, dramatic tones, as if he's discussing fully fleshed-out characters in a 19th century novel; but the movie and the characters simply do not support that sort of interpretation. They don't earn it. The script isn't as rich as Flaubert or Hugo. (This often occurs with Godard's movies: he can talk the talk, but the actual results on celluloid fall short. It's also notable that Godard often discusses the characters in his films in literary terms, but his films veer off into purely cinematic, non-literary zones).

★

Is there a compelling story in *Sauve Qui Peut (La Vie)*? Not much of one. Denise Rimbaud is interested in moving to the countryside to write; she visits a farm[23] and a printer's; she contemplates a new job; and she discusses ending her relationship with Paul Godard. The first part of *Slow Motion* was called 'Imagination', focussing on Denise, the second 'Fear', on Paul, and the third, 'Commerce', on Isabelle.

Slow Motion's characters relate to each other in a casual but cynical, weary, grouchy fashion. There is a barely suppressed anger and self-loathing at work in *Slow Motion* which permeates the film like poison, recalling the oh-so-cool but fraught relationships in earlier Jean-Luc Godard films like *Weekend,* an infinitely superior movie all-round. You find this kind of acting in TV soap operas and every Hollywood drama and action movie: it's as if, lacking some decent guidance from the director, actors slip into that snidey, bitter way of relating to other actors.

Some of the circumstances of the shooting of *Slow Motion* probably influenced the movie: there was plenty of tension on set, Godard lost his temper, was difficult to work with, and according to DP Lubtchansky, Godard and Miéville 'argued all the time' (B, 425).

When the central couple in *Slow Motion* eventually meet (at the end of act one – if we used the conventional dramatic structure of movies, which doesn't always apply to Godard's movies) – they argue fiercely. We've already seen them bickering on the phone, and Rimbaud has talked about leaving – now we see just why.

★

---

[23] *Slow Motion* is a film with a lengthy shot of... cows in a cowshed. The farm girl (Catherine Freiburghaus) bares her *cul* and tells Rimbaud that it's fun when the cows give you a lick.

Marguerite Duras[24] makes an appearance in *Slow Motion* - well, not really. She is heard in voiceover,[25] and in one scene, where Paul Godard is visiting a college and giving a talk, there's some pretence that Duras is in the next room (a playful but rather feeble attempt at including Duras in the film, even though she's simply an off-screen voice). No - I stand corrected: according to Godard, Duras really *was* there, as he explained in 2001:

> in *Sauve qui peut (la vie)* when Dutronc announces to his students that Marguerite Duras is in the next room... we never see her. In fact, she really was there, but she did not want to be filmed - perhaps because of her taste for voiceover in her own films. She came in order to be offscreen.

The idea was to reproduce a real episode where Marguerite Duras had refused to appear at a film festival, in public at least; so *Slow Motion* plays with off-screen space, as also in a scene where Paul is supposedly driving Duras to the airport (but this time, she wasn't there. Godard has often done that - characters, framed in close-up, look off-screen at something or someone that is never seen). It's not, however, the most satisfying solution from a filmmaker of writing around a problem that suddenly presents itself - a performer who refuses to perform. From what we know about Godard, we might've expected him to come up with something a little more compelling than this.

★

Jean-Luc Godard spoke in his video notes of the way he wanted to use music in *Slow Motion* but the music (by Gabriel Yared) is lyrical sometimes, but indifferent and undistinguished more often, and also too fussy and arch.[26] It's also electronic, too, sometimes with piano backed by electronic sounds and synthesizers, which recall Harold Budd or Brian Eno. Except not as good as Budd or Eno. Nowhere near as good. As an experiment, coupled with the slow motion, it's interesting but not wholly successful.

There are short vignettes in *Slow Motion* which involve cameos, and are included one supposes to comment upon the action, or offer alternative versions of the anxious relationships at the heart of the

---

[24] J.-L. Godard had considered adapting *The Lover* by Marguerite Duras in 1982: it would've been a way of making the film he wanted to do about fathers and daughters (in this case, an older man and a younger woman). In the event, *The Lover* turned up as a glossy epic directed by Jean-Jacques Annaud in 1992 - as far away from a Godard movie as one could imagine.
[25] Voicing the expected (and rather predictable) ruminations on gender issues. Why didn't Godard use one of the divine trinity of French feminists, Julia Kristeva, Luce Irigaray or Hélène Cixous?
[26] Gabriel Yared's credits included *Moon in the Gutter, Betty Blue, The Lover, Camille Claudel, Vincent & Theo, Map of the Human Heart, City of Angels, The English Patient* and *The Talented Mr Ripley*.

film. In one, a young woman, Georgiana (Georgiana Eaton), is slapped around the face by a man who yells out 'choose!', to the point where she bleeds (presumably, to choose between him and the biker standing next to him: a girl choosing between two guys). Denise watches as the film shifts into step motion of a C.U. of the woman being beaten. (And at the end of the confrontation, Georgiana takes off with one of the bikers anyway, on the back of a motorcycle). It's an ugly scene, depicting men as brutes.

In another vignette, Paul Godard waits in a cinema queue (to see a better film than this one), and a guy carrying a child on his shoulders exits the theatre behind the queue and cries that there's 'no sound! it's outrageous!' (A replay of the scene in *Masculin Féminin* (a much, much better film!), when Jean-Pierre Léaud complains to the projectionist about the aspect ratio of the cinema).[27]

Another comment on cinema occurs when characters pause and ask, 'where's that music coming from?' (like the woman sitting at the bar near Paul and Denise. That gag, which is reprised several times, doesn't work, because the setting is a noisy bar, where one might expect to hear music, and the joke is clumsily delivered. Anyway, Woody Allen had already shown in *Bananas* that film music comes from a harpist hiding in the wardrobe (a reprise of Marx Brothers jokes). And Mel Brooks had Count Basie and his Orchestra in *Blazing Saddles*. And the Zucker-Abrahams-Zucker comedies feature many great gags about film music).

Yet another vignette in *Slow Motion* (outside the cinema) features a woman trying to be nice and her boyfriend blanking her every attempt. Hell, she's even taken off her underwear so they can play as they watch the movie, but no, he has his nose in a newspaper. Yes, we know that men are heels, but this is adolescent drivel, this is sledgehammer pseudo-feminism: you expect something a little more zingy from the director of *Contempt* and *Weekend*.

One of the more bizarre scenes has Isabelle being cornered in her car by two guys driving a Mercedes, who drag her out of her car, pull her pants down and spank her, while ranting about trade unions and left-wing politics. (A trade union for hookers? Why not?). No one is independent, the pimp insists. This is Godard's version of a-pimp-exerting-his-power scene. It's a brief reprise of the self-righteous, militant anger of the Dziga Vertov Group films).

In a better film these vignettes might enhance the movie, but in

---

[27] Godard had wanted Jacques Tati to play the guy who complains about the film being played without sound; Tati refused, so a bit player was used.

Slow Motion they help it feel as disjointed as a series of student comedy sketches written by a nerd who's swallowed *Das Kapital* for breakfast, and has it in for prostitutes and women in general because he can't get laid and can't afford whores.

There's a return to the sleazy, sadomasochistic world of prostitution in *Sauve Qui Peut (La Vie)* too (which for some critics was a step backwards). With the entry of Isabelle and her story (at the 37-minute mark), *Sauve Qui Peut* sort of explores the power relations between sex and money, buyer and seller, giver and taker, and men and women. (The director had covered the same territory before, and better – in *Vivre Sa Vie*, most obviously. But, yet again, let's remember that this film was not written by the Maestro, but by Anne-Marie Miéville and Jean-Claude Carrière).

And then Isabelle's sweet but fatally naïve sister (Anna Baldaccini) fancies raising some \$\$\$\$[28] from hooking, and asks Isabelle for some advice. Isabelle tells her what she'll have to do with guys, in detail – down to swallowing sperm and licking a guy's ass – Godard is fond of inserting the graphic imagery he can't actually film in the dialogue. (And Isabelle points out that, like her pimp, she'll be taking half of the earnings).

Slow Motion is another Ass Movie from Godard – when Isabelle visits clients, they inspect her behind; a woman exposes her butt to some cows for them to lick; Isabelle is spanked on the rear; Isabelle discussing ass licking with her sister Anna; and the so-called 'orgy' scene includes anal sex.

In one sequence Isabelle visits a portly, middle-aged business-man client (Monsieur Personne – Fred Personne) in a hotel, strips off her pants (for the obligatory 'baring-of-the-ass-in-a-Godard-movie' moment), and is persuaded to play-act his daughter returning from university. It's a scene of desperation, loneliness and degradation – and Isabelle is as much a lonely, friendless soul as the poor, old sod who's abusing her. As this excruciatingly sordid and pathetic drama unfolds, the 1979 film cuts back to images of the city and the landscape – images of life carrying on regardless (but the sound of the sex scene in the hotel runs over the shots, as in the 'orgy' scene). At the end of the skit, Isabelle listens at the door, and it appears that someone, a woman perhaps (maybe the punter's wife), has been watching the sorry saga secretly.

But the viewer shouldn't take it all at face value. Jean-Luc Godard

---

28 Isabelle's sister Anna needs the money to help her friends, who're in jail following a botched robbery.

is always playing (or messing about), often to a much greater degree than film critics acknowledge.

In another sequence, Isabelle visits an address given to her by a schoolfriend (whom she meets in the corridor of the hotel). She goes there and meets a guy working at a film editing machine (classic Godard) who offers her lots of money to travel around the world. What's the catch? Drugs? Money? Crime? There isn't one – this isn't a spy thriller. It's partly an in-joke, too: the location Isabelle visits is in Rolle (at 15, rue du Nord), where Godard and Miéville had their studio at the time.

★

In the silliest scene in *Slow Potion*, Godard and Miéville have four people involved in a human chain of S/M and sexual acts, controlled by a businessman. A naked hooker, Nicole, lies on the floor having her breasts touched by the businessman; when that happens, it's the cue for the prostitute to fellate the tyro's assistant Thierry; cue gasps, and the assistant licking the heiny of another prostitute, Isabelle, who in turn is told to put lipstick on the suit.[29] (The businessman is a miserable, arrogant jerk, a caricature of a brutish bully, who enjoys humiliating his underlings. This is the view *Slow Motion* puts forward: men hire prostitutes in order to debase them).

It's all done in the ironic, nonchalant, offhand, Godardian style, but, as it's covered mainly by close-ups of the businessman and Isabelle beside him, any kind of (sexual) act (or other act) could be occurring (the scene features some nudity, but it's consciously non-erotic or anti-erotic, and after the medium shots, it's all close-ups of heads.) The scene is much more like a schoolboy's idea of an orgy than anything plausible or convincing. (And the businessman, as the boss, inevitably resembles a film director making a porno film: at one point he says we'll add the sound, the 'ahhs' and 'ohhs' of pornography. The boss orchestrating his actors in the 'orgy' very much resembles a film director at work on set).[30]

Critics have deconstructed this 'orgy' along intellectual lines, bringing in the usual critical apparatus of control, representation, voyeurism, feminism, etc. But, really, why bother? (Because the scene includes its own deconstruction. No need for your *Idiot's Guide* to Lacan or Freud or Dworkin or Cixous, the scene provides all of that).

---

29 Julia Kristeva saw this scene as a fantasy for a boss in which he can be both sexes at the same time.
30 The 'orgy' is also, for critics, a parody of capitalism, industry, manufacturing: there's a boss who runs the show, sets the schedule and plans the labour, and the workers who carry it out on his command. Sex as an assembly line. A pleasure factory. Sort of – but the scene isn't worthy of such weighty critical interpretations.

Slow Motion gives feminists plenty to get uptight about – there's prostitution and degradation and women used and abused in some fairly nasty ways. Godard has made the exploitation of the body and soul of prostitution of his earlier films much more explicit in *Go Motion*. Not sexually explicit so much as socially or personally explicit: i.e., the degradations are shown in detail.[31] (And yet, it was all done, and much better – and just as savagely – in *Vivre Sa Vie*). There's an obsessive emphasis on the details of sex acts, too, in *Slow Motion*: in that scene in the hotel, it's about sucking cocks at certain times and licking tushes and all the rest of it.[32]

Slow Motion seems to be more explicit in terms of evoking sexual issues, but it has the same idiosyncratic approach that Jean-Luc Godard undertook in his 1960s movies. It's showing yet hiding, evoking yet negating. During the sex scenes between hookers and clients, for example, the 1979 film pointedly avoids portraying what's going on, and cuts away to empty, banal shots of trucks driving along roads, or a busy city street. Meanwhile, the sex acts are heard in voiceover: the cinematic devices draw attention to the manipulations of cinema.

Remember in *Weekend* how the filmmakers avoided showing car accidents, but always cut to the scene afterwards? Same in *Contempt*, where the car crash itself occurs off-screen. And *Weekend* also features a lengthy sex scene, which isn't depicted, but is related in a monologue (and the words, too, are sometimes drowned by the music, a further obscuring, and the actors are lost in shadows). Hiding, hiding.

Slow Motion cutting to everyday scenes of trucks on roads or people out shopping are a standard, Godardian ploy, and they can be interpreted any way you like. In the midst of prostitute and client scenes, the shots can appear like wry commentaries on making cinema – that films can show shoppers and cars but not sex acts. Or they can appear like images of life carrying on regardless of what occurs indoors. Or that sex acts are just another part of life, like driving along a road. Or even, at worst, as padding (we note that *Slow Motion* is a short feature, at 87 minutes, and Godard has always used padding. Some of the shots are shamelessly used repeatedly – such as the cars driving at night).

★

The slow motion itself is not true slow motion (is anything

---

31 The sex acts include oral and anal sex, exhibitionism, fetishism, and a little S/M. It's not a film about regular heterosexual coupling.
32 And when Isabelle's hapless sister Anna slips into minor crimes (she and her friends tried to rob a jewellery store and failed, and she needs some money quickly), she asks Isabelle's advice about whoring. Isabelle tells her she'll have to put up with sucking wieners and licking assholes and anything the punter wants.

straightforward in Jean-Luc Godard's cinema?). Full slow motion (which video couldn't really reproduce at the time – it's better now) is footage filmed at faster frame rates than cinema's 24 frames per second (48 or 96 frames per second, for instance). But *Sauve Qui Peut (La Vie)* doesn't do that: rather, it uses what's called stepped slow motion or step motion (which's sometimes how video simulates slow motion). That is, frames are extended over a few frames, so it looks more like short freeze frames bunched together. And sometimes Godard does use freeze frames (step motion became one of Godard's favourite devices from this point on). Godard remarked that was why certain actions were employed – like Nathalie Baye on the bike, or Cécile playing soccer, or the curious game played with wooden paddles and a ball – because sport and movement made for better slow motion (Godard also commented that women in slow motion were more interesting than men).[33] And to accompany the stepped motion, the film sometimes employs music, and sometimes sound effects, and sometimes dialogue (using the step motion images as the background for voiceover).

The step motion became the signature shot of *Slow Motion* in its marketing – Nathalie Baye on the bicycle[34] riding along roads in the French-Swiss countryside, or by the Lake. But those images are not representative at all of the film: more suitable would be a wide shot of a bland, late 1970s hotel room with someone talking in the next room, seen through the doorway, on the telephone (the first shot). Or images of city streets – passers-by by day, and cars by night.

★

By the time *Slow Motion* is over, it has passed by with some mildly diverting moments, but how tiresome some of it is. If you've seen other Jean-Luc Godard movies, you know what Godard – and Anne-Marie Miéville – are capable of (*Hail Mary*, for example). Well, they just don't make it work here. *Slow Commotion* isn't even a series of scenes or notes for a film that might be made that would be really fascinating. The viewer doesn't care for anyone or anything in *Slow Motion*. Well, at least, I don't. But then, I don't care every time with a Godard and Miéville film anyway: their movies are not often emotionally gripping, so one is not swept along by the emotion of the narrative or the film. Their movies can be thrilling, witty, intellectual,

---

33 Discussing his technique of slowing down action in *Slow Motion*, Godard said it was much more interesting to slow down a woman's movements rather than a man's; women were more graceful, more subtle, more complex in their motion, said Godard, than men. He called it 'the decomposition of movement'.
34 The Freddie Mercury song 'Bicycle Race' was written about cycling in Switzerland (where Queen were recording in Montreux, around this time). *Slow Motion* is Godard's version of fat-bottomed girls on bikes.

compelling, but not so much emotional. *Éloge de L'Amour* is, *Notre Musique* is, even *Passion* is. But *Slow Demotion*, despite the frantic and violent relationship between Paul and Denise, is among the most emotionally detached of all of Godard's and Miéville's pictures.

The ending of *Sauve Qui Peut (La Vie)* embodies that: Paul Godard, bless him, tries some kind of reconciliation with his ex-wife Paulette and his daughter Cécile, but then the poor bastard's run down by a car (driven by a punter in the car with Isabelle's sister Anna, she's now into prostitution). Godard's injury/ death is staged by an 8 year-old who's just been handed a camera for the first time (the car's not even moving, and Godard falls over the bonnet in step motion. If you walk around any car lot anywhere in the world, you'll see people being run down by stationary cars all the time. I saw three people getting killed this morning by two Buicks and a Lexus. You can imagine the pandemonium when someone comes out of Target to find a dead body draped over their fender. 'But I parked it right by the wall! No one could possibly get run down here!').

The ending of *S.M.* has the appearance of something rushed, or not planned in advance, or, really, something the filmmakers don't want to shoot at all and so they put in as little effort as possible. Even by J.-L. Godard's usual indifference to endings and action, this is extreme. In other words, a middle finger to the film, and a middle finger to the audience, and a middle finger to the filmmakers themselves. Filmmaking as self-loathing.[35]

Death is no ending, Fritz Lang commented in *Contempt*, but Jean-Luc Godard couldn't help returning to it. Here, the scene is served with a triple helping of irony and bile – it even includes some dying words from Paul Godard, a barb aimed at the ending of *Breathless*. Here, the contempt in *Contempt* seems to be about (the) filmmakers for their film, or for being film directors. (The ending – the death of the main character – is not suggested in the previous eighty minutes, and appears not as an arbitrary act of the Gods or fate or destiny or punishment for sins or any other literary artifice, but a bitterly cynical act of desperation by the film and the filmmakers).

Consider how Cécile, a surly teenager *par excellence*, simply wanders away from the car accident – and that's her father there lying in the road! (Paul's ex-wife Paulette is similarly utterly uncaring, and just turns away). Does it make any difference that the Brechtian device

---

[35] Godard had messed up the filming of the scene, according to Roman Goupil, because he rushed it: he didn't like being in the street, being watched, and was still agoraphobic (B, 428). It was also an expensive shot – partly due to hiring the orchestra. The scene was re-shot a week later, without Godard.

of a classical orchestra playing right there in the alley where Cécile walks is used here? Who cares? And then that horrible electronic music crashes in over the orchestra (as the camera moves from the musicians to the actors, a comment on diegetic sound). And Godard and Miéville hold the shot of Cécile and her mom walking away from the camera s-o-o-o-o long. I'm sure everyone in the cinema has left by then. And anyone who's still there will be asleep.

◆

Slow Motion was taken to the Cannes Film Festival, where reviewers panned it. Producer Marin Karmitz cleverly declared that it was a work-in-progress. Screenings for journos organized over the Summer of 1979 helped to promote the movie so that, by the time of its release in October, 'the same journalists who had demolished the film at Cannes in May now delcared it a masterpiece', Karmitz recalled in 2001 (B, 430). But the Maestro hadn't changed a thing.

Slow Motion is not a 'triumphant return' to feature filmmaking, then, for J. Godard and A. Miéville, and, no, there isn't a great film in there waiting to get out, if only it could be re-edited or re-dubbed or re-whatever. And I've read some of the critics on *Sauve Qui Peut (La Vie)*, who have discussed it at length as if it's this fabulously incisive and insightful film, like a modern-day *Battle of Algiers* or *Hiroshima Mon Amour* (if only!). And I've read Constance Penley (a fine film critic) but, no, I can't see the nuggets of Cultural Theory Bliss to be found in this mess of a movie.

But *Row Motion* was important for Jean-Luc Godard's career, because it did well for him around the world, and grossed more than $1 million in its 12-week release in Paris, making it Godard's biggest hit for many years. And Godard was tireless in promoting *Slow Motion*, as he has been throughout his career with certain other films: according to Zoetrope's Tom Luddy he undertook 12-14 days of promotion for the film in New York, doing the rounds of photo sessions, interviews, TV spots, etc (Mac, 268).

And the success of *Slow Motion* was vital in another respect: it helped Godard raise a decent budget for his next project, *Passion*, the first of two feature masterpieces of the Eighties (the other was *Hail Mary*). The first group of 1980s films – *Passion, First Name: Carmen* and *Hail Mary* – were far more successful and compelling than the second set – *Detective, King Lear* and *Grandeur and Decadence*. However, by the late 1980s Godard was already deep into his major work *Histor/ies of Cinema*.

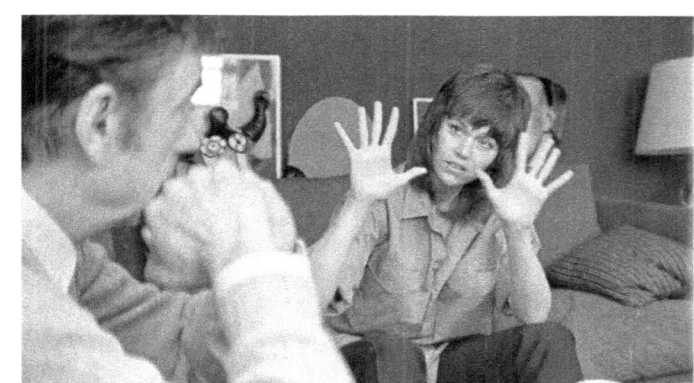
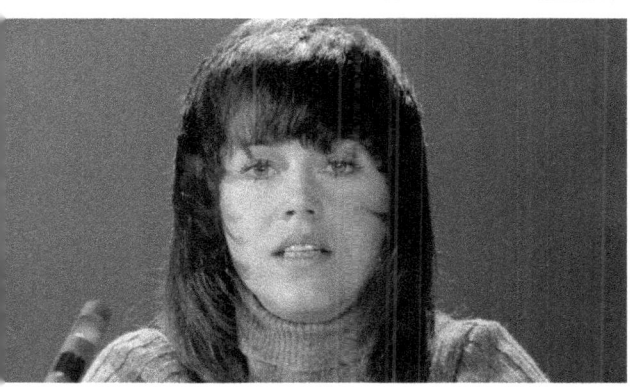

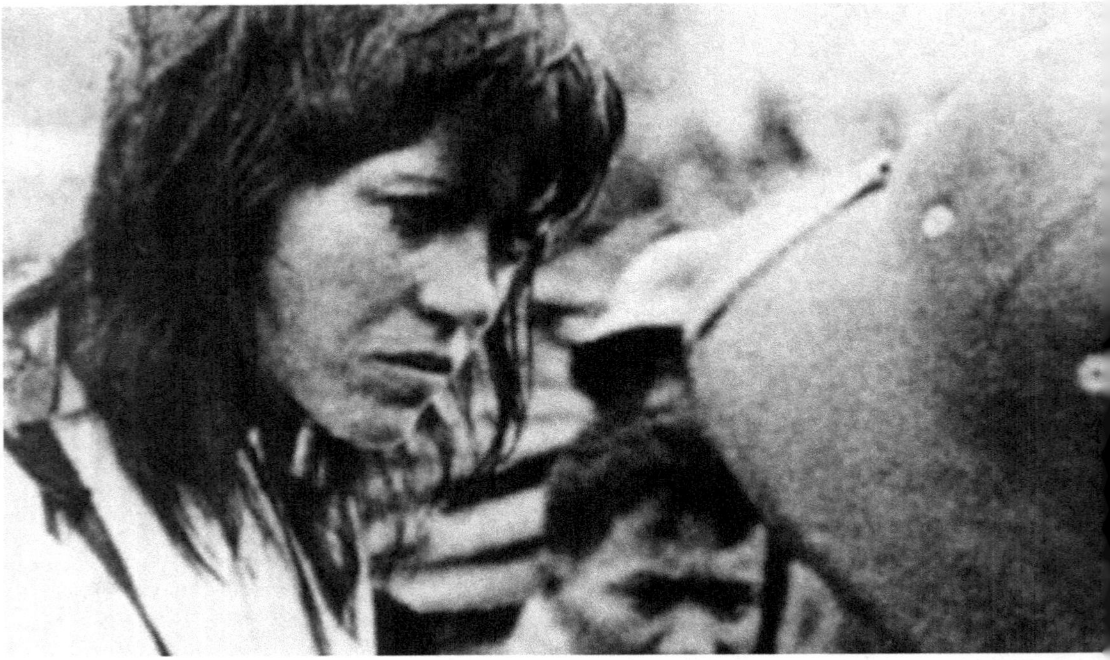

JEAN-LUC GODARD AND
JEAN-PIERRE GORIN
Letter to
Jane

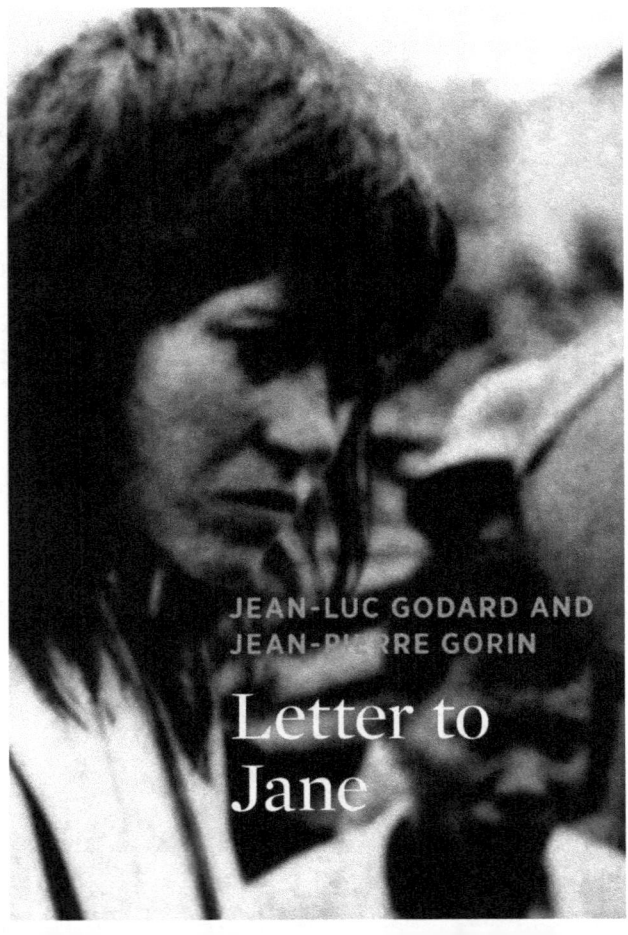

25

PASSION

PASSION

> The reasons that impel me to write are multiple, and the most important ones, it seems to me, are the most secret. Perhaps this one above all: to have security against death...
>
> André Gide, *Journals*[1]

---

[1] A. Gide, *The Journals of André Gide*, tr. J. O'Brien, Secker & Warburg, London, 1948, 306.

Passion (1982) was produced by Alain Sarde, Armand Barbault, Catherine Lapoujade and Martine Marignac, putting together another of those TV-biased, Euro co-productions: *Passion* was produced by Sara Films/ Sonimage/ Films Antenne 2/ Film et Video Production S.A./ S.S.R. Télévision Suisse. That was the familiar pattern of much of Jean-Luc Godard's work from the late 1970s onwards, and it was the same for many filmmakers in Europe who wanted to have their output distributed outside the country of origin (it must be stressed, again and again, how very little film or TV gets shown outside of its country of manufacture. Some of Godard's pieces are difficult to track down, but try with a lesser-known filmmaker and you can forget it).

ADs were Alain Tasma, Gérard Ruey, Bertrand Theubet and Lee Colver; Jean-Pierre Menoud shot the video footage, and Raoul Coutard, André Clément and Jean Garcenot lit the 35mm film; Serge Marzolff and Jean Bauer were art directors; wardrobe was by Christian Gasc, Rosalie Varda and Rosemary Melka; hair was by Patrick Archambaud; make-up by Bernard Minne; Lydias Mahias did continuity; Anne-Marie Miéville was stills photographer and adviser; François Mussy recorded the sound, and Bernard Le Roux mixed it; the Maestro co-wrote (with Jean-Claude Carrière), directed and edited *Passion*. Released 1982.5.26. 88 mins.

The cast included: Isabelle Huppert, Hanna Schygulla, Michel Piccoli, Jerzy Radziwilowicz, László Szabó, Jean-François Stévenin, Patrick Bonnel, Sophie Lucachevski, Barbara Tissier, Magali Campos, Myriem Roussel, Serge Desarnanos, Ágnes Bánfalvy, Ezio Ambrosetti, Manuelle Baltazar, Sarah Cohen-Sali, Sarah Beauchesne and Bertrand Theubet. And with some decent names involved (Schygulla, Piccoli, Huppert), plus the box office success of *Slow Motion*, Sarde and Godard were able to attract a budget of 12 million Francs ($2m plus).[2]

One of the ideas for *Passion* was to have it filmed by Vittorio Storaro, with production design by Dean Tavoularis (the prospect of Jean-Luc Godard joining forces with Storaro, probably the top cinematographer in the world at the time, are tantilizing. One wonders, though, how they would've agreed on lighting – Storaro famously lights his sets with astonishing intricacy, which takes a *long* time to set up, while Godard is all about natural lighting and filming fast. When Storaro works on a movie, he is one of the stars of the show).[3] At the time, Storaro and Tavoularis were finishing up on *One From the Heart*

---

[2] About 60% of the budget Godard had used up prior to principal photography, however, on the pre-production (B, 435).
[3] Storaro was one of a number of DPs, including Henri Decaë, Henri Alekan and Ricardo Aranowicz, who didn't want to shoot with natural light in the Godard manner.

at Zoetrope Studios. Godard's association with Francis Coppola and Zoetrope didn't emerge with Godard making a film, although Zoetrope did distribute *Sauve Qui Peut*.[4] And Godard had joined Coppola on a scouting trip to Las Vegas.

Actually, *Passion does* foreground lighting many times – and even the studio lamps themselves. There are more lamps on display in *Passion* than in any other Godard movie.

Passion hadn't made the impact that the filmmakers hoped with audiences. Many critics regard *Passion* as one of Jean-Luc Godard's finest works, as I do, but in Paris it grossed $300,000 from a 5-week run, much less than expected. *Slow Motion* was worth making if it led to this film, *Passion*. Or the success of *Slow Motion* was necessary if it enabled Godard and co. to produce *Passion*.

★

Passion is a summary of so many Godardian motifs and themes: it's really a montage of J.-L. Godard's *Greatest Hits* from 1956 to 1982. Pretty much everything in the Godard Box of Tricks is here: discussions among workers from the Dziga Vertov Group years; madcap car comedy from *Weekend*; pinball machines; films about films; a man and his love affairs; the beauty of video, etc.

Passion was one of the more difficult of Jean-Luc Godard's movies to bring to the screen. Producers walked out (Marin Karmitz, who produced *Slow Motion,* because he found Godard's treatment 'very aggressive'), actors were fired (Jean-Luc Bideau, originally playing the factory owner), and Godard kept changing his mind about what the film was going to be (this occurred with increasing frequency in Godard's later work). He would bring his actors together, film them improvizing on video, then change his mind again. He set his actors tasks to do (Hanna Schygulla waited tables in a café, Isabelle Huppert worked in a button factory, and Jerzy Radziwilowicz tried to direct a film in Paris but couldn't decide what it was going to be about. Just kidding). Godard filmed them once more on video, improvizing. He brought in writer Jean-Claude Carrière (co-writer of *Slow Motion*) to help with the script. He altered the characters, and changed his mind about who should play what. He made Huppert's character a virgin called Odile, and based her on Simone Weil.

Cameraman Ed Lachman described Godard's restless state of mind at the time: he would fly to L.A., have lunch, and fly back.[5] He carried

---

4 The relationship between Godard and Tom Luddy at Zoetrope was important, though (Luddy is presumably the 'Tom' referred to in *Passion*). Godard had met Luddy in 1968.
5 E. Lachman, in 2002, quoted in B, 437.

first-class air tickets with him all the time: he would tell Lachman, can you meet me next week in Paris? They would meet, talk, but Godard would say he wasn't ready to start *Passion* yet. 'That's how I see him at that time, always in motion'.

In the *Scenario for Passion* (1982), Jean-Luc Godard talks to the camera for ages, pondering on his film *Passion*. This guy can talk like very few filmmakers. Godard can *talk*. And the *Scénario du film Passion* offers an insight to Godard's studio set-up: he's sitting in front of a large screen, vision mixing, pontificating about the white screen, the blank page of the writer, and he's *so* in his element! He's got all his technological toys around him, his images, his films, orchestrating them all like a cinema magician.6

◆

In *Passion*, the Polish director, Jerzy (played by Jerzy Radziwilowicz),7 is trying to make a film which features elaborate *tableaux* based on classical paintings (Jerzy's appearance recalls Paul Godard in *Slow Motion*, and his character looks like a continuation of Paul: long side parting, glasses, jacket – so he's partly yet another Godard stand-in). But he never shoots anything, he cancels every set-up, tells the actors and extras to go home, informs everyone to return again tomorrow.8 Something is always wrong (it's usually the lighting, Jerzy complains, or the actors, or something else. Even tho' we can see that the light is beautiful). His refrain is: 'it's not working, let's try again tomorrow'. It's all rehearsal and no shooting. All preparation and no fulfilment. Jerzy is always on the point of walking out (and he drives everyone to despair: everyone's asking: is he going to shoot anything?).

Many film directors have spoken of film directing as being bombarded with a thousand questions every day. Many film directors don't like shooting – George Lucas and Steven Spielberg are two famous examples. Dick Lester summed the predicament thus:

> The actual day's shooting is bloody hell. To work with a hundred people looking on, saying, 'Go on, show us something, you're getting the most money, you smart ass' is an appalling thing to do day in and day out. It's physically very tiring because you have to charge a hundred people with your own enthusiasm in order to keep the film together. (J. Gelmis, 336)

Thus, Jerzy is in part Godard sending up himself and his

---

6 Godard is at the centre of the filmmaking process in *Scenario for Passion*: this is movie-making as art, created by an artist.
7 There are references to Solidarity and what's happening in Poland, but Jerzy seems unconcerned with it.
8 A car is parked up below the platform in one of the *tableaux*. Why?

indecisiveness, his tendency to want to go in *that* direction, but then in *this* direction, his desire to say *this* but also *that*. Jerzy in *Passion* tries the patience of everybody around him (in his personal life, too). He's the film director as the one person in the production who *shouldn't* be given the job of directing the film. (Of course, there's no script, or we don't see a script – another joke about Godard filming without a script, or writing up the day's filming in the morning).

Jerzy is at the centre of the 1982 film and provides a dramatic focus for the other characters: his sexual relationships with two women (played by Hanna Schygulla and Isabelle Huppert), with hints of further liaisons (such as the maid Sarah), his relations with the producers and the crew, and his opposite number, the C.E.O. of a factory (played by Michel Piccoli). All of these relationships are troubled.

Hanna Schygulla is the glam element in *Passion,* clad in furs, tight skirts and one of those spiky, teased, early 1980s hairstyles. She wouldn't look out of place in *Dallas* or *Dynasty*.

Prior to *Passion*, Hanna Schygulla was best-known for her work with Rainer Werner Fassbinder, with stand-outs including *Effi Briest* and *The Marriage of Maria Braun*. Following Godard's movie, Schygulla appeared in productions directed by Carlos Saura, Marco Ferreri, Andrzej Wajda, Volker Schlöndorff and Margarethe von Trotta.

Michel Piccoli has a constant cough – maybe a joke on the cancerous, Godardian chain-smoker. Yes – because instead of a cigar or cigarette in his *bouche* he has a red rose (and has flowers delivered).

Other characters include Sophie (Sophie Lucatchevsky), Jerzy's long-suffering production assistant, László (László Szabó), his line producer, Patrick (Patrick Bonnel), another assistant, an Italian producer (Enzio Ambrosetti), Sarah the motel maid, Magali (Magali Campos) and Jean-François (Jean-François Stévenin), the lightning guy.

★

None of the people in *Passion* are anything close to 'happiness'. Everyone seems disgruntled, disaffected, dissatisfied or downright miserable (it's Schopenhauerian). Slapstick cat fights are common in *Passion*, as are people being chased down by cars with horns blaring (Jean-Luc Godard has a penchant for silly physical fights among grown-ups – do you think he taps or tweaks people in real life? There's a moment in *JLG/ JLG* where he taps a young woman on the buttocks). Michel and Hanna have cat fights, Sophie yanks the hair of the couple she catches kissing in a car, and Michel harasses Hanna in his car, driving up close to her (cars are like extensions of the body in Godard's cinema, used for fetishization, intimidation and trysts).

Notice that altho' the film-within-a-film in *Passion* (also called *Passion*) is a film about lighting and cinematography, and has several complex and intricate recreations of famous paintings. And yet, altho' this is a movie about the making of a movie, and features several characters in the production team, one character is glaringly missing: *the cinematographer*. The film director is Top Dog on a film set, but the director of photography is Number Two in the chain of command. But where is he or she in *Passion*? On a production like this, the director would be conferring constantly with the DP (and when Jerzy complains, once again, about the light, it's not the frigging sparks and electricians who should take the heat, but the DP and the camera team). Also absent are art directors, set dressers, and the hair and make-up assistants.

Jerzy's line producer, László Szabó (a regular Godard actor), wants the film to have a story, as does the Italian producer (who passionately begs for 'a story, a story, a story!').9 Jerzy says repeatedly complains, 'why does there have to be a story?'10 It's something that Godard has wrestled with throughout his career, the conflicts between fiction and documentary, the make-believe of drama and the reality of reportage. Godard of course wants to have it both ways, like any artist. And in *Passion* he gives in, of course: there *is* a story in *Passion* - in fact, there are multiple stories involving a number of characters. This is one of the striking aspects of *Passion*: it is an ensemble piece, although Jerzy is at the centre. And an ensemble drama means keeping parallel stories up in the air at the same time, no easy thing to do, which requires a lot of work at the script/ conception stage (and many of Godard's films of this period were ensemble pieces - *Prénom Carmen* and *King Lear*, for instance).

The U.S. movie studios want a story too: they'll buy the film if it has a story, as László reports, *pace* Fox and M.G.M. (Throughout *Passion,* László is working away on the phones to save the film; Jerzy seems oddly unappreciative, and doesn't seem bothered whether the production sinks, although he does admit that László is his only friend. Is Jerzy perhaps a portrait of Godard the film director, always at odds

---

9 Languages in *Passion* mix French, Italian and German. The funding for *Passion* comes partly from Italian sources. Impressively, several actors who don't speak French as their mother tongue, such as Hanna Schygulla, speak in French.
10 As to the story, there is no story: you could say, echoing similar Beckettian pronouncements, there never was a story (along with: there is no character, there never was a character). It's the postmodern stance, voiced in the *Ghost In the Shell manga* by Masamune Shirow: there's no one here because there never was anyone here.

with his film crews? He certainly said at the time that he'd struggled with the crews of the films of the period. And he was making the same complaints about film crews 20 years later).

In some films, Jean-Luc Godard deliberately subverts the story and its demands. He can't or won't deal with them. At the same time, many of the films he most admires are very much story-driven, and one of the reasons they are such good films, and have lasted so long, is precisely because they tell stories in a compelling fashion. And it's the same with Godard's cinema: the Godard films that have lasted have tended to have been those that told stories, despite (or in spite of) the film director. Even twenty years after *Passion*, in *Notre Musique* in 2005, Godard was still telling stories. *Notre Musique* is another Godardian film essay, of course, about contemporary politics, and Sarajevo, and music, and the Middle East and all, but at the centre of *Notre Musique* is the story of two young women, Olga and Judith. (Meanwhile, nearly *all* of the movies that Godard went goo-goo over in his published criticism of the 1950s and 1960s were utterly, completely story-driven. And what does Godard do in his critical reviews? He does what every film critic does: he re-tells the stories in the movies!).

In fact, Jean-Luc Godard is a born storyteller, one of the best in the history of cinema. He simply can't help himself from telling stories. As the global media and the whole history of literature and art demonstrate, telling stories is still one of the best ways of exploring a subject, an issue, a theme. And no other filmmaker has staged so many scenes where characters pick up books or newspapers and start to read stories aloud. So the answer to Jerzy's question – 'why must there be a story?' – is simple: *because.* Because there must be.

László is portrayed as a harrassed individual, pressurized by the people above him (such as the moneymen and the producers), who want to get something – anything – filmed and cut. László is often depicted yelling at Jerzy to hurry up – to get in a car, for example. You can feel the pressure from the higher-ups on László to keep the movie production going, and to produce results. There are scenes where members of the film crew bustle into their cars, there's a feeling of urgency, yet nothing gets filmed, and the production winds on and on. (Thus, the crew hasten to the film studio, only to sit around after getting the cast into costume and make-up. The rushing about is ultimately pointless, because somewhere between the café and the film studio, the director goes A.W.O.L., ending up with one of his women).

★

Passion recalls *8 1/2* (1963), as it follows Jerzy the director (but Jerzy is no *alter ego* for Godard, as Guido Anselmi might have been for Federico Fellini – his working methods are quite different). The use of classical art recalls another Italian director, Pier Paolo Pasolini, who, in *La Ricotta* (part of *RoGoPaG,* 1963, which Godard contributed to), mounted self-consciously arty parodies of Renaissance, religious paintings (a *Deposition From the Cross*), filmed in lurid Technicolor.11

There are many other films about the making of films, of course: and *Passion* also resembles the backstage drama, which always has its love affairs, its conflicts, its audition scenes, its ambitious career people, its backbiting. And *Passion* follows the backstage drama closely: there's the producer yelling about spending too much money, there's the arty director reaching for the unknown (with no idea how to get there), there are the affairs with actors, there are disgruntled crew members, and so on. Bickering, in-fighting, gossip. Like the classic backstage drama, there's a pervading air of cynicism and world-weariness. *Passion* is Godard's *42nd Street, All About Eve,* and *The Bad and the Beautiful.*

Jerzy says at one point: 'there are no laws in cinema'. But of course there are, and Sophie doesn't need to remind Jerzy of them (such as: you have to tell a story). One of the clearest is played out in every scene in the TV studio: Jerzy is the Boss, and everything revolves around him. So, there are no laws, but the director is King. He is the law times a million (demonstrated when he walks in to the studio where not much is going on, and at his command people get busy. The A.D.s and line producers constantly admonish the cast/ crew: 'get to work!').

★

The themes explored in *Passion* include the nature of work, representation, narrative, cinema, sexuality, and love. And Europe vs. North Amerika (Jerzy will do anything to keep the financing for his film away from N. Amerika). The dialogue is stuffed with Godardisms. If it boils down to two themes or issues, they are love and work. Love and labour are compared: there's no difference for Jerzy: work is like love, and love is like work. And Isabelle mentions that the gestures and movements of work are like those of love (unusually, Jean-Luc Godard opts not to demonstrate that notion, though). An early conception of *Passion* was subtitled *Work and Love*: Godard wanted to remake *Toni*

---

11 The recreations of famous paintings remind me of many other directors: Peter Greenaway and Derek Jarman come to mind among British filmmakers. Indeed, Greenaway's cinema is virtually a footnote to Godard's cinema, as well as Alain Resnais' and Ken Russell's films. *Passion* forms a template for many Greenaway movies.

(1934), a Jean Renoir film, but couldn't get the rights.

Passion eschews traditional back-story and exposition, as usual in a Jean-Luc Godard film, and the audience has to pick up the information on the characters as it's scattered around the film. *Passion* doesn't make it easy for the audience, and it's denser than many Godard films.

Instead of a story, there are story elements: a couple kissing in a car; a child going to school; workers in front of machines in a factory; a man playing a typewriter like a piano. You can put them together to form a story if you wish, or you can submit to the primacy of the images, and see them just as a series of images and sounds.

◆

Passion begins with a characteristic Godardian shot: clouds, a blue sky[12] and a jet trail, filmed by Godard himself (with the Aaton 35/8 camera designed for him by Jean-Pierre Beauviala), with jerky movements (it's actually not that easy to produce a smooth follow shot of a jet). The music is phenomenal: it's Maurice Ravel's *Concerto For the Left Hand*, and it's the music that's much more to the point than this shot. Intercut with the shot are images of the major characters (with Isabelle Huppert first).

The first famous painting to be recreated inside the most expensive studio in Europe (200,000 Francs a day!) is Rembrandt van Rijn's *The Night Watch* (1642), one of the star attractions in Amsterdam's Rijksmuseum. As the piano music continues, the film includes voiceovers from people discussing the scene being filmed, without identifying them all (curiously Raoul Coutard is included, but that's no different from Godard using the actor's real names for the characters' names. And of course Coutard really likes the lighting of *The Night Watch*. Well, he would, he's probably spent the whole previous day lighting the scene. But Coutard is not seen on screen as one of the crew).

The hair, make-up and costume depts have their work on display here, and for once in static *tableaux*, not as part of a blink-and-you-miss-it scene as usual in cinema: costumes were by Christian Gasc, Rosalie Varda and Rosemary Melka; Patrick Archambaud did the hair; and Bernard Minne applied the make-up.

The scene is truly wonderful, as the camera wanders over close-ups of the actors in costume – folks, these are money shots, production value shots, and also the 'Godard Sublime'. And they're also completely

---

[12] Actually, *Sauve Qui Peut (La Vie)* also opened with a shot of the sky. It does seem to be a favourite Godardian image.

pointless: why reproduce famous paintings? Errr, ummm... *Because*, that's why. But why do it? *Pourquoi?* Because it's something wonderful to do... Critics can discuss endlessly critical issues like the age of simulation and reproduction, postmodern hyperspace, the emptying out of the image, the negative space of the sign, the death of art, the death of the author, and all that. But that doesn't explain or justify why Jerzy or Godard are recreating these paintings. This is the closest we'll get to seeing Godard recreating history.

A search for the lost light of art? The lost spaces of art? How to recreate light itself? A search for the past, but a past that never existed – this is *art, painting*, not history. Painting as the lost maternal realm, *à la* Jacques Lacan and Julia Kristeva? (Certainly the film seems more interested in the light and space of these paintings than their historical context or even the subjects they are depicting. It's an art history lesson, but it's about form, and the image, not meanings or histories).

The allusions to the history of art (and painting in particular) in *Passion* are a typical Godardian quotation, and these scenes are some of the most luxurious and sophisticated in Godard's cinema: Eugène Delacroix, Peter Paul Rubens, Rembrandt van Rijn, Francisco de Goya and Jean Auguste Dominique Ingres. *Passion* orchestrates actors in Biblical costumes, drapes, nudes, angels' wings, horses and horse riders, plus the technical arsenal of cinema: model cityscapes (including Constantinople), cycloramas, cranes and lights.

The recreation of the paintings of Francisco de Goya y Lucientes includes *The Executions of the Third of May, 1808* (1814), *The Nude Maja* (c. 1800), *The Parasol* (1817) and *The Family of Charles IV* (1800). It's a 'Best of Goya', a *Guide To Goya*, an art history lesson in Goya. Movement is added to the *tableaux* of Goya's images, as the TV cameras follow the woman with the parasol walking slowly around the figures.[13]

In all of the paintings, Jean-Luc Godard and his team extend the space of the paintings, showing what is beyond the paintings' frames. They also add movements and gestures within the paintings, dramatizing them, and sometimes altering the gestures of the original works. And the team add elements to the paintings, and sometimes don't include everything in the original image. For instance, there's lots more in Francisco de Goya's *The Executions of the Third of May, 1808* from the victims who've been shot and lie on the ground than there is in *Passion*.

---

13 J.-L. Leutrat has noted that the recreations of paintings consistently depict 'women in movement' (*Des traces qui nous ressemblent*, Editions Comp'Act, Bodoni, 1990.)

But these loving, detailed evocations of classical paintings are romantic, poetic interludes in the film of *Passion*. The 'story' as such – this was the era when Jean-Luc Godard was questioning the whole notion of narrative and why audiences crave stories – involves a bunch of people making the film, people in the nearby factory, and in the motel where they stay.

◆

Other aspects of *Passion* are typical of Jean-Luc Godard's cinema: characters are addressed by the first names of the actors playing them (Jerzy, Hanna, Isabelle, Michel, László). The title of the film being shot in the studios is of course *Passion*.[14] There are lengthy and elaborate takes. Nude women drift about. The location is France/ Switzerland (looking very bland in the towns and wintry in the countryside. Classical music rises behind the dialogue (Wolfgang Amadeus Mozart, Johann Sebastian Bach, Ludwig van Beethoven, Antonin Dvorák, Maurice Ravel and Gabriel Fauré). Sounds stop and start abruptly, or dip out entirely, to be replaced by music. Background noise is loud (making some dialogue indistinguishable. And those bloody car horns! In the age of DVD and home sound systems, Godard's penchant for including very loud car horns is irksome. I wouldn't be surprised that Godard, with his state of the art sound studio down in Rolle, deliberately makes the car horns as piercing as possible).

If *Passion* proves a little tricky to follow at times, that's because Jean-Luc Godard and François Mussy are overlapping dialogue like they've never done before: dialogue overlaps within scenes; dialogue from the factory scenes is laid over the TV studio scenes, and vice versa; and, most disorientating of all, dialogue within scenes is deliberately put out of sync with actors' mouths (and, for non-French speaking folk, there's the added layer of subtitles). So, sound-wise, *Passion* is among Godard's densest works.[15]

If you think it seems like sticking it to the audience, you'd be right. To have dialogue consciously out of synchronization at one or two moments is easy to take (Woody Allen and the Marx Brothers, for instance, have done wonders with it). But across *an entire scene* – and not just one, but *several*. Wow. Jean-Luc Godard sure has some guts.

---

14 The studio or TV station is T.V.F. (it was filmed at Boulogne-Billancourt studios and in Rolle).
15 And music is layered under some scenes: during the discussion of workers possibly striking, Mozart's *Requiem* is played.
   Maybe, as Kaja Silverman suggested, the conversation about the factory is not specific to the workers here, but to all workers everywhere, so Godard deliberately breaks the synchronization between sound and image (1998, 177).
   The other scenes, involving Isabelle and the workers, are also shot in a comical style: Isabelle is chased around the factory floor by Michel and a cop.

◆

There's so much business with cars, *Passion* comes across like a sequel to *Weekend* - *Passion* stages numerous scenes inside and outside cars, and employs cars as bodies, physically interacting with the performers (it's mandatory for an actor to be able to drive to act in a Godard production). There's also a penchant for slowing moving cars - and for people to get in or out of cars while they're moving. And of course we have cars bashing into other cars. And of course scenes in gas stations.[16]

When Hanna and Michel are first introduced, it's in their cars: Michel drives up and talks to Hanna nearby thru the car window. It's the (wing) mirror of the scene introducing Jerzy and Isabelle as a couple. (Again, the staging curiously resembles two people on horseback, as if Godard and co. are doing their version of a horse opera like Godard faves such as *Johnny Guitar* or *Rancho Notorious*. But with cars. In Switzerland. In the rain. With French and German actors.)

If Godard did a cowboy flick, of course it would be with cars not horses. And yet horses *do* appear in this movie - in the recreation of Eugène Delacroix's painting *The Entry of the Crusaders Into Constantinople*. (Horses are not what comes to mind when thinking of a Godard movie! He might adore Howard Hawks, John Ford and Anthony Mann, but nobody hired him to make a Western! But wait - he *did* attempt a WEstern - *Wind From the East*).

◆

Jerzy, looking at a nude woman floating in a pool in front of him (a deaf and dumb actor, played by the divine Myriem Roussel),[17] tells his production manager he's 'looking at the universal wound', the vagina (he asks the actress to make a star-shape in the water - in the irked, impatient tones of the film-director-who-must-be-obeyed). Pro-Godardians and anti-Godardians and feminists can excuse or criticize that comment - but really it's just another Godardian throwaway, deliberately designed to annoy some of the audience. And look at how it's part of a longer sequence (one of the best shots in *Passion*), and how the scene continues with Jerzy discussing women and affairs in a crude manner with László (these two guys are the grown-up versions of the laddish youths in *Bande à Part* or *A Woman Is a Woman*). There's also the element of music in the sequence - the *Requiem* by Wolfgang

---

16 Patrick bumps into someone's precious Japanese car (they yell offscreen, another *Weekend* moment. It's a long rant, but we never see who it is).
17 Godard and co. seem to have fallen for Myriem Roussel - from an extra, playing the Boss's daughter, Roussel appears in many scenes (often fully naked).

Mozart – which adds another layer of meaning (one of the themes of *Passion* is being able to 'see' music and 'hear' paintings. It's as if Jerzy is only able to visualize the *tableaux* when music is playing. And not just any music, of course, but the classical classics, just as the paintings are classics). Music became increasingly important in the later Jean-Luc Godard films – or important in a different way. Now it's not Godard and his producers commissioning 'film music'-type music from film composers, but Godard and his producers selecting existing recordings of classical music (with one or two newer pieces).

As Godard put it, *Passion* was about both music *and* painting, 'neither one without the other'. The subtitle might be 'Passion, the world and its metaphor', Godard suggested in 1983. Certainly *Passion* is rapturous, containing some of the finest sounds that humans have created. Music that good guarantees some cultural value at least: it's probably impossible for a film to be worthless if it contains selections from Mozart, Bach and Beethoven.

✱

Passion is Jean-Luc Godard's Nude Film – meaning, his *Nude Women* film. *Passion* contains more nudity than any other Godard film, although *Hail Mary* and *Prénom Carmen* also feature quite a lot of skin (and Godard included nudity from his first feature, *Breathless* onwards). Much of the nakedness in *Passion* appears in the recreations of classical paintings, of course – the nudes of Goya, Ingres, etc. But there are other nude scenes – a woman appears on the hotel balcony with her child, apparently from a shower; there's a sex scene with the woman bare and the man fully clothed; the maid strips down, etc.

What also comes across very strongly in *Passion* is that Godard and his team have worked through all of these concerns and issues and motifs before – and often much better. I mean, the whole story element about a film director who's dissatisfied with everything in his life and faces pressures from all of the people around him – Godard did it all in *Contempt*. And Godard's also mounted recreations of paintings before. *Passion* does come across at times as the work of someone exhausted, creatively, too uninspired to deliver a really good film.

That's one view: but the recreations of paintings are so beautiful, the filmmakers seem to be revelling in this work. The 'Godard Sublime' is in full effect there. And *Passion*, despite its exhaustion and rehashing of former glories, exerts its own magic. It is a kind of rebirth, too, for Godard's cinema – much more than *Slow Motion* was. It's the same Godardian material but reborn in a different form.

Passion also integrates the cultural concerns – painting and music – with the neurotic relationships seen in *Slow Motion* in a more satisfying manner. The pessimism and self-loathing of *Slow Motion* has been tempered by a more optimistic worldview ('everywhere is beautiful').

Critics have often drawn attention to the contribution of Raoul Coutard again in *Passion*, and his work is delicious, especially in the complex lighting challenges of the paintings (a lighting cameraman's dream project). However, Coutard didn't film all of *Passion* – André Clément and Jean Garcenot are also credited as DPs.

Light is of course one of the recurring motifs of *Passion*, with light being adjusted within shots, and many scenes shifting from light to dark and vice versa. In one scene, at the end of the lengthy sequence shot in the bath set, Jerzy orders all of the lamps to be switched off. It's a way of making manifest yet again the huge arsenal of fakery of a film or TV studio, and the materiality of the scene is beguiling (the doors beyond the cyclorama are opened, so the artificial light mixes with daylight, and the fake sky fuses with the real sky; and *Passion* opens with a lengthy shot of the sky).

But the real *tour-de-force* of technicality in *Passion* is of course the editing and the sound. It has been worked over many times in the sound mix. This is a film that was drastically rewritten in post-production. Jean-Luc Godard is credited as film editor (though he would have had assistants, probably including Anne-Marie Miéville), and François Mussy was his regular sound editor. Just putting all of those voiceovers and parts of dialogue from one scene over another is a mammoth job.

✽

Critics have pointed out the affinities between Jean-Luc Godard and Jerzy in *Passion*. Well, *duh*, they are both film directors! Actually, if you want to point out links between authors and their characters, you have to acknowledge that an author is *every* major character in their works, not just the one that seems the most obvious alter ego. And in *Passion*, Godard is very much the young idealistic worker Isabelle, who rebels against her role in the capitalist system. Oh yes, and he's also Michel, the ageing factory owner. And he's Hanna, the beautiful bourgeois lover of Jerzy and Michel. And so on. Of course. *D'accord*.

Allons-y: in many ways, Jean-Luc Godard is *not* like Jerzy. For a start, although Jerzy's predicament in shooting his film echoes some of the concerns that Godard has faced, as every film director faces – what are we going to shoot today, Boss? – and all those thousand-questions-a-day – no way would Godard (or his producers) have allowed an expensive film production to go so far over-schedule and over-budget (*Passion* is meant to be the sort of film that would have been over-budget and behind schedule from day one of shooting). As far as I know, Godard has never been in the situation of a massive over-spend and over-schedule (and has only occasionally gone over. His budgets, for example, are really tiny).

Another great line in *Passion*, related to money, runs: 'I'm sick of working on a production that produces nothing!' There have been film shoots that ran for weeks then months, stretching on for 150... then 200... then 250 days: *Apocalypse Now, Heaven's Gate, Eyes Wide Shut, Barry Lyndon, Cleopatra, Titanic, Jaws*, etc. On those films, the crew would have Tee shirts printed 'Day 200!' or 'No End In Sight!' That's when fantasies of killing the film director or the film producer become very attractive. It's when the cult of the director and *auteur* becomes unstuck: no one's got the guts to tell the director to give up or walk away, and let someone else finish up the job.[18] And the studio is in so deep it would be silly to stop the shoot.

But Jean-Luc Godard has never been in that situation of running on and on for 100 days or 150 days or more days (200 days for three people in a hotel – *The Shining* – are you kidding?! 400 days for a marital breakdown yarn – *Eyes Wide Shut* – are you nuts?). And even on his more complex films, like *Weekend* or *Passion*, I bet Godard didn't go much over, if at all. And many of Godard's 1960s films were famously staged on schedules of 2, 3, 4 or so weeks (and on budgets of $70,000 or $150,000).[19]

Further, Jean-Luc Godard, faced with those beautiful recreations of great paintings, wouldn't hesitate for a second: he'd be filming them every which way. Which of course, *his* camera does, even while Jerzy's team wait around for instructions from the Boss. Godard simply wouldn't be stuck for ideas with those sorts of toys and costumes and lights and actors to play with.[20] Godard is a completely natural filmmaker who would find something to make out of those ingredients.

There is an irony about the whole film-within-a-film production

---

18 Yet that's what seems to happen at the end of *Passion*, when the production departs for Tinseltown.
19 The shoot of *Passion* hadn't been much fun, Godard asserted, and his conflicts with the crew were a common gripe.
20 Jerzy complains that the light's wrong, but does nothing to fix it with his DP. There are no discussions about how they can improve it. He doesn't shoot tests, for instance, and isn't seen watching rushes. He prefers to sit by the TV monitor in his hotel room and watch the playback of his impromptu opera-mime with Hanna (much to László's consternation).

in *Passion*, though: apart from those lovely *tableaux* of famous paintings, what is Jerzy's film about? And who financed and authorized this particular film? The Italian film producer who comes in and goes nuts presumably signed off on the budget for Jerzy's project. In which case, what did he expect? Didn't he see the script? (One of the best scenes has the Italian producer entering and going crazy about the film being behind schedule and over-budget. Jean-Luc Godard is clearly referring (bitterly) to producers he's worked with, such as Carlo Ponti and Dino de Laurentiis, always with a beautiful woman on their arm (who's much taller than they are!). The producer yells 'where's my money?', 'what have you done with my money?' It's one of the recurring phrases in the film, usually yelled out, as of course it should be. And the best part of the scene has László pointing to props, sets and costumes and rattling off prices, just to wind up the producer. And the prices are in Lire, of course, which always sound like loads – ten million, 20 million. Once again, Godard did all of this in *Contempt* – and better (or the opening of *Tout Va Bien*, when he writes the cheques to pay for the production). I've seen nearly everything that Godard has produced, but I haven't come across the film yet in which Godard has attached price tags to everything in the movie, including the actors, the camera, the tins of film stock, the editing machine, etc.

But we shouldn't take it all too literally, of course: the film production in *Passion* is a comment upon filmmaking, and work in a late capitalist system, so it's not meant to be realistic. Maybe Jerzy is meant to be a parody of those European film *auteurs* like Federico Fellini, who were allowed to shoot expensive movies for months on end (such as *Casanova*, 1976),[21] even when the story or the commercial potential for their projects seemed obscure or limited (and *Passion*, in 1981-82, was being made at a time when a few very costly films had over-run and over-spent: *Apocalypse Now, Heaven's Gate, Raise the Titanic, 1941, Popeye, Superman, Honky Tonk Freeway*, etc).

In his later years, as Ingmar Bergman pointed out, Federico Fellini ended up doing 'Fellini movies', films that he thought approximated to 'Fellini films'. Certainly other filmmakers, such as Andrei Tarkovsky, Steven Spielberg, Brian de Palma, Martin Scorsese and Bernardo Bertolucci, have done similar things.

I don't think God-Art fell into that trap: I think he remained remarkably fresh – *remarkably fresh* for an older filmmaker. He never rested on his laurels, never dined out for decades on former glories

---

21 Much to the aggravation of producer Alberto Grimaldi.

(indeed, he preferred to seldom even refer to them; the past was another time, another world, he often said). Except, maybe, there is a nagging feeling that Jean-Luc Godard is exploring in *Passion* the idea of repeating oneself to the point of weariness, nihilism and career suicide or even personal suicide. *Passion* is thus another of Godard's films about the End of Cinema, like *Pierrot le Fou* or *Weekend* (and several others). At the end of *Pierrot le Fou*, of course, there is Rimbaudian desperation and despair, and both the lead characters die. Except, I think that not only Jerzy's film-with-a-film is exhausted and desperate, but Godard's film itself comes dangerously close.

It's ironic, too, that we never see (parts of) the film that Jerzy is making (that's not uncommon in backstage dramas, though). They talk about it, they shoot it, they keep stopping then starting again the next day, but *Passion* never shows a frame from *Passion*.[22] Instead, all of those lovely painterly *tableaux* are filmed with Raoul Coutard's camera, not Jerzy's. And there's no script, no *Bible* shown. (One of the wonderful things about video, which Godard has spoken about, is its ability to produce an instant image. Yet it's curious that *Passion* doesn't even depict a TV monitor showing the cameras' views. And there's one space in this F200,000-a-day studio that's notably absent, which is the core of any TV studio, and that's the control room.[23] That's where Jerzy, László and their assistants would be holed up for the entire schedule, not on the studio floor with the actors).

The film-with-a-film, the *Passion*-within-*Passion*, is also being shot on video, of course, so there's another layer to the film, involving the relation between the film and the television industries, and even the material aspects, such as the differences between film stock and video footage. *Passion* is thus partly about the fact that, as Bernardo Bertolucci remarked, all films end up on television (so those *tableaux* of paintings are almost a defiance of television, a refusal to be sucked down to the lowest common denominator. And television, of course, wants stories even more than cinema. Or rather, television won't accept abstract, poetic pieces: it only wants stories).

What the film production is actually making is kept vague: it seems to be a European art movie (though on a lavish scale, with its

---

22 Jean-Jacques Beneix, *cinéma du look* director of *Diva* and *Betty Blue*, said that Godard sometimes 'talks better about the movie than he makes the movie. But the minute after I see what he's done, there's a moment of pure intelligence and grace and genius, of how to place the camera' (M. Figgis, 76).
23 Again, *Passion* isn't a literal film of TV production at all. What about those two tables set up right next to the sets – complete with telephones – where the production staff work? An expensive film studio or TV studio would have plenty of offices where the production team would be based.

recreations of classical art). But what the story is, or what the film is about, remains indistinct. The story, in fact, is never unveiled. Remember in *Contempt* how Fritz Lang and Michel Piccoli often discussed the plot of *The Odyssey*? Not in *Passion*: the movie refuses to tell the audience what those stunning classical painting reproductions are for, or how they fit in with the movie.

Another glaring omission are the main actors: there's no Anna Karina or Jean-Paul Belmondo here. Instead, every scene looks like a preparation for something that never materializes. Jerzy and László sometimes talk about the film they're making, but without really saying anything about it.

Casting is another area of contention: Jerzy, László and company occasionally discuss who's going to play particular roles. The Italian producer, for example, insists that his supermodel girlfriend will play the Madonna, but Jerzy nixes that. The film production has been hiring workers at the factory next door as extras (and Jerzy of course wants Isabelle to play a role).

❋

Passion conjures a number of erotic triangles: Jerzy-Isabelle-Hanna; Jerzy-Hanna-Michel; Sophie-Patrick-Magali.[24] Isabelle Huppert is a factory worker, later in a relationship with Jerzy (Huppert is an actor I find really irritating, in the way that the writer John Cowper Powys took a *physical* dislike to Robert Browning, just from reading his poetry.[25] Doesn't everyone have such irrational blindspots and aversions?[26] And Huppert plays Isabelle ten years younger than she is, with a ridiculously unconvincing stutter, really horrible clothes (those yellow tights!), and a wilfully childish demeanour).[27]

---

[24] How is it that the women in *Passion* seem to admire and love Jerzy? He has three women desiring him: Hanna, Isabelle and Sarah the maid. This man must have some secret aphrodisiac hidden from the audience. Or is it because he's the film director, and even ugly, speccy guys become romantic magnets?
[25] John Cowper Powys spoke of disliking certain authors because he disliked their *bodies*, even though he hadn't met them:

> Yes, at bottom the thing is physical. My literary likes and dislikes are physical, quite as much as my personal ones. And this applies to the dead equally with the living. I like and can understand, for example, the physical quality of Wordsworth's flesh and blood, while I instinctively shrink from that of - Browning, let us say! (*Autobiography*, Macdonald, London, 1967, 320)

This notion offers an interesting gloss to the 'writing with the body' of Hélène Cixous and French feminism. Powys, writing decades before politically correct cultural and postmodern theory, was not bothered by steering clear of being 'biologist' or 'essentialist'. If he didn't like a poet's flesh and blood, he said so. Who cares if it's a silly way of critically evaluating writers (literature is actually full of such idiosyncratic and irrational likes and dislikes). At the same time, Powys's notion of disliking writers 'physically' presages the postmodern idea of the 'sexuality of the text', of the text as body.
[26] Keira Knightley, Nicole Kidman, Gwyneth Paltrow, Orlando Bloom and Adam Sandler are also people I find it difficult to watch or hear on screen.
[27] Like that stupid harmonica.

The scene which depicts the relationship of Isabelle and Jerzy is one only Jean-Luc Godard could do: it mainly comprises just two shots: one of Isabelle beside Jerzy's car, talking to him through the window, occasionally playing a harmonica, and occasionally stepping forward to block the sun (a very Godardian touch, unmotivated, and entirely about the visuals, about light). The reverse angle is of Jerzy in his car. He takes out a pen and notebook at one point (though Isabelle is now unseen, appearing as a voice).

That's already unusual – a love scene played with someone in a car and someone next to it, but Jean-Luc Godard adds two further elements: the car is moving, slowly. Why? It's like those scenes in cowboy flicks where two people talk as they travel through the desert, one on a horse, and one walking. But to have a car moving very slowly adds a really odd note to the scene (Godard's cinema is full of 'car acting', acting with cars).

But that's not the most amazing thing about it: what really kicks the scene into Godardland, a world where nothing is as it seems, a kind of *Alice In Wonderland*, European art film-style, is that the two shots *are not cut together*, but simply played one after the other, refusing the shot/ reverse shot form, with Isabelle's voice running over Jerzy's shot (she's doing most of the talking, but Jerzy is heard over her shot). And there's yet another element: the film fades out Isabelle's voice, but shows her talking, and instead Jerzy's heard talking in voiceover – but not to Isabelle, but in his head.[28] I can't think of anyone else editing a scene that way – to *not* intercut the shots at all. In *Passion*, the filmakers're stripping down the basics of film grammar and rebuilding them from scratch. That's an amazing feat in itself, but that God-Art would do that after making *twenty-four features*, is equally striking. His enthusiasm for the act of creating images and sounds is as strong as ever.

✣

Money and work are recurring motifs in *Passion*: in both the factory and the studio. When Jerzy is with Hannah and someone calls on the phone (probably László), he insists that he's working. Is he? Sort of. There's a worker who chases Michel around for the money he's owed. 'Mon chèque!' the guy yells, chasing Michel in silent comedy fashion. Michel, the stingy capitalist *par excellence*, appears to prefer not to pay his workers if possible (and sadly goes to great lengths to avoid the

---

28 Kaja Silverman notes that 'Jerzy and Isabelle's voices defy the categories of voice-over and voice-off. Godard creates a new vocal category with these voices, what might be called the 'voice between'' (1998, 176).

guy). A commentary on the capitalist system, of course, on bosses and workers, but it also very much applies to film production. Crew members hounding film producers for their money is more common than one would think, even in the age of unions. This running gag culminates with the angry guy doing what everybody's been hoping to do: he stabs the director with a knife (but he was trying to nail Michel. A scene where someone physically attacks the film director? Many film crews secretly dream of it. Well, we know, pursing the biographical angle, that Godard has been involved in fights).

While the studio contains scenes that some critics have termed 'sublime' – certainly among the most luscious in Jean-Luc Godard's cinema – the outside world is painfully, desperately banal and ordinary. The buildings are faceless and bland: a motel, a gas station, a forecourt, a factory. They could be anywhere in the Western world from Alaska to Romania. (Altho' the mantra 'everywhere is beautiful' in the 1982 movie is true, much of the human-made environment is anti-beautiful).

❋

There's a sex scene in *Passion,* which's unusual for its explicitness. Sophie is being taken from the rear by the lighting guy Jean-François: of course, the woman is completely naked, and the guy is fully clothed. And as it's a Jean-Luc Godard scene, it's not a simple sex scene: there's no pleasure involved, it seems, and the couple are arguing about production schedules, while Sophie, bent over and flailing her hair around self-consciously, says, 'we must have stories'. And there are a couple of other (male) voices on the soundtrack. (This new sexual explicitness would reach its peak in the following picture, *First Name: Carmen*).

Several of the lengthy sequence shots in *Passion* would take hours to set up and rehearse, and some a whole day. One of the most elaborate takes in *Passion* has Jerzy on a camera crane, lining up shots over the Constantinople model and in front of the cyclorama, the camera sweeping around;[29] the shot continues with Jerzy climbing off the crane and encountering a host of people clamouring for his attention. He puts them all off, increasingly violently – extras in costume, crew members, László his producer, the Italian producer, etc. At the end of the shot, Jerzy ends up wrestling with an old guy dressed

---

[29] A version of the crane shot had been filmed by Godard on the set of Francis Coppola's film *One From the Heart.* Godard and his team also shot two *tableaux* from paintings on the *One From the Heart* set: *The Fall of the Damned* by Peter Rubens, and *The Newborn* by Georges de la Tour. For *The Newborn,* 50 babies were used, but Godard decided to employ dolls instead, because they made less noise (B, 436).

as an angel, evoking *Jacob Wrestling With the Angel* by Eugène Delacroix (the whole shot may have been building up to this particular image – the filmmaker wrestling an angel, like Jacob in the *Bible*).

Another lengthy shot in the film studio depicts a procession comprising soldiers, half-naked women, and several characters (it's a recreation of Eugène Delacroix's *Entry of the Crusaders Into Constantinople*, 1840). At one point, one of the soldiers goes A.W.O.L. and starts to chase one of the half-naked women (played by Myriem Roussel) around the studio. The proximity of those beautiful women is just too much for some of the soldiers.[30]

In this episode the 1982 movie also mounts another intricate sequence shot involving images of the soldiers riding around the miniature of Constantinople, carrying off naked women, and panning around to show Patrick talking to the lighting guy's daughter. As they look at an art book, Patrick gives a mini-art history lesson about Eugène Delacroix. The evocation of Delacroix's art leads into nature – an image of Hanna in a kind of greenhouse or indoor garden, spied on by Michel. A woman in a garden being observed is a motif from mediæval or Renaissance literature and painting, yet another allusion in a film packed tight with them. But the following scene is pure Godard: Hanna being chased by Michel in his car (until she explodes).[31]

During the Eugène Delacroix art recreation, Sophie is dancing along the lighting gallery, and embracing her new-found love, the lighting gaffer, Jean-François. On the studio floor, extras are shoved onto the stage by Patrick – the treatment of the extras is violent and exaggerated at times, included presumably to emphasize the master-slave relationships of the labour market. During the painting *tableaux* shoots, one of the phrases shouted is, 'to work!' On this film, everyone is an assistant director, eager to chivvy everyone else to get to work.

Another of the elaborate recreations of famous paintings is based on the art of Jean Auguste Dominique Ingres, well-known for his female nudes and bathers, which's what *Passion* delivers. The *tableaux* collage *The Valpinçon Bather, The Turkish Bath*, and others.[32] And movement is added to the painting again, as the bather (the sublime Myriem Roussel again) enters the scene and takes her place within it. The paintings threaten to move and become theatrical. The re-enactments of the paintings can't seem to resist moving. And some-

---

30 It's a comment on history, and on the representation of history in art, yes, but it's also a swipe at film extras, who are occasionally derided by filmmakers.
31 Hanna, not the car.
32 The film alters some details: the towel is red, the turban is white.

times the actors in the *tableaux* rebel and start chasing women around.

While operatic music plays (Wolfgang Mozart's *Requiem* again), the camera tracks around the pool and the bathers. Characters muse on the links between work and love, sex and labour. There's no difference? One is like the other (maybe – but tell that to people cleaning their seventieth toilet halfway through a ten-hour shift in an office block in São Paolo).

The film studio as factory, the factory as film studio. The studio as 'dream factory'. (The production hires (some of) their extras from the factory next door). Jerzy mentions that he exists in an 'in-between' zone, in between two women, much as the film exists in between the factory and the studio, in between work and love. ('Everyone is searching. Everyone is in between', says László, a classic Godardism).

At one point, Isabelle complains that films never show people at work, which's true. And people at work in factories. The filmmakers stage her dialogue with movement – the camera follows Isabelle walking, and behind Isabelle people are shown at work. (It's one of Godard's oldest mantras – his films have been depicting people at work from the early days).

A scene with many of the main actors grouped around a pinball machine (oddly it has the U.S. rock band Kiss on the side) is a call-back to Godard's early 1960s films.

★

One of the more intriguing scenes in *Passion*, and a scene specifically designed to make film and cultural critics go gooey, has Jerzy and Hanna watching a playback of Hanna (and Jerzy) mock miming to W.A. Mozart's *Mass*. This lengthy sequence (in which Hanna can barely bring herself to look at herself), shifts into a love scene – a love scene played against a love scene. And this is a private film that Jerzy has made, recording his lover on video (not film), which has instant playback (it seems as if it were shot earlier in the same room, although of course it probably wasn't). The love scene coalesces all sorts of issues – take your pick: love > sex > mirrors > voyeurism > video > television > identity > women > men > masculinity > femininity, etc, and any number of philosophers: Lacan > Freud > Hegel > Barthes > Derrida > Brecht > Heidegger.

The scene is recapitulated later in *Passion*, this time with Jerzy watching Hanna on the screen on his own (while László's beside him, on the phone yet again – the film producer's default position – film producing as tele-sales). Now Jerzy's talking about the relationship between art and death, video and death, art/ video and memory, video as memoralization: 'don't forget me... I'll forget you', Jerzy murmurs, and the stepped frames technique from *Slow Motion* is employed, with Schygulla's face slowed down (it's like a mini-demonstration of Godard at work, editing, reviewing rushes and manipulating them with video devices).

❋

The lengthy scene in *Passion* where Isabelle and her chums discuss working at Michel's factory is a reprise of the famous episode in the career of Jean-Luc Godard, the Dziga Vertov Group period with Jean-Pierre Gorin and company. The scene is a return to the Marxist-Leninist Therapy Group, with Isabelle appearing as the stuttering idealist who hopes to stick it to the Boss.

The opinions voiced by those present in the room are augmented by other voices – that would make the scene dense enough, but the scene is edited out of sync. Thus, we see people talking but hear someone else. Sometimes, the mis-match is one of timing, of a few seconds - resembling when image and sound lose sync during film projection.

Again, it can appear as another instance where the filmmakers are being difficult for the sake of it, or to reveal the mechanisms of cinema. The device adds a layer of self-conscious commentary, which we have come to expect from Godard's work. (But do we need the mechanisms of cinema, of images coupled with sounds, to be exposed yet again? Hasn't most of the audience already been there and done that? I certainly don't need another lecture on how cinema works! I've given 100s of them).

However, the content in the dialogue isn't so surprising, with the workers voicing political/ ideological opinions familiar from the Dziga Vertov Group pieces. But these are nice, middle class Swiss and French youngsters, not like the self-consciously intense radicals depicted in the Dziggy Verty Group films. So nobody raises their voice – they might be discussing where to buy the cheapest Swiss cheese. [33]

◆

Sarah, the contortionist maid at the motel, is another of Jean-Luc Godard's young dreamers. There's a scene where Sarah brings Jerzy some food and the dalliance between the older director and the young maid begins.[34] Sarah asks if Poland is beautiful, and Jerzy responds, rightly, *partout c'est beau* (an optimistic and poetic Godardism:

---

33 Have you tried Monoprix? Leclerc? Géant? Carrefour?
34 It continues in the kitchen, over soup.

'everywhere is beautiful'). That modest scene sets up the final scene, where Sarah, at the last moment, opts to go with Jerzy to Poland.

Passion is no different from many Jean-Luc Godard movies in having a dissatisfying ending. The ending 'doesn't work', as Jerzy would put it. *Why should there be a story?* the film asks. And therefore: *why should there be a decent ending*? *Passion* ends with the production breaking up: László takes the show to California to complete it (presumably with most if not all of Jerzy's footage junked, and a new director and team hired), but Jerzy chooses to stay behind and head back to Poland. (The decision to stay is dramatized in a simple but effective scene: Jerzy talks with Isabelle in her apartment, while László taps on the window impatiently outside in the cold, returning a number of times (he's literally shut out). Eventually, at the end of the scene, Jerzy opens the window and László tells him they've got the go-ahead to shoot in the U.S.A. – in Josef von Sternberg's light, László adds. He's got the plane tickets. But even that's not enough to convince Jerzy (who has been determined to avoid North America throughout the production – *pas l'Amérique*, as they put it).

Incredibly, in a scene at Isabelle's apartment, following the above scene, Jerzy chooses Isabelle over Hanna (well, Jerzy and Isabelle deserve each other: they can be miserable together). And, once again, it's filmed in a manner that opposes Hollywood formulaic cinema with every breath: a single take, a medium shot, set in the hallway, in a pool of light that one of the DPs has lit from above, up the stairs (allowing everything else to drop into black). Isabelle and Hanna talk first, when she calls round to see Jerzy and bring back his jacket which she's mended; Hanna realizes that Jerzy's chosen Isabelle over her (opting for dreary, predictable Huppert over glam, sophisticated Schygulla!). Eventually, Jerzy deigns to come downstairs, and re-affirms his decision. The camera trucks in for a *very* big close-up of Hanna and her *au revoir* (which's repeated and s-l-o-w-l-y). And out of the blackness of the corridor, a beat later, Michel appears, and converses briefly with Isabelle. It's all quite muted and downbeat, compared with some of the rest of the film.

The lovemaking of Isabelle and Jerzy that follows veers from the sublime to the chilly. Cold? No, Arctic. Both Jerzy and Isabelle are about as downcast as you can get having sex. They might be contemplating a joint suicide. At one point, Jerzy asks, 'from behind now?', and Isabelle talks about him not leaving marks on her virginal body. The film hints at sado-masochistic sex without showing a thing.

It's not the anal sex or S/M that's disturbing, but the way that Jerzy approaches Isabelle (with barely-suppressed hostility and *ennui*), and the way that Isabelle submits to him like Joan of Arc about to be burnt at the stake. (Sex as painful martyrdom in the Existential manner of Ingmar Bergman and Carl Theodor Dreyer).

But Jean-Luc Godard and his team don't show the lovemaking, of course. Instead, during each part of the sex act, the 1982 film shifts to the TV studio again, with the sublime images of the recreation of El Greco's *Assumption of the Virgin* (1608-13) standing in for the tupping. It's a suitably religious and high-powered *tableau* with which to finish *Passion*: images of angels, naked cherubs, Virgin Marys, and assorted figures (a nude woman has been added that's not in El Greco's painting. Yes, but that's typical of Godard).

To enhance the religiosity of this sequence of symbolic cross-cutting the film plays Gabriel Fauré's *Requiem*, and both Jerzy and Isabelle recite the *Agnes Dei* to each other before they get down to it (ridiculous! – but this is Godard, after all). Kaja Silverman and Harun Farocki reckon that the film is really staging an Immaculate Conception in the bedroom, with Isabelle as the Virgin Mary.[35] The continuity between Isabelle and the Madonna is certainly suggested (the film cuts from big close-ups of both women); and many of the tropes are religious. I'm not so sure that Harun Farocki is right to suggest that Jerzy tupping Isabelle anally constitutes an Immaculate Conception via the ass – anal sex as a sacred act, with the anus as the 'universal wound' Jerzy talked about, not the vagina. (But Godard's cinema has many references to anal sex, of course. The idea that sodomy could lead to the birth of Jesus is going to upset some Christians – their point being that the Virgin Mary wasn't taken at all).

★

The parting of the ways at the close of *Passion* comes in the next group of scenes, when everyone seems to be on the move, everyone is 'going home' (except only Jerzy appears to be really 'going home' – back to Poland; the 'home' of everyone else isn't revealed). The last evocation of the world of cinema occurs in a curious sequence in some fields and woods, with a light covering of snow. Some of the crew and some of the extras – still in costume – wander about aimlessly or throw snowballs. Lights are dotted about on stands, and props lie

---

35 Kaja Silverman noted that some commentators thought that El Greco had originally planned to paint an Annunciation not an Assumption, so the lovemaking hints at the Annunciation.

around, and there's a scaled-down galleon with red sails on a trailer (the scene's a recreation of *Pilgrimage To Cytherea*, 1779, by Antoine Watteau). The circus of filmmakers has left town, and this's what's left. (By the way, this is not what behind-the-scenes looks like on a Godard movie!).

As Hanna searches for Jerzy,[36] she passes by pastoral images – sheep, snow, trees. There are images out of Michelangelo Antonioni (figures walking on roads in fog). In this world of cars,[37] people set off along highways on foot (there's a brief shot of a plane at an airport). Isabelle hooks up with Hanna, and off they head for Poland (a hopeless quest. Anything involving Jerzy is hopeless). The setting continues with the countryside, now in deep, frozen snow. Characters are passing through the world like solitary beings, occasionally bumping into each other. So Jerzy comes upon the maid Sarah (she dances along the road). Sarah is a rare personality in Jean-Luc Godard's cinema: she doesn't want to get into cars. Jerzy persuades her by telling her that his car isn't a car, it's a flying carpet. And they leave for Poland (a ride into the sunset ending for a Godard film which doesn't have someone being shot or a fumbled gun battle).

Fin.

---

[36] You have to wonder at Hanna's persistence in pursuing Jerzy: he's the classic womaniser and dilettante, who can't commit to anything, including his own film, or any of the other people around him. He's also about as much fun as attending three funerals in a row.

[37] Cars, always cars with Godard. Maybe he really wanted to be a racing driver.

26

PRÉNOM CARMEN

FIRST NAME: CARMEN

Said is missaid. Whenever said said said missaid. From now said alone. No more from now now said and now missaid. From now said alone. Said for missaid. For be missaid.

Samuel Beckett, *Worstward Ho*[38]

---

[38] S. Beckett, *Worstward Ho*, Calder, London, 1983, 36.

Prénom Carmen (1983) was written by Anne-Marie Miéville. That's important to remember – and that Jean-Luc Godard's films of this time were very much collaborations between Godard and Miéville. So the script,[39] the narrative, the characters, the themes and issues – they come as much from Miéville as from Godard. However, this is a remaking/ reworking of existing *Carmen* material, including movies, fiction and operas.

Prénom Carmen was produced by Alain Sarde for Sara Films/ JLG Films/ Antenne 2 Films, with many of the usual Jean-Luc Godard collaborators at work on it: Mussy, Garcenot, Coutard, Menoud, etc. Editing by Fabienne Alvarez-Giro and Suzanne Lang-Willar, costumes: Renée Renard, make-up: Laurence Azouvy, hair: Catherine Crassac, and A.D.: Richard Debuisne. The cast included: Maruschka Detmers, Jacques Bonnaffé, Myriem Roussel, Christophe Odent, Bertrand Liebert, Alain Bastien-Thiry, Hippolyte Girardot, Valérie Dréville and Odile Roire. It was made in Paris and the Parisian surroundings, and in Trouville, Normandy. In Venice it won the Golden Lion in 1983. Released: Sept, 1983. 85 mins.

Isabelle Adjani was due to star in the film,[40] but pulled out. Colin MacCabe cites an incident where Adjani was very disappointed with the way she was being filmed by Raoul Coutard, but there were clearly other reasons. Adjani was very concerned with how she would look – Godard was insisting on no make-up (again). Adjani demanded camera tests. According to Anne-Marie Miéville, Adjani complained that Coutard 'was a misogynist and didn't know how to photograph women'. Hadn't Adjani seen Coutard's 1960s movies?

So, Jean-Luc Godard was faced with another major casting crisis, with his main star walking out after a week of shooting. But it wasn't the first time that it had happened (or the last time). And Godard and Miéville were able to recover. The Dutch actress Maruschka Detmers (b. 1962.12.16) was cast in the lead role, but that wasn't entirely a happy choice – Detmers didn't really fit the part, she was way out of her depth artistically, and was reluctant to strip.[41] That's a significant drawback in a picture with many scenes played partially nude, as well as sex scenes (Jacques Bonnaffé, though, twenty at the time, her co-star, didn't seem to mind disrobing, and plays the part of the doomed lover well). The nudity was probably one of the reasons that Isabelle Adjani

[39] Actually, there was an audio cassette rather than a script this time: it included Godard's description of what the film would be, plus Beethoven's *Quartets*.
[40] Adjani via producer Sarde.
[41] Godard acknowledged in 1983 that Adjani wouldn't have done 3/4 of the things Detmers did. However, in *L'Éte Meurtrier* (Jean Becker, 1982), Adjani was 'stark naked for much' of the film, remarked David Thomson.

dropped out (when Adjani did *La Reine Margot* [1994], for instance, which required sex scenes, she kept most of her clothes on, and Adjani disagreed with Godard about how she would be filmed).42

Maruschka Detmers, it must be said, isn't one of the most satisfactory of Godard's leading actors – like Gérard Depardieu in *Hélas Pour Moi*, Detmers seems uncomfortable in some scenes, and not only the nude ones, as if she isn't sure about the character she's playing, or what Godard requires of her. In 1984, Detmers explained that she was after psychological motivations and detailed direction, which Godard didn't provide in his style of directing. He wanted Detmers to listen to the music and follow it.43

And Maruschka Detmers is miscast – the actress (20 years-old at the time of filming) doesn't convince as a mysterious *femme fatale*, or as a girl who's a criminal and can wield a gun, or as a Goddess that a guy would go to Hell and back for. Detmers just looks like an average, European woman with big hair. And her acting skills are simply not up to the task. Adjani's mega-star quality is sorely missed (and why didn't the producers go with Myriem Roussel?).

Other problems surrounding the production of *Prénom Carmen* included re-scheduling to accommodate Myriem Roussel's schedule, and Jean-Luc Godard falling out with the Prat Quartet. This clearly wasn't an easy film to make for Godard.44 (However, Jean-Pierre Beauviala, the camera-maker who developed the Auton 35-8 camera with Godard, commented in 2002 that the Maestro thrived on conflict: 'he needs drama; he needs discord; he needs provocation; he needs conflict; he needs difficulties; he needs to yell at people – he needs to be unhappy' [B, 453]).

Jean-Luc Godard said he produced *Prénom Carmen* partly because he feared that *Passion* would be a financial failure.45 Signing up a big star like Isabelle Adjani was central to the new project. So when the money walks out, that's a major setback. (And, when *Prénom Carmen* didn't seem to work, he could've moved to another movie, and on and on, an endless cycle of making films in order to ensure the previous one succeeds. And Godard did just that with *Je Vous Salue, Marie*, making *Détective* to shore up his Madonna movie).

---

42 Maruschka Detmers, though, starred in a film a few years later which featured nudity – *Il diavolo in corpo* (1986). That was probably Detmers' best-known work – she appeared in films and many TV dramas after this.
43 And Godard's conception of Carmen is not the fiery gypsy of the Bizet opera.
44 Or did Godard realize halfway thru making *Carmen* that, *merde*, he'd already produced this movie twenty years ago? And so much better.
45 *Carmen* was now in the public domain at this time – hence the other *Carmen* productions.

First Name: Carmen is also one of those Godard movies which can seem terrible or brilliant on repeated viewings. Sometimes it can appear so shoddy, or throwaway, or indifferent to its audience; at other times, it's gripping, witty and lyrical. *Carmen* is one of those movies where you wonder if Ingmar Bergman was right: 'Godard is a fucking bore'.

❋

Prénom Carmen absorbs a number of influences – Prosper Mérimée's story *Carmen*, Georges Bizet's opera *Carmen* (1875), the film *Carmen Jones* (1954), which both Miéville and Godard liked, Ludwig van Beethoven's *Quartets*, Beethoven's notebooks, Jean Giraudoux's *Électre*, and Auguste Rodin's sculpture. The 20th Century Fox movie of *Carmen Jones* was based on the Broadway stage play, a black musical with lyrics by Oscar Hammerstein (however, all four stars had their voices dubbed). A film of Bizet's *Carmen* was released a year after *Prénom Carmen*, with Julia Migenes-Johnson and Placido Domingo in the leads, and there was another *Carmen* project released in the same year, a Spanish film directed by Carlos Saura. Bizet's opera was set in Seville in 1820; it was first performed in Paris in 1875.

The central relationship, and the pivotal drama of *Prénom Carmen*, is the mad love, the fatal love, the impossible love between Carmen and Joseph. Carmen (Maruschka Detmers) is a *femme fatale*, a Goddess figure, a sadistic temptress, a terrorist with an unspecified organization, and a criminal. Joseph (Jacques Bonnaffé) is the hapless cop who falls in love with Carmen.

Jean-Luc Godard has a cameo, appearing as Uncle Jean,[46] a film director who's taken to holing up in a hospital, unwilling or unable to work (he manages a few words a day at his typewriter, including the Samuel Beckettian phrases 'mal vu, mal dit').[47] It's a character previously played by Samuel Fuller in *Pierrot le Fou*, Fritz Lang in *Contempt*, and Jerzy Radziwilowicz in *Passion*.

It's one of Jean-Luc Godard's best performances in his own movies – still stylized and affected, but also very funny. Some of the best comical moments in *Carmen* occur in the Uncle Jean scenes as Godard

---

[46] It's Godard as he has appeared on screen in many of his films: the familiar figure, with his trenchcoat, black-rimmed glasses, curly, black receding hair, intent stare, and trademark cigarette or cigar.

[47] Beckett published his late trilogy, *Company, Ill Seen, Ill Said* and *Worstward Ho* around the time of *Prénom Carmen*. There are numerous affinities between Beckett's prose works and Godard's late films – melancholy, lyricism, the past, asceticism, austerity, etc. The text of *Ill Seen, Ill Said* is 'ill said': it is unfinished, distorted – Beckett always emphasizes the incompleteness of his texts, and the limitations of language something that's deeply in tune with Godardian philosophy.

As well as the notion of 'mal vu, mal dit' in the writings of Samuel Beckett, there is also Stéphane Mallarmé and Ludwig Wittgenstein in *Prénom Carmen*.

ruminates on his usual passions and *bête noirs*: cinema, capitalism, Mao Zedong, politics, leftism, popular culture, etc. The scene in the café with Uncle Jean and the leader of the terrorist group, Fred (Hippolyte Giradot), has some great jokes. (It's apt that Carmen links cinema and terrorism, cinema and politics: she tells Uncle Jean she wants to make a movie using his beachfront apartment, but it's really for the terrorist group to use). *Prénom Carmen* explores cinema as terrorism, and terrorism as cinema.

Uncle Jean in hospital is another of Jean-Luc Godard's depictions of the film director – again, the familiar trope of the filmmaker who can't or won't (or doesn't) make films anymore (Uncle Jean has the first significant scene in the picture). It's a film director who hides in a hospital in order to escape making movies.

Inevitably, an erotic dalliance, sometime in the past, is suggested between Uncle Jean and Carmen (a replay of the father-daughter, pseudo-Freudian narrative Godard hoped to film in this period). And of course Uncle Jean has an attractive nurse who looks after him (and of course there's some anal humour – Uncle Jean talks about sticking a finger up her ass and counting). The nurse later becomes Uncle Jean's assistant, with a running refrain of 'I write it down' to anything that's said, another familiar Godardian joke (and she does so – writing it down in a notebook).

✹

Godard and Miéville opted to use to Ludwig van Beethoven's music instead of Georges Bizet's music because they didn't want the film 'to be just like a photocopy'. For Godard, the Carmen story was about

> the music and the body, and the script comes from that realization – the lovemaking between the music and the body.

For Gerald Mast and Bruce Kawin, *Prénom Carmen* is

> Part romance (the classic temptress who lures a man to his doom), part movie parody (cops and robbers), and part tactile exploration of eroticism (like *Breathless*), *First Name: Carmen* was the first Godard film in fifteen years to attempt his earlier balance between human spontaneity, emotional intensity, and reflexive commentary on the way images are shot, edited, ordered, and synchronized with a soundtrack. (363)

Prénom Carmen revolves around these familiar Godardian themes: the body, in particular the female body, and love, the impossibility of it, and music, the eternal beauty and nourishment of it. There are elements of the thriller, the political thriller, and other genre components, but *Prénom Carmen* is really about an erotic relationship that's falling apart.

And, once again, Godard and Miéville depict the relationship as a very physical, very tense experience. Godard and Miéville have their actors engaging in a constant play of physical interaction.[48] The two leads are grabbing each other, pushing each other, slamming windows on each other. They grapple on the bed, then Carmen twists herself free. They shove into each other one moment, then they're caressing tenderly the next. You're never sure how serious it all is – it appears as a game, as if these lovers are really children play-acting lovers; but there's also an undercurrent of anxiety and resentment. It's love as a battleground, with hostility not far from love, and obsession driving everything.

※

Prénom Carmen plays with sound effects in the usual asynchronous, Godardian manner: the sound of seagulls by the sea is played over a shot of Paris at night, for instance, and the sound of the sea over images of cars on a freeway. Ocean noises cut into several scenes, drowning out the dialogue. Sometimes actors are speaking on camera but we hear something else. Sometimes we see the musicians rehearsing but hear other sounds. Sound from a previous scene continues into the following scene. *Prénom Carmen*, however, is rare among Godard's feature films in *not* having numerous captions and intertitles.

And there are *so many shots of the sea*. So many, in fact, *Prénom Carmen* might be regarded as a documentary about the ocean at Normandy with the additions of a love story and a crime caper intercut with it. *Prénom Carmen* isn't just cutting to the sea shot low from the sandy beaches of Normandy as linking images between sequences, but in the middle of scenes. The images of the ocean go far beyond lyrical refrains or hooks, to become striking flows of the natural world into the narrative of the film. However, some of those images are left on screen for a *long* time – giving the impression of filler (it's the same with the repeated takes, as if the filmmakers are padding out the movie to feature length).

The more one considers Jean-Luc Godard's whole body of work, the more one sees how much he likes to train his cameras on water – on the River Seine, on Lake Geneva, on the Mediterranean Sea, on the North Sea and on the Channel (one of the signature shots of Godards's

---

[48] The acting style Godard wanted was not psychological or emotional, but comprised actions and gestures performed precisely, and dialogue that was word perfect.

later work is of Lake Geneva seen from a car). This is a movie director in love with rivers and oceans – a hundred years earlier he would have been an open-air painter (or maybe a Bohemian, Symbolist poet haunting the cafés and bordellos of Paris).

※

The 1983 film returns to the Quator Prat Quartet rehearsing Ludwig van Beethoven's music (the late *Quartets* – numbers 9, 10, 14, 15 and 16) many times – it's one of the recurring motifs of the film[49] (Uncle Jean voices the audience's question: how does the Quartet fit into the film? Well, it doesn't fit on the ordinary, narrative level). Part of it is Godard and Miéville simply wanting to use music in the foreground of a film. It's something Jean-Luc Godard has struggled with right from his earliest films. *A Woman Is a Woman*, for example, was an attempt at a musical, a try at staging a musical in a modern film. In *Prénom Carmen*, part of the goal must be to have the audience listen to music (and also perhaps to watch music being performed and rehearsed).[50]

Miéville and Godard put Claire (Myriem Roussel), Joseph's girlfriend, into the Quator Prat Quartet, as a way of dramatically linking the music and the narrative, but it's a minor association.[51] There is virtually no interaction, for instance, between Joseph and Claire: *Prénom Carmen* is all about Joseph and Carmen.[52] *Prénom Carmen* is Carmen's picture: she dominates the action, and drives most of the narrative. Joseph is doomed to follow her around, to do what she says, to do anything she wants.

Aside from a very brief scene where Joseph and her brother collect Claire in a car (after a music rehearsal), the link between Claire and Joseph is conjured up more in the editing, as the film cross-cuts between Carmen and Joseph together and Claire rehearsing with the musos. Claire tries to get through to Joseph during a break in his trial. Claire is present in the gun battle in the hotel at the end, though, and sees Joseph there, and weeps as she continues to play. (Claire delivers solemn Godardisms aloud during the rehearsals, which the strict band leader would definitely *not* allow if he, not Godard, had been running the rehearsals!).

---

49 Federico Fellini had directed a movie about an orchestra rehearsing which delivered political/ ideological statements – rare for Fellini (*Orchestral Rehearsal*, 1978).
50 For Richard Brody, the music scenes comprised 'the most revelatory depiction of musical performance in the history of cinema' (B, 453).
51 Roussel practiced the violin, with and without the Quartet, as well as listening to music, overseen by Godard. However, notice that the camera frames out her left hand on the fretboard.
52 Richard Brody suggested that Godard intended *Prénom: Carmen* to be about 3 couples: Joseph and Carmen, Godard and Myriem Roussel, and Godard and Carmen (B, 448).

※

First Name: Carmen features the Obligatory Gas Station Scene In a Godard Movie (paragraph 23.8 in Godard's film contracts specifies: 'at least one afternoon will be spent filming in a local gas station').[53] And this's also when the couple're fleeing the crime scene, another mandatory Godardism. (A typical bit of Godard-type business has Carmen urinating in the restroom while Joseph and a fat guy eating from a jar are right there: it's Godard's joke on criminals on the run being handcuffed together, his crude, schoolboy version of *It Happened One Night* or *The 39 Steps*).

The plot in *Prénom Carmen* is centred around the doomed erotic relationship of Carmen and Joseph, but there are some action scenes. Well, *Godardian* action scenes – which means the action is gleefully (or rather, miserably) subverted. In the first reel, for instance, there's a big heist scene and gun battle. Narratively, it's where Joseph hooks up with Carmen – i.e., that's what the scene is there for, script-wise (and we see Carmen in her mobster guise). But Godard and Miéville play it wholly for comedy – though it's the savage, not particularly funny kind of comedy that's Godard's speciality. As the gun battle rages, there are people sitting about reading newspapers, wholly untroubled by the chaos (until they're shot). It's Godard's John Woo/ Sam Peckinpah scene. A cleaner appears to mop up blood, stepping over corpses.

The trial of Joseph following his arrest is played as a comical sketch – Godard doing the Marx Brothers and harking back to his Dziga Vertov Group days (when the Maoist-Leninists staged the trial of the Chicago radicals). During the court case Biblical quotes are hurled about.

※

Prénom Carmen is another of Jean-Luc Godard's films about a couple on the run, and hiding from the law. It's another riff on and a kind of updated sequel to films such as *Pierrot le Fou*. When the lovers hide away in a house right next to the sea, for instance (staged at Trouville in Normandy), it's *Pierrot le Fou* (and *Summer With Monika*) all over again. The same gestures and motifs are employed: sharing cigarettes, walking on the beach, making love. (Other references to *Pierrot le Fou* include Joseph correcting his name – Joseph not Joe – the name Fred (from the gun-runner and romantic rival), and the 'tragic' ending, as the lovers expire).

There's a new explicitness to the sex in *Prénom Carmen*, or a

---

53 And cast and crew will receive free fuel.

graphic quality that's depicted on screen rather than, as is usual in Jean-Luc Godard's cinema, talked about or suggested offscreen. No, Godard and Miéville are not moving into hardcore porn territory, but they do include a scene of Joseph masturbating over Carmen in the shower, with both actors nude. And Godard and Miéville have Maruschka Detmers and Jacques Bonnaffé play many of the scenes in the house by the sea and in the hotel semi-naked (in Hollywood films, semi-naked means topless – in European art films, it means bottomless. And Godard loves to see pubic hair (as he admits), which Detmers provides plenty of).[54]

And there are moments of lyricism, too, in amongst the fraught relations between the lovers – images of the couple caressing each other on a mattress, or framed against the setting sun. A shot of the sea at sunset – another Godardian van Gogh[55] moment. In the antagonistic relationships that Godard and Miéville depict in their films, there are always moments of beauty, quietude, even joy. You need that in a story based on *Carmen*, you need to show that the lovers care for each other, otherwise the rest of the story doesn't have so much resonance. Once again, when you put aside the pushing and the shoving, the sudden eruptions of aggression, the emotional outbursts and snarled putdowns, there is tenderness in the depictions of love in Godard's cinema. It's not conventional, it's not what most audiences or filmmakers would think of as ways of portraying love, but it is love.

So *Prénom Carmen* builds to something of an action climax: there's the big scene with most of the cast present; there's a detective in a trenchcoat and his flics; there's Carmen and Joseph; there's the terrorists with their guns, preparing to kidnap someone; and there's the Quator Prat Quartet in the restaurant, playing Ludwig van Beethoven (thus bringing together the two sections of *First Name: Carmen*). Of course the gun battle, when it comes, is depicted in Jean-Luc Godard's usual throwaway manner (with his odd selective viewpoints which obscure the action).[56] In amongst the chaos of this chaotically-filmed scene, there are all sorts of looks, in a series of tight close-ups: between Uncle Jean and Carmen; and between Claire and Joseph (Carmen is oddly immobile in this scene – or perhaps the film had only that single close-up of Maruschka Detmers to play with).

But what really counts is the lead-up to the abortive kidnapping,

---
54 There are concessions, however – scenes which would be performed nude have Detmers in underwear (such as the hotel scenes).
55 Van Gogh is cited by Uncle Jean a couple of times.
56 Godard has a penchant for angles or shots which restrict the point-of-view of the audience – he will often film key dramatic moments with walls or bodies or plants obscuring the action.

the lengthy scenes involving Carmen and Joseph, with other guys threatening Joseph's hold over Carmen (such as the terrorist leader, Fred, or the butler (Alain Bastien-Thiry). Turns out that Carmen has been Fred's lover all along – again reminiscent of the romantic betrayal in *Pierrot le Fou*, where the rival was called Fred). Here the relationship is highly erotically charged but also impossible and doomed. There is a lyrical scene of Carmen and Joseph embracing and kissing (a rare moment of a tender erotic kiss in Godard's cinema), to the sound of a Tom Waits song (and the film mixes Waits and Ludwig van Beethoven together, creating an unusual juxtaposition).[57] There's an iconic image of Joseph's hand on the TV screen, with its white noise[58] (there are TVs in every room in the hotel scenes, but always showing nothing but static, another wry Godardian commentary on the media). Both Carmen and Fred inform Joseph emphatically that 'it's over' (and they can't get rid of him).

There are numerous beats to the decline and fall of the love affair in the Parisian hotel scenes, with the lovers in yellow dressing gowns, or nude, with Carmen in red panties, with characters entering and leaving rooms, or embracing on the bed, or standing by the window. It's all carried out like Jean-Luc Godard's previous erotic-domestic scenes, in *Contempt* or *Pierrot le Fou*: characters are always partially dressed, or undressing, or getting dressed, or entering bathrooms, or leaving bathrooms, or staring into mirrors, or brushing their hair. In *Prénom Carmen*, there's a new sexually graphic quality to the relationship (or an underlying terror/ self-loathing: Joseph caressing Carmen's bare buttocks, or desperately masturbating over her in the shower. 'You disgust me,' she tells him as they lie on the floor of the bathroom, meaning: 'I disgust myself', or: 'we disgust ourselves'.[59]

Joseph is of course doomed from the start: he has no centre, no sense of himself, no identity, no work and nothing to do unless it revolves around Carmen. She doesn't 'complete' him, like a soul-mate or a lover, like lovers who are two halves of a whole in the Neo-platonic model, she *is* him, and without her he is literally nothing. As he says, when she tells him she's going out, when they're staying in the hotel, what shall I do all day?

Poor Joseph. A lost soul. As Arthur Rimbaud said, 'je est un autre', *I is an other*. And when the other is the lover, you're dead we could cite

---

[57] Maybe Tom Waits was used because Godard had been involved with Zoetrope, and Waits (among others) had provided the music for *One From the Heart*.
[58] Joseph might be caressing the TV screen – in *The Simpsons*, Bart and Lisa love TV so much, they hug their precious television set.
[59] 'Tu m'emmerde' or 'je me dégoût' are recurring imprecations in Godard's cinema.

Julia Kristeva, Jacques Lacan or any philosopher of your choice here, and ponder on the links between love-identity-desire-loss-separation-death, etc). Carmen's the *femme fatale* who's stolen his soul. So, as in tragic theatre, there's only one solution for Joseph: he has to kill her. But in doing so of course he kills himself: he shoots Carmen at the end of the hotel battle scene, and is taken away to prison.

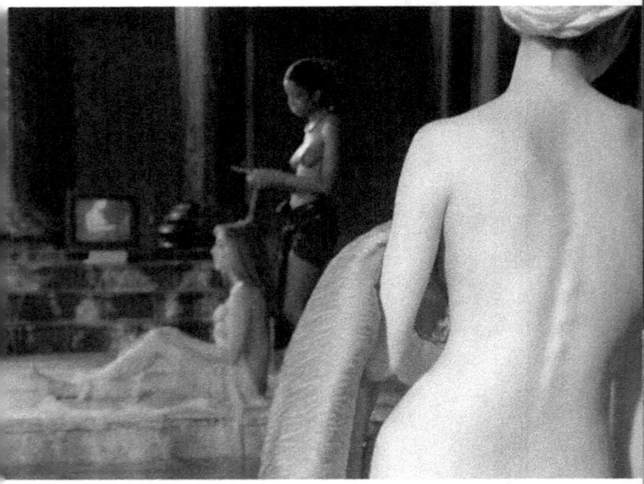

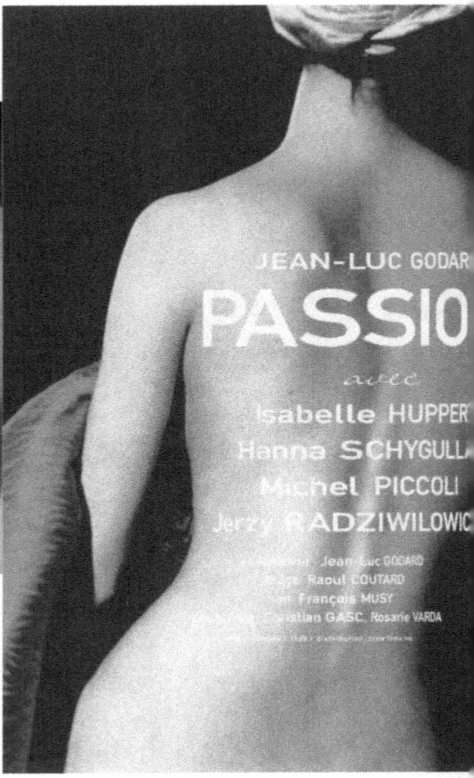
JEAN-LUC GODAR
PASSIO
avec
Isabelle HUPPER
Hanna SCHYGULL
Michel PICCOLI
Jerzy RADZIWILOWIC
Jean-Luc GODARD
Raoul COUTARD
François MUSY
GASC, Rosarie VARDA

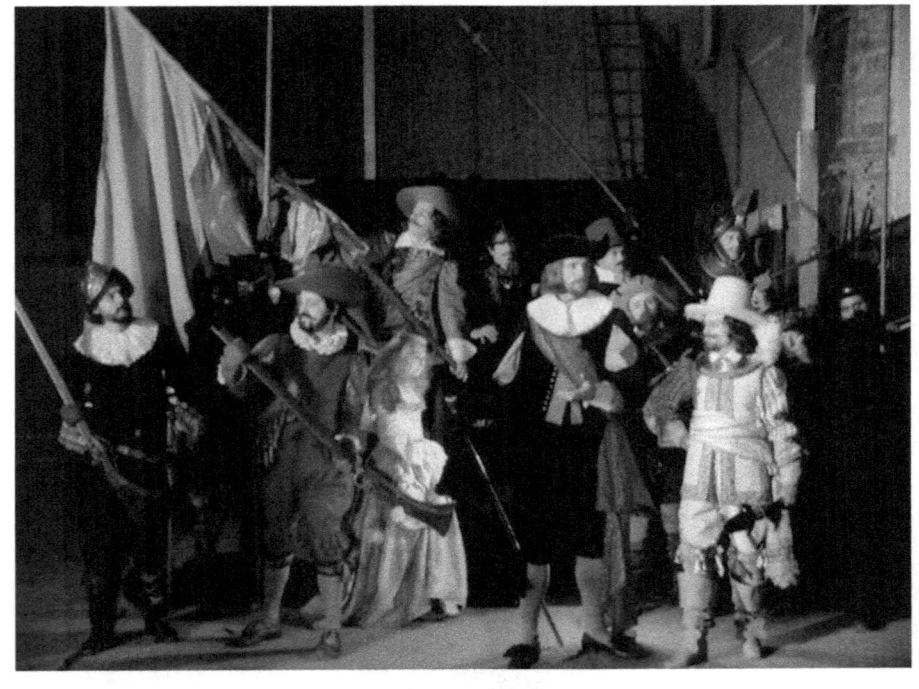

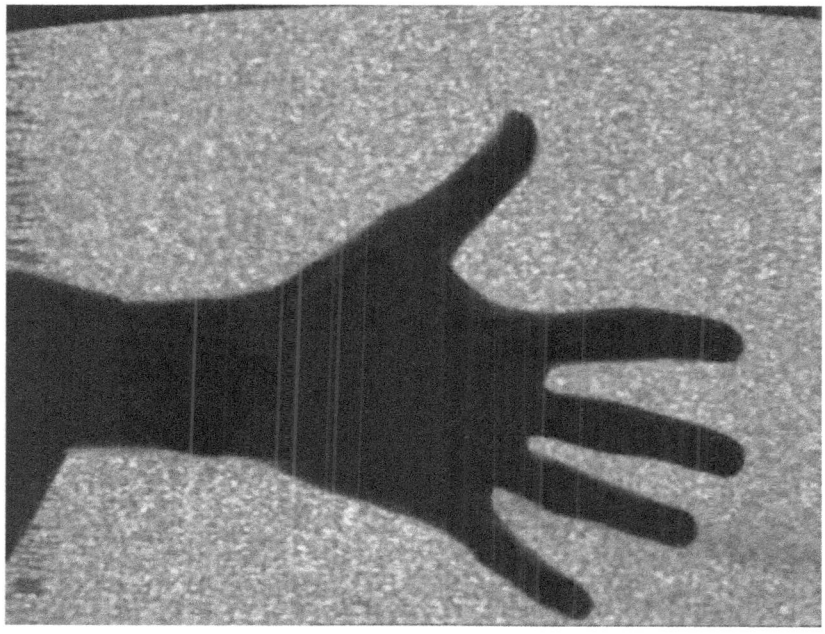

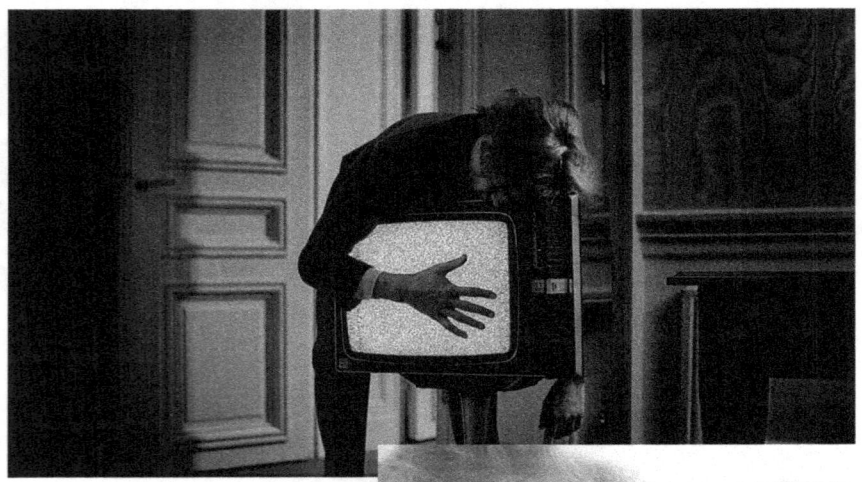

27

JE VOUS SALUE, MARIE

HAIL MARY

...cinema is neither an art nor a technique, but a mystery. That's what differentiates it from painting, literature or music, all arts when undertaken by artists. Cinema is close to a religion.

Jean-Luc Godard[1]

---
[1] J.-L. Godard, interview, Montréal, 1995.

Je Vous Salue, Marie (*Hail Mary*, 1985) was made for Pégase Films/ S.S.R/ Channel Four/ Sara Films/ Jean-Luc Godard Films. It was produced by Alain Sarde and Yves Peyrot. *Hail Mary* was filmed between January and February, 1984 (tho' some scenes are clearly Spring and Summer),[2] and filmed on Eastmancolor thirty-five millimetre film stock by cameramen Jacques Firmann and Jean-Bernard Menoud, edited by Anne-Marie Miéville (Godard's wife at the time) and Godard, with sound by François Mussy. François Pélissier and Philippe Malignon were ADs and unit managers.[3] Released: January 23, 1985. 107 minutes.

Je Vous Salue, Marie starred Myriem Roussel and Thierry Rode as a modern-day Mary and Joseph in Godard's radical interpretation of the *New Testament* story. The rest of the cast included: Philippe Lacoste and Manon Andersen as the Angel Gabriel plus helper, Malachi Jara Kohan as Jesus, Juliette Binoche as Juliette, Anne Gautier as Eva, Johan Leysen as the Professor, plus Serge Musy and Georges Staquet.

Jean-Luc Godard financed the project himself (it cost $600,000). Halfway through, due to rising debts, he was obliged to stop shooting and direct another film (*Détective*), which he was reluctant to do.[4] (I'm glad he did – ten *Détectives* could have been made just so we could have *Hail Mary*. However, making some low-power movies just to cover the cost of the one you really want to make does seem an odd and wasteful venture). Godard said they went over-budget partly because of trying to capture images from nature:[5]

> we set up a camera and were waiting, waiting, waiting, until a certain time when you got the exceptional in everyday, natural things. (1993, 120)

Is that budget correct? $600,000 seems too much for this kind of film, and for the budgets of Godard's movies of the period. There are no stars in *Hail Mary*, for instance, and the material – the *Bible* – cost nothing (the *Bible* is 2,000 years out of copyright!).

Hail Mary apparently contains 300 shots and lasts 79 minutes (*The Book of Mary*, which precedes it, is 28 minutes long). 300 shots in 79 minutes gives some idea of the slow cutting style of *Hail Mary*

---

2 Some scenes were filmed later; and the 2nd unit material, of the landscapes and skies, are in Summer. Some of the material is library footage.
3 For much of *Hail Mary*, the crew was so small it comprised not much more than DP Menoud, sound man Mussy, a production manager and an assistant.
4 Wheeler Dixon is right when he says that one of the most interesting aspects of *Hail Mary* 'is simply that Jean-Luc Godard chose to do the project', and that he made *Détective* so he could complete *Hail Mary* (161).
5 It might've been tempting to use library shots, which Godard did in other projects. And also to plump for shots they couldn't film, like images from deep space.

(some Hollywood features in the 1980s used many more – by the 1990s, over 1,000 shots wasn't uncommon, and some films would reach 2,000 or more).6 For a European art movie, which tends to be slower-paced, 300 shots over 79 minutes is a much slower and more thoughtful kind of pace (though not as slow as a film like *The Sacrifice* (Andrei Tarkovsky, 1986), which is two-and-a-half hours long and has only 115 shots. The figure of 300 shots for *Hail Mary* comes from David Sterritt. I'm not sure: it looks like more).

Je Vous Salue, Marie (and many of his other later films) was filmed in Switzerland because, Jean-Luc Godard explained, he had made so many films in Paris, because Paris had been used so many times (also, Godard has always been a part of the two countries, France and Switzerland, and had a Swiss passport). And many of Godard's later films were based in and staged in Switzerland (he called Switzerland his 'studio of exteriors', with its 'forests, lakes, snow, mountains, wind').7

I like *Hail Mary* very much partly because it contains so many images that I use in my own films. When it was made, in the mid-1980s, I was shooting lots of Super-8 film of the same imagery: sunsets, the moon above cities, streets and cars at night, trees, close-ups of water (and beautiful women, too). 8

Myriem Roussel recalled that Jean-Luc Godard had originally wanted to cast her in a film of a father and daughter, an old project which Godard worked on with Roussel on video. But it was abandoned, partly because, Roussel said, 'it demanded far too much personally that I was certainly incapable of and perhaps he was too'. The project would have required the actors to live it before filming it. 'You have to live things before you film them', as Roussel put it, which's one of Godard's maxims (Mac, 290-1). So they made *Hail Mary* instead. (I wonder, though, if some of the father-daughter video project found its way into *Hail Mary* in the form of the relationship between Professor Johannes and Eva. which of course echoes a father and a daughter, as well as a psychoanalyst and his patient. And father-daughter material (including the relationship between a Freudian analyst and his patient, with hints at incest) appears in several projects of the post-1979 period in Godard's career).

---

6 David Bordwell is the undisputed expert on this subject – see his book *The Way Hollywood Tells It*.
7 Godard in *Le Point*, Mch 24, 1980.
8 And I used the same imagery in my documentaries, such as *Andy Goldsworthy* (2005).

Jean-Luc Godard had Myriem Roussel watch movies such as *King of Comedy*, *The Passion of Joan of Arc*, *New York, New York*, *Pauline At the Beach* and his own films (that is, the preparation for *Hail Mary* included studying the *History of Cinema According to Godard*). He gave her collections of images and texts to look at. Godard also asked Roussel to keep a journal for three years prior to making the film.

Myriem Roussel stayed in Nyon, near Rolle, Jean-Luc Godard's base, where the film was made. Godard would pick her up and drive her to the set, explaining what he looking for. Godard was after a Bressonian kind of non-acting, performance without theatricality. He wanted Roussel to extract any self-conscous performance from her role. He didn't want training, skills, tricks.

Myriem Roussel, though, wanted to act: she said that her relationship with Jean-Luc Godard began to fall apart during filming, partly because of the conflicting demands that Godard made on her (he was also filming her on video).

Unfortunately, Myriem Roussel felt like she was at the centre of an awkward love triangle between Godard and Miéville: 'there was him and her, him and me; the three of us, it wasn't working', Roussel said in 2003 (B, 459). Earlier, Anne Wiazemsky had also felt awkward when she was married to Godard, but Miéville was around.

Myriem Roussel said the preparation with Jean-Luc Godard for *Hail Mary* was intense – he was writing letters to her 3, 4 or 5 times a day, for instance. And they spent hours on the phone. 'It was exhilarating and exhausting', Roussel later recalled (1985).[9] The relationship felt like a real psychoanalytic project to Roussel. Godard wanted the total fusion of the personal and emotional with the professional and artistic. (And Roussel, 22 at the time of filming, is playing Mary at around 17).

Incredibly, Jean Marais, an icon of French cinema, was being considered for the role of Joseph by Jean-Luc Godard at one point. Marais was amazed – a Joseph that old would've been very unusual, to say the least (Marais was 71 at the time). However, Joseph is always cast older than Mary, in every single movie of the *Gospels*. But not that old! (Perhaps Godard was still thinking along the lines of his father-daughter or psychologist-patient concepts).[10]

According to some of the Christian Fathers, Joseph was already

---

[9] For Roussel the mingling of the personal and professional aspects of the production, plus the length of the schedule, was too tiring, and too much.
[10] Jean-Luc Godard also considered asking Bernard-Henri Lévy if he wanted the part. A French philosopher, 35 at the time, Lévy declined, saying he 'very afraid' of Godard – that he might be falling a trap of Godard's making (B, 458-9).

very old (over 80) when he was with Mary (so maybe Jean-Luc Godard's idea of casting Jean Marais wasn't that crazy. And some thought that Joseph was impotent). But the point made by theologians in Christian history is that Joseph and Mary did not have sex after they were married, or after the Madonna'd given birth. And they didn't have any other kids. So the Virgin Mary always remained a virgin.11

Why Thierry Rode? A virtual unknown, Rode had far less experience than many of Jean-Luc Godard's male leads (Roussel knew Rode in Paris). True, Rode was no Léaud, Brialy, or Belmondo, no star or even star-in-the-making, but he did suit the everyman approach Godard was after. He looks and acts like a regular guy, and Godard did want 'an ordinary couple... who accept the extraordinary in an ordinary way'.

As with some previous films, Jean-Luc Godard produced a short preparatory film, in which he discusses the film he wants to make. Aside from those discussions, and a scene of Godard and Miéville at work, most of the twenty minute short *Petites notes à propos du film 'Je vous salue Marie'* concentrates on Myriem Roussel. The camera lingers over her face as if it can't tear itself away to look at anything else. Roussel's beauty eats up the lens: it's extraordinary.

In *Petites notes à propos du film 'Je vous salue Marie'*, the Maestro gives Myriem Roussel one or two things to do, like ironing, or reading a scene with an actor, or discussing the role, but most of all the film focusses on big close-ups of Roussel (occasionally dissolving them into Leonardo da Vinci's drawing of St Anne, and, curiously, Giulietta Masina in *La Strada*, 1954).

From the outset, even before the cameras had rolled, *Je Vous Salue, Marie* was a controversial film. A range of institutions, organizations and individuals protested against the film (as usual, many of these hadn't seen it, or had misunderstood it). The controversy surrounding *Hail Mary* resulted in the film being banned, or withdrawn, and theatres being picketed; it was banned in Brazil and Argentina; in North America some 5,000 people (or 8,000, according to other reports), demonstrated against the film at its premiere at the New York Film Festival, at the Lincoln Center.12 J.-L. Godard wasn't at the

---

11 The perpetual virginity of the Mother of God was defined as dogma at the Lateran Council in 649 A.D. and confirmed at the 6th General Council in 680, held in Constantinople.

12 Myriem Roussel encountered people picketing the film at a Strasbourg cinema: 'There were five men, including a priest, and they hadn't seen the movie. I said to one man, 'I'll give you $3 to go inside,' but it was impossible to have a dialogue with them.'

public screening. New York's Archbishop, John O'Connor, denounced the movie. (Decades years later, I'm sure many people *still* haven't seen the film; a similar controversy surrounded *The Last Temptation of Christ* in 1988, and though a major studio released it – Universal – I bet few people who protested against it have actually seen it.)

Hail Mary created controversy by taking such as a secular, 'realistic' approach towards the sacred (such as when it depicted the Blessed Virgin as a gas station attendant). There were bomb threats, 5,000 protesters reciting the rosary to cinema queues, and the 'film bears the distinction of being the first ever condemned by a Pope (Pope John Paul II), and being the first instance in 400 years that a Pope directly intervened in the suppression of a work of art' (Steven Dubin, 93).13 In Massachussetts the film was withdrawn from a Boston cinema, but was shown in Cambridge, MA to good reviews.

When Pope John Paul II wanted the film banned from Roma, Jean-Luc Godard said he was happy to 'respect his wishes' if he 'didn't want a bad boy running around in his house', the 'house of the church', Rome (1998, 168). According to the Pope, *Hail Mary* 'distorts and offends the spiritual meaning and historical value of the fundamental theme of Christian faith'. Godard also stated (at the Berlin Film Festival):

> It's a real story, Mary's story about life coming down from the sky. We've had lots of films about Jesus and the Bible, but none about Mary. Why? The Church should have made this film.

It was surprising that a European art movie (i.e., a small movie in global terms – compared to the big movies in 1985, which were: *Back To the Future, Rambo, Rocky 4, Out of Africa* and *A View To a Kill*), could provoke such a violent response. Jean-Luc Godard's reaction was that *Hail Mary* was 'only a movie' (as Alfred Hitchcock used to say); for some commentators, *Hail Mary* was clearly not 'just a movie', it was a serious,14 uncompromising exploration of the themes of spirituality and religion in contemporary society, not part of Godard's 'comeback' in the early 1980s, announced in films such as *Sauve Qui Peut* and *Passion*, but part of a radical, complex moment in Godard's cinema.

---

13 Also on *Hail Mary*, see J. Strong: "*Hail Mary* leaves council offended, box office booming", *Chicago Tribune*, 17 April 1986; W. Smith: "Ecumenical crowd of protesters pans *Hail Mary*", *Chicago Tribune*, 5 April 1986; M. Wilmington: "*Hail Mary*: A Godard Pirouette", *Los Angeles Times*, 20 November 1985
14 'No one who has seen the film can doubt the fact that it is, at base, absolutely serious', commented Wheeler Dixon (162).

Jean-Luc Godard said he felt at times as if he were being punished for trying to film the Virgin Mary's life during the making of *Hail Mary*, as if the interdiction was from the Madonna Herself: 'there were days when we were punished, punished for having wanted to do it: 'That's not true, that mustn't be shown, thou shalt not show my face and belly like that".[15]

There were times when Jean-Luc Godard felt like cancelling the whole enterprise, and giving co-producer Alain Sarde his money back. One of the things that kept him going was Anne-Marie Miéville (1985b).

Part of the controversy stemmed from how the movie depicted the Virgin Mary: she is shown naked in many shots, and there are close-ups of her hand in her pubic hair, or examining her breasts. No movie exists anywhere that includes close-up images of the Virgin Mary's vulva. I wonder also if the voiceover that Mary speaks upset viewers as well as the nudity also upset some viewers: she talks about the Father and the Mother fucking to death over her body, and about anuses and cunts.

It's certainly true you haven't seen the Mother of God's pubic hair and buttocks in close-up in a film before. Or any other parts of the sacred body apart from her face, hair and hands. Think how offensive some viewers would have found it, though, if Jean-Luc Godard had set his film in Biblical times: if Mary had been clad in the usual robes and cowl. Seeing the Virgin Mary taking off the traditional, Biblical robes and washing herself or touching her vulva might've been even worse for some spectators. For Myriem Roussel, the nudity was partly about Mary's femininity:

> Mary is a virgin, but Mary is a woman, too. For me, the decision was to show her in 1985 as an actual contemporary person. Maybe if we'd set the film in Biblical times, it could be shocking but not now.

Because what you actually *see* (rather than what you *think* you saw) is a young, Swiss woman undressing and contorting on a bed naked. You see a modern woman's body, and she's in a modern bedroom in a modern apartment, with modern women's clothes, etc. Is it really the Virgin Mary, then? Well, no; rather, it's a very stylized, updated and reworked interpretation of an account written years after the events of something spiritual or divine (i.e., very abstract/ metaphysical) that might have happened two thousand years ago. The

---

[15] J.-L. Godard, interview, *Art Press*, Feb, 1985.

film does not show *facts*, or pretend to be historically authentic. It's not *recreating* the story of the Madonna (as most religious movies do). It's a modern-dress, updated or parallel version of the Christian story, and not just any modern version, but a version produced in a self-conscious, heavily stylized manner by a very idiosyncratic, European filmmaker and set in a particular time and place. It's not meant to be literal; it's not the *Bible*; but it is meant completely sincerely or seriously (though the filmmaker is not a believer).16 Rather, it's exploring some of the issues and emotions the story of the Virgin Mary suggests to the filmmaker. 17

In 1993, Jean-Luc Godard opined (*pace Histoire(s) du Cinéma*):

> The cinema is of the order of a revelation as the Church describes it. Something that happens within. I prefer to say 'a mystery', that's all... I've adapted a quotation from Wittgenstein. Referring to Christianity, he said: 'Whatever happens, believe'. I've simply added that the same is true of cinema.

It's certainly unusual to use the story of Mary and Joseph in the *Gospels* for an exploration of sexuality and the body. A prostitute and a client, yes, or two lovers, yes (familiar Godardian charas), but the Virgin Mary and St Joseph?!

> And in the sixth month the angel Gabriel was sent from God unto a city of Galilee, named Nazareth, to a virgin espoused to a man whose name was Joseph, of the house of David; and the virgin's name was Mary. And the angel came in unto her, and said, Hail, thou that art highly favoured, the Lord is with thee: blessed art thou among women. And when she saw him, she was troubled at his saying, and cast in her mind what manner of salutation this should be. And the angel said unto her, Fear not, Mary: for thou hast found favour with God. And, behold, thou shalt conceive in thy womb, and bring forth a son, and shalt call his name JESUS. (*The Gospel of St Luke*, 1:26-32)

Je Vous Salue, Marie is an exploration of spiritual issues, a modern version of the *Gospels* and the *Apocrypha*, depicting well-known scenes from Christianity, such as the childhood of Mary, the Annunciation, and the Virgin's life with Joseph, events which have been portrayed thousands of times in European art, in mediæval manuscripts, in *Books of Hours, Hours of the Virgin Mary*, Renaissance paintings, and so on.

---

16 What sets *Hail Mary* apart for Wheeler Dixon from Jean-Luc Godard's other works of the time was 'the absolute seriousness of the project, and the intensity with which Godard presents his subject matter' (156).

17 For a Godard movie, Wheeler Dixon noted that the story was 'surprisingly straight-foward' (154). The reason is partly because it's the most famous story in the Western world. No notes on the plot are required for the audience, as with many other Godard films.

When a filmmaker like Jean-Luc Godard tackles the Annunciation and Nativity of Jesus Christ, you know it's not going to be a conventional, rose-tinted approach. Rather, it's radically different from all other cinematic interpretations of the *Gospels*: the Annunciation takes place in a gas station at night, in a noisy, chaotic, and aggressive scene; Mary is a garage attendant; she plays in a college basketball team;[18] her boyfriend, Joseph, is a taxi driver who misunderstands her and wants to at least see her naked if he can't make love with her; there are other women, such as Juliette, one of Joseph's girlfriends (Godard invented this character, adding an erotic melodrama to the Marian myth – the obvious inspiration, though, is Mary Magdalene); a subplot, unconnected spatially and narratively to the main plot,[19] involves the adulterous affair between a student, Eva, and a married science lecturer, Professor Johannes.

Why did Jean-Luc Godard invent characters such as Juliette and Gabriel's young helper? For the same reasons other screenwriters do: to fill out the script, to give characters other people to talk to, to create dramatic tensions, to explore themes and issues from other angles, etc. For instance, it's much more interesting having Gabriel with a sidekick, especially the humorous relationship developed for the film, where the young helper has to remind Gabriel of his dialogue, and correct him when he says the wrong thing. The helper is thus a kind of equivalent for the holy spirit or holy ghost (sometimes visualized as a dove in Renaissance art), as well as more obviously a cherub or young angel.

Introducing Juliette is not completely successful, I reckon, from a narrative and dramatic point-of-view, but her presence does add spice to the relationship between Joseph and Mary. And Juliette does give Joseph someone to talk to away from Mary: otherwise, the film would be largely about Mary and Joseph, with them running over the same issues time after time. (The romantic triangle is a very modern, clichéd dramatic addition to the Biblical story – and very typical of Godard's cinema – he'd been presenting this sort of adolescent, romantic rivalry for over 25 years by the time of *Hail Mary*).

Instead of concentrating, as the *Gospels* and the *Apocrypha* do, on Mary and Joseph, and her relation with her parents, Anne and Joachim, Jean-Luc Godard focusses on Mary and Joseph, and introduces a rival in love, Juliette, which alters the Biblical story, and

---

18 The basketball scene had symbolic aspects for Godard: he very much wanted Roussel to learn basketball. It was about the ball, the pregnant belly, of motherhood.
19 It does intersect when Eva and Johannes take a taxi driven by Joseph.

changes the emotional, dramatic (and theological) emphasis.[20]

And both women have a right to be angry with Joseph – because Joseph points out that he and Mary have been together for 2 years (he mentions this when he's complaining about not having touched sexually her for 2 years). If so, then Joseph was still having a relationship with Mary when he was also dating Juliette. This guy is never satisfied – because although he keeps begging for consummation from Mary, he must have been having sex with Juliette recently, too (she talks about getting married, for instance, and that she's not afraid). Maybe it's yet another case of wanting what you can't have – that Joseph desires Mary precisely because she's unattainable, or because she withholds physical affection from him. Meanwhile, he and Juliette are tupping. Which means that, from this masculinist point-of-view, from Joseph's p.o.v. that is, *Hail Mary* exhibits the crummiest kind of sexism. (But Godard has included such erotic triangles throughout his film career. Despite the nods towards (second wave) feminism, some of Godard's movies are distinctly chauvinist).[21]

▼

As the narrative of *Hail Mary* progresses, there are disquisitions on religion, spirituality, art, death, sex, evolution, science and metaphysics. There are direct allusions to writers such as Friedrich Hölderlin, Martin Heidegger and William Shakespeare.

The characters read books (and read aloud from books) to a striking degree – but this is not unusual for a Jean-Luc Godard movie, of course. They bring each other books. They carry books. Mary often reads aloud from a book, as so often in a Godard movie, and also seems to be looking to books for inspiration and confirmation.

No one else had, 'til then, made a film about the young life of the Virgin Mary, her pregnancy, and her relationship with Joseph. Previous films had concentrated on depicting the Madonna's early life always in relation to Jesus, as an episode in the story of Christ. Events such as the Annunciation and the lead-up to the birth of Jesus had been seen before (in *The Gospel According to Matthew* (1964) or *Jesus of Nazareth* (1977), for example), but not Mary on her own.

Renaissance art, though, in paintings, altarpieces and mediæval *Books of Hours* and *Hours of the Virgin*, had a long tradition of portraying aspects of Mary's life, such as her parents, Anne and

---

20 The narrative becomes one of sexual rivalry; the dramatic configuration of two women and one man tends to focus attention on the man, on his viewpoint.
21 For Laura Mulvey, there's an ambiguity about how *Hail Mary* views its heroine, which can't help objectifying the woman (and her body), which contradicts the religious themes.

Joachim, her birth, her childhood, and the more familiar Annunciation and Nativity events (many depictions were based on the apocryphal *Book of James* and *The Golden Legend*). Not only are parental figures excised in the main in *Hail Mary* (tho' Mary's Pa is featured), but all of those older characters you find in Biblical/ Christian stories are absent – the elders of the temple, the priests, the Pharisees, the Magi, etc. The Doctor and the Professor stand in for them (as modern equivalents).

It's significant that *Hail Mary* doesn't show Mary's mother, St Anne, an important figure in Christianity (although she is seen in the preceding film, *The Book of Mary*). St Anne with Mary, Anne and Joachim, and the birth of Mary were popular subjects in Northern European Renaissance art (and in Leonardo da Vinci's deeply mysterious painting in the Louvre Museum, of *St Anne, the Virgin and Child*, and the London drawing in the National Gallery).

Instead, *Hail Mary* gives Mary's parents a minor role – her mother may be the figure towards the end, in the Nativity scene (but she barely makes an impression), while Mary's father, who runs the Shell gas station, is a shadowy figure who hardly features in the film (he's there at the Annunciation, struggling with Gabriel, and later, when Mary's manning the garage at night, he asks her to note down the pump numbers).

There are many other ways that *Hail Mary* could have constructed the narrative of Mary's childhood, Annunciation, pregnancy and childbirth. Although *Hail Mary* deals with what second wave feminists and Jungian psychologists term 'women's mysteries' (conception, childbearing, birth, child-rearing), Mary is firmly ensconced in a masculinist world.[22] There are no significant women in her life: apart from Joseph, her ineffectual and irritable boyfriend, there's the even more temperamental Archangel Gabriel, plus her father, and the child inside her. The only woman who has a marked effect on her existence (apart from Gabriel's young helper) is Juliette, and she's a rival for Joseph's love (Juliette derides Mary by calling her the Princess – *Hail Mary* uses the familiar high school trope of the bitchy rivalry between girls, with Juliette feeling plain and inadequate next to Miss Perfect).[23]

True, the parallel story, of the Professor Johannes and the student Eva, proffers a substantial female character; however, in the Professor<–>Eva relationship, the Professor does most of the talking

---

[22] Feminists, even if they disliked *Hail Mary*, agreed that Jean-Luc Godard succeeded in evoking the Virgin Mary.
[23] Juliette Binoche can play glamorous, but in *Hail Mary* she's given a plain, no make-up look.

by far (he is continually enunciating – it's a standard Godardian sexist set-up: the wise, older man lectures and pontificates, and the younger, female acolyte's job is to listen respectfully; remember that Godard had considered making two films prior to *Hail Mary*: one about fathers and daughters (and specifically also about incest), entitled *Fathers and Daughters,* and one about Sigmund Freud and Dora, relationships which chime with those of the Professor and Eva (and other characters in Godard pictures of this era). At first Godard had wanted to do father-daughter incest (also couched within an adaptation of *King Lear*), then moved on to Freud and Dora, and finally to God and his daughter – not one to shy away from ambitious subjects, Godard). Further, when the Professor Johannes decides to leave her, Eva crumples like a soap opera queen, pleading with the Professor not to leave her alone, begging him to abandon his wife[24] and son for her (hell, how many times have we seen that particular scenario in movies?).[25]

The Professor is linked with Adam, the first man – hence his continual disquisitions on the origins of life and on cosmology (the first time we see him lecturing). Adam and Eve are evoked in other Jean-Luc Godard films, such as *Contempt*. Godard has always been intrigued by a primal heterosexual couple, the mythical, eternal lovers (and he has put lovers in a central position in most of his movies).

The Virgin Mary was called 'the Second Eve' or 'the New Eve' in mediæval theology, the woman who would redeem, like Christ, the sin of Eve[26] and the 'fall' of Adam (Johannes mistakenly calls Eva 'Eve' a couple of times,[27] although Eva[28] means Eve anyway). In a later scene, Eva is shown nude, eating an apple,[29] with the Professor, at the Paradise Villa.

In terms of dramatic construction, the script of *Hail Mary* is striking in one respect: it leaps forward to six years or so after the events in the bulk of the movie, something Jean-Luc Godard's scripts don't tend to do. The typical Godard flick, from the 1960s or the 1980s, takes place over a few days, sometimes weeks, but rarely longer. Leaping ahead in time is something that many movies do without thinking anything of it, but Godard avoids that sort of retroactive,

---

24 His family seem to be back in Czechoslovakia (he mentions Prague).
25 Woody Allen is a shameless re-user of that old chestnut.
26 The Madonna's virginity frees her from God's punishment of painful childbirth, which all women inherit, as the *Bible* puts it (*Genesis,* 3: 16).
27 Mis-naming someone is a recurring Godardism.
28 Jean-Luc Godard may have been referring to the angelic salutation which Gabriel says at the annunciation – *Ave Maria gratia plena* – in which the word *Ave* (*hail*) is *eva* or Eve backwards.
29 Eating an apple pops up in the Heaven section of *Our Music.*

even nostalgic approach. It's too smug, it's too confident that it knows what the future will bring: no, Godard's cinema says, the future is always uncertain, so his films steer clear of jumping into the future for a happy ending.

For some critics, the first half of *Hail Mary* concentrates on Joseph's story, on his reaction to Mary's new spiritual and physical state, on his desire for her body and sex, and his wavering between Mary and Juliette. For me, Jean-Luc Godard's focus on Joseph's predicament is a way into Mary's story, but Mary remains absolutely the centre of the 1985 film, from start to finish. Although Joseph and Juliette are the first characters the spectator meets (in scene 1), from the first time she's seen, at the basketball court (in scene 2), Mary dominates the film (and Juliette Binoche, radiant as she is,[30] is no match in close-up for Myriem Roussel, whose beauty eats up the screen).

It's not stated if Mary and Joseph have been dating together for a long time (it's two years according to Joseph). But the Doctor does say that Joseph seemed to be serious about Mary, as if they have something of a history of being together.[31] So has Mary being sexually withholding herself from Joseph since the beginning of their relationship? Or is it a new development? Have they already been having sex (though not intercourse), or at least kissing and touching? The film doesn't say so. (Mary withholds a kiss when Joseph grapples her on the hood of the taxi).

Juliette is a somewhat peripheral character, who has few scenes and even less screen time. She's there as another pretext for Joseph's emotional confusion; she's much more concerned about Joseph's affection for Mary than Mary is about Joseph's feelings for Juliette. Joseph himself doesn't have a *human* rival for Mary's love: his rival is divine. Mary's new relationship is between herself and God, and it's the extraordinary nature of this spiritual relationship that Joseph struggles to understand. (God's love also has an anthropomorphic form, the Archangel Gabriel, and Joseph squabbles and fights with Gabriel as if he were a romantic rival).[32]

It's not a love triangle, then, but an erotic-spiritual quartet (comprising four people or entities, Mary, Joseph, Juliette and God/

---

[30] Binoche would make a good Mary – later she starred in *Mary* (Abel Ferrara, 2005), a movie with religious themes that also used the Christian story.
[31] And Joseph mentions two years.
[32] Wheeler Dixon pointed out that Gabriel reprises the antsy character of Joseph Balsamo in *Weekend*.

Gabriel, and three relationships: Mary and Joseph, Joseph and Juliette, and Mary and God – plus another one Joseph can't fathom, Mary and the child growing inside her).

If *Je Vous Salue Marie* was transferred to a contemporary, North American setting, this love triangle between Mary, Joseph and Juliette would become the standard banal melodrama of Hollywood teen high school dramas. Mary would become the high school jock, a virginal do-gooder, a bit bratty, played in the mid-1980s by, say, Molly Ringwald (who appeared in Godard's next film but one after *Hail Mary*, *King Lear*), while Juliette would be her rival, louder, more confident, immoral, and perhaps the leader of a girl gang. No chance of *Hail Mary* becoming anything like *Pretty In Pink* or *The Breakfast Club*, though: *Je Vous Salue Marie* is a very 'French' film, the characters are sullen and serious, given to philosophizing at length, the polar opposite of aspirational teenagers in Hollywood movies.

However, Jean-Luc Godard has made already made moves towards pop soap opera by introducing the character of Juliette in the first place, and by giving Mary and Joseph the characterization of young people. They don't chew gum, fiddle with their cel phones, listen to pop music, or watch TV, as they do in Hollywood teen films, but they are still young French/ Swiss people, and still part of popular youth culture (basketball is one of the few self-consciously 'modern' elements that the film allows the lead characters to have).

Joseph is in many ways an archetypal Godardian character: a youth with relatively simple desires, who wants to see Mary naked, who wants her body, who's promiscuous, who can't decide between Mary and Juliette. He's the kind of character Jean-Pierre Léaud played in *Masculine/ Féminin*: intense, dissatisfied, lazy, reading books, with dark glasses – all classic, Godardian traits.

Jean-Luc Godard was not a 'believer' – a cursory glance at his *œuvre* reveals a tirelessly questioning, irreverent, rebellious personality.[33] Nevertheless, Godard was very interested in religion, in the *Bible*, in Catholicism, just as he wanted to explore politics, or capitalism, or popular culture.[34] And he was interested in how the divine and the spiritual would function in the contemporary world: Mao and Marx in the Sixties; God and Mary in the Eighties. Godard

---

[33] 'I'm not a believer, it's not a film about religion', Jean-Luc Godard admitted of *Hélas Pour Moi* (in S. Tipot, *La Croix*, Sept, 1993.)
[34] Françoise Dolto's book *L'Evangile au risque de la psychoanalyse* is an influence on *Hail Mary*. In it, Godard found a description of Mary and Joseph which fascinated him: 'she spoke of Mary and Joseph in a way that I had never heard before. It seemed very cinematic: the story of a couple. And I'm very traditional. I've always made love stories and stories of couples' (1985b).

said the *Bible* was an amazing book, how it speaks of events that are happening today. An atheist, highly sceptical, Godard admitted that something larger than himself was required: 'somehow I think we need faith, or I need faith, or I'm lacking in faith' (1993, 119).

There are numerous discussions in *Hail Mary* about virginity: indeed, if you took away the religious elements (impossible, but if you could), you would see a film about a heterosexual couple who have their relationship thrown into turmoil when the woman becomes pregnant but insists that she hasn't had sex with anyone. And not with her lover, either.

Virginity. Purity. Sex. Conception. Pregnancy. Children. *Hail Mary*, even without the Christian, religious elements, is a fascinating exploration of grand themes like an immaculate conception and virginity and purity. (The dogma of the Immaculate Conception – contested between the Franciscans and Dominicans in the Middle Ages, was generally accepted by the 16th century – means that the Virgin Mary is *free from Original Sin*.[35] No stain.)

Hence the two scenes in *Hail Mary* where Mary's virginity is physically tested – by her Doctor and her boyfriend, who both examine her internally (in this movie, the test of virginity is the archaic one of whether the hymen is still intact). Because Godard and Miéville have rightly judged that one of the biggest issues in the Christian story of Mary is how a virgin became pregnant. So Joseph is not so much a character in *Hail Mary* as a function of the plot and the script, there to ask the same question: 'how?' (not 'why?', but always 'how? – 'why?' is beyond him, and Mary struggles all the time with the '*pourquoi?*' of it all).

The scene with the Doctor is a way of including authority figures, which in Biblical times might have been priests or rabbis or village elders. The Doctor's examination and confirmation of Mary's virginity is vital to the drama of *Hail Mary*.

Notice how Godard and Miéville simply leave out one enormous factor in *Hail Mary*, which a Hollywood movie would surely include: Mary and Joseph don't involve anyone else in their miracle. Mary becomes pregnant while she's still a virgin, but there are no scenes of Mary going to specialists, and no confrontations with her parents. A Hollywood movie would probably include those sorts of elements, and there would be scenes of the media circus (TV crews and journalists)

---

35 Original Sin stems from the first time that humans disobeyed God.

coming to Switzerland to interview the miraculous couple.[36] And Mary confides to no friends or relatives (aside from the Doctor).

But this's part of the conceit of *Hail Mary* – in this mid-1980s movie, the audience has to (kind of) pretend that Christianity never happened. There are no scenes in churches, for instance, and no images of Christian symbols and tropes (no crucifixes, no clergy, no *Bibles*).[37] A world in which Christianity never occurred might make a fascinating movie, if filmed by Jean-Luc Godard. But it isn't incorporated here because it would make *Hail Mary* far too complex – and it's already complicated enough – thematically, psychologically, theologically, spiritually, you name it. Staying with the conceit of the events of the Christian *Gospels* taking place in the modern world is plenty to be going on with.

▼

'What happened? How did he take Mary's secret? How did he cope with this violence?' Jean-Luc Godard asked about Joseph. 'I wanted to present the two of them as an ordinary couple, an archetype of a couple, who accept the extraordinary in an ordinary way.'[38]

One or two more recent movies have also tried to explore this area, which has always been left out of the religious epic films of the 1920s-1970s. In those older, filmed interpretations of the Christian story, Joseph simply accepts it all. In 2006's *The Nativity Story* (dir. by Catherine Hardwicke, and distributed by Hollywood's New Line Cinema), Joseph acts hurt and insulted when Mary returns from visiting her relation Anne pregnant. Mary's parents arrange an angry meeting between the couple, with Mary's Pa demanding that Mary explain herself, and what about poor Joseph? he wants to know. But a little Hollywood lovin' comes to the rescue, and Joseph accepts Mary, despite her being pregnant.

In 2000's *Mary, Mother of God*, meanwhile, the Virgin also returns from staying with Anne for several months with child, but Joseph here is much quicker to forgive and accept Mary. However, he too has the male huff and puff and grand sulk, storming around their (rather luxurious) house.

And Godard and Miéville too stage scenes in *Hail Mary* of Joseph getting angry and insulted that Mary gets pregnant while professing to 'know no one'. And the lust that Joseph feels for Mary is far, far more

---

36 That's how Federico Fellini would play it – he enjoyed staging scenes of crowds and the media descending upon sites of miracles (such as media circus surrounding the vision of the Virgin Mary in *La Dolce Vita*.
37 Japanese animation would not be able to resist images of stained glass or crucifixes.
38 J.-L. Godard in *La Croix*, Jan 24, 1985.

explicit and intense than *any* movie about the Christian story or the *Gospels*. He *really* wants to have her, just like Michel with Patricia in *Breathless* or any of Godard's male characters.

Hm-mmm, Jean-Luc Godard's interpretation of the story of the Virgin Mary is far, far more eroticized than any other version. In *The Nativity Story* or *Mary, Mother of God* or *Jesus of Nazareth* or any other recent approach to the Christian myth, of the 1990s to 2020s, Mary and Joseph are never shown kissing. Not even kissing on the forehead or hand. And barely a hug either. Oh no.

But Godard and Miéville have scenes where Joseph physically inspecting Mary to test if she's a virgin! And the climax of their movie has Mary standing naked from the waist down in front of Joseph! And they include dialogue such as, 'I'm a woman... though I don't beget my man through my cunt'.

Wow.

☆

'Jesus has appeared often on the screen. But no one has told the story of Mary and Joseph', Jean-Luc Godard remarked. Indeed, it is surprising that the Madonna hasn't had more films made about her life.[39] The task Godard set himself was to imagine the early life of Mary and Joseph, including their conversations:

> What could they say to each other? It's a major problem, because from the *Bible* we know of only two or three words that Mary spoke, and from Joseph absolutely nothing. And they must have talked together! So it was difficult to invent the dialogue, because nobody knows. (1993, 121).

There is much more detail on Mary and Joseph's life together in the ancient *Apocrypha*, but Jean-Luc Godard was basing his film more on the Biblical *Gospels*, on the generally accepted interpretations of Mary and Joseph.

Actually, there *are* some films which deal with Mary's early life, and Jean-Luc Godard would have known about them: one is *The Gospel According To Matthew* (1964), without question the greatest film about Christ (directed of course by Pier Paolo Pasolini, and produced by Alfredo Bini). This beyond-beautiful film contains sequences which deal with the early days of Mary and Joseph. [40]

---

[39] 'If I were ever to film the life of Christ,' Jean-Luc Godard said in 1965, 'I would film the scenes which are left out of the *Bible*' (G, 222). Well, he didn't film the life of Christ (what a pity!), but he did film the early life of the Virgin Mary and, as expected, staged the scenes he wanted to see but which weren't in the *Gospels*.
[40] Myriem Roussel watched *The Gospel According To Matthew* in preparation for the film, at Godard's behest, and also a film Godard loved, *The Passion of Joan of Arc*. She also studied the *Bible*.

The other one is *Jesus of Nazareth*, the all-star, TV mini-series of 1977 (another Italian production), which depicts the young Virgin and her life with Joseph. And, since *Hail Mary*, there have been further TV shows and films about the Madonna. For instance, the Italian company Lux Vide has produced a *Bible Collection* of TV movies centred on figures such as Jesus (*Jesus: The Bible*, Roger Young, 1999), Mary Magdalene (2000), Judas, Simon, St Paul, etc, and their *Mary, Mother of Jesus* (1999) is about the Virgin. And *The Da Vinci Code* (2006) phenomenon, along with the surprise success of *The Passion of the Christ* (2004), have spearheaded renewed millennial interest in Christian themes in cinema.

Without doubt *The Gospel According To Matthew* is the greatest of all movies dealing with the Christian story. It's the movie everyone has to see if they're going to depict the life of Christ. And of course, Pier Paolo Pasolini was very influenced by Jean-Luc Godard, and that's plain to see in *The Gospel According To Matthew* – the jump cuts, the handheld camera, the to-camera looks and monologues, the rapid editing, the abrupt ellipses, the use of real people, the pop music soundtrack, etc. In its way, *The Gospel According To Matthew* is among the most Godardian of movies which Godard didn't direct.

You can't simply pick up the *Bible* and walk onto a film set and start filming it. The amount of work in adapting the *Gospels* and other Biblical texts that you see in *Hail Mary* is considerable: the writers have thought about the characterizations, how to update the famous scenes, how to explore the themes and issues in the modern era, and a thousand other items.

And, Godard being Godard, *Hail Mary* works *against* or *in opposition* to the *Bible* and to the many interpretations of Biblical material in cinema (and other media, such as music and painting, two of Godard's passions). It's the same approach that Godard has taken with most of his other movies: in writing a thriller film, for instance, Godard deliberately works against the accepted/ received view of what a thriller is. So Godard wouldn't produce a regular or mainstream religious film, because none of his films or TV shows have been mainstream.

★

Je vous salue, Myriem.

Hail Mary is a pæan to the female nude, to one particular body, that of the Virgin, and of the actress who plays her, Myriem Roussel (Roussel, with her large eyes and dark looks, recalls Anna Karina).

Roussel's performance is magnificent – it's the performance of a lifetime; she was 22 at the time of filming in Spring, 1984 (she was born on February 2, 1962, in Rabat, Morocco.)[41] Roussel had also appeared in *Prénom Carmen* and *Passion*; Godard had cast her as one of the extras in *Passion*, the deaf and dumb girl by the pool. and in *First Name: Carmen* she carries the subplot about music. Since *Hail Mary*, Roussel has done mainly television: *Carte de presse, Tote leben nicht allein, Jules, Maître Da Costa, La crim', Le grand Batre, Diane, femme flic, Avocats & associés* and *La vie devant nous*. I haven't seen those shows, but it is a pity that Roussel hasn't pursued a higher profile film career, because she is in the same league as Juliette Binoche, Isabelle Adjani and Irène Jacob.

Rarely has the female nude been so lovingly photographed in a film. Sometimes Jean-Luc Godard has been criticized for sexism, of using the female nude for titillation or cheap effects. There is some truth in this (it's *de rigeur* in a European art film to have a nude woman wandering through a scene – she nearly always *just happens* to be attractive, too. Odd how European art filmmakers don't cast unappealing people for those nude walk-ons).

In *Hail Mary*, though, Jean-Luc Godard moves well beyond that, into a new realm of exploration which has nothing to do with eroticism or pornography, or even conventional depictions of sexuality or heterosexuality. It's true, it's still a situation of clothed, male fiilmmaker/s looking at the nude, female actress (and the older man gazing at the younger woman),[42] but there's much more going on here, to do with the relation between the soul and the body, spirituality and sexuality, religion and the individual, the immanent and the transcendent, the miraculous and the everyday.

Je Vous Salue, Marie is not about conventional (hetero)sexual relations at all; it is not a soap opera starring St Mary and St Joseph (although the middle section of the film, the bickering between Mary and Joseph, can appear like an emotional melodrama – but that's largely stemming from Joseph and his inability to grasp exactly what's happening with his girlfriend Mary; *Hail Mary* is about being unable to imagine what a woman is, Godard said [1993, 121]i.

Mary is photographed in a variety of situations: washing herself crouched in the bath; getting dressed and undressed; in a Tee shirt and underwear, pressing her hand over her vulva; clad in a cotton, Summer

---

[41] Somehow it's apposite that the Virgin Mary should be played by a Moroccan, a North African woman.
[42] The scenes of Mary naked, writhing in bed, were filmed by Jean-Luc Godard himself – only the director and the actress were present.

dress; there is a key shot, medium close-up, of her naked torso; and in the most agonized scenes, Mary is shown writhing on her bed, arching her back, or doubled up.

Jean-Luc Godard admitted he liked to look at naked women (yes we guessed that), but he was trying for something else in *Hail Mary*, to portray a naked woman in a non-pornographic or aggressive way ('our purpose was to try and shoot a woman naked and not make it aggressive, not in an X-rated picture way' [1998, 169]). He referred to the tradition in Renaissance art of depicting the Madonna with a naked breast, and the controversy that caused. But Godard also acknowledged that the nudity ran the risk of being received as 'sinister', or a 'sin' (ibid.). Godard said he was after something like an anatomical drawing, or to encourage the viewer to see flesh, rather than a naked woman (ibid.). Godard also admitted: 'I'm a man, still, I like to look at women naked!' (ib., 170).

☆

Je Vous Salue, Marie is a densely poetic, allusive film. There are many, many shots of the sun, of sunsets, of cloudy skies, of the moon in different phases, of trees, fields, big close-ups of flowers, water, and many shots of a lake (from above, on a shoreline, and so on). A shot of shallow water over sand, with the sun glittering on it, recurs, as do visuals of the sky, of sunsets, and of the moon: these images suggest outer space, the cosmic, the galactic (Jean-Luc Godard was interested in science and speculative thinking, including cosmology). He explained in an interview:

> What we wanted to show in *Hail Mary* was signs in the beginning. Signs in the sense of signals, the beginning of signs, when signs are beginning to grow. Before they have signification of meaning. Immaculate signs in a way. And not just to give a feeling of nature, in order to be poetic, but to show the physical process of making nature possible. A philosophy of nature, just as we tried to show the spirit and flesh of Mary. (1993, 120)

The influx of natural imagery in *Hail Mary* takes the narrative far away from the usual Godardian *milieu*, of Parisian streets and cafés. These can be seen as both documentary shots and hyper-symbolic, at once the natural world and intimations of the cosmic, the infinite, the sublime (Friedrich Hölderlin, one of the most æthereal and sublime of poets, is cited at one point, and some of the landscape images include the snowy peaks of the Alps in the distance – Hölderlin famously tramped over the Alps,[43] a journey which some reckon hastened his madness).

☆

The human body and the natural world of fields, flowers and trees are not the only sites of spiritual inquiry in *Hail Mary*: there are many shots of suns, moons, skies, lakes, seas and close-ups of the sun shining on water. Notions of outer space, distant stars and other worlds are suggested by this imagery. The divine, the transcendent, the sacred are also evoked in these images of skies, moons and suns. As Mircea Eliade rightly noted, the sky is an image of transcendence and the sacred *par excellence*; thus, if one wants to suggest the divine or the transcendent in a film, a shot of the sky is one of the easiest, the clearest and the most direct ways of doing it. If one can't film God, then an image of the sky can be one of the best ways of evoking the deity. In a conventional film, a picture of the sky might not connote much of the mystical at all, but in a film called *Hail Mary* it probably has spiritual undertones, and in this particular movie, there are cuts back to images of the sky (in a variety of states, from clear blue to cloudy to sunset to nighttime) many, many times.

Another recurring motif in *Hail Mary* is the circle and the sphere: Mary's belly, her womb, the moon, the sun, a basketball, an apple, the eye, the face, the mouth, the vulva, and the anus. Jean-Luc Godard emphasizes the circularity of his imagery by cutting from one circle to another.

> We used it metaphorically: the woman as circle, and the plane flying toward it. That's one signal: coming to a woman's centre. But at a certain point there's no difference between metaphor and actuality. (1993, 120)

In the pictures of Mary on her bed in her room, her belly is prominent; in one shot, she lies still, but her belly, in the foreground, rises and falls under the bedclothes. When Eva (and also Mary) eats an apple, it is an obvious reference to Adam and Eve in Paradise.

☆

Time for a quotation from Friedrich Hölderlin. This is from *The Death of Empedocles* (third version):

---

[43] Hölderlin usually walked on his travels, including as a tutor. He walked, for example, to Hauptwyl, crossing the Alps in January, 1800. Poems of this time ('Sung Beneath the Alps' and 'Homecoming') depict snowy, Alpine scenes. The journey to his last engagement as a private tutor, to Bordeaux in January, 1802, took over a month on foot (Hölderlin armed himself with pistols for the hazardous journey). Not much is known about Hölderlin's time in Bordeaux. There are rumours about his life there, and intimations of his oncoming mental disturbance.

Ja! ruhig wohnen wir; es öffnen groß
Sich hier vor uns die heilgen Elemente.
Die Mühelosen regen immergleich
In ihrer Kraft sich freudig hier um uns.
An seinen vesten Ufern wallt und ruht
Das alte Meer, und das Gebirge steigt
Mit seiner Ströme Klang, es woogt und rauscht
Sein grüner Wald von Thal zu Thal hinunter.
Und oben weilt das Licht, der Aether stilt
Den Geist und das geheimere Verlangen.
Hier wohnen ruhig wir!

(Yes, we live peacefully; and vastly here
The holy elements reveal themselves.
Ever the same, the untoiling joyously,
Surely and powerfully stir around us.
On its firm shores advances and reposes
The ancient sea, and the great mountains rise
With music of their springs, the green woods flow
And roar and rustle down from vale to vale.
And at the top light lingers, Aether stills
Our minds and the more secret of our longings.
Here we live peacefully.)[44]

Yet Jean-Luc Godard's cinema has always had a heightened sense of the environment, whether city or country. The poetic shots of skies, seas, suns and moons suggest the Virgin's inner world, its turmoil and pain, but also its beauty, its magic. *Hail Mary* offers a sometimes spectacular view of the inner landscape of the protagonist, making *Hail Mary* one of the great religious films, on a par with any of the religious classics (such as those helmed by Robert Bresson, Andrei Tarkovsky, Carl-Theodor Dreyer or Luis Buñuel).

The nature imagery in *Hail Mary* is also suggestive of a divine presence, imagery of the spiritual or the divine. The 1985 film doesn't show God, or anything resembling a miracle or divine intervention in the usual manner (no flying angels, no beams of light, no holy dove/ghost), but it does explore the world beyond the human world, something larger and mysterious (and it *does* portray a miracle – Mary's pregnancy).

A non-believer, J.-L. Godard is not going to state that those images of the giant, round sun are meant to indicate the deity or a divinity, but these sorts of images have for millennia been indicative of spiritual or divine presences. You don't need to be an expert in (Jungian) symbolism to know that when the 1985 film cuts from Mary at the Annunciation to an image of a giant, orange sun, it's suggesting the divine.

---

[44] *Hölderlin's Songs of Light*, tr. M. Hamburger, ed. J.M. Robinson, Crescent Moon, 2000.

For David Sterrit, Jean-Luc Godard's films are aiming to explore something beyond psychological realism, or images, or inner, emotional selves. Rather: 'something more profound and mysterious – a 'something else' that can only be approached through oxymoronic genres... and eccentric creative processes... I wish to underscore again the importance of an aggressively ungraspable edge to the Mobius strip of Godardian cinema, which pursues philosophical goals far beyond those sought by the over-whelming majority of narratively and psychologically oriented films.' (2002)

To achieve the many beautiful natural events in the film such as particular cloud effects, or kinds of sunlight, or a jet passing the sun, Godard said the camera was set up and the crew waited and waited. It's an unusual (and expensive) way of making films, and was one of the reasons that *Hail Mary* went over-budget.

One of Jean-Luc Godard's new ways of using the camera in *Hail Mary* was to look for 'centres' or 'points' to concentrate the lens on, rather than framing. He didn't want conventional framing, or to talk in terms of framing. But even a brilliant communicator like Godard found that difficult to explain to the crew: 'I can't manage to explain to a camera operator that there's no frame, that there's a point to find'.[45] And if you look at some of Godard's later movies, conventional photographic framing is sometimes dispensed with: camera operators instinctively frame up shots with pleasing proportions out of traditional art and perspective. But Godard's movies contain some odd compositions, which professional cameramen would probably alter.

☆

According to Myriem Roussel, many times Jean-Luc Godard sent the crew home without having filmed anything (that has happened before). Godard found this film tough to make – he said he filmed the whole story 'four or five times',[46] and also shot many more takes than usual (Godard has never liked doing too many takes: if he gets it first time, that'll do). But it's also probable that the remaking of the film several times improved it (not the many takes, but rather than continual polishing of the material).

Jean-Luc Godard wanted to involve the crew, as he had tried to do in earlier movies, in discussions about the subject of the movie – virginity, the birth of a child, and man-woman relationships – but they wouldn't respond satisfactorily (understandable – Godard is a director who intimidates even seasoned veterans and philosophers).

---
45 *Art Press, Spécial Godard*, Dec, 1984/ Jan, 1985.
46 In *Libération*, Jan 23,1985.

There were times, Myriem Roussel recalled, when Jean-Luc Godard wasn't sure how he wanted shoot this sacred story. They would rehearse the dialogue the night before, but sometimes Godard on set would admit that he didn't know quite what to do: 'he simply didn't see the frame that he wanted, or what he wanted to show, or why this sequence now and not another,' Roussel remembered in 1985 (B, 461). That too has happened on quite a few Godard movies.

*

As well as the dense layers of imagery, the soundtrack of *Je Vous Salue, Marie* is a rich collage of voiceover, dialogue, sound effects (such as water, dogs, birds, animals, bells, traffic, wind), and music. Soundwise, *Je Vous Salue, Marie* is extremely complicated, moving abruptly from silence to crashes of the ocean or thunderous chords, or music stopping as suddenly as it came in (sometimes in very short bursts, erupting in a gap of 2.5 seconds between dialogue). Jean-Luc Godard said he didn't use 'vertical sound', with each track distinct from the others, but 'horizontal sound', 'where there are many, many sounds but still it's as though every sound is becoming one general speech, whether it's music, dialogue or nature sound' (1993, 121).

In terms of music, Johann Sebastian Bach (1685-1750) and Antonín Dvořák (1841-1904) predominate. Jean-Luc Godard said *Hail Mary* could be seen as a documentary on Bach's music.[47] 'I tried to put in all sorts of Bach: violins, church music, piano, choral' (1993, 121). (It had to be Bach, Godard said, not Ludwig van Beethoven or Wolfgang Mozart, for historical reasons, and also because Bach suits any situation).[48] The music cuts in and out abruptly in some scenes, unmotivated (in the Annunciation scene, for example). Sometimes the music swamps the dialogue, and sometimes the background sounds, such as birds or traffic noise, drown out the dialogue. Often the sounds or music from a previous scene carry over into the next, or, more commonly, the sounds from the next scene impose themselves on the scene now playing. Sometimes this created harsh tensions (the sound of noisy cars over shots of Mary in bed), or some startling juxtapositions. Indeed, by the mid-1980s, very few European filmmakers were so skilfully radical with sound – Rainer Fassbinder was dead, Ingmar Bergman had apparently ceased activity for a while after *Fanny and Alexander*, Bernardo Bertolucci was soon to embark on his epic but

---

[47] The first 15 minutes are a medley of Bach's greatest hits, commented James Williams (in M. Temple, 2004, 295).
[48] 'Bach's music can be matched to any situation. It's perfect', remarked Jean-Luc Godard, 'even when you play it backwards.' (And you can bet that Godard has probably tried playing Back backwards!).

very conventional 'Oriental trilogy', François Truffaut died in the year of filming (1984), and Andrei Tarkovsky would be dead within a year of *Hail Mary* being released. But when it comes to the application of sound effects, music and voice in cinema, virtually no filmmaker can even equal Godard's achievements.

Some sounds recur many times in *Hail Mary*: the sound of wind (loud, chaotic); the sound of birdsong; a singular bird cry, resembling a crow's 'caw'; traffic noise; and the splash of a stone in water, which usually occurs with a shot of some shallow water with the sun shining on it. Some off-screen sounds might've been recorded in a hotel foyer, a train station, a shopping mall – they are busy, chatty sounds of crowds and activity, which are not explained or justified (evocations of the community, perhaps, the crowds who are always seen in the villages in a Biblical story).

The sound of the wind blowing hard, for example, is a wonderful concept: it erupts over shots of Mary or Joseph (among others) and comes out of nowhere, with no motivation, and no diegetic justification. But it's the particular *quality* of the wind sound effect that Jean-Luc Godard and his sound team (headed up by François Musy) have chosen: it sounds like it was recorded on some moorland or mountain – a flapping, agitated wind sound, which suggests an other-worldly realm. And wind and air are of course intimately linked to gods (like the deity Zeus in Ancient Greek mythology), and also to concepts such as divinity and divine power and creativity (the creative breath of life, the Creative Word of God, 'let there be light', and so on).

In terms of sound and music, *Hail Mary* has one of the most complicated sound mixes in cinema of the 1980s and after. True, there may not be as many channels of sound in the mix as a contemporary, Hollywood blockbuster, but the combination of music, sound effects and voices is far more complex than 99.9% of Hollywood movies.

Hail Mary is particularly brilliant in its use of voiceover (mainly from Mary, but also from the Professor Johannes, and Joseph), and the many ways in which the narration relates to the image (I think Godard himself is heard too – when the title card 'AT THAT TIME' comes up, and the director is saying let's continue with our story). The philosophizing in the narration is another layer of complexity in *Hail Mary* – and in a film that already possesses one of the most dynamic combinations of image and music, image and sound effects, in cinema for many years.

*

The sheer intensity of spiritual emotion, the exploration of religious imagery in *Je Vous Salue, Marie* may be surprising to some who come to the film knowing only Jean-Luc Godard's Sixties movies, who know only the Godard of Maoism and Marxism, the radical political filmmaker, or the Godard who ironically and savagely satirizes consumer capitalism and popular culture. It's certainly unexpected that Godard would contemplate divinity and spirituality. The move from ideology and politics to religion and spirituality could be seen as a 'softening', a lessening of the power of analysis, a step backward into conservatism. Not at all. In its way, *Hail Mary* is as radical as any of Jean-Luc Godard's movies. (Godard himself said, *pace* people being brought up by militants and Maoists, that his religious upbringing was just the same as having a political background).[49]

If Jean-Luc Godard isn't a 'believer', he is totally fascinated by the story of Mary and Jesus in the *Gospels*. You just wouldn't bother to make a film about the girlhood and Annunciation of the Virgin Mary if you weren't fascinated by the story in the first place (you wouldn't, because it takes months and months to make a film – and 600,000 dollars, and you invite attention from religious groups).

A comment made by Jean-Luc Godard back in the Sixties offers an insight here: if he made a film from the *Bible*, Godard remarked, he'd be interested in the things that films don't show, in the acts and dialogue that went on in between the famous moments. You can see in *Hail Mary* that Godard is intrigued by what Mary and Joseph would have said to each other. How *did* Joseph react when Mary told him she was pregnant, even though he knew they hadn't yet had intercourse? And then if she insisted that her child was divine, that it hadn't come from coupling with a man? (Actually, that wasn't such a crazy concept back then: mothers conceiving by the gods wasn't unknown – you find it in Homer, and in Ancient Greek mythology, for instance).

A way of looking at *Hail Mary* and how it works is to take out the religious aspects – the story from the *Gospels*, the hints at divinity. If you didn't know it was about the young Mary and Joseph from the *Gospels*, how would it play? Then it becomes a teenage melodrama, with a romantic plot. It then becomes about a boy who loves a girl but she won't have sex with him (or even kiss him), and he's got another girlfriend but he doesn't like her as much (although she's thrown herself at him and told him they could get married).[50] And then his girlfriend

---

49 Sort of – or is this yet another apology by the Maestro for his very bourgeois origins in a wealthy Swiss family?
50 Juliette wishes perhaps that she could've snared Joseph by telling him she was pregnant, as out of a Thomas Hardy novel.

tells him she's pregnant but they haven't had sex. And it's all so frustrating and such a mess but he can't give up Mary because he's nuts about her.

So if you take out the Archangel Gabriel and God and the Christian/ religious aspects of the story, it's a very different movie. But it's still a fascinating tale – it's still about a woman who's a virgin who becomes pregnant. It might still be about miracles, but without the religious baggage. It's about conception and pregnancy – the how and the why. And it then becomes about young people talking about sex, and conception and contraception, and what would happen if the girl became pregnant. (The movie could drop the direct Biblical references, and it would still be compelling).

Take out the religion and the Christianity and God and all and you've got a young person's sex drama. But put back the religion and the Christian story and all and you've got this enormous weight of religion and two thousand years of theology and everything else and it becomes a gigantic story (and a very controversial item). It's no longer about a small group of young people in a Swiss town in the mid-Eighties.

Part of the genius of *Hail Mary*, then, is how skilfully Jean-Luc Godard has updated the Christian story, placing it into a believable contemporary context. That has been done before (and since), of course: in *Jesus Christ Superstar* (1973), the story of Jesus is played out by a bunch of young hippies in Israel. In *Jesus of Montréal* (1989), the Passion Play is put on in contemporary Canada. And many films have taken up messiah myths, Christ-like heroes, and other Christian metaphors: *Akira, Star Wars, E.T., The Terminator, Nausicaä of the Valley of the Wind, City of Angels, The Matrix*, etc (there's a whole sub-genre of contemporary films which rework Christian mythology, and another sub-genre which have taken up Satan and devilish tropes). But when Jean-Luc Godard tackles the Christian story, you know it won't be a traditional or conventional telling.[51]

*

The central section of the 1985 film largely concerns Mary and Joseph, with both of them trying to come to terms with what is happening to her. While she is troubled, doubtful, she also seems to accept her situation (her initial reactions include surprise, even shock, but they soon pass); Joseph is much more confused and anxious. He

---

[51] For Wheeler Dixon, *Hail Mary* was not a re-telling of the Christian story, but 'a *rebirth* of the vision of the divine. One might also call the film a vision of the second coming of Christ, or a reaffirmation of the centrality of God in matters of daily existence' (162).

can't understand how she can be pregnant. 'Miracles don't exist. Kiss me', he demands. When she wants to stay intact, withholding physical affection, he's bewildered, and angry. 'Kiss me... just once', he says; her reply by turns bemuses and infuriates him: 'I do kiss you. You should trust me'. Myriem Roussel explained Mary's behaviour thus: 'It's not that Mary hates men or that she's scared of sex. It's only because she has been chosen for that special birth. She's predestined to act that way.'

The battle of wills, centred around sex, with Mary telling Joseph she does kiss him, in spirit, and Joseph wanting much more than being kissed spiritually, from afar, takes up much of the central segment of *Je Vous Salue, Marie*.[52] In some scenes he is angry, insistent; he forces her down on the hood of his taxi, but she won't kiss him and turns her head away twice. Joseph accuses Mary of fooing around, unable to accept that she can have conceived any other way. 'A child must come from somewhere!' Joseph says, over a shot of the sky. During a telephone argument, Mary quotes from *Hamlet*, which Joseph doesn't understand.

On one level, the spiritual struggle in *Hail Mary* is reduced to soap opera, to a banal melodrama, to yet another rendition of a man pursuing a woman, the oldest story in the world. At the same time, their arguments, discussions and struggles embody the very core of Jean-Luc Godard's project. Mary has to accept her destiny wholly, and Joseph has to recognize its importance.

The emotional apotheosis occurs when Mary allows Joseph to touch her, and express his love for her (and she for him). It's a tender scene, the dramatic culmination. After it, the 1985 film depicts Mary's 'dark night of the soul', and then relates the birth of Jesus and his early childhood. It takes the couple, Mary and Joseph, into early middle age, now a (holy) family, with Mary a proud mother and Joseph a dutiful husband and worker-father (and at the climax of the film, the music is allowed its own climax, after being halted so often).

The finale of the life of Christ in cinema is always the Crucifixion followed by the Resurrection. A few films go a little further, and portray the life of the disciples afterwards (as in *Jesus of Nazareth* and *The Last Temptation of Christ*).[53] But what could be the climax of the Blessed Virgin's life? Not the birth, nor the death of Christ: rather, her

---

[52] Charles Warren notes that 'making love, living sexually at all, is an aspect to Mary that Mary is curious about, wants and shies off from, projects and creates' (in M. Locke, 1993).

[53] And some films, like *The Passion of the Christ* (2004), turn the flagellation of Christ into a 20-minute bloodbath.

Assumption into Heaven, presumably (when the Madonna was received bodily into Heaven).

'Let the soul be body. Then no one can say the body is soul, since the soul shall be body'. The body is always on display – the soul cannot be photographed. This is the dilemma of any visual artist, the depiction of the divine. Renaissance painters used the convention of the halo to indicate a person's divinity (and the reactions of onlookers); in the Biblical movies and sword-and-sandal epics of the 1950s and 1960s, several techniques were deployed, including glowing lights, choral music, special effects, and, again, the adoring gaze of onlookers (the quickest, easiest and perhaps most convincing of all dramatic devices).

The approach in *Hail Mary* is to use images from the natural world (moons, suns, skies, seas) as symbolic/ religious equivalents: hence, whenever a character in *Hail Mary* starts talking or thinking theologically, the film cuts to a shot of the moon or the Lake.

As Jean-Luc Godard and his cinematographers Jacques Firmann and Jean-Bernard Menoud cannot photograph Mary's soul, they concentrate on her body; seen naked in many shots, it connotes not only sexuality, but notions such as innocence and virginity (in traditional symbolism, nudity means the natural, the paradisal, birth, creation, resurrection in rebirth, renunciation, and unveiled reality). It is these connotations that *Hail Mary* hopes to evoke, not the obverse ones of lust, shamelessness, vice.

Jean-Luc Godard, as a materialist, would stress Mary's body anyway, above her soul or the idea of the spirit in her body. What the viewer sees, materially, in *Hail Mary*, is the body of the woman; for Godard, the body is still the ground of being, the site of all human activity and thought. (You can't control how viewers experience a film, though, and many viewers probably see Myriem Roussel's naked body and not much else. It just so happens that Roussel has a beautiful body, too: you could cast all sorts of women as the Virgin Mary – she doesn't have to be a slim, curvaceous 22 year-old. And the other nude body on display in *Hail Mary*, Anne Gautier, who plays Eva, also happens to be attractive. But, as Godard admitted, 'I like to look at women naked!').

UN FILM DI JEAN-LUC GODARD
JE VOUS SALUE *Marie*

INCLUDE IL CORTO 'IL LIBRO DI MARIA' diretto da Anne-Marie Miéville

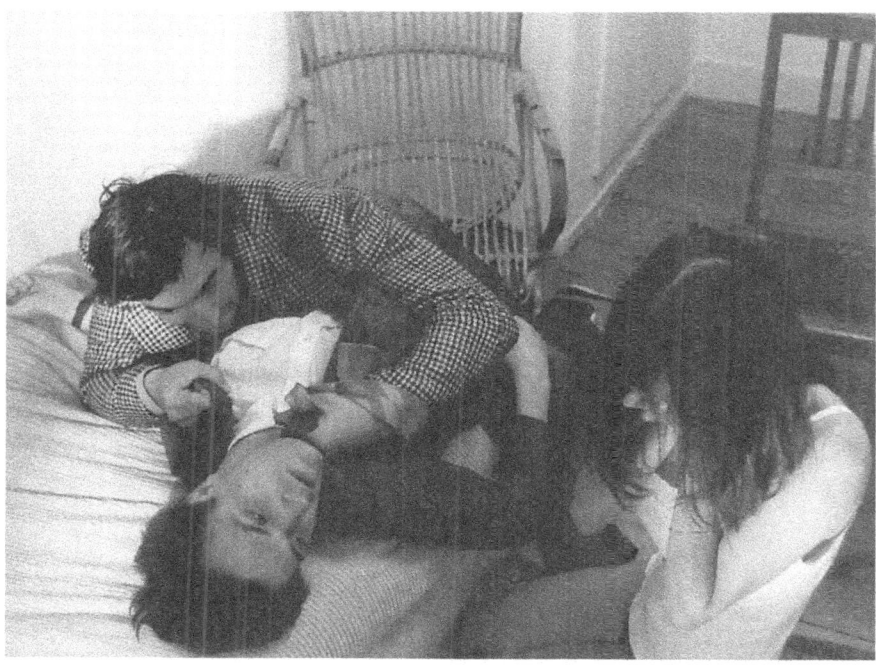

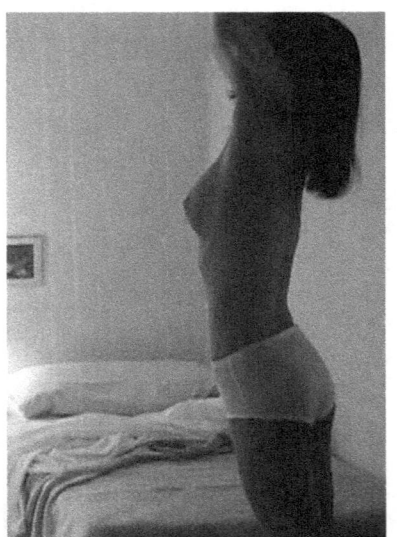

28

DÉTECTIVE

DETECTIVE

What's important is not that things should be filmed in any particular way, but simply that they should be filmed and be properly in focus.

Jean-Luc Godard[1]

---

[1] Quoted in P. Braunberger, 1987, 183.

Difficult to know what to say about *Détective* (1985), a 95-minute, 35mm feature film that Jean-Luc Cinéma Godard made with Anne-Marie Cinéma Miéville in order to pay for and complete *Je Vous Salue, Marie*. By any standards, *Détective* is a minor Godard and Miéville film (but if it helped to get *Hail, Mary* finished, all the better).

Alain Sarde, Richard Debuisne and Philippe Setbon co-wrote the script with Miéville and the Master. Christine Gozlan and Alain Sarde produced; the DPs were Louis Bihi, Pierre Novion and Bruno Nuytten; editing by Marilyne Dubreuil; make-up by Jean-Pierre Eychenne; sound by François Mussy, Bernard Leroux, Pierre Gamet and Bernard Chaumeil; music by Arthur Honegger, Ornette Coleman, Franz Liszt, Frédéric Chopin, Emmanuel Chabrier, Franz Schubert and Jean Schwarz. Released: May 10, 1985. 95 mins.

The cast included Laurent Terzieff, Johnny Hallyday, Jean-Pierre Léaud, Claude Brasseur, Nathalie Baye, Aurelle Doazan, Alain Cuny, Pierre Bertin, Stéphane Ferrara, Emmanuelle Seigner and Julie Delpy. Several of the actors were well-known in France.

This is one of the finest casts in a Godard movie.[2] One of the pleasures of *Detective* is seeing so many actors from previous Godard movies being gathered in one place. It's a cast brought together to help to sell a movie – name actors, plus three cute girls.

Detective is Godard's *Grand Hotel*,[3] his Sherlock Holmes or Agatha Christie mystery, where a bunch of eccentric characters arer gathered in one place. It's typical that Godard doesn't solve the mystery, though – both Isidore and William find out who killed the Prince, but we aren't told.

Characters, stories, dramas, situations – Godard and Miéville remain as uninterested in those narrative elements in a film as ever. No characters in the usual sense, then, no proper introductions of characters, or plots, or themes, no goals or quests or problems clearly marked, and virtually no 'story', zero drama and not much in the way of situations or confrontations. (And yet, Godard and Miéville do the narrative work in the first ten minutes of introducing all of the major characters, just like a regular film. Or is it really that they introduce the well-known actors? That is enough, however, in this sort of wilfully eccentric pseudo-mystery-drama – the first reel actually does introduce most of the main characters).

So, putting those considerations aside, what about the other

---
2 They are required to smoke – the film was sponsored by Gitanes and Marlborough.
3 Wheeler Dixon: 'this is *Grand Hotel* meets *A Night At the Opera* and *The Big Sleep*' (165).

elements in *Détective*?

All present and correct, from the Godard Box of Tricks: classical music # overlapping sound # intertitles (the opening credits run on as captions well into the film) # Paris # hotels # partial nudity # cameras # guns # cafés, etc.[4] It's all there, all the familiar furniture and bodies and faces and gestures and dialogue of a Jean-Luc Godard and Anne-Marie Miéville film. Classical music thunders and plinks throughout many scenes in *Détective*, but often it doesn't fit at all with the emotional timbre of the scenes – and this is demonstrated strikingly when the music is suddenly cut out and the scenes revert to the ambient sound of the hotel rooms (but the score is superb from all of those dead[5] (i.e., out of copyright) composers). At one point Johnny Hallyday yells at the pianist to quieten down (which he does). But pop icon Hallyday doesn't sing in *Détective*.

But Jean-Luc Godard's heart isn't in it, as with *King Lear*. It's as if he can't be bothered, and would much rather be working on something like *Hail Mary*. With that film, one can sense Godard's and Miéville's committment and passion with every frame. In *Détective*, some scenes look as if Godard had handed out a bit of dialogue on a scrap of paper to the actors at the start of the day, given a few instructions to the camera and sound crew, then left for the restaurant with Miéville, and let the team get on with it (apparently, Godard wasn't in the best of moods during the shooting of *Détective*).

This is another movie which seems to have been constructed specifically so it could be filmed *entirely* in a single hotel[6] (with other locales within walking distance), like Godard & co. had done recently with *Slow Motion* and *First Name: Carmen*. A movie where the director can tell the crew to meet in the room next to his at two p.m. to shoot a couple of scenes, then he can go back to watching soccer or tennis on telly, and smoke those endless cigars...

But that would be enough for Godard: a fancy hotel and a bunch of actors. The Master can cook up a story around that. or at least some bits of business for the actors to do each day.

❋

What are the narrative and dramatic elements in *Détective*? Do we care? Do we need to know?

---

[4] A new addition to the Godard arsenal is the computer: in the hotel room characters, including the boxer, mess about with a computer. There's an early drawing programme on it, with an image of Nathalie Baye sketched with dots.
[5] The intertitles superimpose the word 'MORT' over the caption crediting the composers (and 'alas').
[6] And it's a fancy one, too – well, you might as well live comfortably, and let the financiers foot the bill.

OK, here's the plot: some hotel detectives, Uncle William (Laurent Terzieff)[7] and Isidore Neveu (Jean-Pierre Léaud) hole up in a hotel room and film the people on the street outside with a video camera and a monitor, accompanied by an 18 year-old girl, Ariel (Aurelle Doazan,[8] with whom they both have affairs – yes, it's the older man and much younger woman again in a God-Cinéma-Art movie). There's some narrative guff about the murder of a 'Prince' in the hotel two years ago.

One of the stars – Nathalie Baye – is Françoise, married to an ageing airline pilot, Émile, who resembles Charles Aznavour (Claude Brasseur);[9] there's something about money being owed to or by the Chenal couple.[10] There's a young boxer, Tiger Jones (Stéphane Ferrara), with a girlfriend called Princess of the Bahamas (Emmanuelle Seigner) who's often half-naked (providing the requisite Godardian T. and A. – which's utterly gratuitous), and hangers-on who include Julie Delphy, who spends her time playing the clarinet.[11] (During *Detective*, Godard asked Emmanuelle Seigner to go topless, which she did (on her first day of shooting), but she drew the line at full nudity, which Godard asked for on the third day (she was born in 1966, so was 18 at the time). Seigner claimed that Godard told her: 'but I only hired you because you had a nice ass'.[12] So she left. And Godard, as reliable as ever, duly included every single one of Seigner topless shots. And also a scene where boxer Jones gently bats each of the Princess's breasts with his gloves on – practising his left and right swings. Later, Seigner had no problem appearing nude in many movies – such as *The Ninth Gate* and *Bitter Moon*. Seigner married Roman Polanski in 1989).

Ariel is also seen semi-naked in several scenes, and Isidore Neveu's young aide also strips off her top (which Ariel sees and huffs off jealously). The double standard is alive and well in *Detective*: when Johnny Hallyday changes into a suit, for instance, it's off-screen (while the camera stays on Nathalie Baye). But when Ariel changes into a dress, she's in front of the camera, and when the Princess tries on different tops in an early scene, she's on display topless.

There's an ageing Mafia boss (Alain Cluny), suave and refined and grey, who's also addressed as Prince (part of the Sicilian Mafia,

---

7 Godard had considered Laurent Terzieff for the lead in *Breathless*. He would've been great.
8 Not every actor can do Godardian acting – you expect Cluny and Léaud to be comfortable with it. But a newbie like Doazan also gets it, and delivers a charming, wide-eyed teenager.
9 You may recognize Claude Brasseur – he was Arthur, one of the boorish youths in *Bande à Part*.
10 And Francoise is even portrayed as a hooker – tho' her husband doesn't know, as if we haven't seen that a million times before in a Godard movie.
11 The film alludes to fellatio – a man's hand grasps the clarinet as Delphy plays it.
12 In *Le Temps*, Geneva, January 12, 2000.

he's also called the Accountant. Cluny is certainly an elegant sight in pristine suits, as he was in films such as *La Dolce Vita*). His associates include a young girl, a young guy and a bodyguard, Angelo. And there's a boxing promoter with a stupid name, Jim Fox Warner (Johnny Hallyday), Françoise's one-time lover who brushes her off (the Chenals are on the verge of separating). Françoise and Warner have a romantic and fraught past (when the hubby's away on a flight, they rekindle their romance).

※

The setting for these groups of people is the Hotel Concorde in St Lazare, in Gay Paree. The plots interweave a little, but the plots themselves aren't particularly important (they're certainly not interesting). Along the way are portraits of people, but only cursory ones, half-involved, and indifferent, as if the film is always having its eye caught by other things going on in other hotel rooms. Without any dramatic shape, the vignettes simply pile up, one upon the other.

One of the references in *Détective* is to the William Shakespeare film that Jean-Luc Godard was to make two years later: the young woman with the detectives, Ariel, is carrying a Norman Mailer book (in an elevator), and she and Uncle William spend time discussing the Immortal Bard, or reading aloud from Shagspur (the two detectives call her Ariel, and Uncle William is addressed as Prospero. There are piles of copies of *The Tempest* on the table, which Uncle William chucks around later – books seem made to be thrown about in a Godard movie. Françoise and Jim also read books).

And there's a typewriter, *d'accord*, which Uncle William patters away on, and every time Isidore or Ariel enter the room, they go to the tripecutter and pull out the paper (which's always blank), and rip it up. William turns out to be the writer who can't write, a recurring Godardian motif (but not something the Master has ever suffered from!).

The references to *The Tempest* seem more fitting for a late Jean-Luc Godard project than having our man direct *King Lear* – in particular seeing Godard as a Prospero figure, a magician who breaks his staff and buries his books and retires to the Island of Rolle.[13]

In one extraordinary sequence (the best in the movie), Uncle William and Ariel read aloud from a dual-language edition of *The Tempest* play at the same time – Ariel reading the French text and

---
13 There are also references to Joseph Conrad and *Lord Jim*, which Françoise explains she used as a life guide – open it anywhere and the book would tell you something useful. And André Gide too: Françoise reads aloud from Gide's *L'École des femmes*, after going through a pile of books in the usual Godardian manner.

Uncle William reading the English translation on the facing page (they read a sentence each). That's such a simple performance idea, but it's so effective. It's a brief shot, but somehow says so much about literature and translation (especially when the characters reading aloud are identified as Ariel and Prospero).

As well as the Bard, there're references in *Detective* to Joseph Conrad (*Lord Jim*), André Breton, Léo Ferré (his song 'Richard'), lines fron the poet René Char, Antoine de Saint-Exupéry (*Viol de Nuit*), André Gide (*L'École des Femmes*), and nostalgic reminiscences of 1930s adventure tales by Edouard Peisson and the Orient Express. And lengthy, on-screen quotations of films such as *Beauty and the Beast* (Jean Cocteau, 1946) and an Erich von Stroheim picture (*The Last Squadron*, George Archainbaud, 1932). Lines from movies are also quoted in the soundtrack (with no indication given of their relation to the movie we're watching).

In amongst the fractious relationships in *Détective*, the conflicts and suppressed anger, there is quite a bit of tenderness on display too: characters are often embracing each other, stroking their fingers along necks, as if, no matter how vicious the betrayals of the past were, there's always the desire to reach out to the beloved when they're right in front of you. And the film replays a favourite Godardian motif: someone of the telephone saying 'oui... oui... oui!' in the tones of a lover, in answer to unheard but possibly sexual questions (along the lines of: 'will you do this?').

※

Among the most satisfying aspects of *Détective* is the wonderful Jean-Pierre Léaud, who's never given a bad performance, and is always worth watching. In *Détective*, whatever scene he's in, even if he has little to do, he effortlessly steals it. And in *Détective* it's moving to see a middle-aged, paunchy Léaud, quite different from the passionate, effusive, mercurial Léaud of Godard's early films, such as *La Chinoise* and *Masculin/Féminin*. Yes, but Léaud is *still* passionate, effusive and mercurial in *Détective*.

And Jean-Pierre Léaud is kind of the hero of the piece (he is the detective of the title) – it's Léaud who solves the mystery of the murder of the Prince (though he clumsily shoots his partner Uncle William in the process, who has also solved the case). Yes – *Détective* ends with a shoot-out, and yet again it's depicted in the Godardian style of not really bothering. Warner is shot, William is shot, Émile shoots the Prince's aide Angelo, but is shot himself (an echo of Claude Brasseur's demise in *Bande à Part*. Notice that the Prince himself isn't seen being shot). But where a Hollywood thriller would employ 200 shots to cover the scene, and a Hong Kong movie would use 400 (and numerous stunts), Godard uses four or five – and they're partial views too![14] (Godard is the anti-Sam Peckpinpah, the anti-John Woo).

※

A film like *Détective* can't have a satisfactory ending in the conventional narrative manner, but it hasn't promised it. either. Never once does *Détective* announce itself as thrilling thriller, or a dastardly detective tale. It's a Jean-Luc Godard film, irredeemably a Godard film (although Godard co-wrote it with Miéville, Sarde and Serbon).

But *Détective* is very watchable (mostly), not least due to the great cast that producers Alain Sarde and Christine Gozlan have assembled. The actors do their best with the very little they're given by the Creator and his collaborators – to say the roles in *Détective* are under-written would be an under-statement. But it doesn't matter, because the film takes the viewer along quite happily, and there are many jokes and witty asides along the way. OK, it's not *Grand Hotel*, but it is an enjoyable though minor film. And even when presented with hotels rooms and restaurants and a few actors – elements which are seemingly banal – Godard and Miéville can conjure up some inspired scenes. For instance, the beautiful close-ups of Hallyday and Baye embracing, or Baye and Brasseur (these close-ups are as impressive as those of Ingmar Bergman).

And the 1985 film ends on a deeply optimistic note: it's the romantic couple again, the lovers of Jean-Luc Godard's cinema (Isidore and Ariel), and they're sitting in a car, and after a brief exchange, as she works out what to say, she asserts: 'love is eternal' (Léaud embraces her). It's not only an echo of the gooey, sentimental ending of *Alphaville* (where Karina and Constantine drive off into the sunset), it's also Godard and Miéville once again stating the primacy of love.

What is *Détective* about? Several themes are explored: eternal love; being haunted by the past (and unable to escape it); the idea that lots of money can solve anything (all of the characters know it can't); being given One Last Chance; the younger generation vs. the older generation; and the decline of La France.

---

14 And elements such as police cars and ambulances are all done with sound effects and references in the dialogue. There's no need to hire an ambulance for the day on a Godard film – it can all be fixed in post-production.

29

KING LEAR

KING LEAR

King Lear (1987) was wr. & dir. by Jean-Luc Godard for Menahem Golan and Yoram Globus and Cannon Films. Tom Luddy was assoc. prod.; sound by Stanley B. Gill and François Mussy; Hervé Duhamel was A.D.; and Sophie Maintigneux was DP. Released: Sept 15, 1987. 90 mins.

Legend has it that Godard made the deal for *King Lear* during a very brief meeting at the Cannes Film Festival in 1986.[15] It sounded like an intriguing proposal: Jean-Luc Godard takes on William Shakespeare's *King Lear*, starring Burgess Meredith, Molly Ringwald, Peter Sellars and Woody Allen, and scripted by Norman Mailer. Actually, Godard wasn't particularly interested in Shakespeare, and hadn't read the play.[16]

King Lear's central characters were Peter Sellars as William Shakespeare, Jr. the Fifth, veteran Burgess Meredith as the aging patriarch, Don Learo, up-and-coming 'bratpack' actress Molly Ringwald (she had previously appeared in the teen romance *Pretty in Pink*), and Jean-Luc himself as a Fool/ Professor. (Secondary characters included Leos Carax, Suzanne Lanza, Freddy Buache, Michèle Pétin, Juliette Binoche and Julie Delphy).

Tom Luddy acted as a go-between for Jean-Luc Godard and the producers. *King Lear* was not released in France until 2002 (although it had been shown in New York City). Norman Mailer knew the movie was going to be a tough assignment, and that not much of his contribution would probably be used. He and Godard would meet and discuss the project in New York, but there was no script from Godard. Godard was not interested in reading the play, Mailer recounted. Mailer said it was his idea to have Lear as a Mafia don, Don Learo. But Godard never looked at Mailer's script (B, 494). For Mailer, in 2000, working on *King Lear* with J.L.G. was 'probably the most disagreeable single experience I've had in all these years as a writer' (B, 505).

As one would expect from the one-time guru of French New Wave cinema, Jean-Luc Godard's version of *King Lear* was not your standard Shakespearean adaptation. No elaborate sets or costumes, no grand set-pieces, no sword fights, no over-the-top acting, no bloody deaths, no intricate monologues, no 'how now, my Lords?', 'I prithee, sirrah' or flowery Shakespearean language, and very few actual lines of Shakespeare. Instead, what detractors saw was a bunch of recognizable

---

15 The crew included Hervé Duhamel, Sophie Maintigneux, Isabelle Czajka, and François Mussy.
16 While making *King Lear*, Godard reckoned he had crossed the Atlantic 70 times (by Concorde). That's a huge number of meetings. His travel expenses added to the movie's costs.

actors sitting around in hotel rooms, restaurants or wandering out onto balconies, a couple of characters pontificating about anything but the Bard, all intercut with nice but not particularly outstanding shots of lakes, mountains and skies, and accompanied by snatches of birds' song and classical music. In other words, it's the same movie as *Detective* and many others.

King Lear does look as if the actors and crew didn't venture out of their hotel much, but simply staged the film inside, with a skeleton crew being sent out to capture Peter Sellars wandering around and writing in a notebook (far too much of *King Lear* is just that: Sellars in a wood, by a lakeside, sitting on a rock, or wherever, not doing much above writing in a notebook.) Sellars can be regarded as a co-author of the movie: Godard acknowledged that Sellars had kept the film going, and Sellars had brought in actors like Molly Ringwald (she had appeared in *Tempest* (Paul Mazursky, 1982), which had a vague Shakespearean theme, and starred one of Godard's favourites – John Cassavetes). But altho' Sellars was an important collaborator for *King Lear*, it didn't leadn on to more collaborations.

Whereas in a masterwork like *JLG/ JLG* Jean-Luc Godard and his team produced an entrancing film essay, from very similar elements, in *King Lear* there are too many scenes of the filmmakers just messing about. In one lengthy take, Peter Sellars walks in a wood (near Rolle), followed by individuals who skip out from behind the trees and mime Sellars walking and writing in his notebook (they were models that Godard was using in a TV advert). That looks like a bit of stage business that Sellars, not Godard, improvized on the day – Sellars being a theatre director – and do you know what? It's pointless, and boring. Oh, I know not every Godard film can be as sublime as *Bande à Part* or *JLG/ JLG*, but this's just feeble.

Jean-Luc Godard's own attempt at a comical/ ironic/ satirical/ whatever performance was just plain embarrassing: he sported a ridiculous accent (he's doing a cliché mob boss, or Burgess Meredith), spoke out of the corner of his mouth, chomped on his trademark cigar, and wore dreadlocks made from wires, plugs and connectors. There were cameos from Norman Mailer and Woody Allen[17] (Godard had made a film, *J.L.G. Meets Woody Allen*, the year before. Allen wisely

---

[17] It was Tom Luddy's plan to keep promoting Allen to ensure money from the producers, Menahem Golan and Cannon. The interview film between Godard and Allen was partly created to maintain Allen's interest (B, 495). Godard even considered having Richard Nixon appear, discussing power and politics: he offered half a million dollars for a day's shooting. Allen appeared as a film editor working with a needle and thread, and reciting *Sonnet* no. 60. 'It didn't make any sense to me,' Allen said, 'but I knew I was in good hands'.

kept his contribution to a single scene and a shot or two. There was more, but it was cut out).

Peter Sellars is a rather bland presence in *King Lear* (Jean-Luc Godard isn't the only director in *King Lear* who can't act),[18] but Burgess Meredith is great – it actually would be wonderful to see Meredith doing King Lear as a mob boss. Meredith's Don Learo talks about the only way of doing *King Lear* in the contemporary era – as a gangster movie. He talks about gangsters like Bugsy Siegel and the foundation of Las Vegas. (Many of those elements come from Godard's unmade *The Story* project, with its view of America as a Las Vegas-ized entertainment culture).

It's not the only conception of *King Lear*, of course. Probably the most famous version of *King Lear* as a Mafia movie were the *Godfather* films; Francis Coppola had consciously worked in elements of William Shakespeare into his *Godfather* films (particularly the third movie of 1990).

Jean-Luc Godard had been associated with Francis Coppola's Zoetrope Studios in the early 1980s (and had an office there). Godard was signed by Zoetrope to direct *Bugsy Siegel*[19] (for $250,000), with Robert de Niro and Diane Keaton, which didn't emerge; later, Godard was due to make *The Story* (a.k.a. *The Audience*) for Zoetrope, but that too came to nothing (it emerged later as *Passion*). Zoetrope did distribute Godard's *Sauve Qui Peut,* which was marketed as Godard's triumphant return to feature filmmaking. (that was Godard's way of returning Zeotrope's investment).

❋

One of the interesting things about Jean-Luc Godard's *King Lear* was that it was acted and filmed in English. Gone were the subtitles; the familiar Godard intertitles (white lettering on black) were also in English ('virtue and power', 'power and virtue', 'King Lear: An Approach'). Godard had used American actors before (such as Jack Palance), but there were almost no attempts at speaking in French by the American actors (altho' Jane Fonda does in *Toiut Va Bien*). Seeing *King Lear* in English meant that non-French speaking spectators had a different viewing experience of a Godard film: they weren't scanning the subtitles in case they missed something (even the 'easier' Godard films could be dense and 'difficult' to follow).

---

18 Like Godard, Sellars had been associated with Zoetrope Studios: he was set to direct *On the Road*.
19 A movie, *Bugsy*, appeared in 1991, as a Warren Beatty star vehicle (plus all-star cast). It was run-of-the-mill Hollywood entertainment – if only Godard had got there first.

However, you wouldn't recommend *King Lear* as a first Jean-Luc Godard film to see: some viewers, watching the first five or six minutes, would walk out. It looks as if a Godard assistant has put the film together from dull images of people in hotels or restaurants, with Godard coming in during post-production to record a bitter voiceover to stitch the images together.[20] (Godard used the same technique in earlier films such as *Made In U.S.A.*).

Norman Mailer, one of at least four 'Great Writers' in the film (the others being Shakespeare, William Shakespeare, Jr., and Godard himself), was only on-screen for a few moments, in two takes (of the same shot) at the beginning of the film (his daughter Kate also appeared). The contractual details and comments on the acting by Godard in voiceover give some indication of the mess the film became. The filming was 'a train wreck', in Tom Luddy's opinion (Mac, 330). (However, Jean-Luc Godard's insistence of putting on a really silly voice for the narration ruins it). Maybe the shots of Mailer were there out of spite, or because Godard wanted to show off another celebrity in his film (Clint Eastwood,[21] among other actors, was also considered for the part). There had been a big bust-up between Mailer and Godard at the start of photography, after which Mailer left (but was still paid $500,000). Which left very little $$$$ for the rest of the movie.

There's an interview with Mailer in the 1970 book *The Film Director as Superstar* (Mailer had made some films by then – *Wild, Beyond the Law* and *Maidstone*), in which Mailer waxes lyrical about Godard: 'in a funny way, I think Godard approaches films in the same way that I do. Which is, he loves these myths'. Mailer called *Weekend* 'one of the best films I've seen in years... In a way, what he was talking about was the death of the 20th century'. But Mailer added that *Weekend* 'isn't pretentious enough, isn't grandi-loquent enough. The man has a vision. There are parts of that film that to me are like Hieronymous Bosch. I'd never been a Godard lover until I saw that film. It converted me. But I still think there are some terrible things in it. I think Godard is tiresome. He delights in boring the people he attracts' (103-4).

The hints of an incestuous relationship between King Lear and his daughter was the deal-breaker for Norman Mailer, according to Godard and Golan (B, 496-7). They are there in the play, and some theatre productions have brought them out, but Mailer didn't want to be

---

20 The readings of Shakespeare were by Ruth Maleczech and David Warrilow (recorded in Philip Glass's studio in Gotham).
21 *Détective* had been dedicated to Eastwood.

part of that kind of approach.

With the departure of Norman Mailer, J.L.G. came up with a number of possibilities: Prince and Sting would appear (!); he offered the lead to Lee Marvin and Rod Steiger; he had Al Pacino and Paul Newman read lines.

❋

The usual motifs of middle-to-late period Jean-Luc Godard were in plentiful supply in *King Lear*: the off-screen sounds of birds (seagulls and crows being a favourite);[22] shots of Lake Geneva; characters leafing through books; references to the history of image-making (in painting, cinema, etc, with many images of Giotto's angels in the famous *Lamentation* painting); people staring at the water; shots of Romantic landscapes, mountainscapes, lakesides; characters taking notes; lengthy takes; cuts to black leader; intertitles; overlapping dialogue; a variety of voiceovers; and complex interactions between narration, music, sound and image.

Among the many themes addressed in *King Lear* were writing, 'great' literature, painting, artistic production, capitalism, and French vs. American culture. *King Lear* was also very much, like all of Godard's cinema, a film-within-a-film, a film-about-film, a film about the history of cinema, and a film about the problems of making a film.

It wasn't *King Lear* at all, of course: it was a bunch of notes about possibly making a movie barely related to *King Lear*. The Maestro just wasn't interested in William Shakespeare, and didn't appear to know much about the play or Shakespeare in general. You can see that he's picked up on some lines in the play and other Shakespeare plays and done a Godardian riff on them. The quotation of 'nothing', a famous line in *King Lear*, became one of those Godardian plays on words, and part of the inter-titles: 'NOTHING', 'NO THING'.

Lacking in *King Lear* were nude or semi-nude women, compared to all of Godard's previous films since *Slow Motion* (maybe Molly Ringwald, 18 at the time, refused the statutory disrobing in a Jean-Luc Godard movie; though the filmmaker did turn in some big close-ups of Ringwald, with her large pouty mouth, and shots of her asleep). And there is a lithe young woman who makes some dance shapes before running out of frame.

But if the visuals and staging and so on in *King Lear* looked as if Jean-Luc Godard couldn't be bothered, at least the post-production

---

[22] Colin MacCabe calls the soundtrack of *King Lear* a masterpiece (Mac, 330). I wouldn't go that far, but it certainly is the soundtrack that saves *King Lear* from being what American producers call 'a piece of shit'. Maybe *King Lear* is one of those movies to project without the picture – just play the sound.

showed some promise, with a variety of voiceovers being orchestrated, which livened up the bland imagery. Meredith, Ringwald, Sellars, Godard and others provided narration.

As well as William Shakespeare, other ghosts in *King Lear* included dead directors: Méliès, Lang, Renoir, Mizoguchi, Welles, Pagnoll, Pasolini, Cocteau, Bresson and Truffaut (there were black-and-white stills of the *auteurs*). And painters: Giotto, Piero, Vermeer, Renoir, Leonardo, Morisot, Blake, Rembrandt, Goya, Angelico, and Manet (there were cuts to paintings, and shots of Cordelia[23] leafing through art books. And she goes to sleep with her hand on a book about Gustave Doré, an artist beloved of filmmakers). This material is right out of *Stor/ies of Cinema*, which Godard was preparing around the same time.

❄

After an hour of *King Lear*, you get the feeling that Jean-Luc Godard has made all the points he wants to make, and is running out of ideas fast. There's some messing about with images in a TV studio, on TV monitors (as in *Passion*). Peter Sellars lights a firework sparkler in front of the TV screens, and there's a close-up of a photocopier at work. It's all rather pathetic, really. If a film student delivered this kind of footage for a film course assignment, you'd give them a 'C', tell them they need to do better, and send them away to do it again.

I know some critics loved *King Lear* – Timothy Murray calls it 'a stunning portrayal of the challenges of the cultural loss of property and the recovery of a 'certain power' in the new social field of cinema'.[24] No. *Contempt* is stunning, *Hail Mary* is stunning, *Bande à Part* is stunning, but there's no way anyone could call Godard's *King Lear* stunning.[25] Wheeler Dixon regarded *King Lear* as 'by any measure, a brilliant and groundbreaking film' (173). Oh dear, no, no.

Ça suffit.

---

23 Originally, she would've been played by Norman Mailer's daughter Kate.
24 T. Murray, in M. Temple, 163.
25 Godard worked over-time to get the movie ready for Cannes in 1987. Reactions were mixed. Producer Golan was furious that one of his private telephone conversations had been included (B, 505). Ultimately, *King Lear* didn't make much of an impression.

CLAUDE BRASSEUR
NATHALIE BAYE
JOHNNY HALLYDAY
DÉTECTIVE
A FILM BY JEAN-LUC
GODARD
WITH LAURENT TERZIEFF • JEAN-PIERRE LÉAUD • ALAIN CUNY
DEDICATED TO: JOHN CASSAVETES • EDGAR G. ULMER • CLINT EASTWOOD
spectra

DÉTECTIVE

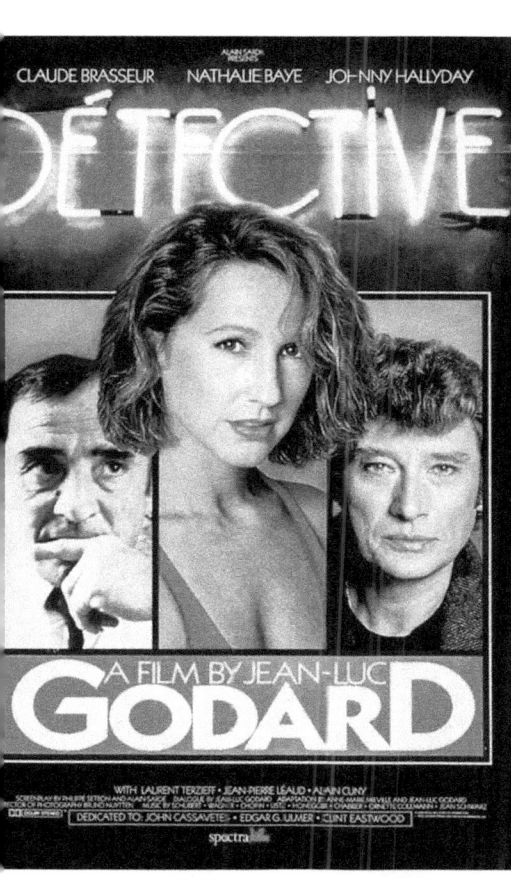

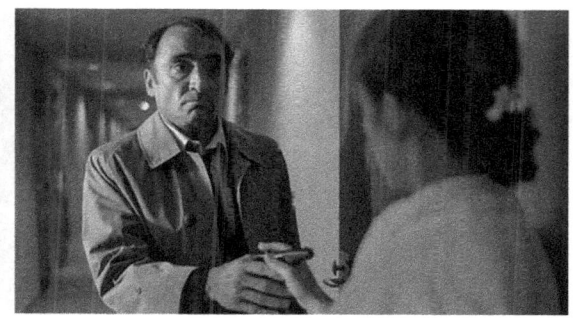

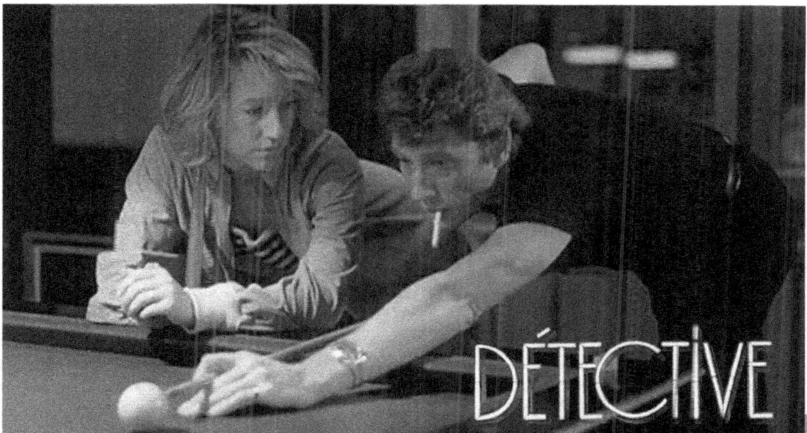

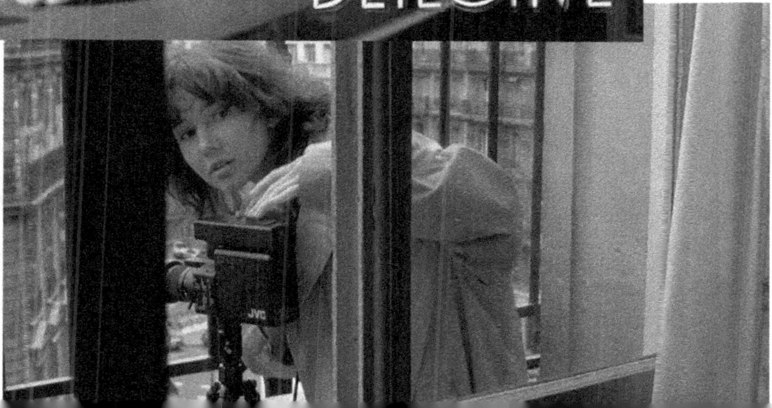

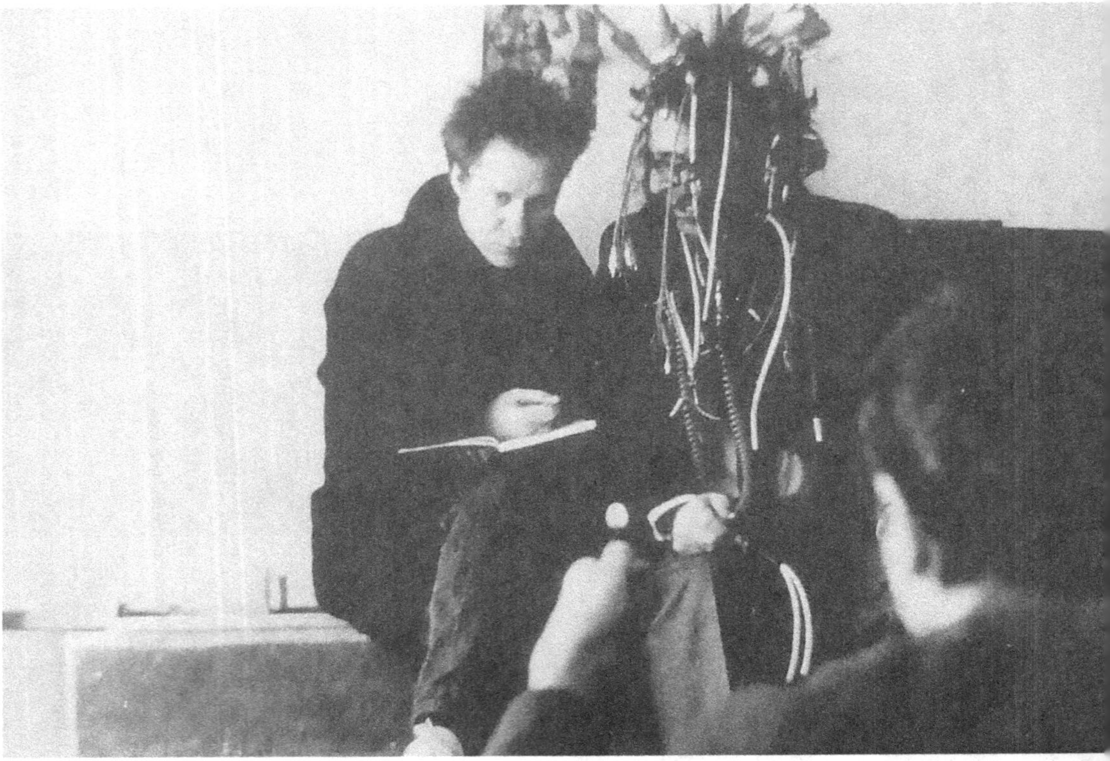

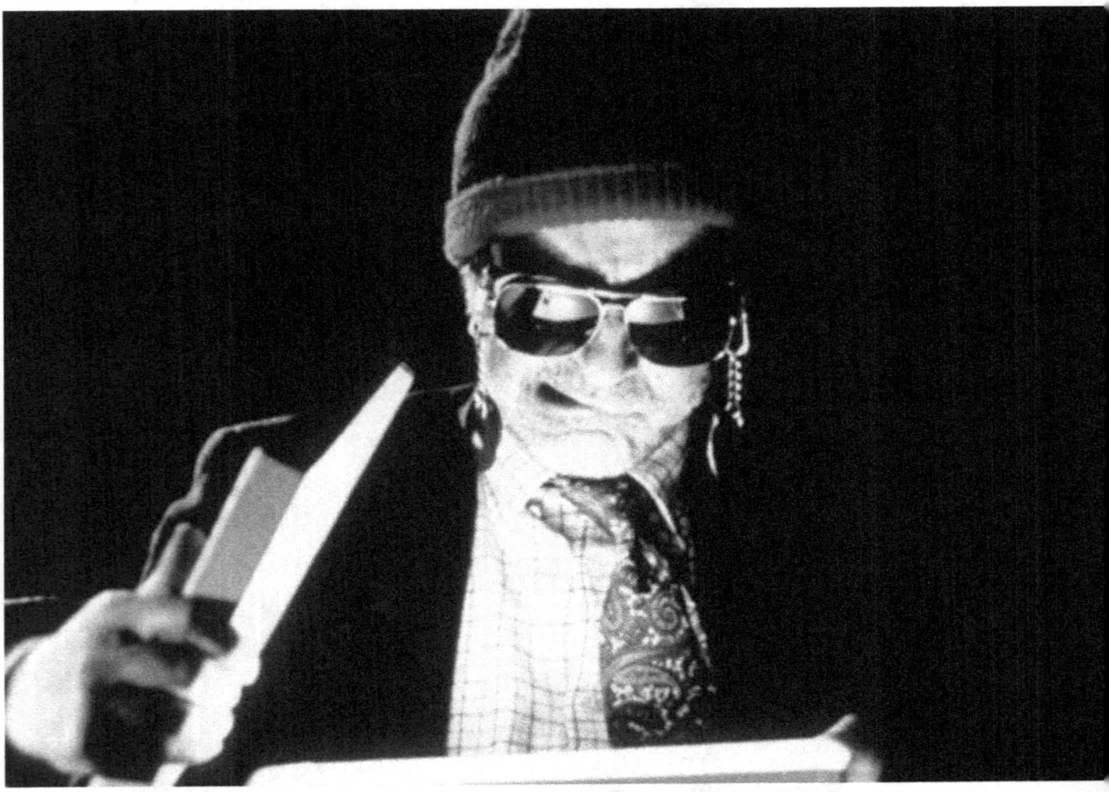

30

HISTOIRE(S) DU CINÉMA

(HI)STOR(IES) OF CINEMA

Jean-Luc Godard produced an epic history of cinema, between 1989 and 1998, *Histoire(s) du Cinéma* (which means *Stor(ies) of Cinema*, as well as *Histor(ies) of Cinem*a).1 This was a major work, and has generated a good deal of critical comment. As well as being a history of cinema, it was also a history of the age – and a history of Godard himself. It was completed in 1998 (but may develop further): there were five audio CDs (from Edition of Contemporary Music Records),2 a video release of the 8 parts on video from Gaumont (running to 266 minutes), and a boxed set of 4 books from Gallimard.3 A 90-minute 'best of' film was edited for cinemas: *Le Moment choisi des Histoire(s) de cinéma*, 2004).

Histoire(s) du Cinéma was produced by Canal Plus/ Centre National de la Cinématographie/ France 3/ Gaumont/ La Sept/ Télévision Suisse Romande/ Vega Films (plus Godard's own companies: Peripheria, Sonimage and JLG Films). Pierre Binggeli and Hervé Duhamel were DPs. It was broadcast in full on Canal + in 1999.

There were eight parts/ chapters in the histories of cinema enterprise:

1. 1A *Toutes les Histoires* (51minutes)
2. 1B *Une Histoire Seule* (42m)
3. 2A *Seul le Cinéma* (26m)
4. 2B *Fatale Beauté* (28m)
5. 3A *La Monnaie de l'Absolu* (27m)
6. 3B *Une Vague Nouvelle* (27m)
7. 4A *Le Contrôle de l'Univers* (27m)
8. 4B *Les Signes Parmi Nous* (38m)

The *Histoire(s) du Cinéma* project was one that Jean-Luc Godard could not leave alone. He kept tinkering with it for months, to the point where it seemed obsessive to outsiders. 'I would have added, to the six hours, two hundred hours of annexes, like little footnotes', he admitted. (Easy to run to 100s of hours, when the movies quoted are 90-120 mins long, and you want to use longer extracts).

When *Histoire(s) du Cinéma* was complete, Jean-Luc Godard re-edited the earlier material to match the later work. He could've gone on

---

1 It was originally intended for schools.
47 E.C.M has also released the soundtrack of *Nouvelle Vague*. It was typical of Godard to remark (of *Nouvelle Vague*) that the soundtrack on its own would be better – even better than the images on their own (in *L'Humanité*, May 19, 1990).
3 Godard wanted *Histoire(s) du Cinéma* to be released on DVD, but it was released on video instead (by Gaumont). There were also 4 CDs. And there was a book, published by the prestigious press Gallimard.

and on, layering image after image. Even as it is, *Histoire(s) du Cinéma* looks highly worked-over: you can see how Godard and his team have gone back over each episode and enhanced it visually and aurally.

An enormous undertaking, Godard set to work on *Histoire(s) du Cinéma* in 1985, when he signed with Gaumont. One of the biggest tasks was to screen a huge number of classic movies, to find the parts he wanted to use.

The soundtrack includes composers such as Franz Schubert, Arvo Pärt, Igor Stravinsky, Dimitri Shostakovitch, Anton Webern, Arthur Honegger, Bernard Herrmann, David Darling, jazz and pop (John Coltrane, Otis Redding, Leonard Cohen), and of course the famous 'B's: Ludwig von Beethoven, Bela Bartók and Godard's beloved Johann Sebastian Bach.

In *Histoire(s) du Cinéma*, Jean-Luc Godard delivered a poetic document of cinema in his highly idiosyncratic style of overlays and endless quotations, a montage style all his own, which combined multiple voices, layers of sounds and music, sound clips from films, captions, and an endless stream of visuals (interspersed with images of Godard at work in his offices, typing or writing or talking). *Histoire(s) du Cinéma* was a super-dense collage of photos, music, sounds, movie clips, and written texts, taking in prints (Rembrandt, Doré), paintings (Turner, Moreau, Renoir, Goya, Grünewald, Delacroix, Kandinsky, van Gogh, Uccello, Klimt, Gentileschi, Giotto, Botticelli, Angelico, Fuseli, Caravaggio, Blake, El Greco, Piero, Monet, Manet, Picasso, Byzantine ikons), writers (Rimbaud, Céline, Brecht, Bataille, Faulkner, Flaubert, Duras, Valéry, Hugo, Dante, Ovid, Aragorn, Malraux, Proust, Gide), *ciné*-heroes like Henri Langlois, newsreel, pornography, television, and complex video techniques, such as super-impositions, irses, masked frames, visual mixes, flash cuts,[4] repeated phrases, and echo and reverb effects on voices and sounds. And it's Godard's vision, his narration, his philosophy, his ideas, and his emotions that unites it all, that makes it all work. Certainly there are very few filmmakers on the planet who could've pulled it off.

Histoire(s) du Cinéma plays with text in a dazzling manner, too, with words revealed in numerous ways, and also cut up into shorter phrases, in classic, Godardian fashion (from 'histoires' to 'toi', for instance, or 'cinemoi'). Many times the phrases are the titles of movies, or the titles of classic novels, as are the phrases that the voiceover

---

[4] The strobing effects (out of white as well as black) become irritating.

repeats. Some of the captions reprise word games from the 1960s movies. In one segment, the accent atop a letter is moved slowly across the screen, so it becomes 'né'. Godard is without question the most word obsessed, letter obsessed, phrase obsessed filmmaker in history.

Histoire(s) du Cinéma also layers sounds densely: there will typically be music plus a sound clip from a movie, plus Godard or an actor in voiceover. Sometimes two voiceovers. Godard also included scenes of actors reading texts.

This is Godard's *Last Will and Testament*, his theological apology and partial *Gospel*, and his eulogy and memorial – to cinema... to his life's work... to life itself.

No one else could have made it – no one else *would* have made it. Throughout *Histoire(s) du Cinéma*, Jean-Luc Godard provides a constant voiceover. Sometimes he's just repeating the phrase 'histoires du cinéma' (occasionally with silly bits of echo added). The repetitions become redundant quickly. But if you think Godard has run out of things to say, and has taken to mouthing the title of his documentary (or the poignant title of a fave film), don't be fooled: this man can talk about cinema longer and more knowledgeably than any other filmmaker in the history of cinema. And, sure enough, he starts up again, talking, talking, talking, as only Jean-Luc Godard can.

And of course there were plentiful references and images from all of the great filmmakers in *Histoire(s) du Cinéma*: Griffith, Chaplin, Méliès, Pasolini, Truffaut, Whale, Gance, Dreyer, Disney, Antonioni, Welles, Fellini, Carné, Eisenstein, Rossellini, De Sica, Hawks, the Marxes, De Mille, Murnau, Bresson, etc (and particular favourites like Hitchcock, Lang and Welles, plus the Three Jeans – Cocteau, Vigo and Renoir, and scenes such as the end of *Duel In the Sun*, a cowboy and a guitar in *Johnny Guitar*, Natalie Wood and John Wayne in *The Searchers*, Jimmy Stewart rescuing Kim Novak in the Bay in *Vertigo*, the ball in *The Leopard*, the monster in *Frankenstein*, Joan of Arc burning at the stake, are repeated many times). Plus *Bicycle Thieves, Notorious, Apocalypse Now, Persona,* Disney cartoons, *Man Hunt, Theorem,*[5] *Snow White, The Passion of Joan of Arc, Sunrise, Frankenstein, Only Angels Have Wings, Scarface, The Night of the Hunter, King Kong, Rear Window, Umberto D, Amarcord, Stromboli, Senso, Nosferatu, The Lady From Shanghai, Macbeth, Die Nibelungen, Metropolis, Salò, The Hawks and the Sparrows, The Gospel According To Matthew,* etc. And countless images of film stars. Oh, and quite a bit

---

5 A scene featuring his former wife, Anne Wiazemsky.

of porn – people fucking insome vintage b/w porn, and some porn on video. For Godard, the (hi)stor(ies) of cinema must also include the history of pornography (of course – porn was produced from the get-go of cinema, and porn is at the forefront when any new tchnology or delivery system is introduced).

Nearly all of the films included came from the 1910s-1960s, and most were from Europe and the U.S.A. (Godard happily included many clips and sounds from his own movies, including *Pierrot le Fou, Le Petit Soldat, Contempt, Alphaville, Hélas Pour Moi, Passion, Band of Outsiders, One Plus One, King Lear,* etc). Although he didn't like to see his own movies (as with many artists), he did sometimes watch them – at the Montréal retrospective of his cinema, for instance, in 1977.

No one can miss that half or more of the film references are from 'Ollywooood cinema: this from a man who loudly complains about U.S. colonialism and consumerism and corruption and conformism and capitalism (all the naughty words beginning with 'C').

Numerous N. American filmmakers are pointedly *not* included in *Histoire(s) du Cinéma*, including the most successful film director in history, Steven Spielberg (one of Godard's *bête noires*). So, no Scorsese, Allen, Cameron, Lucas, Coppola, etc.

Histor/es of Cinema is wilfully eccentric compared to the standard documentaries on cinema: Bertrand Tavernier produced a story of French cinema in 2016 (*Voyage à travers le cinéma francais*), which included Tavernier chatting affably in interviews with clips from films, plus his voiceover. Martin Scorsese, Ken Russell, Federico Fellini[6] and others have taken a similar approach to personal accounts of film history. Well, that's just too conventional – too 'bourgeois'! – for Godard. (But we might wish that many other filmmakers had produced their own interpretation of the history of cinema – Kurosawa, Pasolini, Bergman, Coppola, Paradjanov, Fassbinder, and Welles, for example).

Throughout *Histoire(s) du Cinéma,* we often enjoy the quotations from movies more than anything in the documentary itself: the outrageous ending of *Duel In the Sun,* for ex, as Jennifer Jones crawls thru the dust towards Gregory Peck, or the matchless ballroom scene from *The Magnificent Ambersons,* or Lillian Gish on the ice in *Way Down East,* or Gene Kelly dancing in *An American In Paris,* or the dreamy boat trip in *The Night of the Hunter.*

An eccentric format was developed by Godard for this project:

---

6 One of the most enjoyable personal accounts of cinema is Federico Fellini in his *A Director's Notebook* of 1969 and his *Interview* (1987). Also, *Amarcord, 8 1/2* and *City of Women,* for instance.

there are several prestige TV formats which we could conceive Godard helming about the history/ story of cinema: obvious choices: a series of interviews between Godard and filmmakers, historians, critics, actors, etc. Godard could shoot the breeze (*circa* mid-1980s) with Samuel Fuller, say, or Lauren Bacall (we would love to see Godard chatting with Anna Karina, for instance, about their 1960s collaborations in cinema). Another obvious choice: Godard is interviewed on a range of cinematic topics (by several guest interviewers, perhaps). Obvious choice no. 3: Godard presents explorations of his ten best films from selected years (as he did in his film criticism), or his top 100 films. Because *Histoire(s) du Cinéma,* succulent as it is, doesn't discuss any particular movie for more'n a very short time.

Histoire(s) du Cinéma presents a selective view of the origins of film which emphasizes photography and painting and literature and high art and misses out what many regard as the true origins of cinema – in vaudeville, theatre, street entertainers, puppet shows, travelling players, funfairs, side shows and circuses. And, in the world of publishing: magazine serials, Victorian penny dreadfuls, sleazy newspaper stories, etc. But no, *Histoire(s) du Cinéma* and Jean-Luc Godard doesn't want to admit that cinema could come out of circuses and clowns and theatre and farce and pantomime and folk art and trashy, popular fiction – that's just not hi-falutin' enough. (Godard insists here that cinema isn't communication, and didn't arise from communication, nor is it entertainment).

Some of the collections of film quotations are grouped in themes: people in water or in boats, for example, or sex, or corpses (plenty of corpses – cinema is filmed death, as Godard asserted, and there's plenty of newsreel imagery of dead bodies).

*

Jean-Luc Godard appears a good deal in *Histoire(s) du Cinéma*: sometimes he's in photos, sometimes he's sitting in his offices, just smoking (including in slo-mo). In one scene he's shirtless, wearing a cap. And he's always smoking a cigar, of course. And often at his typewriter, or handwriting at a desk. It's kind of bizarre. If Steven Spielberg or George Lucas included images of themselves in a documentary just doing nothing, sitting about and solemnly muttering a phrase like 'the magic mountain' occasionally, critics would laugh at them. But with Godard, it's 'art', it's 'serious'.

Yet, when Jean-Luc Godard stops prattling or lecturing the audience, *Histoire(s) du Cinéma* can be moving, in a way that his films not always are: when the filmmaker shuts up and lets the music and images work their magic, the effect is emotional. This is where *Histoire(s) du Cinéma* achieves greatness. There is a hommage to Italian cinema, for instance, that is absolutely breathtaking (partly because *Histoire(s) du Cinéma* allows the images to flow without narration, while a song by Ricardo Cocciante plays). And as one would expect, *Histoire(s) du Cinéma* discusses the New Wave at length.

Histoire(s) du Cinéma has received some of the most ecstatic reviews in Godard's career, with comparisons to Dante Alighieri's *Divine Comedy*, no less! Antoine de Baecque called it 'unrivalled' and 'æsthetically peerless... the culmination of our time'.[7] 'So strong is his love of the cinema that Godard communicates it to us like a trance', opined Jacques Siclier.[8] It has been the subject of dossiers and special issues of publications such as *Art Press*, *Le Monde*, and of course *Cahiers du Cinéma* (several issues).

James Williams, raving about one of the best-known parts of *Histoire(s) du Cinéma*, where Liz Taylor and *A Place In the Sun* is montaged with newsreel footage of the concentration camps and a Giotto painting (*Noli me tangere*), spoke of

> a new and unheralded form of touching across form, encompassing art, cinema and video – a kind of hyper-tripping and troping by Godard such as that the various elements banal and divine are stretched to their limit and reversed.[9]

When the issue of the Shoah is raised in *Histoire(s)*, once again Jean-Luc Godard comes across as possessive about it, as if only *he* has the moral right, the highest level of intellectual sophistication, and the God-like perception to discuss the Holocaust. It's like who uses the word *justice* first in an argument: Godard gets in there first, evokes the abomination of World War Two, and with that behind him he can shoot anyone else down.

Cinema should have shown the concentration camps, but no one wanted to see them: this was one of Jean-Luc Godard's recurring issues in his later work. His notion was that if the Holocaust had been filmed, and had been *seen*, it might've helped to avert later catastrophes: but 'it started again, so to speak, Vietnam, Algeria – it's not finished – Biafra, Afghanistan, Palestine', Godard remarked in 1995.[10] Nothing was 'unfilmable' for Godard, even if it was the Holocaust. Everything could

---

7 In M. Temple, 2004, 122.
8 J. Siclier, *Le Monde*, May 6, 1989.
9 J. Williams, in M. Temple, 135.
10 In a speech in Frankfurt, when Godard accepted the Theodor Adorno prize (B, 564).

be and should be filmed, for Godard.

The Second World War looms large over *Histoire(s) du Cinéma* (Jean-Luc Godard also refers to many other conflicts of the modern age), and its effect on Western society (and also on European cinema). *Histoire(s) du Cinéma* comes back to Germany, Adolf Hitler and the Holocaust many times. Godard was certain that footage of the Germans killing victims existed; it would be film of the unfilmable (but nobody had tried to find it). The failure to recover the footage of the concentration camps and to make movies about the Shoah resulted in the death of cinema in Europe and the triumph of N. American movies, for Godard. WWII saw the U.S.A. victorious over the cinemas of Europe: Germany lost the war, and North Amerika won the cultural war. In this idiosyncratic and controversial Godardian view, both Germany and North Amerika attempted a political colonization of Europe: and Godard aligned North Amerika with Germany in terms of right-wing, fascistic and military ambitions. Adolf Hitler used the war to wipe out European Jews, and the U.S.A. used the war to wipe out European culture (cinema included).

It was the Italian cinema (and *Rome: Open City* in particular) that resisted North Amerika's colonization of European cinema, Godard reckoned. Anything that *resists* Amerika is valorized in Godard's worldview.

❋

Stor/ies of Cinema is great for playing Spot the Film Quotation – a parlour game popular with Gitanes-puffing, Left Bank intellectuals and Berkeley film geeks. But *Stor/ies of Cinema* is Spot the Film Quotation at a very high level – this is beyond Trivial Pursuit or Strip Poker. You don't get any points for identifying *Vertigo* or *The Magnificent Ambersons* or *The Rules of the Game*, for example. Oh no, you've got to work *much* harder than that! (But you do score if you can recognize *Wind From the East* or a painting by Gustave Moreau). The prize? A box of cigars and a year's free admission to the arthouse of your choice).

Of course, absolutely no one else on Earth would be able to identify every single film source, except the God of Cinema Himself. There is a thrill, if you love cinema, of seeing images from *Intolerance* or *Way Down East* or *North By North-west*, within this particular cultural context.

I guess the filmmaker had to use well-known movies to a degree; otherwise, if everything was a quotation from an obscure work, which hardly anybody would recognize, it wouldn't be so effective. You need those quotations from *On the Town* or *Citizen Kane* or *Rome: Open City*.

※

Let's have a look at some of the episodes:

Episode one of *Histoire(s)* – *How I Became a World-Famous Film Director (On 5 Francs a Day)* – a.k.a. *Toutes les Histoires* (1988, 51 mins) – begins with the Maestro sitting in a room at his Brother typewriter, pecking out phrases with his forefingers like 'the rules of the game' and 'the heart of darkness'. He is in a serious frame of mind, as if being serious and sombre is the only way to think of cinema, or to present cinema, or to analyze cinema. (Meanwhile, the machine sounds of the tripecutter printing out the words on paper is over-used: include it once or twice, yes, we get the idea, monsieur – but that *very* irritating noise continues throughout *Toutes les Histoires* and into the subsequent episodes. Godard also reprises the bizarre sight of mics moving about on mic stands from *Alphaville*).

Later, Jean-Luc Godard is seen next to shelves of books. Just like one of his charas, he picks up volumes and reads aloud ominous phrases from them (or seems to add them to his typed text).

In *Stor/ies of Cinema,* each episode quotes from other episodes – partly, perhaps, as a kind of reminder of the previous installments (a regular practice in television, where audiences have to be updated constantly). Or it might be more padding from the Godster.

So titles are repeated, as are captions (why waste a good caption on one outing?). And there are multiple quotes from the same bits of *Duel In the Sun, The Leopard, Vertigo,* etc (sometimes documentaries re-use the same film clips because they can't afford different clips from a movie. But in Godard's case, it's unlikely that the producers paid for the clips he used, so if he's repeating them it's for effect).[11]

There're extracts from a torrent of films, including: *Citizen Kane, La Strada, Alexander Nevsky, Battleship Potemkin, Rashomon, The Rules of the Game, On the Town, Ben-Hur, The Birth of a Nation, Nosferatu, Die Niebelungen, Metropolis, Haxan, A Place In the Sun, Othello, Beauty and the Beast, An American In Paris, Dracula, Orphée,* Hollywood musicals, porn, etc.[12] (The first quote from Godard's own movies is, appropriately enough, a close-up of the divine Anna Karina from *Band of Outsiders*, from the scene in the Metro, and Karina kissing Belmondo in *Pierrot le Fou*).

---

11 Or it could be more padding.
12 *Toutes les Histoires* demonstrates that North America and Europe will be the primary areas of study in *Histoire(s) du Cinéma*.

Charlie Chaplin is one of the first figures to be trotted out before the eager viewer in *Histoire(s) du Cinéma* (a British filmmaker!), followed by, in the first installment: Sergei Eisenstein, Federico Fellini, Géorges Méliès, Orson Welles, Irwin Thalberg, Jean Renoir, Fritz Lang, Erich von Stroheim, F.W. Murnau, Akira Kurosawa, George Stevens, John Ford, Jean Renoir, Charlie Chaplin, D.W. Griffith, Max Ophüls, Robert Flaherty, the Marx Brothers, Jean Cocteau, etc, and actors such as Liz Taylor, Lon Chaney, Rita Hayworth, Humphrey Bogart, Alexander Dovzhenko, James Cagney, Orson Welles, Marlene Dietrich, Fred Astaire, Gene Kelly, Laurel & Hardy, Bela Lugosi, etc.

And painters such as Gustave Moreau, Vincent van Gogh, J.M.W. Turner, Edouard Manet, Francisco de Goya, Henri de Toulouse-Lautrec, Géorges Seurat, Claude Monet, Rembrandt van Rijn, etc.

And figures such as Vladimir Lenin, Howard Hughes, Daniel Defoe, André Gide, Joseph Conrad, Adolf Hitler, André Malraux, F. Scott Fitzgerald, etc.

Howard Hughes is a curious choice for our attention, consuming several moments in 1A: *Toutes les Histoires,* forming a sort of mini-documentary on the famous tycoon (cue images of planes, *Only Angels Have Wings*, Jane Russell, and Hughes in his bizarre recluse persona).

World War II, Adolf Hitler and the death camps are also part of ep. 1 of *Histoire(s) du Cinéma* (topics which the documentary returns to several times). World War II looms over this incredible documentary series as the most oppressive and damaging spectre that will never ever be vanquished (when the first episode seems done with WWII, it lurches back into view again. It can't keep away from it. The scenes from World War Two newsreel footage remind us that for Godard and for so many other people, the war wasn't just the defining event in their lives, it has never gone away, never been subsumed underneath whatever followed it. Indeed, it often seems to me that we are still living in the shadow of WWII).

✻

There's no doubt that the first installment in *Histoire(s) du Cinéma* is an absolutely spectacular piece of television. The director has decided to go all-out, and include pretty much everything he can – and not only from cinema, but from painting, from literature, from political life and even more celebrity culture.

Toutes les Histoires is a barrage of material that threatens to overwhelm the viewer. Jean-Luc Godard doesn't hold back – he gives it his all (which is considerable). *Toutes les Histoires* announces that

Histoire(s) du Cinéma will be a history of the 20th century as well as the history of one particular artform or industry.

And so on for seven more installments.

*

When *Histories/ Stories of Cinema* moves into chapter two (entitled: *Cigar Commercial II: How I Learnt To Smoke Like a Movie Mogul = Une Histoire Seule, A History Alone*, 1989, 42 mins), it seems to be more of the same (hell, it *is* More Of The Same!). The enigmatic flow of images and sounds doesn't alter much, or announce a new theme, and the narration by Mr Godard refuses to clarify (or explain) the documentary but continues to pontificate at length (as well as to repeat certain phrases, just in case we don't get it the first time. We do, actually, Uncle Jean, we *do* get it the first time and we don't need/ require/ want repetitions: we are very, very clever, and very, very quick at consuming TV/ cinema/ ideas/ anything).[13]

Now the Master of Ceremonies quotes from his own *Contempt, Wind From the East* and *Weekend,* along with a massive flood of other movies, including Hitchcock, Pasolini, Murnau, Lang, De Mille, Griffith, Disney, Renoir and the rest of the Immortal Gang (he's still sitting at his typewriter, picking books off shelves and tap-tap-tapping away. Godard presents scriptwriting as lesson one on a secretarial course at a local college: first, buy a typewriter; second, learn to type with two fingers; third, and most important of all, you must type while holding a cigar between your teeth. If you can't do that, you fail. There are no refunds).

Stor/ies of Cinema expands its remit to include disquisitions on religion and philosophy as well as cinema and 20th century atrocities.

*

The *Third Lesson of the Gospel According To Jean-Luc Godard* (2A: *Seule de Cinéma*, 1997, 26 mins) contains an interview, or a sort of discussion, between Godard and Alain Bergala. In typical Godardian style, the conflab is filmed entirely from one angle, with the Master of Cinema framed on the far left, between Bergala and the camera. The two men don't talk *to* each other but *at* each other. And, dialogue aside, the scene is more about smoking, about lighting cigars and Marlborough cigarettes, and about tapping them out in ashtrays like nervous patients (the inmates have been allowed to smoke while they chat in a side-room in a mental asylum).

---

13 Or Maybe an exec at Gaumont told Godard that television audiences require constant reminders of what the hell they're watching (there being 2,089,202 TV channels in France alone).

Whatever Alain Bergala says in the discussion, Godard trumps it, and his presence dominates. It's a stitch-up, like the chat in the hotel between Godard and Michel Piccoli in another film documentary, *2 x 50 Ans de Cinéma Français* (1995).

And that's not all: *Stor/ies of Cinema* allows the conversation to fade in and out; it muffles it with music and sound effects; and it obscures the two men with images. In other words, the standard format of all television everywhere – people talking in rooms (whether it's drama, news, soap operas or chat shows) – has been Godardized, given the God-Art treatment (well, you wouldn't expect Godard to deliver a straight-up television interview or discussion).

Elsewhere in 2A: *Seule de Cinéma*, Julie Delphy turns up to declaim pointedly while doing a bunch of banal things: reading a book... taking a bath...[14] studying her contract with Périphéria/ J.L.G. Films... she harangues someone off-screen with assertions about cinema... And, with its customary eccentricity, once an actress has been hired to recite filosofikal verbiage, *Stor/ies of Cinema* cuts away to other things, and also drowns her voice out with film quotations, or Godard's on-going interview with Bergala.

The quotations come thick and fast in episode 2A: *Seule de Cinéma* – *ciné*-folk such as Keaton, Laurel & Hardy, Truffaut, Disney, Hawks, and more porn; plus more literati: Poe, Baudelaire, Joyce, Faulkner, Homer, etc; plus more painters: Klimt, Turner, Courbet, Böcklin, etc; plus more film stars: James Dean, Fred Astaire, Robert Mitchum, Jerry Lewis, etc.

1955's *The Night of the Hunter* (which was directed by a Brit, Jean-Luc!), receives a lengthy quotation – it's the scene where Robert Mitchum chases the kids into a rowing boat, and they elude him. With typical eccentricity, however, the film quote has its soundtrack replaced with something else.

✻

In the next episode of *Histoire(s)* – 2B: *Fatale Beauté* – Anne-Marie Miéville pops up to talk about time and space. I think. I'm not sure. Because it's difficult to remember anything that Miéville says: she has the tone, the appearance and the delivery of the European intellectual (of course she wears black, she smokes, she's in a nice, neat hotel room), but what she actually means, and how you can apply anything that Miéville says to anything, is a mystery. Any intellectual, if you pay them 20 Euros and a pack of Gauloises, can rattle off

---

14 Delphy isn't eroticized, however, as she was in *Detective* (altho' she is filmed in the bath, for absolutely no reason whatsoever).

pseudo-filosofikal monologues like this (we all can – it's easy), but, like the other present-day material in *Histoire(s) du Cinéma*, it amounts to very little.

Meanwhile, among the film references in 2B: *Fatal Beauty* are Chaplin, Murnau, Walt Disney, Sarte, Gustave Doré, Henry Fuseli, Pierre Renoir, and Géorges Seurat. Plus films such as *The Searchers, King Kong, Duel in the Sun, Bicycle Thieves,* and *The Magnificent Ambersons.* And the Maestro's own *Contempt, First Name: Carmen, Weekend* and *Band of Outsiders.*

❊

One of the most moving montages in the output of Godard is the pæan to Italian cinema in 3A: *La Monnaie de l'Absolu,* which the Maestro reckons was a genuine refutation of both Amerikan and Deutsch political domination. The films in the beautiful Italian *hommage* include *Umberto D, La Terra Trema, Rome: Open City, Pigsty, Francesco, The Hawks and the Sparrows, Amarcord, Theorem, Stromboli, Bitter Rice, Bicycle Thieves, The Swindler (Il Bidone), The Leopard, Senso,* and *La Strada.* (However, as Italian directors such as Elio Petri pointed out, America had already been colonizing Italy culturally from the 1930s – via Hollywood cinema. That is, before World War Two. And after the war, *teenagers in Europe <u>wanted</u> all things American*).

The tribute to Italian cinema overshadows everything else in episode 3A: *La Monnaie de l'Absolu,* which also includes references to *The Birds,* newsreel, and artists such as Goya, Bosch, Leonardo, Hopper, Manet, Corot, Morisot, and Piero, and writers such as Zola. *Pierrot le Fou* is quoted, too. Robert Schumann's *Kindersehen* plays underneath some of the scenes as a counterpoint to the doom-laden music cues assembled for the war-torn images.

Episode 3A is all about death, how photography and cinema can capture it and process it. WWII, as the ultimate manifestation of mass death thus far in history, is referenced throughout the installment. So that *Stor/ies of Cinema* might be called *How Cinema Saw World War Two.* The war is the Year Zero for Godard, when the contemporary era really began, or when it was fixed for good. And evoking WWII for Godard inevitably means the concentration camps (with the Resistance as a footnote). [15]

What is cinema? What can cinema do? are some of the questions

---

15 Godard maintains that no great movies were produced during WWII. Not true, of course: *Casablanca, Rebbeca, To Have and Have Not, Shadow of a Doubt, The Grapes of Wrath, The Great Dictator, The Life and Death of Colonel Blimp, Double Indemnity,* etc. And how about *The Maginificent Ambersons* and *Citizen Kane?*

raised in episode 3A. And the answers are deliberaterly vague: something mysterious is what cinema is, and what cinema can do is... something (*quelque chose*).

In one bit of unsatisfying business filmed in this episode of *Histoire(s) du Cinéma* (3A: *La Monnaie de l'Absolu*), a woman reads aloud from a book and is approached by an old man who says something to her. We might recognize the man – Alain Cuny – but the woman (Marie Dea) isn't introduced properly or given a close-up. We need footnotes here, or more pointers: for ex, the woman is reading some Emily Brontë poetry, and Cuny is replaying a moment from a 1942 picture (*Les Visiteurs du Soir*).

❊

Episode 6 – 3B: *Une Vague Nouvelle* – is More Of The Same, but with some wistful, wry comments on the French New Wave and what it all meant. Well, we know that Godard doesn't like to go back and talk about those times. It's another age to him (and his reluctance shows here). But maybe his producers (Canal+/ Centre National de la Cinématographie/ France 3/ Gaumont/ La Sept/ Télévision Suisse Romande/ Vega Films) reckoned that as he knew many of the participants of the *Cahiers du Cinéma* crowd, and because he is known for being part of that period in film history, he really should address it. So here is Truffaut and Karina and Langlois and Cocteau and quotes from films such as *The 400 Blows* and *Alphaville*. But Godard's account of the Nouvelle Vague in *(Hi)Stor/ies of Cinema* is not just tinged with melancholy (as expected), it's curiously disssatisfying, with a make-do quality.

Ep. 3B: *Une Vague Nouvelle* also brings in *Touch of Evil, Rear Window, Vertigo, Snow White and the Seven Dwarfs, Beauty and the Beast* (1946), *Faust* (1926), *Frankenstein, Johnny Guitar, The Passion of Joan of Arc, Joan of Arc* (1948), *The Gospel According To Matthew* (the Sermon on the Mount sequence again), more pornography, more death camps newsreel, and perhaps the greatest film ever made, *Sunrise*. Among Godard's own works, we have *One Plus One* (the big beach ending), *King Lear, A Woman Is a Woman* and *Passion*. And figures such as Marilyn Monroe, Adolf Hitler, Lewis Carroll, Sergei Eisenstein, the Lumières, Erich von Stroheim, William Blake, Alberto Giacometti, Sandro Botticelli, Fra Angelico, and F.W. Murnau.

❊

Hitch gets his own shrine in *Histoire(s) du Cinéma*, in episode 4A: *Le Contrôle de l'Univers* with several quotations from his flicks

(*Psycho, The Wrong Man, The Birds, Rebecca, Vertigo,* and *North By Northwest*), and he's heard speaking (in voiceover);[15] it's in the production of the images, Godard reckons, that Hitchcock reigns supreme – not in his stories/ charas/ suspense (which is, of course, the kind of filmmaker that Godard aspired to be, but Hitch would never have neglected narrative and character to the extent that Godard did). Hitchcock is about the only British (nay, *English*) film director quoted in *Histoire(s) du Cinéma,* along with Charlie Chaplin. No Powell & Pressburger, Alexander Mackendrick, David Lean or Ken Russell here!

Elsewhere in ep. 4A*: Le Contrôle de l'Univers* we have the odd juxtaposition of hardcore porn (group sex) intercut with *Freaks* (1932), of all things. Meanwhile, early porn (showing people fucking) is superimposed over images of people kissing in classic movies (a comment, perhaps, on what mainstream, commercial cinema refused to show but suggested instead, or a depiction of the above and the below – regular cinema above, and the moral underbelly of cinema below).

Among the *ciné*-folk cited in 4A*: Le Contrôle de l'Univers* are Fassbinder, Truffaut, Lang, Bresson, Cocteau, Welles, Monroe, and films such as *Frankenstein, Nosferatu, Macbeth, Duel In the Sun, The Leopard, The Searchers, The Lady From Shanghai, Joan of Arc,* and Godard's own *King Lear, For Ever Mozart,* and *One Plus One* (the Camber Sands ending again).

✼

The eighth and final episode of *Histore(s) du Cinéma* – 4B: *Les Signes Parmi Nous* – rounds off our *Adventures With Uncle Jean* with some song-and-dance numbers and a slushy Happy Ending. No, not really. But actually, *yes.*

Yes, Jean-Luc Godard can be as sentimental as 'Ollywoood cinema – in his movies and in this document/ essay/ artwork. He talks about love, folks, he talks about friendship, and he talks in a wistful, nostalgic manner about his passion for *le cinéma.*

But he also includes more images of death, of mangled corpses, of bodies being hurled into open graves in the concentration camps. Few works of art go from the ecstasy of being alive to the horror of being very dead so often and so aggressively. And using the Holocaust as one of its chief examples. Sure, many documentaries explore issues such as death, but few keep returning to the Final Solution of the Nazi regime with such a dogged insistence.

Anyway, among the references in 4B: *Les Signes Parmi Nous* are

---

16 Hitch talks about the style and form of cinema. Yet it's typical of Godard that over Hitchcock speaking he adds a woman reciting, *and* his own voice pontificating!

An American In Paris, On the Town, Nosferatu, The Lady From Shanghai, Nanook of the North, Citizen Kane, Macbeth, The Searchers, Duel In the Sun, A Streetcar Named Desire, Red Desert, Madame de..., and of course newsreel (WWII, the Spanish Civil War), and pornography.

The Color of Pomegranates makes an unusual (and very welcome) appearance (a rare instance of a more recent Russian movie), and a quote from a Japanese classic, *In the Realm of the Senses.* Plus Godard's own *Pierrot le Fou, Alphaville, King Lear, Hélas Pour Moi,* etc. Filmmakers such as Chaplin, Welles, Eisenstein, Fassbinder, Keaton, etc. And figures such as Botticelli, Rimbaud, Bosch, Sartre, Bataille, Emily Dickinson, Stalin, Hitler, and the Virgin Mary.

❋

Thus, dear friends, *Histoire(s) du Cinéma* reaches the end of its 8-chapter run with a gradual fade into the Great Nothingness (the Existential concept of nothingness is discussed in the voiceover). But there's no 'ending', in the usual sense: like most other Godard video/film projects, *Histoire(s) du Cinéma* simply stops.

❋

CRITICISM OF *HISTOIRE(S) DU CINÉMA*.

Omitting cinema from regions outside of North America and Europe (and Russia) is a massive flaw in *Histoire(s) du Cinéma*, if you consider it to be a documentary on the whole history of cinema, including world cinema. So there's very little Japanese or Chinese or Indian or African or South American or Australian cinema. And Russian cinema tends to be the famous early works (Eisenstein, Dovzhenko, etc).

Further niggles arise when you watch *Histoire(s) du Cinéma* closer, such as:

• why are the readings out loud, the voiceovers and the quotations *all* delivered in solemn and serious tones?

• why is the music so sombre?

• why is the mood so downbeat?

• where are the comedies and the comedians?

• why are so many film genres neglected?

• why is animation mostly left aside?

• why are there so many nervy, rapid vision mixes between two images?

• why is there so much repetition?

• why are none of the quotations/ sources identified?

Emphasizing the serious, non-smiling aspect of the stories and histories of cinema is a major lack – but then, comedy and humour is under-valued *everywhere* in film criticism (and by awards and festivals). *Histoire(s) du Cinéma* might be a monument to cinema, a farewell to cinema, an oration at a funeral[17] to cinema, but that doesn't mean that comedic films have to be shoved aside so that we all have to act like we're attending a wake, dressing in black, staring downwards in humility and despair, and whispering requiems from André Bazin or Siegfried Kracauer.

Director Lina Wertmuller said:

> I always fear the representation of power in a totally serious light because power itself requires this seriousness to be terrfying... Why should serious political points necessarily be made in a serious manner? This is not the only way to present political problems. (in D. Georgakas, 132)

There are numerous further niggles with *Histoire(s) du Cinéma:* despite the screen being splattered with captions, virtually no sources are identified. No sources for the film clips, no sources for the 100s of photographs, no sources for the paintings, no sources for the newsreels, no sources for the quotations in voiceover and on screen.

Even the most ardent cinema lover, the most passionate film buff, will not be able to identify all of the film/ video clips, or all of the faces peering out of old, b/w photos. Any film fan can spot a Hitch or a Welles or a Cocteau quote or clip, but *Histoire(s) du Cinéma* features, for ex, obscure films from the 1920s from France.

Some of the juxtapositions in *Histoire(s) du Cinéma* are simply too pat: for instance, cross-cutting scenes from *Metropolis* and *Die Nibelungen* with newsreel images of World War One – making the too-obvious links between the images of the hero Siegfried on horseback from German mythology with soldiers in the trenches in WW I.

Is it enough for the Maestro to sit in his office in Rolle, staring into space and mouthing the titles of classic novels in a meaningful manner? *The Counterfeiters... The Magic Mountain... Great Expectations....*[18] In *(Hi)Stor/ies of Cinema* Godard feels it is enough merely to point at something and his work is done. Similarly, film critics who loathe the spoof movies of Jason Friedberg and Aaron Seltzer (*Date Movie, Epic Movie, Vampires Suck*, etc) complain that they think it's funny just to reference something (look, it's Michael Jackson! look, it's

---

17 Philippe Sollers regarded *Histoire(s) du Cinéma* as a memorial, a funerary document for cinema, and found Godard's non-stop meditation and cogitation irritating.
18 We know he hasn't read all of *Great Expectations* or *The Magic Mountain!* Only the first and last pages!

a cretinous pop idol show!).

The padding is glaringly obvious in *(Hi)Stor/ies of Cinema* – not only the typewriter scenes, but the endless shots of a Movieola running celluloid[19] thru it, the many repetitions, the re-use of captions, and Godard's default position for padding out anything – fades to black (fade out – 3 seconds, fade in 3 seconds. It's not only the black, the fades take up time). You have to admit that even a genius like Godard has *not* found a satisfying means of illustrating some of his material in *(Hi)Stor/ies of Cinema*.

The scenes of J.-L. Godard sitting at a typewriter and typing a single sentence are the equivalent in documentaries of dramatizing something (this is an aspect of drama-documentaries that is regualrly negatively criticized). If this is so, then Godard is dramatizing is the act of writing; he's insisting that films are really made during the scriptwriting (he depicts himself writing, though very slowly – one sentence every five minutes!).

Now, many documentaries can't help repeating themselves: you will see the same images repeated in many documentaries. Incredible as *(Hi)Stor/ies of Cinema* is, it *does* return to shots of a K.E.M. too many times, it *does* use the scenes of Godard at his typewriter, and it *does* use too many repetitions and fades to black too often.

Stor/ies/ Histor/es of Cinema is a post-production piece – it's put together in the main in the editing suite and the dubbing/ mixing studio. The footage filmed specially for the documentary is bitty, sometimes banal/ inconsequential, and, worst of all for a filmmaker of Godard's abilities, uninspired and, well, *boring*. Yes, even a director as imaginative as Godard can, even when faced with the incredible subject of the story/ history of cinema, produce boring material.

Boring? Surely not! Much as we love this astonishing filmmaker, those lengthy shots of the man sitting at a typewriter, bare-chested and sucking on that infernal baby's pacifier, and occasionally intoning phrases like 'the magic mountain...' or 'the counterfeiters...', is not the equal of Dante Alighieri's *Divine Comedy*!

Women sitting at tables and reading aloud from books now comes across as fantastically dull and uninspired; it was fun and novel in the 1960s, but in the 1990s? Coming from almost any other filmmaker, this would be derided as misconceived and deliberately obscure. (Godard has always been shameless about his padding in his works: in his modernist phase (early 1960s), he could repeat the same shot, and

---

[19] Ironically, this pæan to celluloid was edited and filmed on video (and the 100s of effects are video effects).

get away with it. But it was still padding).

You can pause for dramatic effect after each momentous phrase, like this: ... ... but it ain't happening. I think audiences of film fans, like us, should be *absolutely slaughtered* by a 266-minute documentary from a genius like Godard The Great And Powerful on the (hi_stor(ies) of cinema. It *should* be the equal of the great documentaries, and in parts it is. But it also needs someone to come along with some scissors and say *no, no* and *no!*

Or does Jean-Luc Godard take such a ridiculously grave approach to the his/tor(ies) of cinema because he realizes that he's wasted so much of his attention on frivolous and superficial entertainment? He and his *Cahiers du Cinéma* pals raved and raved about North American cinema even tho' they must've known that 95% of it was dumb, silly popcorn. The movies that Godard and his cronies enshrined were at least half of the time glamorous but empty spy capers, macho, ultra-conservative Westerns (which completely endorsed the Great American Dream), and glitzy but goofy musicals. Oh, we love those movies, but they are not grand, high art, they are not of the order of Sophocles' plays or Friedrich Hölderlin's poetry.

But if you talk about stupid American movies in a low, whispery voice, and use sad, plinky piano music from the Edition of Contemporary Music record label, you might get away with audiences taking you straight and seriously. It's the same in film criticism: use words like *postmodern* or *liminal* or *scopophilia*, and you can kid yourself that you're dealing with the greatest cultural achievements in the history of the world, instead of vacuous North American and European movies which endorse and celebrate the Western/ American way of life, which celebrate Western/ American capitalism and consumerism, and, worst of all, uphold the aggressive militaristic and corrupt ideological policies of Western/ American societies.[20]

---

20 *The Searchers* and Disney cartoons, cited several times in *Histoire(s) du Cinéma*, can be seen as no less fascistic and reactionary than *Star Wars, Rambo* or *The Terminator*.

JEAN-LUC GODARD

HISTOIRE(S) DU CINÉMA

LA MONNAIE DE L'ABSOLU

31

NOUVELLE VAGUE

NEW WAVE

INTRO.

Nouvelle Vague (*New Wave*, 1990) was wr./ dir. by J.-L. Godard (Jacques Audiberti's novel is credited as a source); Alain Sarde produced; William Lubtchansky was DP (among others); Godard edited; Anne-Marie Miéville was art dir.; costumes by Ingeborg Dietsche, Marie-Françoise Perochon and Melusine Shamber; make-up by Josée De Luca; hair by Patrick Villain; A.D.s: Claude Chiquet and Jean-Marie Gindraux; sound by Pierre-Alain Besse, Henri Morelle and François Mussy; and script girl: Hélène Sébillotte. The cast included: Alain Delon, Domiziana Giordano, Jacque Dacqmine, Christophe Odent, Roland Amstutz, Cécile Reigher, Laurence Côte, Joseph Lisbona, Véronique Müller, Joe Sheridan, and Hubert Ravel. Released: May 23, 1990. 90 mins.

New Wave was the first significant appearance of Edition of Contemporary Music Records' music in a Godard movie (the soundtrack of *New Wave* was duly released by E.C.M.). In typical Godardian style, the composers are identified only by their family name in the film's credits. After this, when Godard needed music for his most of his movies and documentaries, he simply reached down an E.C.M. CD from the shelf in his editing suite in Rolle).

Nouvelle Vague contains most of the motifs of Godard's late work: Switzerland (filmed in all seasons), numerous car scenes, actors drifting about, lost in their own contemplations about Lord Buddha knows what, actors delivering arch, self-conscious dialogue (much of it literary quotations), actors bickering and nudging each other,[1] actors engaged in pointless activities, intertitles on black, unidentified offscreen voices, black leader, pretentious references,[2] a boat on a lake, shots of water, trees, clouds, fields, roads, horses, etc... *Nouvelle Vague* is a movie riffling thru the Godard back catalogue (a factory scene from *Passion* > a boat scene from *Pierrot le Fou* > gangster movie quotes from *Breathless*), and sorting through a pile of CDs of the melancholy music on the Edition of Contemporary Music record label.

Among the movie references in *New Wave* are *To Have and Have Not* (1944), *Diary of a Country Priest* (1951), *Sunrise* (1927), *The Rules of the Game* (1939) and *Leave Her To Heaven* (1945). Painting is evoked several times, as usual in a late Godard outing, with a canvas of *The Naked Maja* by Francisco de Goya (1797-1800 – actually in the

---

[1] Here, a maid is continually berated by the head waiter (and in front of the customers in a restaurant). No one can do nervous tension in the workplace like Godard! He is quite brilliant at the debasement and agony of work, and of labour relations.
[2] Among the cultural refs. in *New Wave* are Friedrich Schiller, Fran cisco de Goya, Vincent van Gogh, Aristotle, Robert Bresson and Dante Alighieri.

Prado, Madrid) being one of the hyper-situated objects (in the scene at the airport, where it's delivered to the business tycoon P.D.G., played by Jacques Dacqmine).

FIRST, THE GRUMPY RESPONSE.

I find this a very dissatsifying movie, even tho' it was directed by Jean-Luc Godard and stars Alain Delon (two factors which ought to make it worthwhile on some level).

For the legions of the undead who dislike Godard's cinema, *Nouvelle Vague* offers plenty of ammunition: the impeccably-dressed, ultra-bourgeois people,[3] who do nothing but languidly drift about (they don't have to work, they're well-off, but they're all miserable, spoilt, pointless and bland); the incessant dialogue (in every scene with the gardener he's yakking non-stop – to nobody in particular);[4] the pretentious quotes from classic authors (much of the dialogue is quotation); the poncy reading-aloud from books; the lack of dramatic conventions (no story, no characters, etc); the disjointed editing and sound (overlapping dialogue), etc.

And at times watching *New Wave*, you might wonder why you're bothering at all. ('The party's over' for Godard, declared Vincent Canby in the *New York Times*).

This movie contains a higher percentage of Pretentious Prattle than most Godard movies. At least five of the main characters spout embarrassing drivel.

Nouvelle Vague is swamped by chatter, but it doesn't find the images or the dramatic situations to go with that endless blah-blah-blah (a recurring issue in Godard's later films). For too much of the time we are looking at the smug, too-perfect bourgeoisie nattering and nattering (much of the dialogue is arrogant or hostile). And too much of it is delivered in the familiar, self-conscious, Godardian style, as if actors who've been cast in a Godard-directed picture are now turning up having learnt how to speak how actors are supposed to speak in a Godard movie (maybe they watched earlier Godard movies and thought, well, that's how you're supposed to be in a Godard movie. Indeed, it's striking how early in Godard's film career actors settled into that solemn form of self-conscious declaiming).

We also have the bullying behaviour of characters towards each other, their sarcastic witticisms barely concealing the spite underneath.

---
3 As Pier Paolo Pasolini put it, the bourgeoisie are always wrong.
4 Godard uses the gardener to drift into shots and utter some choice witticisms. It might be a Greek chorus motif, but no Greek chorus was ever this pretentious.

Meanwhle, the underlings of the bourgeoisie are pushed around by their superiors. (Lawyer Raoul Dorfman (Christophe Odent) in particular is an aggressive little prick).

✳

One of the problems with *New Wave* is that the initial narrative set-up is fudged. So the Man (Roger Lennox) is someone who came back to life, or was revived somehow. Anyway, it's a spiritual return of some kind. But how this is dramatized is clumsy: he's walking along a highway, some vehicles whizz by, horns blare, and the Man scurries aside. Is there an accident? Who knows? – none of it is visualized. Instead, the emphasis is on the Woman (Contessa Elena Torlato-Favrini) encountering the Man at the roadside, which's where their relationship begins.

The same incoherent and awkward anti-dramatization occurs in *Woe Is Me* – the set-up there has Gérard Depardieu as God, or a divinity. That's one of the core layers of *Woe Is Me*, which the audience really needs to get, but it's similarly messily handled.

Thus, *New Wave* is yet another Jean-Luc Godard movie which works better if the viewer has read a summary of the film beforehand. Maybe like the *Star Wars* crawl.

However, even armed with a two-page summation of the movie (which would, ironically, be as long as the treatment that Godard likely penned for this film), watching it is still not a simple task. *New Wave* is scrappy and ungainly, lumbering from painterly lyricism (oh, oh, how exquisite is Switzerland in Summer!), to snippy snarking amongst people with too much time on their hands, and to pompous references to Aristotle, Vincent van Gogh, Francisco de Goya or Friedrich Schiller. (At its worst, with its indifferent evocations of cold relationships between the white, European middle-class and too-slick, empty tracking shots, it resembles a bad Peter Greenaway movie – when Greenaway made pretentious copies of the pretentious Alain Resnais).

The setting of *New Wave* is a grand mansion beside Lake Geneva; it's another evocation of the bourgeois environment that Jean-Luc Godard grew up in, but now chilly with frozen emotions and life reduced to the contemplation of the business practices of global capitalism. The gathering of wealthy types in the country house recalls *The Rules of the Game*.

The boat on the Lake sequence, which occurs twice, may be a reference to *Sunrise* (1927), one of Godard's favourite movies, which includes a famous scene where George O'Brien contemplates drowning his wife Janet Gaynor,[5] as well as *Leave Her To Heaven* (John Stahl, 1945). In the first boat scene, the Contessa swims and Lennox falls in, apparently drowning (while Elena looks on impassively, not offering to help). In the second boat scene, the Second Lennox watches Elena in the water, seeming indifferent to her struggle to remain afloat.

Lennox Mark Two arrives in *New Wave* (known as Richard), a version of the popular double or *doppelgänger* theme in cinema and literature. This Other Lennox is a brilliant business operator, and is soon taking charge of the Contessa's business deals. The other characters, such as the patriarch P.D.G., loudly express their irritation and impotence at this new arrival.

SECONDLY, LET'S BE NICE.

New Wave is a film of beautiful images – a mythical vision of Switzerland and Lake Geneva from the man who's photographed it more in international movies than anyone else in recent times. (Switzerland in High Summer is a mass of green foliage – this is where all those endless months of endless rain pay off).

The camera drifts slowly laterally (and when a crane's been hired for the day, it floats upward, into the trees – a recurring Godardian visual motif in his recent work. A camera taking a voyage around a tree). Once again, Godard displays his miraculous talent for photographing the world and turning it into... cinema. His eye for imagery is so distinctive, so incisive, so compelling. (For some the shots and images may be bursting with supermeaningfulness, so incandescent with sublime, postmodern value... for others they're empty of everything. For instance, there's an elaborate tracking shot along the ground floor of the manse, looking in thru the windows (a favourite sort of Godard staging). As the camera reverses direction and dollies the other way, a maid moves from room to room switching off the lamps. Is it profound? Or simply nothing?).

Two attractive people appear in *Nouvelle Vague* – French icon Alain Delon[6] and Italian actress Domiziana Giordano (known for her appearance in *Nostalghia*, 1983).[7] They play the Eternal Couple in Godard's cinema (dubbed 'Him' and 'Her', the Man, the Woman) – in earlier incarnations, they might've been Jean-Paul Belmondo and Anna Karina (*circa* 1964), or Marcello Mastrioanni and a French

---
5 Incidentally, the characters in *Sunrise* are known as the Man and the Wife.
6 One might imagine that Alain Delon would've appeared in one of Godard's 1960s movies – he was very much a part of the scene in French cinema.
7 She acts with her hair – those pretty cascades of curls. She fiddles with it, or flicks it.

starlet (these were going to appear in earlier versions of *Nouvelle Vague*). Delon and Giordano are certainly an alluring couple in *New Wave*. (Meanwhile, characters observing the couple from the wings seethe with resentment: how *dare* they be so happy? Surely, the Godard Couple are supposed to be at each other's throats?).

Alain Delon looks lost – but that fits his characterization, of course, as the loner or drifter who's given a new chance at life. How do you play this kind of allegorical character? Delon – or Delon as directed by Godard – has not come up with a satisfying solution.

Sure, it's Alain Delon, but his star image this time doesn't bring the role to life. From his brilliance in *Rocco and His Brothers* and *The Leopard* (to cite two famous and really fantastic Delon movies) to this, an under-written characterization *par excellence.*

Jean-Luc Godard is a film director who prefers to cast actors who 'just get it', who know what to do without being told. But it didn't work this time.

❈

Nouvelle Vague is one of the first of the later Jean-Luc Godard movies to feature a character who appears in every subsequent movie: a middle-aged or elderly white man dressed neatly in a suit and carrying newspapers under his arm. He is a businessman, or a journalist. These are the bosses – smug, patronizing, powerful – that Godard's characters in the 1960s movies loathed (the factory bosses attacked repeatedly in the Dziga Vertov movies). And now they've become the main characters, weary and cynical but with social power. The business folk in this film are so rich they've bought Warners (that's likely a reference to the sale of Warner Brothers and its businesses iin 1990, when Warner Communciations merged with Time, Inc to become Time Warner).

Are these confident, in-control men Godard's tribute to his father perhaps? Or to Roberto Rossellini, a smart filmmaker that Godard admired? Or has Godard reversed his attacks on the bourgoisie and decided that they aren't so bad after all? And, anyway, he himself hails from a well-off, Swiss-French bourgeois family. So is he going back to his roots?

32

HÉLAS POUR MOI

WOE IS ME

As in war, you have to improvize, but not in any old way. First you have to be aware of what you're doing. You look at what you're doing, and you listen to what you're saying. Or perhaps you listen to what you see, and look at what you're hearing... that's the New Wave.

Jean-Luc Godard[8]

---

[8] Quoted in A. Riding, 18.

+++ When your lead actor walks out of your movie halfway through a six week shooting schedule,[9] that would be a disaster for many film productions (and he isn't replaced). But it's not a problem for Jean-Luc Godard, who simply rewrites the film, and salvages the rest of the schedule. The producers (Alain Sarde, Christine Hutin, Benoît Rossel, Christine Gozlan and Ruth Waldburger) get round the departure of Gérard Depardieu[10] (another big star, one of the biggest names of recent French cinema)[11] by cutting to a shot of a book and a Paul Klee postcard, for instance, or a terrace, in the middle of a scene involving Depardieu, or using a take of Depardieu's voice only, over other shots. And Depardieu doesn't appear until 11 minutes into the film. There's also plenty of black leader, with voices, sound effects and music, and intertitles – further methods of stretching out a film, as well as replacing an actor (Godard has had to stretched out films before). The rough cut of *Woe Is Me* had come in at only 60 minutes – too short, and a sure sign that a movie's in trouble. That's because rough cuts (a.k.a. first assemblies) are *always* way too long (Godard has never had to cut down a four-hour rough cut to two hours!).

The prospect of Gérard Depardieu playing God in a movie directed by Jean-Luc Godard had potential – unfortunately, the movie is milk spilt on sand, and the juicy, milky concept rapidly seeps away, lost forever. The film doesn't give the famous Nose anything to do. This is a car wreck of a movie, if viewed in conventional terms, yet it has elements that compel.

Hélas Pour Moi (a.k.a. *Woe Is Me*, 1993) was produced by Alain Sarde, Christine Hutin, Benoît Rossel, Christine Gozlan and Ruth Waldburger for Les Films Alain Sarde/ Vega Films/ Télévision Suisse Romande/ Périphéria (Godard and Miéville's own company). The Maestro scripted the film, basing it on Jean Giraudoux's play *Amphrytrion 39*.[12] DP: Caroline Champetier (and 5 others), editor: the Master, art dir. and production management by Anne-Marie Faux, costumes by Valérie De Buck, make-up by Thomas Nellen, sound by Pierre-Alain Besse, François Mussy and Nathalie Vidal.

The cast included: Gérard Depardieu, Laurence Masliah, Bernard Verley, Aude Amiot, Roland Blanche, Marc Betton, François Germond

---

9 In some accounts, *Hélas Pour Moi* was shot in eight weeks.
10 That nose! It's nose acting.
11 Godard had met Depardieu back in 1977, and had discussed a couple of possible projects. There was a link with Marguerite Duras, too: Depardieu had appeared in two of her movies (B, 399).
12 There were 37 interpretations of the myth written before Giraudoux took it on, according to the playwright, with Godard's being the thirty-ninth. Godard also drew on *Amphitryon* by Heinrich von Kleist and *Amphitryon* by Molière.

and Jean-Louis Loca. Released: Sept 8, 1993. 84 mins.

Many in the team were regular Jean-Luc Godard collaborators, but the real stars of the show were the film editors and the sound editors and mixers: Bernard Le Roux, François Mussy, Pierre-Alain Besse and Godard. Why? Because *Hélas Pour Moi* was a film rescued or re-made or re-birthed in post-production.

+++ The lead actor walking out *and* the replacement of the main actress was only one aspect of the production that hampered *Hélas Pour Moi*: Godard seemed to lose confidence in his movie, and tore into the screenplay, prior to shooting. There were 18 sequences (a magical number in Hebraic mysticism), and Godard dropped 8 or 9 (B, 551). Godard wanted to delay shooting for a year while he worked out what to do (a recurring Godardian strategy), but Gérard Depardieu wasn't available then. So Godard and co. shot the film in Summer, 1992.

Laurence Masliah was another late-hour replacement. According to Caroline Champetier, Godard's original choice, Dutch actress Johanna Der Steege, had fallen in love with Godard, but Anne-Marie Miéville wasn't having any of it. She had Godard replace Der Steege. According to Godard, it was because Der Steege couldn't speak French (B, 550). But he wasn't so keen on Masliah, either (neither am I).

Jean-Luc Godard is a master at constructing a movie out of outtakes, fluffed takes, the beginnings and the ends of takes, using doubles, and numerous pieces of audio. He's been in this game for a long time, and he's a veteran at bending and shaping footage into something else. On this occasion, however, the end results are poor.

Jean-Luc Godard acknowledged that *Hélas Pour Moi* was not complete, not the film he intended to make, and could be regarded as a failure.[13] It was another of Godard's filmic propositions, a film which suggested how a film might play. (One of Godard's waspish remarks about *Hélas Pour Moi* runs: 'we've seen that the film was somewhat abandoned. But, after all, the Son of Man was also abandoned'. Only God-Art would compare his film to Christ! And many filmmakers would be laughed at, or taken too seriously and denounced as blasphemous).[14]

Despite that, Jean-Luc Godard still liked *Hélas Pour Moi,* and

---

13 Godard described *Hélas Pour Moi* as a premature baby, born too early, because once you get the money in cinema, you have to start shooting. You can't wait around (in M. Tranchant, "Jean-Luc Godard", *Le Figaro*, Aug 30, 1993.)
14 Godard likes to quote big Biblical statements: at the beginning of *Passion* Isabelle Huppert, working at a machine in a factory, asks 'God, why hast thou forsaken me?'

remarked that there was something in it which worked for him. He spoke about the 'pure present' tense of the film, where the only shot that mattered was the current one on screen, yet that present shot depended on what went on before, or what is about to come. But because you didn't know what that shot would be, it didn't help. The film seemed to be reaching into a future it hadn't yet manufactured.

+++ Still, all of that philosophizing about *Hélas Pour Moi* isn't going to save it from confused film critics. The critics weren't mad about *Hélas Pour Moi,* to put it mildly, and the film performed poorly on its release in September, 1993.

• Gérard Depardieu was uncomfortable in his role, and looked 'as miserable as a beached whale', quipped Amy Taubin.15

• 'There's little hope that anyone will stay awake,' said M. Stouvenot in *Le Journal du Dimanche.*

• 'a shambles. It exaggerates and irritates', moaned F. Julien in *V.S.D.*

• 'both arrogant and poignant', averred A.C. in *Les Échoes.*

• 'an irritably, grumpy film in a foul mood,' G. Lefort & O. Seguret complained in *Libération.*

• 'a garrulous film and a wall of silence', admitted *La Tribune Des Fossés*' S. Chemineau.16

The film critics were right to a certain extent: you wouldn't choose *Hélas Pour Moi* as a great way of introducing an audience new to Jean-Luc Godard (ditto with *King Lear, Tout Va Bien, Detective* or any of the Dziga Vertov Group films). For quite a bit of *Hélas Pour Moi* it's difficult to make sense of what's going on if you employ the usual approaches of cinema. This certainly isn't *Gigi* or *Jules and Jim* or *Astérix and Obélix.*

+++ Quite a bit of *Hélas Pour Moi* involves people wandering aim-lessly around the lakeside in Switzerland or sitting outside cafés at night, or in video stores, or in and out of doorways, with conversations going on all over the place, but nothing like recognizable narrative elements, such as

(1) a hero and a heroine and a rival/ villain,

and (2) a story.

Or: (3) characters in the usual sense of any kind;

and (4) a story of any kind.

---

15 A. Taubin, "All My Sons", *Village Voice,* Sept 27, 1994.
16 But *Le Monde* (Régis Debray and Jean-Michel Frodon) liked it.

The constant flow of dialogue is about everything and nothing. Everyone's speaking, but no one saying anything. (And don't expect any of the other elements of conventional movies, like conflicts/ goals/ motives/ relationships, etc, and even the themes and issues're presented in a smashed mirror fashion. If you don't mind getting your fingers cut to bloody ribbons, you can pick the pieces up, and see if there really is a 'mystery' here).

Woe Is Me is a collection of fragments of nuggets of shards of pieces of what might once have been a story – in a different era on another planet in another galaxy in another dimension.

The central relationship, which took up much of the narrative of *Hélas Pour Moi*, was between a man and a woman, the central Godardian impossible/ romantic relationship – between Simon Donnadieu (Depardieu) and Rachel Donnadieu (Laurence Masliah). The scenes between Simon/ God and Rachel formed the central drama of *Hélas Pour Moi* (they took place at a to-die-for lakeside house, complete with verandah overlooking the Swiss Lake. The *milieu* of *Woe Is Me* is very bourgeois[17] – a world of nice cars, nice houses, and nice clothes, where nobody works for a living. The Maoist/ Marxist/ Militant Godard of the 1968-1973 era is long forgotten – this is a thoroughly bourgeois, Imperialist environment. If you haven't got a suit and tie and a flashy car, don't bother turning up).

Here we have the central sequence in a Godard movie where the romantic couple move warily around each other, grouch and bicker, intone pretentiously, correct each other's dialogue ('that's a good sentence'),[18] pad about restlessly, put on dressing gowns, etc (*Contempt* offers the supreme example of the big romantic couple arguing scene). Extraordinarily, whole parts of this sequence are played over a shot of a Paul Klee picture in a book, or over black leader, or other empty shots, Godard's outrageous solution to Depardieu departing.

Godard added the character of the publisher Abraham Klimt (Bernard Berley) late in the production. The scenes and conversations between Aude (Aude Amiot), a poet, her boyfriend and Klimt commented upon the central narrative (Aude was one of the more intriguing of Godard's later characters, but, like everyone else in *Hélas Pour Moi*, she's not really a character at all).

Bernard Berley said that Godard had called him after two months of filming, telling him that 'the film was a complete failure', and he had

---

17 The influence of Anne-Marie Miéville is very apparent.
18 Can we rewrite that line, Jean-Luc?

decided to add a new character and rework the film.[19]

The addition of the publisher/ detective character Abraham Klimt aims to turn *Hélas Pour Moi* into something of a mystery to be solved, but it doesn't really work (it took its cue from *Detective* – a mystery in the past that is solved in the present day). Critic Lætitia Fieschi-Vivet has tried to interpret the film as a mystery, but it isn't convincing: the film just doesn't bear up to such an analysis. The structure hints at flashbacks and a past to be excavated, but those are only hints, suggestions of a story (Godard doesn't do flashbacks, except in one or two films where a short montage is inserted to liven up the proceedings).

So A. Klimt has to *explain* the 'mystery', in voiceover, but the film doesn't *show* it – because there isn't enough footage to depict it. (There *are* good movies of mystery constructed largely from narration and ambiguous (off-screen) suggestions, but this isn't one of them).

As Pascal Bonitzer put it in *Trafic*, in *Hélas Pour Moi*

> there is therefore a before and an after, except that, as is often the case with Jean-Luc Godard, the tenses get mixed up. There is no ending possible because everything is already over and at the same time has never begun.[20]

With its depiction of God inhabiting a man, and its explorations of religious, metaphysical and philosophical issues, *Hélas Pour Moi* appeared as a kind of sequel to *Hail Mary*. It might've been a fascinating companion piece to the 1985 movie. The film ruminated on similar issues – especially those to do with belief (not religious belief, necessarily, just the need to believe). Again, recall Godard's rewriting of Ludwig Wittgenstein: 'whatever happens, believe'. And that sense of just believing in something also has to apply to the viewer coming to *Hélas Pour Moi* itself: to watch this film, you just have to believe.

+++ Few of the characters are identified clearly in *Hélas Pour Moi,* which doesn't help. Who are these people? What are they doing there? Clearly, it doesn't matter much. There's Max, the young guy with the Elvis haircut who works in the video store... there's Angélica, a gorgeous, blonde woman at the centre of a *ménage à trois*... there's Aude, the slim, female poet, an angelic commentator on the film...

---

19 In "Mon tournage avec Godard", *L'Événement du Jeudi*, Sept 2, 1993
20 P. Bonitzer, "Dieu, Godard, le zapping", *Trafic*, 8, Fall, 1993.

there's A. Klimt,[21] the portly, middle-aged publisher/ investigator... and then there's Rachel and Simon Donnadieu, the holy couple ..

And there are a host of minor characters that drift in and out of the film, seemingly designed to further irritate viewers already irritated by the movie. *Hélas Pour Moi* is a film which requires a printed summary before consumption, like an *avant garde* opera. With previous Jean-Luc Godard outings, critics could forgive the lack of narrative/s, the sketchy characterizations, the incompleteness of the films because there were other elements to enjoy: beautiful people like Anne Wiazemsky, Jean-Pierre Léaud, Myriem Roussel and Anna Karina, or crazy arty happenings, or witty asides and jokes... But in *Hélas Pour Moi* those pleasures, for the average cinema-goer, are thin on the ground. *Hélas Pour Moi* is very much for the converted, and even then it's a struggle. (The *editing* in the 1960s masterpieces is *fast*, which helps, too, but in *Hélas Pour Moi*, to pad out the film, it's *slow*, but not slow-interesting, it's slow-boring).

+++ The love-making of Simon and Rachel when it comes is suggested in a rapid montages of images: a woman stroking her mound with a still picture of sunlight on rippling water super-imposed over it; a sunrise; the sun; patches of black; and what appears to be a porn flick filmed off a TV monitor, depicting genitals doing what they do during intercourse. An impressionistic rendition of fucking. kind of rapturous, with these flashes of the natural world and the sun (it's also a replay of the poetic, spiritualized approach Godard and Miéville took with *Je Vous Salue, Marie*).

Godard and Miéville want to have it both ways, as at other times in their film careers. Thus, what happened in the 1993 film may not have happened; maybe Simon left, but maybe he didn't; maybe he came back, maybe he didn't; maybe he was Rachel's husband, and maybe he wasn't. Or maybe he was both all the way through: simultaneously there and not there, simultaneously Rachel's husband and not her husband.

+++ The discussions in *Hélas Pour Moi* take in God, religion, cinema, painting, and the impossibility of love. A film about men and women and asses and clouds and skies.

And the usual Godardian motifs: pinball machines, cinema, TV

---

21 *Woe Is Me* is a kind of anti-cinema: Klimt is introduced in a fantastically boring manner, walking along a road in one direction, then walking back towards the camera. As if the filmmakers are trying to make the emptiest, most pointless shots possible.

monitors, gas stations, trains – and cars, *d'accord*.

There are literary and philosophical references to Seneca, Stéphane Mallarmé, Giacomo Leopardi,[22] St Paul and the *Bible*.[23] (At one point, Aude quotes St Paul to Abraham Klimt about no image existing – as she's remembering or recreating what happened when God inhabited Simon. That may once again be to cover over images that weren't shot after Gérard Depardieu left).

Only in a Jean-Luc Godard film can some students ask their teacher 'Romanesque – what is it exactly?'[24] (Aude and her boyfriend appear to have turned up at the teacher's house to ask her precisely that. And, bless 'em, they won't leave until they've got the answer!).

+++ Music was again a beguiling element in *Hélas Pour Moi:* it was by Johann Sebastian Bach, Dimitri Shostakovitch, Ludwig van Beethoven, Heinz Holliger, Arthur Honegger, Peter Tchaikovsky, Keith Jarrett and David Darling. Slow-moving viola and cello[25] was the signature music of the film, stately and lyrical and melancholy. Very loud piano chords act as stabs in the score, as do the repetitions of thunder claps (one of the sound editor's go-to sounds in many a movie). The soundtrack is by far the most attractive element in *Woe Is Me*.

Indeed, the score of *Hélas Pour Moi* was one of Jean-Luc Godard's densest: sometimes there were two voiceovers, on top of the dialogue within the film, sometimes additional voices over scenes, sometimes voices were deliberately drowned out (a favourite Godard device),[26] and the sound mixers also played with the stereo picture, putting voices on each channel (the multi-layered soundtrack was further complicated for non-French speaking audiences by the subtitles: when a film is this complex, in terms of sound, subtitles just don't cut it. Films like this would be an absolute nightmare to dub into another language).

Hélas Pour Moi orchestrates a variety of voiceovers, including those of deities. There's also the croaky voice of a demon, which may be God's voice (it recalled the treated voice of the super-computer in *Alphaville*). And Gérard Depardieu also puts on a cracked voice when he's with Rachel (for those sarcastic exchanges that're a part of every romantic couple scene in Godard's output).

---

[22] Godard had read Giacomo Leopardi's poem 'To the Patriarch', God's view of life on Earth.
[23] Walter Benjamin, Gershom Scholem and Jewish mysticism were also influences.
[24] A reference to Godard's mother, in the character of Madame Anne Monod.
[25] David Darling's signature sound.
[26] Godard acknowledged that it was sometimes difficult to follow the different parts of the story. That certainly enhances the mystery element.

The use of offscreen sound in *Hélas Pour Moi* is again stupendous – plenty of thunder rumbles this time. Characters walk on and quote from philosophers (a man walks on and states Tertulian's *credo absurdam* – I believe because it is absurd – a favourite saying of Godard's).

The imagery was beautiful in *Woe Is Me* (the camera team included Caroline Champetier, Julien Hirsch, Laurent Hincelin, and three others). The images were the familiar Godardian ones of lakes, mountains, cafés, cars, trains and railroad stations. It's all very painterly – a trend in Godard's later work. *Woe Is Me* includes numerous shots looking thru doors and windows – it's Godard's version of Dutch painting (Pieter de Hooch, Jan Vermeer, Gerrit Dou, Gerard ter Borch), where domestic interiors were composed of shadowy, receding rooms.

Poetic lateral tracking shots unfurl which seemed to be part of some bigger, European, art cinema epic, but amounted to... nothing but beautiful, lateral tracking shots (pretty but utterly empty). Within them, very little happened: actors stood about along a wall beside a Swiss lake as a pleasure boat[27] rode past, or they walked past trees.[28] Very luscious, but luscious for what purpose? Maybe it's enough now for a film to merely gesture towards lyricism, beauty and mystery (but for a filmmaker with a C.V. like Godard, absolutely not).

Of Jean-Luc Godard's later films, Jonathan Rosenbaum remarked that while Godard was better than ever at creating images, lighting shots, and filling the screen with colours, sounds and actions, he seemed to have less reasons, without his Marxism or cinephilia, for stringing those images together (1992). That might be true of films such as *Détective, King Lear* and *Hélas Pour Moi* – a heap of broken images that might be assembled by the spectator into something else (if they could be bothered).

However, once again Jean-Luc Godard and his team are re-inventing cinema, or reminding viewers yet again of the materiality of cinema: there's a close-up shot of the too-pretty blonde woman by a lake changing from over-exposed to regularly exposed to under-exposed in steps of f-stops (or grading achieved in post-production), an astonishing revaluation of the possibilities of cinema.[29]

The film also experiments with out of focus images, and using a

---

27 That boat pops up in several subsequent Godard movies, including *Goodbye To Language*.
28 And a guy spied on some lovers.
29 For Armond White, 'this portrait shot takes on a poetic quality that is determined solely by the light'.

long lens. There's another self-reflexive shot which draws attention to the mechanics of cinema – the classic one of a character walking into focus from far away (this's the intro shot of Laurence Masliah as Rachel,[30] held for a long time). Moments like this lift *Woe Is Me* into another realm: if only it could stay there! But it's far too flimsy, and the film doesn't have the strength to sustain those heights of the poetry of cinema for more'n a beat or two of its angelic wings.

There are plenty of intertitles and word games. Some of these were Biblical quotes, some were philosophical statements, some were puns in the usual Godardian manner. And there was *lots* of black (more than the usual, Godard movie). The film was divided into 'books', though that didn't make much difference to an already very confused narrative.

Actions are repeated, varieties in what might have happened: Rachel approaching Simon – wading through the water, or swimming up to him, or she's already on the pontoon at the Lake. (Folks, once again these alternative takes of the same action may have been included to expand the film following the re-think and departure of Gérard Depardieu. The clue to this is in the narration, the conversation between Klimt and Aude, which was part of the re-shoot, and the guy on the pier is likely a double).

The 1993 movie is filled with padding – there are several shots which try the patience of diehard Godardians (such as Abraham Klimt walking along country roads which go on and on).

Little bits of business occur – a man practising his tennis swings; a guy juggling fruit; a film editor frantically searching for another shot of a car on a road to fill in ten more seconds of the movie.

Hélas Pour Moi is a film that flashes from light to dark regularly, that obscures then reveals things, that creates noise on the soundtrack then reduces it to a single sound, that is at once self-consciously vague and self-consciously clear. The suggestions of mystery and vagueness that stem from the film's troubled production and its incomplete realization aren't always to the point. How much of *Hélas Pour Moi* is the result of conscious planning and execution, and how much of it is a rescue job?

There are shadowy figures, not identified, who may be God's accomplices (though they appear ambiguous, more like threats than angels). This seems to be a reprise of the conceptualization of the Archangel Gabriel in *Hail Mary* as a very modern guy. When a hat is passed to Depardieu's Simon and he puts it on (from the angel-like

---

30 With ridiculously bushy, back-combed hair.

figure who arrives by train), that is presumably the moment when God enters Simon (the film deploys a loud music cue at this moment).

Hélas Pour Moi employs a number of visual *caches* (masks) as well as the aural ones. That's a recurring Godardism: to deliberately obscure the screen, to withhold information from the viewer. Godard has always enjoyed compositions in which actors are obscured by props or doors or whatever. In an already very enigmatic film such as *Hélas Pour Moi*, it makes it even more enigmatic. But if an audience is having difficulty following the film in the first place, it isn't going to appreciate being even more confused by wilful obscurations and *caches*.

+++ Towards the end of *Hélas Pour Moi*, when the film turns to trains and train stations, with new (and unidentified) characters ruminating about Godardian concerns like philosophical theology (or theological philosophy), we seem to be in the realm of re-shoots. Very little of Gérard Depardieu appears in these scenes (all that remains are odds and sods of bits of fragments of shards of ashes swept off the cutting room floor). We're left with new characters (including Abraham Klimt), though Rachel does turn up on her bike.

At this point, *Hélas Pour Moi* becomes inconsequential and self-consciously a failure, and that feeling of looking forward to the next shot which Jean-Luc Godard talked about which he liked about *Woe Is Me* disappears too (it's now 'woe for this film', not 'woe is me'). Of the cinema of poetry – I mean the poetry of cinema – there is only really one true instance in the third act, and that is the lengthy shot where Simon, Rachel and some other people appear at the lakeside, and Simon wades into the water, around a boat, as the camera tracks to the left. It's a classic, Godardian mobile shot, with offscreen sounds, a conversation with an offscreen character, an unusual piece of action (why does Simon wade into the water?), and a lengthy take which culminates with a tight M.C.U. on Rachel and Simon on the quay in the foreground. (This might have been a way of incorporating a walking-on-the-water sequence which Godard wanted to include in *Hélas Pour Moi*: he and DP Caroline Champetier had experimented with visual effects to achieve it. There would also have been a major visual fx sequence involving God witnessing 'all the battles of history').

In the last minutes of *Hélas Pour Moi*, the black leader seems to come thicker and faster, as if the live action footage of the film will fade away and leave nothing but black with white captions, and let the soundtrack – the voices, the music, the sound effects – do the work (that's not a bad idea, and a Godard film of nothing but black and titles and sounds would still be compelling. Indeed, Godard's later cinema is perfect for turning into a radio play, or a CD).

33

J.L.G./ J.L.G. AUTOPORTRAIT DE DÉCEMBRE

J.L.G./ J.L.G. SELF-PORTRAIT IN DECEMBER

> In jüngern Tagen war ich des Morgens froh,
> Des Abends weint' ich; jetzt, da ich älter bin,
> Beginn ich zweifelnd meinen Tag, doch
> Heilig und heiter ist mir sein Ende.
>
> Friedrich Hölderlin, 'Then and Now'[31]

---

[31] 'In younger days each morning I rose with joy, | to weep at nightfall now, in my later years, | though doubting I begin my day, yet | always its end is serene and holy' (*Poems and Fragments*, 22-23).

J.L.G./ J.L.G. – Autoportrait de Décembre (1995) was an hour-long autobiographical film, made for Gaumont/ Périphéria/ J.L.G. Films. It was written by, produced by, directed by and featured Jean-Luc Godard ruminating on life, death, art, cinema, politics, ideology, philosophy, literature and popular culture.

The crew for this miniature masterpiece were: DPs Yves Pouliguen and Christian Jacquenod, costumes by Marina Zuliani and Corrine Baersiwyl, sound by Pierre-Alain Besse and Benoît Hilbrant, the AD was Thierry Borders, and Godard and Catherine Cormon edited it. Appearing were: Geneviève Pasquier, Denis Jadót, Brigitte Bastien, Elisabeth Kaza, André S. Labarthe, Louis Seguin, Bernard Eisenschitz and Nathalie Aguillar. Released: March 8, 1995. 55 mins.

Jean-Luc Godard recalled that '*J.L.G. on J.L.G.* was a film I shot very quickly because one day I read in the contract: "Delivery in a month."' Godard had a film owed in his contract with Gaumont: the result was *J.L.G./ J.L.G.* (Gaumont supported Godard for years).

J.L.G./ J.L.G. was one of Godard's late film-essays; shots of Godard sitting in what appeared to be his apartment in Switzerland, reading or writing or talking to the camera were intercut with images of Lake Geneva, or snowy fields, a snowbound road, or trees, or a park, or distant hills (many of these images appeared to be places from Godard's childhood). The shifts between interior and exterior, between the life of the mind and the life of the world outside, recalled Godard's cinematic tactics in *Hail Mary*. For much of the film Godard was seen in shadow, or from behind, so that his face was obscured.[32] One wishes that other filmmakers, like Tsui Hark, Stanley Kubrick, or Woody Allen, had produced such a revealing, intimate self-portrait as *J.L.G./ J.L.G.*

J.L.G./ J.L.G. was full of quotations, mainly from other writers: Jean-Luc Godard was seen pulling down books from the many shelves that lined his apartment/ studio, leafing through the pages and reading a few lines aloud (from Ludwig Wittgenstein, Denis Diderot, Fyodor Dostoievsky). Often Godard would use the quote as a springboard for his own reflections. The quotations continued on the soundtrack: there were many excerpts from movies (presumably some were Godard's own films, some from Hollywood productions, and references to Jean Vigo, Roberto Rossellini, and Nicholas Ray), adverts and television programmes. Music, as one would expect from a Godard film, ran

---

[32] For Jim Hoberman, *J.L.G./ J.L.G.* was 'charged with death, absence, silence', the artist isolated in a home of books and videotapes ("*Germany Year Nine Zero* and *J.L.G. By J.L.G.*", *Village Voice*, Jan 24, 1995).

throughout: symphonies, piano music, Gregorian chant, and choirs (mainly by Arvo Pärt). The familiar heavy stab of piano. Painters were cited, of course: Jan Vermeer, Peter Paul Rubens, Diego Velásquez, Egon Schiele, Enerst Kirchner, Pierre Renoir, Francisco de Goya, Paul Cézanne, etc.

Jean-Luc Godard also included a TV set in the background of some images (sometimes with a camcorder in the foreground, filming it); a couple of shots concentrated on paintings (a slow pan across some reproductions of paintings taken out of artbooks and scattered on a table (including some Egon Schiele and Francisco de Goya images, and mostly of women, with Godard ruminating on sex); a later shot had Godard lighting a Diego Velásquez painting with a match, as if in a power black-out, and watching himself in a nearby video camera, a self-portrait within a self-portrait, the camera as mirror). (Many of the scenes are under-lit to the point of darkness. Although *J.L.G./ J.L.G.* looked like Godard had filmed it himself, Yves Pouliguen and Christian Jaquenod were the DPs).

In one scene, which consisted of a shot of Jean-Luc Godard's hands, some paper and pens on a table, Godard demonstrated the concept of stereo, stereo vision and stereo hearing, sketching out overlapping triangles in black and red marker pens, talking about the blind, and animals, the mystic hexagram, then moving on to the Star of David (contrasting Israel and Palestine). That scene seems specially designed to make cultural critics twitch with anticipation. Godard is such a tease! (And, yes, critics have duly analyzed that scene. But why? The scene contains its own commentary, it's own meta-text, and its own hyper-meta-post-analysis).

This is Godard as Professor Godard, the visiting teacher, who'll come to your college and lead a class in Modern Cinema. It's Godard performing one of his 'blackboard' sceness (which began in earnest in *La Chinoise*).

Writing, as well as reading, was a constant motif in *J.L.G./ J.L.G. – Autoportrait de Décembre*, with many images of Jean-Luc Godard writing: at a table writing, or drawing diagrams, or scribbling in a notebook by Lake Geneva (the sound of bombs stood in for thunder in these scenes). The intertitles of *J.L.G./ J.L.G.* were also handwritten, single phrases on lined notepaper which Godard flicked through to announce each new section of the film-essay (about as cheap as you can get for optical captions, filming your own handwriting. But of course the handwritten element enhances this self-portrait. And, anyway, the budget is what the budget is, as Godard often remarked, and if you can't afford flashy captions, a pen and paper will do).

J.L.G./ J.L.G. mainly consisted of Jean-Luc Godard alone in his dimly-lit apartment; in one sequence he was seen walking along the shore of Lake Geneva (two takes are used); in another, playing tennis at an indoor court; in another scene, in what seemed to be an open-plan office (a kind of recreation of the Sonimage/ Périphéria offices, his production company in Rolle, a brief insight into Godard and Miéville's filmmaking operation), he employed a 'blind' female editor (who comes for a job) to help him with his editing (he went through a scene, sifting through a roll of 35mm film stock; Godard sits at the editing table, demonstrating editing in a pointedly silly manner. It's a self-conscious demo of the film editor's job – using a film that Godard had recently completed, *Woe Is Me* in 1993).

Although he was on his own mostly, Jean-Luc Godard did manage to include a beautiful, young woman, as was his custom. Here, the woman was the 'cleaner', Cassandra or Brigitte (Brigitte Bastien), seen wandering around Godard's apartment with a feather duster, wearing cut-off denim shorts which emphasized her rear (which the Master prods). Like Godardian characters in the 1960s films, the woman was shown reading aloud from a book as she walked around, and declaiming in Godard-speak as she dusted the bookshelves. (A satire of how filmmakers are officially judged and assessed by society occurs when some petty bureaucrats visit his offices to take stock of the place. There are shelves of books on French cinema, they note, a whole shelf devoted to Jean Renoir, a shelf to Italian cinema, and a shelf to Russian cinema. You can assess the stature of an intellectual by the size of their library. Who's got the biggest book? The most books? The most obscure books?).

Light, fire and smoke were also running themes: Jean-Luc Godard was seen smoking his trademark cigars, and lighting them often; in one scene he is writing a letter on Sonimage-headed notepaper, in near total darkness, by lighting matches periodically; in another, he studies a postcard of a Diego Velásquez painting by the light of a match (exploring the video camera's ability to film in very low light. And he's filming into mirrors, something that filmmakers can't resist doing).

The 1994 film is augmented by plenty of off-screen sounds, the usual Jean-Luc Godard retinue of birds (that bloody crow!), people, films, feet, and waves. Godard often whispers, and also puts on his silly, low voice (which makes his lisp worse).

J.L.G./ J.L.G. contains the usual package of Godardisms, including the notion that everyone speaks the rule, no one speaks the exception. It cannot be spoken, except in art (or life).

There was also Jean-Luc Godard's customary sly humour in *J.L.G./ J.L.G.*, such as Godard getting the name of his female 'cleaner' wrong, speaking about France (in English) by Lake Geneva (how J.L.G. has spent his life living between two kingdoms, Switzerland and France), trying to grab his coat from an old crone talking in Latin[33] in a snowy forest (a bit of William Shakespeare maybe?), and waspish comments such as, 'Europe has memories, America has Tee shirts'.

The first bit of voiceover is another tease: Lord Godard explains about a typical film production: run through rehearsals, check I know my lines by heart, improve my acting, organize a dress rehearsal. But of course, Godard does none of those things!

At the end of the 1994 film-essay, over a shot of verdant countryside, Jean-Luc Godard simply affirms that he's a man, no more or less, and no better or worse than other men. This is one of Godard's recurring statements: he's not 'special', he's not different from anyone else.

---

[33] Godard has a thing about Latin, wishing that he'd learnt it as a child, so he could communicate clearer Well, he *could* learn it. (He also said he couldn t set a film in Ancient Rome because he didn't speak Latin).

34

ELOGE DE L'AMOUR

IN PRAISE OF LOVE

Éloge de L'Amour (*In Praise of Love,* 2001) showed none of Jean-Luc Godard's powers of creating provocative, idiosyncratic and passionate cinema were undimmed by age (he was over seventy). The production companies were Télévision Suisse Romande/ Arte France Cinéma/ Avventura Films/ Vega Films/ Canal Plus/ Périphéria (Godard's and Miéville's company). Alain Sarde and Ruth Waldburger were the producers. David Darling, Ketil Bjornstad, Georges Van Parys, Maurice Jaubert and Arvo Pärt provided the music,[34] sound was mixed by François Mussy and Gabriel Hafner, Raphaelle Urtin edited it. Marie-France Thibault did the costumes, the DPs were Christophe Pollock and Julien Hirsch, casting by Stéphane Foenkinos, and the ADs were Christophe Rabinovici and Fleur Albert. The crew of *In Praise of Love* was 4 or 5 people, Godard said. Released: May 15, 2001. 97 mins.

In the cast were: Bruno Putzulu, Cécile Camp, Jean Davy, Françoise Verny, Audrey Klebaner, Jérémie Lippmann, Claude Baignières, Rémo Forlani and Lemmy Constantine.

Elogie de l'Amour also features a catalogue of former Jean-Luc Godard associates in small roles (many were non-actors), including Rémo Forlani, who wrote the fake screenplay for *Pierrot le Fou,* the *Figaro*'s film critic, Claude Baignères, critic Noël Simsolo, Marceline Loridan-Ivens, Philippe Loyrette, Jean-Henri Roger (from the Dziga Vertov days), and Lemmy Constantine (from *Alphaville*). The locations in *Elogie de l'Amour* – back in Paris this time – are also stuffed with personal and professional associations for Godard.[35]

Éloge de L'Amour was shown at the Cannes Film Festival and the New York Film Festival (where Jean-Luc Godard's films had been badly received before). The response to *Éloge de L'Amour* was much more favourable than usual – from most critics. But not for all film critics, though: Gerard Peary in the *Boston Phoenix* commented of the *Éloge de L'Amour* screening at Cannes:

> The theatre was full. Many [critics] remained outside, sulking in the hallway. We inside looked eagerly to the screen: at last, *In Praise of Love*! But as the picture unfolded – cryptic epigrams, glib anti-Americanisms, the sketchiest of narrative, shadow characterizations, and melancholy pretension everywhere – many of us realized... that we had been had!

Godard went further with promoting *Elogie de l'Amour* than he

---

[34] Not personally – alas, Godard didn't phone up Arvo Pärt and ask him to compose a ravishing, minimalist score. If only!
[35] Including cafés on the Boul Mich (like La Favorite), where Godard and Jean-Henri Roger met during the late 1960s, and La Liberté, famous for its links to Jean-Paul Sartre.

usually did: he seemed to be everywhere, in every newspaper and magazine, in the run-up to the release in Paris.

•

Jean-Luc Godard remarked that *In Praise of Love* had been difficult to make, partly because, he admitted, 'I was a bit lost, but I kept trying to do it anyway. In fact, you have to just do it and then you have to cut later'. *Éloge de L'Amour* turned out to be 'a long, disjointed shoot, in several sections, and the mixing was difficult. It was something of a strain.' The film was made at different times, and Godard said he had been searching for a way of completing the film. It began in 'February, then in September. Then in Brittany. At that point, I didn't know what I wanted to do.'

There were problems with the film crew. Or, rather, with Godard's relations with the crew. He hankered after people on set he could talk to (meaning, *his* kind of conversation, about philosophy and ideas and culture and all).

Despite the trouble with actors, the over-long schedule, and getting the script right, *Elogie de l'Amour* scored a hit with its lead actor, Bruno Putzulu (b. 1967), a rising star. And Putzulu and Godard got along famously (both were keen followers of sport). Putzulu gets the Godardian style of acting spot-on (many actors deliver what they think the Maestro wants, which isn't always the same thing).

The actress Bérangère Allaux became a later Muse for J.-L. Godard, though the relationship was not reciprocated (she was 45 years younger than Godard). Allaux was a first-year drama student and Godard developed a 'terrible crush' on her, during the pre-production of *For Ever Mozart*, as Richard Brody relates, 'which exerted a powerful influence on his behavior' (B, 568). Godard had planned to make a movie at Allaux's college in Strasbourg, École nationale de l'art dramatique: it would've involved Allaux and her class. But there was some resentment or jealousy among the drama students, who said they'd prefer to make a movie with (yawn) Quentin Tarantino.

The first version of *Elogie de l'Amour* would have featured an older man and two prostitutes: Godard wanted to include sex scenes and violence.[36] The story would've had an older man leaving a younger woman for an older woman. The scenes proved too hardcore for his actors, Jacques Bonaffé and Bérangère Allaux, who refused to do them. According to Allaux, there was an uncomfortable moment in Godard's office at Périphéria in Switzerland when the director said he wanted to

---

[36] In the end, Godard confessed that he was glad he didn't make that version: 'it's very bad, it's horrible, fortunately I didn't make it'.

see them both naked, and they undressed (B, 579). It's certainly outside the norm at a casting session or pre-production meeting for actors to be asked to undress (for a regular movie, anyway).

When the actors walked away from the second version of *Elogie de l'Amour* (which was the same story, but more from the young woman's point-of-view), director Godard reworked the material again, this time focussing on age differences in romantic relations (now there would be a young couple, a middle-aged couple, and an old couple).

Elogie de l'Amour was unusual in going thru so many revisions at the script stage (unusual for Godard). The indecisiveness also extended to the filming, which became protracted (Godard prefers to shoot quickly, if possible – some of his 1960s movies had been staged in two weeks. But Godard can do more in two weeks than 1,000s of other film directors can do in 16 weeks, or 40 weeks. During the time of *In Praise of Love* Godard said he wasn't so fond of filming – it was the search he enjoyed).

Another draft of *In Praise of Love* had the picture split into two parts, the second was entitled *Elogie de l'Amour*, about a young couple who fall out when their grandparents want to sell the rights to the story of their life of being in the Resistance (Isabella, their granddaughter, approves – she's an actress, and wants to be in the movie version. The rights are going to be bought up by Steven Spielberg. Her boyfriend Ludovic disapproves). This part of *In Praise of Love* was titled *Voulez-vous faire du cinéma.* (The couple form the old part of the three ages of love).

There were problems with another actor in *Elogie de l'Amour* – J.-L. Godard wanted Marie Desgranges to undergo a personal, psychological relationship with him, which he had done b4, with, for example, Bérangere Allaux and with Myriem Roussel. It didn't work out, and Godard fired Desgranges.

❋

Éloge de L'Amour contained most of the Jean-Luc Godard hallmarks: a soundtrack that cut in and out abruptly; overlapping sound; dialogue drowned out by background noise; bursts of classical music; cuts to landscapes; freeze frames; slow motion; step motion; actors reading aloud from books; C.U.s of book covers; black leader (repeated many times); ironic, multiple voiceovers; cars and trains; pop culture and 'high' culture references (painters and writers); images of contemporary Paris;[37] and disquisitions on familiar Godardian

---

[37] Godard said he wanted Paris to look 'timeless' in *Éloge de L'Amour*.

subjects: Hollywood, Amerika, France, history, war[38] and mortality. And the usual retinue of Godardian oppositions: France<->Amerika,[39] European cinema<->Hollywood movies, cinema<->history, perception<->reality. And plenty of allusions to painters, writers, and filmmakers (including Max Ophüls, Henri Langlois, Henri-Louis Bergson, Simone Weil and Robert Bresson).[40]

In Praise of Love is a haunted film that exists in a netherworld of memories; everything seems to be relic or a partial survival of something from the past (WWII, the Resistance, the death camps, the Bosnian War, etc). *Elogie de l'Amour* doesn't have a present tense, no feeling of being alive in the here and now (no matter what the characters may say or do). Edgar comes across as a ghost navigating a world of ghosts – everyone he meets seems to exist only momentarily in the present day. The old guys he hangs out with (his grandfather (Jean Davy) and Mr Rosenthal – Claude Baignières) talk continually of the past, and the art that they deal in is all Old Masters (aren't there any New Masters? Doesn't anybody make new art anymore? Has everything already been done – and a long time ago?).

In *Elogie de l'Amour*, Paris appears as a Land of the Dead in which nobody is alive anymore and everyone is a spectre (the black-and-white photography, perpetually under-lit and struggling to retain any light, is reminiscent of barely-lit Godard films such as *Alphaville* and *Le Petit Soldat*).

There is no Movie-Paris quite like this Paris in *Elogie de l'Amour*; as in *Alphaville*, Jean-Luc Godard makes Paris his Land of the Dead. But the genre, thriller elements of *Alphaville* – the man, the gun, the trenchcoat, the girl, the henchmen, the shadowy organization – are long gone, replaced by an uncertain narrative which anyway isn't a narrative but is all preparation for some other project.

With its excavation of the past, or the ambiguous relation with history, *Elogie de l'Amour* came across at times like a narrative or fictional version of *Histoire(s) du Cinéma* (some of the same video techniques were used). That is, if you took one of the installments of *Histoire(s) du Cinéma* and turned it into a film script with a plot, it might resemble *Elogie de l'Amour*. Sort of – well, it would be the usual Godardian thing of notes for the preparation of a script of a possible film. Notes for notes for notes. Eternal preparation for a film that

---

38 'The thin line between entertainment and war', as Rage Against the Machine put it: 'the front line is everywhere'.
39 'You wanted America', someone tells someone else in *Elogie de l'Amour*, 'and you got America' (meaning the colonization of Europe by Amerika following WWII).
40 At one point a woman reads aloud from Bresson's *Notes On Cinematography*.

would never be made, that could never be made, but the obsessive note-making would be sufficient. For now.

But the search itself is a beguiling element in *In Praise of Love*: Edgar is looking for something and can't quite articulate what it is. Godard said he enjoyed the search for a film, even before the script was written. The gap, *si vous voulez*, between the title and the idea, or btn the idea and the screenplay (the title came first and a vague notion of what the movie would be about. Godard has started with titles before).

So this is the early stages of pre-production, way before completing a script, or casting actors, or signing contracts. Now, if you could leap from this stage in filmmaking up over full pre-production and land in post-production, missing out the rest of pre-production and all of the filming, Godard would be happy (and so would filmmakers such as George Lucas, Woody Allen and Steven Spielberg. Yes, even Spielberg doesn't delight in weeks of filming).

Anyway, if you approach *In Praise of Love* as a film of a search (for notes for a film of a search for a film), the scrappy, unfulfilled aspects of it fall away – precisely because it's a search (a quest for the miraculous, 'a search for magic', as Pier Paolo Pasolini put it). Then we are not looking for (or demanding) a story and characters and themes and all. And once we put aside those demands from a Godard movie, it can be more rewarding.

We also see a director directing in *In Praise of Love* in a sometimes more conventional manner (compared to the anguished Jerzy in *Passion*, for example). We see Edgar directing Eglantine and Perceval as the young couple of the movie in a room. But then maybe it isn't conventional after all – Edgar appears distanced, aloof, and turns away from the actors to talk to them while looking out of the window.

*

The use of music in *Éloge de L'Amour* is outstanding – truly Godard and Miéville are masters at deploying music in films. Lyrical piano music, melancholy cello and viola, washes of strings, and early pop songs. The music helps *In Praise of Love* to become, for me, deeply moving. It's a bittersweet film, at once sad and optimistic, a eulogy or elegy but also a pæan to some of the good things in life (like art, like music, like people, like love). The music enhances the ghost-like quality of *Elogie de l'Amour*, its air of lamentation and wistful nostalgia (underlined by the selection of music, of course).

Éloge de L'Amour, Jean-Luc Godard explained, was about love between young people, and someone (a director) who wants to make a project about love. Love in *Éloge de L'Amour* was meant to be about all kinds of love: Godard said: 'I wish we could consider all forms of love: love between a man and a woman, love of fellow man, love of France, love of things'. And love of three ages – young, middle-age and old. But in *In Praise of Love* it is erotic, romantic and heterosexual love that the film is considering, as Edgar states when he interviews actors: the four aspects of love are: (1) meeting, (2) sex, (3) separation, and (4) reconciliation. In the event, *Éloge de L'Amour* did not really illustrate those four moments of love. Edgar appeared to abandon his play or film about love, and when the film shifted back two years, he was now writing a cantata based on the writings of Simone Weil, and the French Resistance, and the Second World War.

Memory and the past are clearly great fascinations for Jean-Luc Godard in *Éloge de L'Amour:* he explores the past at length, but not only his own past, or his own relation to the past. It's history, but not Godard's history (there are hints of links to Godard, though, in the references to Henri Langlois, and in many of the locations used for the film. At times, *In Praise of Love* is like Godard's tour of the Paris he used to know, the Paris he put into many movies). Edgar's notion that someone moving into the future inevitably erases their former self has autobiographical resonances.[41]

✳

As in other later Jean-Luc Godard films, nothing much 'happened' in *Éloge de L'Amour,* in the conventional sense: people sat in rooms and talked; they got in and out of cars; they drove around in cars; they read out aloud; they walked Paris's streets; they talked by the River Seine; they walked along train lines.

But Godard's undiminished power to manipulate sound and image meant that *Éloge de L'Amour* was mesmeric cinema. There were moments of intense poetry, such as when the narrative cut away from a group of characters discussing Kosovo or Hollywood to a seascape or a roadside scene in late Autumn which, accompanied by plangent music, was beautiful. In *Éloge de L'Amour,* Godard demonstrated again that, despite the biting assaults on popular culture (with North Amerika as the prime target), despite the downbeat distantiation (or wholesale withdrawal) from modern life, the love-hate relationship with filmmaking, Godard was still profoundly romantic. As with other late Godard films, there was a wistful melancholy submerged below the narrative surface of *Éloge de L'Amour,* a romanticism and barely

---
41 It chimes with Godard's preference for viewing the past (the New Wave days) as not only long gone, but also of another era, which has little resonance for him now.

disguised utopianism and idealism. Underneath the hard, bleak exterior of Godard's films, as with Samuel Beckett's Existential pessimism, there was an idealistic soul.

What's extraordinary about Jean-Luc Godard's cinema, as a few commentators have noted, is just how much of it deals with *love*. Different kinds of love, but mainly romantic love, the love between a man and a woman. The impossibility of it, of course, but also the mystery of it, and the inescapable desirability of it. Love, one might say, is among Godard's primary themes, and one could argue, drawing on numerous examples, that it is his primary theme above all others.

And that certainly comes across in *Éloge de L'Amour*, although it doesn't really show any couples as such, or couples doing the things that couples do, like kiss, or talk, or go out to eat or watch movies, or tup, or argue, or whatever.[42] Oh, there *are* couples in *Éloge de L'Amour*, but they're not depicted in anything like conventional terms (the couple are called Eglantine and Perceval, though only Eglantine, yet another in a long line of Jean-Luc Godard's actresses with big eyes and a pale, oval face (Modigliani, Botticelli, Velasquez), makes an impression).[43]

And yet *Éloge de L'Amour* is about love, as the title suggests. The film's title, which came first, Jean-Luc Godard explained, has 'love' in it, a rarity in Godard's cinema. An elegy of love, an elegy about love. It is certainly strange, in a way, to be talking about love in relation to Godard's cinema, which's a cool, ironic, distanced and modernist/postmodernist form of cinema. But the more one sees of Godard's fascinating body of work, the more one realizes that love is a theme, an issue, a feeling, a trope, that never goes away. (Love comes back as persistently as his need to make films).

❉

The first part of *In Praise of Love*, lasting over an hour (i.e., most of the film), was set in contemporary Paris and was filmed in black-and-white. This was a conscious nod back to Jean-Luc Godard's black-and-white films of the 1950s and 1960s, of course. And many of the scenes were filmed at night, in the rain, and were *extremely* dark, inevitably recalling the daring low-light levels of *Alphaville* (and much of Godard's late work).[44]

---

42 There is a couple chattering on the bench behind Godard when he makes a brief cameo in Paris at night.
43 Tho' Perceval does some acrobatic tumbling. It's the kind of thing that Godard might've found out during casting and put in the film. He enjoys physical tricks (like the juggling in *Woe Is Me*).
44 Bernardo Bertolucci regarded Godard's later work as 'like a fantastic diamond which has an interior light, because it doesn't need light from the sun and its own inner light radiates outwards. So it's sublime and far away' (in I. Halberstadt).

Éloge de L'Amour had a crisp, lyrical look, the black-and-white photography giving Paris in the rain a gleaming sheen. And Jean-Luc Godard has his cameos: sitting on a bench on a Paris street at night, or sweeping the ground around some actors.

It's not all central Paris and glamour in *Éloge de L'Amour*: Jean-Luc Godard excavates some post-industrial zones of Paris, such as the disused Renault factory by the river (dubbed an 'empty fortress'). Numerous echoes of past Godard movies occur here (including the images of strikes and workers in *Tout Va Bien*, and the long dialogue scene played with the actors' backs to camera, reprised here from *Vivre Sa Vie*).

Early scenes defined Edgar as the major character, as he remained throughout the film. But, as usual in Godard's later work, his profession or purpose, even his name, was kept deliberately shadowy and ambiguous. He appeared interchangeable with an art dealer, a film or theatre director, a writer, a painter, and a composer. Edgar is controlling the narrative in many scenes: his voiceover is explaining about stories and beginnings[45] and the four moments of love.

There are lengthy scenes where Edgar, always offscreen, interviews potential cast members. These are exactly like casting sessions – and Edgar directs them like casting sessions (an insight into Jean-Luc Godard's casting process, perhaps). With Edgar's offscreen voice explaining (and commanding,) the film concentrated on close-ups of unidentified actors. (In fact, they *were* auditions, filmed in 1999. But it would've been Godard asking the questions off-screen, as usual. This is why some of the candidates look uncomfortable – being interviewed by someone like Godard on camera is definitely intimidating!).

Edgar seems to have been an identification figure for Godard, but everything he does seems to be preparation – for something is never finished, never quite clearly defined, and something he doesn't seem sure about at all. Indeed, Edgar's restlessness is apparent in every scene, as if Godard instructed Bruno Putzulu to remain in perpetual unease.

✽

Painting is another familiar Godardian layer to *Éloge de L'Amour* – Edgar's father is an art dealer, and the scenes with father and son are full of paintings and references to painters (scenes in art galleries, shots of paintings and drawings).[46] Discussions about art and

---

45 That's classic Godard: to make conscious the filmmaker's concerns with stories, with how stories start – you see it at the beginning of *Tout Va Bien*, for instance, or *Bande à Part*.
46 Vlaminck, Corot, Rembrandt, Brueghel, etc.

business, the business of art, the art of business.[47] The past is inescapable here, too. It's as if you can't move an inch in *Éloge de L'Amour* without being submerged in memories and the past and a sense of history. Every image appears weighted down with memories and personal and historical associations. *Éloge de L'Amour* is a film soaked in history.

Painting was increasingly a theme in Godard's later films: in particular, he explored how digital video imagery could evoke painting, with its heightened, saturated colours reminiscent of Impressionism, Post-Impressionism, Fauvism and Expressionism. Godard was happy to adjust the contrast, brightness and saturation of video images so that his shots of Lake Geneva or mountains resembled a canvas by Pierre Bonnard, Claude Monet or Emil Nolde. (Remember how Godard was a keen painter in his teens, and his mother Odile organized an exhibition for him in Mortriant).

One could make a book of Godardisms from *Éloge de L'Amour* alone. Every single character speaks in Godardisms of one sort or another: it's a feast of gnomic, pithy one-liners, and although *Éloge de L'Amour* is a melancholy movie, some are humorous. For instance:
- 'we're jesters. We out-live our problems'
- 'things are right in front of us. Why make them up?'
- 'every desire must meet its lassitude, its truth'
- 'you can only think of something if you think of something else'

One of the recurring quips in *Éloge de L'Amour* was a classic Godardism: whenever 'Americans' were referred to, interlocutors demanded clarification: did they mean South Americans? The people of Mexico or Brazil, or Canada, which are also 'United States'? And the explanations came: no, I mean the Americans of North America, the North Americans. You see?, came the response, a country with no name, with no history, which has to borrow its history from other places. Classic Godardian thinking (but this sort of anti-Americanism really irks American critics).

There is plenty of black leader in *Éloge de L'Amour* – a practice Jean-Luc Godard has always employed, but much more so in films such as *Hélas Pour Moi* and *Éloge de L'Amour*. And, as usual, Godard was peppering his film with captions over black (repeating phrases such as 'de quelque choses' or 'de l'amour', in Courier font, the typeface used for film scripts).

Of his treatment of the colours in *Éloge de L'Amour* in post

---

[47] Once again, North America is a reference point in the commercialization of art, with pointed cuts to the U.S. flag hanging outside a building.

production, Jean-Luc Godard said, 'I love impressionism, in cinema and particularly in video', and he enjoyed playing with the colours as a painter would (he also cited the Fauvists). The mix of black-and-white film and colour video really worked – maybe because they were so different.[48] There was no attempt to fuse them together, like the transitions from black-and-white to colour (or vice versa) in many other movies. If *Éloge de L'Amour* was disjointed in some respects in terms of its fragmented narrative, there was no disjunction between black-and-white and colour. (As well as colour video, the filmmakers also employed many superimpositions, some quite slow dissolves, and step motion and slow motion – these were the video techniques of *Histoire(s) du Cinéma*).

The shift from black-and-white celluloid to colour digital video was announced in a dramatic fashion in *Éloge de L'Amour*, with a long shot of the ocean in Brittany, with the colours exaggerated, so the screen was all oranges and reds. And not only the heightened look of the sea, but also a big, oceanic sound on the track.

❉

Godard noted that there's a point around an hour into a film where there's a lull (meaning in his own films – in other movies, it's typically between 60 and 90 minutes in a four-act, 120-minute movie). Hence this was the point in *In Praise of Love* when the film was shifted into colour and into the past. (This also arose from the reworking of the movie, and the addition of the Brittany sequence).

The time shift is *very* unusual in the cinema of Godard. Altho' his works in any medium are haunted by the past, and obsessed with history more than almost any comparable filmmaker, most of his theatrical movies exist in an eternal present day. But *In Praise of Love* went back into the past (indicated by a caption). In addition, the present tense scene in Paris in the first part of the film move ahead in time, so that the scenes at the old Renault factory, for example, were set in the past.

At that point, the narrative of *Éloge de L'Amour* shifted back two years, but still stayed with Edgar. Now he was visiting Brittany, by the sea, in particular two people who fought in the Resistance in World War Two. The film's move away from Paris accompanies a deeper exploration of the past, in particular the war and the Resistance. This section of *Éloge de L'Amour* has plenty of books being cited, as well as

---

48 The video was filmed using the new DV (Digital Video) cameras: Godard had his DP (Christophe Pollock) use the cameras like a Japanese tourist. He wanted that vacation footage look, as if Berthe had filmed Brittany herself. Originally, Godard had wanted to use 70mm cameras, but they proved too expensive.

images of book covers. (A recurring image of *Éloge de L'Amour* is a blank book, which Edgar leafs through as if looking for clues – very Godardian, very Existential – it's the kind of thing that might crop up in a student film or an adaptation of Albert Camus or André Gide).

The narrative of *In Praise of Love*'s Brittany section also included a couple of North Americans (driving a green Lotus sports car), and another who arrives in a helicopter, who were buying the stories of the French Resistance members to be re-made by Hollywood (with Juliette Binoche to star). This part of the film illustrated Jean-Luc Godard's relentless anti-Americanism and anti-Hollywoodism by depicting the uneasy relationship between the Yanks and the French.

The granddaughter (who was amenable in the early drafts) is very hostile to the idea of G.I. Joe buying the rights to the story of her grandparents' French Resistance adventures. Berthe is the one who snipes at the unwelcome foreigners with comments about the 'America of the North' and such.

Did I mention trains? *Éloge de L'Amour* is full of them: Edgar walking beside train tracks; trains whooshing by at night; Edgar riding trains and reading (trains rattle throughout Godard's later cinema). Off-screen sounds included: telephones ringing; trains; cars; car horns; rain; waves.

The homeless and vagabonds are another narrative element in *Éloge de L'Amour*, as Edgar and his aide Philippe move through the underworld of Paris at night, searching. Their quest takes them to the regions of the under-class of Paris, the cleaners and the homeless. A search for a woman, which ends up at a railroad works, where she is cleaning the trains (Edgar becomes fascinated by the woman, and tries to persuade her to become part of his project. She repeatedly refuses).

War is another significant element in *In Praise of Love*, as it had been in *Hélas Pour Moi*, *JLG/ JLG* and *Histoire(s) du Cinéma*, and would be again in *Notre Musique*. In particular two wars: not the Vietnam War this time (tho that is cited several times), but WWII and the Balkans. The war in Yugoslavia, Albania and the Balkans in the Nineties would haunt much of Godard's late cinema. It was a conflict that was right inside Europe, the 'new Europe' – it wasn't happening in some distant territory like Vietnam.[49] It was a conflict with so many tragic echoes down the centuries, and very acutely of World War Two (in particular the notion of 'ethnic cleansing' and the Nazi death camps). It was a conflict that Europe nations reacted badly to, as Jean-

---

[49] Godard's films, though, don't make so many references to the calamities of, for instance, Africa in the 1990s – Algeria, Ethiopia, Rwanda, etc.

Luc Godard commented elsewhere.

*

Scenes are staged in the familar anti-dramatic style of Godard's later movies: for ex, in many scenes Bruno Putzulu simply stands staring out of the window, or he moved restlessly but pointlessly to another window (pointlessly in dramatic/ cinematic terms). There is no attempt at dramatic presentation, even tho' these are actors playing characters (not 'themselves' – I doubt that Putzulu looks glumly out of windows and mutters lines such as, 'every desire must meet its lassitude, its truth'. Or maybe he does now? Maybe after you've appeared in a Godard movie, you gaze off into the distance in the middle of shopping in Géant hypermarket (in the baloney section) and utter pithy witticisms such as 'death is no ending', or 'you must fight on two fronts at the same time – the Cheese Front and the Ham Front').

Coming from a film director who's capable of remarkable staging and blocking, the dramatic approach of Godard's later work can be very underwhelming. We are a *long* way from the highpoint of Godard's career, action-wise and staging-wise – *Weekend*.

The static presentation suits the material, of course – a melancholy, introspective and guilty exploration of melancholy, introspection and guilt. Everyone's a criminal, nothing is pure, corruption is everywhere, World War Two was everybody's fault, we are all guilty, no one escapes, ageing is horrible, and clinging onto memory is the final consolation for folk moving into their seventies and eighties.

Was life really richer/ deeper/ better before World War Two? In some of Godard's later works, there is a sneaking suspicion that WWII corrupted the Western world for good (our man was 9 years-old when WWII started. Part of Godard has that guilt-ridden, 'I wish I was there' feeling you find in other people who lived through it but didn't really participate significantly in WWII – that Godard sort of kind of wishes he'd been nineteen in 1939, and had joined the French Resistance).

This whole thing in late Godard of sitting on chairs and talking, or sitting at a table and talking, or wandering aimless around a room and talking, becomes wearisome. If Godard had opted to film some of the incredible stories from the French Resistance, even in a ten or twenty minute section within a movie, instead of having people leaf thru books or look at old photos, we could well see something truly remarkable.

Can you imagine a Godard movie actually *set* in the Forties? Instead of yakking about the war, and looking at ye olde photographes, we'd see recreations of the French Resistance, of the dangers of the underground movement, and visualizations of the issues that Godard wants to explore. Godard is fascinated by history, is always talking about history, but he refuses to dramatize it, preferring to evoke it with dialogue, photographs, film clips, captions and all.

Jean-Luc Godard's later works *are* remarkable, but they work on the viewer in a very intellectual, very philosophical, very talky manner. And, crucially, they rely a good deal on the audience knowing a good deal about the subject matter. For ex, in *In Praise of Love*, characters evoke the French Resistance by mentioning it in dialogue, and the audience has to fill in everything else (altho' we do see some photos from the period, and one of the characters does relate a teensy bit of a story about being in the Resistance). But how powerful *In Praise of Love* could be if, instead of only talking about the Resistance, or showing a few stills, it shifted into visceral dramatizations of those WWII days in the manner of *Le Petit Soldat*? (Godard's reply might be that he's already made *Le Petit Soldat*, and there's no need to do it again. Or he might say, OK, *you* go and make that Great Film about the French Resistance! Sure – and yet, and yet – there's part of Godard that wishes *he* had been given the money to make *Schindler's List*).

JEAN-LUC GODARD AND STEVEN SPIELBERG

Steven Spielberg was one of Jean-Luc Godard's *bête noires*, the embodiment of all that was wrong with 'Ollywooood: Godard called Universal's *Schindler's List* (1993)50 a film 'du Max Factor' (he took on Spielberg because the name was a modern icon). In *Éloge de L'Amour,* Godard's commentary made waspish remarks about Spielberg, and Hollywood, and Amerika ('Amerika of the North').

One of Jean-Luc Godard's complaints about Hollywood cinema was that it plundered other countries' stories and didn't have a history of its own to examine (or exploit). *In Praise of Love* cited *Schindler's List* as an example of 'Ollywooood colonizing other nations' history. Godard's views chime with those of the anti-American sentiments that

---

50 *Schindler's List* was based on a novel by Thomas Keneally (b. 1935). Steven Spielberg had bought the rights to Keneally's *Schindler's Ark* in 1982. Several directors were linked to the production, including Roman Polanski, Billy Wilder and Martin Scorsese.

were voiced during the 1992 G.A.T.T. talks and coalesced around *Jurassic Park* (1993) and other Hollywood blockbusters and movies which were popular in France, and taking too much of the share of the theatrical box office.

For Jean-Luc Godard, *Schindler's List* was phony. The phoniness extended to Steven Spielberg's choice of black-and-white instead of colour, which seems to be 'more serious'.

> To him it's not phony, I think he's honest to himself, but he's not very intelligent, so it's a phony result. [Spielberg] uses this man and this story and all the Jewish tragedy as if it were a big orchestra, to make a stereophonic sound from a simple story. (1998, 182)

Steven Spielberg, Jean-Luc Godard asserted, was simply 'not capable. Hollywood is not capable' of presenting historical fact (ibid.). Godard compared Spielberg to William Wyler, and reckoned that Wyler had been able to pull off the kind of thing Spielberg had attempted but not achieved (in a film like *The Best Years of Our Lives*).

Of Steven Spielberg, Jean-Luc Godard recalled:

> I've never met him, I don't know him, I'm not so fond of his films, and at the time I was critical of him when he reconstructed Auschwitz. As an artist and auteur, I felt it my duty to point a finger at him.[51]

Godard forgets that Steven Spielberg didn't write *Schindler's List*, didn't create the characters, the story or the themes, and did not originate the project – it had been offered to other directors (thus, *Schindler's List* is not an *auteur* product, certainly not the way that Godard makes his movies). Altho' Thomas Keneally and others attempted writing a film script of the *Schlinder's Ark* book, it was Steve Zaillian[52] who deserves most of the credit for the script[53] – and thus, in a film like *Schindler's List*, for the *whole movie*.

The Holocaust and the concentration camps have long fascinated Jean-Luc Godard (he relates part of his fascination to his father). *Schindler's List*, meanwhile, polarized film critics the world over, and inspired many debates over history, the war, Nazism, memory, and the Shoah. It's easy to see how and why *Schindler's List* riled Godard, as it

---

51 On why he doesn't like Spielberg's films, Godard said: 'That would take too long to explain. I no longer enjoy making comments in my work about films from the past. Show me a film in a screening room, then I'll make comments.'
52 Tom Stoppard called Zaillian 'the best scriptwriter I had come across, almost ever' (J. Baxter, *Steven Spielberg: The Unauthorized Biography*, HarperCollins, London, 1996 381).
53 Certainly, Zaillian's script is one of the great strengths of *Schindler's List*, with an extraordinary eye for detail that provides the opportunity for many telling moments, which Spielberg exploits.

did so many people. I can appreciate all of the sides of the arguments surrounding *Schindler's List*, but there's no denying that it is a most extraordinary film by any standards, and you can bet that many a European *auteur* secretly wished their own serious films could reach such a wide audience, or instigate so much debate.

I wonder, too, if Jean-Luc Godard found *Schindler's List* so irritating because it was another case of North American cinema colonizing European history and using it for its own, commercial, sentimental ends (I wonder if Godard thought, if anyone's going to get $22,000,000 to make a film about the Holocaust in Poland, it should be *me*). Yes, but Godard wants to have it both ways, as usual: hasn't Godard's own cinema happily raided North American culture (and not just North American movies) throughout his entire career?

If Jean-Luc Godard filmed *Schlinder's List* in the manner of *The Little Soldier* or *Weekend*, it could be incredible. But that's not how Godard made movies in the 21st century.

❉

Jean-Luc Godard challenged Steven Spielberg to a debate at the Locarno Film Festival. Needless to say, the American declined; it might have been safe to bet who would have triumphed in that confrontation – Godard, on his home, European, turf. However, Spielberg, partly due to countless appearances in the media, on film shows, documentaries and interviews, is well-versed in media soundbites, debates and marketing, and knows his cinema history at least as well as Godard. (But I'd still put my money on Godard!).

Roger Ebert countered Jean-Luc Godard's denunciations of Steven Spielberg by pointing out that Spielberg had probably done more to honour the survivors with his Holocaust Project than any director, living or dead. Also, Godard claimed in *In Praise of Love* that Spielberg hadn't paid Emilie Schindler for her contributions to *Schindler's List;* but Ebert wondered: has Godard sent her any money, because he used her too? (From what we know of Godard, it's very unlikely he would've sent any $$$$ to Schindler's widow).

Steven Spielberg's committment to the subject of *Schindler's List* was driven home by his subsequent philanthropic work with the Holocaust survivors' archive (Survivors of the Shoah Visual History Foundation), a non-profit Los Angeles organization staffed by volunteers, sited on the studio lot (funded with donations by Spielberg, M.C.A./ Universal, Time Warner, N.B.C. and the Lew Wasserman Foundation).

And Steven Spielberg's other contributions to charities and worthy causes far exceeds that of Jean-Luc Godard (indeed, Godard and charity or Godard plus philanthropy are not words you put together). Spielberg was also involved with the Righteous Persons Foundation, launched with $6m of the profits of *Schindler's List* (aimed at commemorating Gentiles who had rescued Jews in the Holocaust); Synagogue 2000; $3 million to the Holocaust Museum; $500,000 to the Fortunoff Video Archive for Holocaust Testimonies at Yale University; Anne Frank's House in Amsterdam received $250,000 towards its restoration; and the University of Sussex, G.B., was given £65,000 for a centre for German-Jewish Studies. Spielberg also funded Elizabeth Swados' film on anti-Semitism, *The Hating Pot*, Bill Moyers' TV series on the *Bible*, and Jon Blair's *Anne Frank Remembered* documentary.

Godard does share one significant element with Spielberg, and that's a devotion to celluloid. Spielberg has always edited his films on film, with his regular editor Michael Kahn, and has said he will keep editing on film until it's no longer possible. Godard (and Bernardo Bertolucci and Oliver Stone) has the same affection for the old-fashioned, non-digital ways: of *Éloge de L'Amour,* Godard remarked:

> I cut it all the old-fashioned way. We transferred the DV images to 35mm. Digital editing imposes too many manipulations for my taste. The hand doesn't have much to do. I like to take the time to rewind and rethread the film during editing. In the so-called virtual, you never rewind, you're there immediately. The time to rewind, which is vital in relation to the film's subject, must be lived out. It is precious. You have more time to reflect.

In a 1963 interview, Jean-Luc Godard mused on the possibility of making a documentary about the concentration camps which would focus on the actual organization and means of dispensing with humans on a mass scale. Such a film, which would ask questions like 'how to load ten tons of arms and legs on to a three-ton lorry?' or 'How to burn a hundred women with petrol enough for ten?', would be 'intolerable', Godard admitted, adding: 'the really horrible thing about such scenes would not be their horror but their very ordinary everydayness' (G, 198). Since 1963, there have been documentaries about the camps, and *Schindler's List* had its documentary aspects.

The Holocaust came to obsess Jean-Luc Godard in his later work, especially in *Éloge de L'Amour* and *Histoire(s) du Cinéma* (in amongst the rush of images in *Histoire(s) du Cinéma,* the footage of the concentration camps overwhelms everything else). The death camps were an event beyond history or above history or rupturing history. An event that couldn't be encompassed. Hence Godard's attacks on those who've tried to depict the Shoah on film (such as *Schindler's List* and *Shoah*). There are hints that Godard would take on the Holocaust in his earlier films – the women who're tattooed with numbers in *Alphaville*, a conversation in *Masculin Féminin*, and the investigator character in *Une Femme Mariée*.

But the Holocaust *should* have been filmed, Jean-Luc Godard insisted, and it still must be put on screen. (Godard made similar remarks of 9/11, criticizing French broadcasters for showing the Twin Towers collapsing, but not the people falling to their deaths.)

Cinema should have shown the concentration camps, but no one wanted to see them: this was one of Godard's recurring issues in his later work. His notion was that if the Holocaust had been filmed, and had been *seen*, it might've helped to avert later catastrophes: but 'it started again, so to speak, Vietnam, Algeria – it's not finished – Biafra, Afghanistan, Palestine', Godard remarked in 1995.[54]

Jean-Luc Godard's attack wasn't confined to *Schindler's List*, though: Godard also regarded the film *Shoah* (Claude Lanzmann, 1985) as a failure (even though he later called it 'a very great film'). And *Shoah* is of course one of the very few films about the Holocaust that many critics agree is a worthy attempt at depicting the impossible. But no, not even *Shoah* was good enough for Godard. He attacked Lanzmann in articles, too (such as in 1998). It's as if no film has got the concentration camps right for Godard, not even films such as *Night and Fog* directed by Alain Resnais. *In Praise of Love* was thus Godard's reply to *Shoah* as well as *Schindler's List*.

---

54 In a speech in Frankfurt, when Godard accepted the Theodor Adorno prize (B, 564).

DELON ■ GODARD

NOUVELLE VAGUE

ジャン＝リュック・ゴダール
アラン・ドロン

ヌーヴェルヴァーグ

ALAIN SARDE presents NOUVELLE VAGUE
JEAN-LUC GODARD

ELOGE
DE
L'AMOUR
Un Film di JEAN-LUC GODARD
UN FILM DI JEAN-LUC GODARD, CON EDGAR BRUNO PUTZULU, JEAN D'ORMESSON, CÉCILE CAMP, JEAN LACOUTURE, JEAN-HENRI ROGER, AUDREY KLENABER, CLAUDE BAIGNÈRES, JEAN DAVY, FRANÇOISE VERNY
PRODUZIONE: JEAN-PIERRE VINCENT FOTOGRAFIA: JULIEN HIRSCH, CHRISTOPHE POLLOCK MUSICHE: KETIL BJORNSTAD, DAVID DARLING, KARL AMADEUS HARTMANN, MAURICE JAUBERT, ARVO PÄRT, GEORGES VAN PARYS
www.revolverboom.com

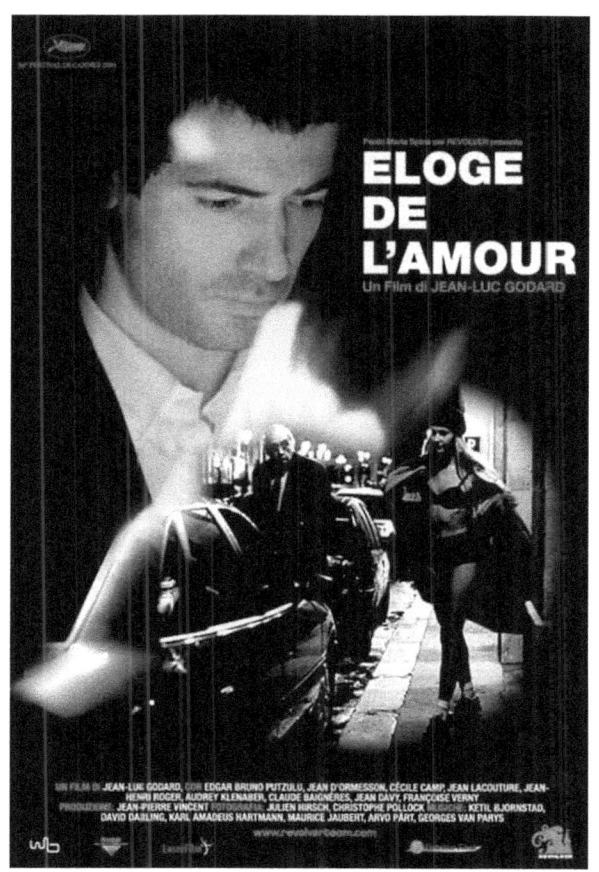

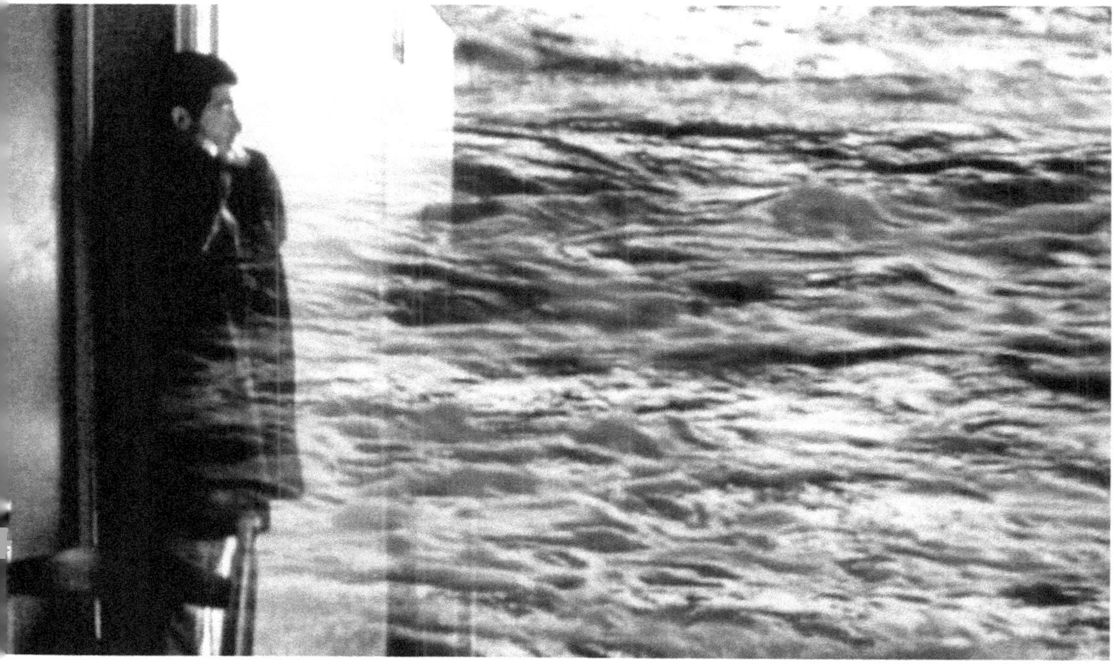

35

NOTRE MUSIQUE

OUR MUSIC

Music expresses the spiritual, and it provides inspiration. When I'm blind music is my little Antigone; it helps to see the unbelievable.

Jean-Luc Godard[1]

---

[1] Godard, quoted in J. Douin, 1994.

2004's *Notre Musique* (*Our Music*) was wr. and dir. by Godard, prod. – Alain Sarde and Ruth Waldburger, DP – Julien Hirsch, casting – Douchka Papierski and Richard Rousseau, art dir – Miéville, A.D. – Aurélien Poitrimoult, and sound – Gabriel Hafner and François Mussy. Released: May 19, 2004. 80 mins.

In the cast of *Our Music* were Sarah Adler, Nade Dieu, Rony Kramer, Simon Eine, George Aguilar, Jean-Christophe Bouvet, Ferlyn Brass, Leticia Gutiérrez, and Aline Schulmann, plus a cameo from Mr Cinema himself (there are no known performers at all in *Our Music*, only the Master).

Other figures appear in *Notre Musique* – they're not 'characters': Ramos Garcia (Rony Kramer), an interpreter, Mahmoud Darwish, a poet, an ambassador (Simon Eine), and some Native Americans (George Aguilar and Leticia Gutiérrez). Real people appeared, including Juan Goytisolo, a Spanish writer, Mahmoud Darwich, a Palestinian poet, Pierre Bergounioux, a French author and sculptor, and Gilles Péqueux, a French architect.

Notre Musique was an impressive meditation on a variety of themes, including Palestine, Israel and the Middle East, Sarajevo and Bosnia in the 1990s, cinema, images, poetry, war, WWII politics and ideology. One moment the film included a discussion of modern democracies, in another moment television, in another Homer. Greek literature and poetry, and in another painting.

There was a plot to *Our Music*, but that wasn't what the film was about, or what the film *was* in itself. Veering between drama, documentary and meditation, *Our Music* was another of Jean-Luc Godard's film essays, a poetic exploration of several contemporary subjects. The sheer range of topics that Godard touched on in *Notre Musique* was amazing, reaching back to the birth of writing in Ancient Sumer. It was a film of someone with a large scale of vision, not limited to Western Europe, or to the early 21st century.

Like *Contempt* or *Éloge de L'Amour*, *Our Music* employed a number of languages, including English, French, Spanish, and Hebrew. There were scenes of simultaneous translation, a favourite Jean-Luc Godard device. Poetry was a significant ingredient in *Our Music*, particularly the role of poetry in national cultural identity. Poetry as the music of a people, the language of a people. Homer was deployed as a key reference, with comparisons made between the Trojan War of ancient times and the contemporary, Balkan/ Bosnian conflict.

Notre Musique was originally going to be based around musicians associated with Edition of Contemporary Music Records (and its founder, Manfred Eicher), and music itself, but the film changed when the production moved to Sarajevo. However, the notion of music remained:

> so I called it *Notre Musique* [Godard explained]: theirs, ours, everybody's. It's what makes us live, or makes us hope. One could say 'our philosophy' or 'our life', but 'our music' is nicer and has a different effect.

Our Music contained plenty of music, including Jean Sibelius, Arvo Pärt, Alexander Knaifel, Hans Otte, Ketil Bjornstad, Meredith Monk, Komitas, Gyorgy Kurtag, Per Oddvar Johansen, Valentin Silvestrov, Oyvind Braekke, Peter Tchaikovsky, Trygve Seim, Anouar Braham and David Darling. Manfred Eicher of Edition of Contemporary Music Records was an important collaborator on *Our Music*, helping the Maestro to organize the distinctive soundtrack for the production (the list of composers on its own demonstrates how important music was to *Our Music* – 'our music').

※

Our Music opened with one of Godard's finest pieces of editing, and one of the greatest ten minutes in recent cinema.

It was a montage of horrific images almost too intense to watch, taken from Hollywood movies, newsreels, TV news shows, documentaries, government films, home movies, and films from around the world. This segment was entitled 'Part 1 – Hell'. Piano music and voiceover was laid over the imagery (with some footage slowed down or frozen; many video images had the colours exaggerated, as in *Histoire(s) du Cinéma*).[2] Godard said that he had edited the first part, 'Hell', last – and had put it together after the music was in place. The images were chosen to fit with the music.

It was a montage of devastation on a global scale that is as incisive and traumatic as any I've seen, and was almost unwatchable in its intensity. The intercutting of footage of bodies being bulldozed in the concentration camps with Hollywood Westerns of charging cavalry, Native Americans, Africans being shot (from *Zulu*), and Napoleonic wars was unbelievably disturbing. Vietnam, the Balkans, the Gulf War, Hiroshima, Israel, Palestine, Sarajevo, tanks, jets, guns, bows and arrows, swords, cannons, explosions,[3] trenches – the mixing of images from the war zones of the 20th century has been done before, but in *Notre Musique* the effect was unrelenting.

---

2 Indeed, some of the images had already been seen in *Historie(s) du Cinéma*.
3 An immense battery of explosions, like the endings of a thousand action movies.

Also, it was rare to see documentary and newsreel footage intercut with Hollywood and commercial movies – most montages of this kind stay with the documentary angle. The fusions of real war footage with Hollywood's version of wars and battles seems outrageous, and creates numerous unsettling resonances in the viewer. (Is this Godard's answer to *Saving Private Ryan* (1998)? As if Godard said: y*ou want to see how to open a film with epic carnage? I'll show you how to do it*).

Cutting fiction films of wars and battles with documentary footage of them is part of Godard's critique of the global media, how history becomes mere fodder for entertainment, how Hollywood cannibalizes history (or substitutes movies for history). Godard uses an extreme subject like world wars as an exaggeration, in order to make a point.

And now the black leader, added as pauses between the images, had a real impact, rather than acting as padding.[4] Now you were almost fearful of what the movie would show you the next time it cut from black to the next image.

We have seen these images in other contexts, often on their own, but rarely have so many images of death and destruction been cut together quite like this. The juxtapositions were incredible: nature documentary footage of monkeys running and leaping out of a river were intercut with soldiers wading in water and (in another clip) emerging from the sea in war-time (making a vivid link between apes and humans), and children playing at war with wooden sticks as rifles mixed with real war footage.

As B.B. said (Bertholt Brecht, not Brigitte Bardot), 'the wickedness of the world is so great you have to run your legs off to avoid having them stolen from under you'.[5] *Our Music* is partly about that sense of catastrophe.

Our Music was a film of using the camera like a scientific instrument, Jean-Luc Godard explained, because only a camera could record certain things: 'like using a stethoscope to examine reality. The camera makes possible certain things. Literature and painting are different, and allow other things'. It was a kind of filmmaking which exploited the act and experience of using a camera, of trying to find what it was that cameras could record, rather than other tools.

Our Music also showed Jean-Luc Godard brilliantly orchestrating the technology of cinema, creating montages with only music, or with voiceover intercut with dialogue, and deftly moving from documentary

---

4 There *is* padding in *Our Music*, however – the repetitions of the same downtown areas of Sarajevo, for example (the same tramways, the same street market, the same row of stores and banks).
5 B. Brecht, *The Threepenny Opera*, I, 3.

to fiction. Godard is among the most accomplished editors in the history of cinema. Very few filmmakers, even those renowned for their editing skills, can compare with Godard's mastery of montage. (One reason is simple: Godard has a mind as sharp as a bayonet, and a very intellectual one, too, with a broad range of cultural references. Thus, he can make all sorts of thematic links which are beyond most film editors. Also, Godard is *fearless* as a filmmaker, and he will bring together elements that many editors wouldn't dare to do, knowing that their efforts would be rejected by producers, executives, studios, etc).

❋

Jean-Luc Godard appeared in *Notre Musique* – once again, playing himself; this time, he's visiting the Balkans to give a lecture on text, the image and history. Fact and fiction blurred, as Godard interacted with the fictional characters (it was a recreation of a lecture Godard had given in 2002 in Sarajevo).

But what's going on? Is Godard softening as he gets older? The Maestro is actually portrayed as friendly, shaking people's hands, and even smiling! A smiling Godard! And there's even a classroom of cute kids learning about Mostar Bridge (and it's filmed without sarcasm!).

Inevitably, Godard returned to one of his favourite subjects during the lecture, the shot/ reverse-shot structure of conventional cinema (illustrated with photographs from *His Girl Friday* (1939), and references to Honoré de Balzac, a favourite with the *Cahiers du Cinéma* crowd. Godard had pioneered challenging to the shot-countershot approach of conventional cinema). It's a failure, Godard asserted, to distinguish between two things, between a man and a woman (yet Godard used the shot-reverse-shot structure in *Our Music,* during a conversation with Olga about suicide).

The Maître also discoursed on his idiosyncratic notion of the image – how the image can only contain its power within itself. The lecture scene was also a look at Godard the Travelling Filmmaker giving talks for classes of students. (An unusual departure for Godard saw him actually dramatizing a piece of history – the appearance of the Virgin Mary to the child Bernadette. The girl was shown a book of religious paintings to find out who she'd seen, and *Our Music* portrays a girl leafing through an artbook).

❋

The visit to Sarajevo and the Balkans (comprising 'Part 2 – Purgatory' of *Our Music*) featured bombed and abandoned buildings, trams, cars, snow. Burnt-out buildings. Mostar at night. A broken world (the cultural/ literary event of the European Literary Encounters, based in Sarajevo, was part of the inspiration for this section of *Notre Musique;* Jean-Luc Godard attended in 2002, and it helped to inspire the script).[6] One problem with *Our Music* is obvious: it is impossible for anything to follow the opening ten minutes, and to go from 'Part 1 – Hell' to something more like regular narration.

Our Music was filmed in particular places with a personal resonance for the filmmakers. As Jean-Luc Godard explained, these weren't just any streets: 'we wanted the camera to welcome the places we loved'.

Musings on culture and the past: a pile of books (filmed in the ruined Sarajevo library), references to Hannah Arendt, Franz Kafka, Spanish poetry and, inevitably, the French Resistance. Native Americans were another historical and cultural element. Again, used without dramaziation: the film simply wheels them on, in costume, as if that is enough. And, without, those haunting faces, it sort of is. (But the Native Americans do deliver Godardisms, like: doesn't the white man realize that we are all strangers on the same land? And they obviously represent displaced people – displaced by one of Godard's primary targets, North Amerikans).

The imagery of *Our Music* was very familiar from all of J.-L. Godard's work: airports, jets, cars, streets, buildings, cityscapes, rivers, bridges, trams – always the contemporary, Western world in Godard's movies (despite his near-obsession with history). Always the emphasis on modern technology, on contemporary imagery, on signage, on modes of transport, on travel, and the migration of people. Plenty of scenes, too, of people talking at tables with coffee, cigarettes and wine, as if the film were a perpetual discussion in an urban café between well-informed intellectuals. And there's Godardian dialogue a-plenty.

But there was also pastoral imagery in *Our Music,* as if Jean-Luc Godard couldn't excise the significance of the natural world. Images of grass and woods, a river, a lake, slow tracking shots of flowers. Those images contrasted vividly with the images of war-torn Sarajevo, the buildings wrecked by fire, bullets and bombs.

The smashed Mostar bridge was a central motif in *Our Music* (no need to gloss the bridge as a symbol). Many times the film comes back to the bridge and the water and Judith Lerner photographing it (there was also some incredible video footage of the bridge being destroyed).

---

[6] There have been other films on the Balkan war – Godard rightly dismisses *Welcome To Sarajevo* (1997), a drearily predictable, right-on liberal film. But Theo Angelopoulos's *Ulysses' Gaze* (1995) is a fascinating exploration of Sarajevo and the former Yugoslavia (it also features a film director, played by Harvey Keitel, as the lead character).

❋

Our Music focussed on two young women (who were originally meant to be the same woman). One is Judith Lerner, played by French-Israeli Sarah Adler, a journalist travelling about the Balkans, taking photographs and interviewing people about issues such as the Middle East. Olga Brodsky (Nade Dieu) is a French Jew of Russian descent, a student who attends Godard's lecture (the two women are another doubling of characters).

The reason for the second young, female character Olga Brodsky was because the actress Sarah Adler didn't want to perform the scene with the bomb suicide.[7] That doesn't put off a filmmaker like Monsieur Godard – he simply invented a new character[8] (and had the suicide reported in dialogue, as if acknowledging Adler's reluctance to play the scene. But it's possible that Godard wouldn't have filmed it anyway). It's a shame that Adler didn't carry on, because she is convincing as an idealistic, young woman (and she has amazing, very dark eyes).

And it's a cheat which adds needless confusion to *Our Music* – for the second young woman, casting directors Douchka Papierski and Richard Rousseau selected an actress who's too close in appearance to Sarah Adler (they have the same serious demeanour, and even brunette hair parted in the middle over their foreheads).

❋

In Sarajevo, Judith Lerner tries to persuade the ambassador to get behind a text she's written; like all politcos, the ambassador vacillates.[9] Godard's unique form of staging continues in *Our Music*: the camera stays on a close-up of Judith throughout the scene, while the ambassador walks to and fro in between her and the camera (i.e., to suggest his presence).

It's a typical example of Godard's refusal of the shot-reverse-shot conventions of cinema. A scene like this if it was staged in television or film anywhere on Earth would include: a wide shot of the two actors and the room (possibly two or three wide shots, solely for variety's sake); close-ups of the ambassador *as well as* Judith; and possibly some point-of-view shots (it's Judith's scene, so a shot from her viewpoint of the ambassador might be included in the shot list of coverage).

No – Godard uses none of that: just one close-up on Judith is enough. And it works (and instead of taking an afternoon to film

---

7 No stripping off for the central female character, either, as in other Godard films.
8 So the two women are swopped 2/3rds into *Notre Musique*; sort of (in fact, Judith returns for a while).
9 That's part of the job of a civil servant – to listen, to be polite, but to do nothing.

those wide shots, reverse angles and p.o.v. shots, it's done in half-an-hour).

※

It was no surprise that *Our Music* ended up at Lake Geneva, a favourite Jean-Luc Godard location, with a lengthy and largely visual sequence, 'Part 3 - Heaven'. The entry into Heaven occurs with a pathetic death, like so many other Godard films: Olga Brodsky dies when she enters a cinema[10] in Jerusalem saying there's a bomb in her bag, and she's shot by the police after the theatre is emptied (there was nothing in her bag, of course, but books - the book as bomb).

Here *Our Music* explores notions of terrorism and political resistance, but also considers a recurring Godardian topic: suicide, and suicide among young people. (Jean-Luc Godard hears about Olga's demise as he's watering flowers in his garden from Ramos Garcia, presumably he's back in Rolle - it's a portrait of Godard-as-Gardener).

'Part 3 - Heaven' moved into mythical territory. Olga Brodsky has been making a film[11] - she is a version of the younger Godard, of course, and this section may be her film; or it might be Olga's experience of the after-life. The after-life is introduced with a shot of Olga walking in woodland in full Summer growth (Switzerland looks abundant and richly green: there is a thematic cut from the pretty flowers in the garden at Godard's place to the woods by the Lake). Lengthy tracking shots and unexplained appearances of an assortment of characters place this part of the film in that familiar Godardian zone of heightened, Brechtian theatricality, as in *Weekend* or *Pierrot le Fou*. We see people reading books, playing *poi*, and volleyball (with a symbolic red among the clothing). Olga shares an apple with a guy sitting beside the Lake, Godard's version of Adam and Eve in the Garden of Eden (once again).

There's nothing realistic here, and the atmosphere of the countryside (next to the Lake in Switzerland) and the music gives the scenes an affecting melancholy. But, although Olga Brodsky's death is a kind of suicide in political terms, an act at once mysterious (it isn't dramatized at all), and unexplainable, the scenes beyond death, in Heaven, are life-affirming, even transcendent. They are part of that spiritual element that Godard has been exploring since the late 1970s.

※

Suicide: Jean-Luc Godard explained that he didn't want to link

---

10 A Godardian space - a place he's claimed as his own.
11 This is a replacement for Judith as a writer: both young women hope to interest older men in what they've created (Judith with the ambassador, Olga with Godard). This continues the father-daughter theme in Godard's later work.

Olga Brodsky's suicide with terrorism, so much as with suicide as a philosophical problem. 'She has to do something that I'd be capable of doing myself. And I think about suicide often, in the abstract, as a philosophical problem', Godard remarked. He was also consciously recalling the suicide of Michel in *La Chinoise*, and also quoted the same text by Fyodor Dostoievsky (suicide is a recurring theme and motif in Godard's cinema, back to his first film, *Breathless*).

It was a suicide with books, with the books that Jean-Luc Godard called his friends:

> And it would be done in the name of peace, with my friends the books. I am an image who has his friends, the books, in his pocket. And I said to myself, that I can do.

Jean-Luc Godard also added that though the film seemed downbeat, it was actually meant to be positive:

> It's true that it's rather cheerful compared to others; those who have called it pessimistic are wrong. On the contrary, it's rather childlike and optimistic.

However, hearing about the crucial dramatic event of the suicide in Jerusalem in a phone call is a really lame effort, short-changing the character of Olga, and not doing justice to the themes. (The suicide scene begs to be visualized).

❈

Our Music was, like *Éloge de L'Amour*, oddly emotional, when one got beyond (i.e., discarded) the disjointed narrative and the unusual form of the movie.[12] It's something to do with the way that Jean-Luc Godard orchestrates the film's components, and uses music and silence to underline an emotional exploration of the world. These films – *Our Music* and *Éloge de L'Amour* – are not cold, detached film essays about contemporary Europe or world politics – they are moving poetic films about how contemporary events are affecting groups of people, and how people are coping with the rapidly changing world of modern times.

It certainly gives *Our Music* an incredible force, too, that it begins with ten minutes of extraordinarily intense footage of conflicts throughout history. It relates the conflict in contemporary Sarajevo/ Bosnia/ Balkans/ former Yugoslavia to wars across history. It's as if

---
12 Richard Brody called *Notre Musique* 'a diatribe under the guise of a meditation, a work of vituperative prejudice disguised as calm reflection, a work of venom dressed up as a masque' (B, 623)

the world has always been at war, as if war is one of the central experiences of the human condition, as if humans can't stop making wars.

And *Our Music* also deals with the consequences of war: it focusses on groups of people who visit war zones (like Sarajevo), or who are grappling with complex, volatile issues like Israel and Palestine and Middle Eastern politics. And it closes with one person's response to the agonized conflict in the Middle East, when Olga performs a revolutionary act, her act of suicide.

Olga Brodsky's suicide is very Godardian: it's a young student who says she's got a bomb in her bag in a cinema (a symbolic Godardian location). But, somehow, the film transcends that very Godardian scenario, and moves into a kind of mythic political arena that's also very contemporary and very emotional.

In terms of the film, Olga Brodsky says very little (though she has an expressive face, and the requisite Godardian large eyes and pouty mouth), yet she makes a deep impression. She has far less to say, for instance, than Judith Lerner, who interacts with ambassadors, film directors and poets, yet her death, related offscreen, makes a strong impact – partly because she is a continuation of Judith's character (altho' had her suicide/ shooting been dramatized, it might've given the movie a powerful injection of drama. And it would've book-ended the film with the incredible Hell-On-Earth montage of the opening reel).[13]

---

[13] And it's Judith, presumably, or Olga perhaps, who speaks in voiceover in 'Part 1 – Hell'.

36

FILM SOCIALISME

SOCIALISM

Socialism (2010), a.k.a. *Film Socialisme,* was produced by Alain Sarde, Ruth Waldburger and Sophie Sallin. DPs: Fabrice Aragno and Paul Grivas. Sound mixers: Gabriel Hafner and François Mussy. In the cast were: Jean-Marc Stehlé, Agatha Couture, Mathias Domahidy, Quentin Grosset, Olga Riazanova, Maurice Sarfati, Patti Smith, Lenny Kaye, Bernard Maris and Marie-Christine Bergier. It was filmed digitally (and in the 16:9 video format, not Godard's usual 4:3 ratio). Released: 2010.5.21. 102 mins.

So *Socialism* is a movie directed by Jean-Luc Godard aged eighty (it began filming in 2008). So what is it? It's not a conventional movie, by any standards. Not a fiction, a story, a documentary, a polemic, propaganda, advertizing, or even a film-essay. It's 'Godardian', I guess.

You have to wonder what viewers who'd never seen a Jean-Luc Godard movie would make of *Film Socialisme*. When passionate *cinéastes* and Godard Disciples watch it, they can fill in 100s of elements from other Godard flicks, as well as 1,000s of intertextual references. But a New Viewer would likely be confused, irritated and ultimately bored. Where are the explosions? The heroes and the villains? The car chases? The dumb-ass humour? The join-the-dots storyline? (Quite a few film crrritics were bewildered, disappointed, irritated and angrified by *Socialism*).

You won't recognize anybody in *Film Socialisme,* but, yes, that is former U.S. punk-rocker Patti Smith who pops up briefly (singing, of course!).[14] The setting (of the first half of *Socialism*) is the *Costa Concordia* ship on a Mediterranean Cruise; an unusual but entertaining location for a Jean-Luc Godard movie.

So it's *National Lampoon's French Vacation* with guest star Uncle Godard, it's Holiday Time on a Mediterranean cruise with the New Wave's sole survivor, France's hottest director, the one and only, ladies and gents, please welcome...

Socialism is not vintage Jean-Luc Godard, and not the finest among his later works (it's a far lesser outing than *Elogie de l'Amour* or *Our Music*, for instance, the two big movies preceding it. There is none of the deep emotion that runs through those wonderful movies).

The first half is by far the more intriguing; parts of the second half test the patience of even the most ardent, masochistic Godardians. (Note the running time: 102 minutes, not the 75 or 80 minutes of

---

[14] Accompanied by guitarist Lenny Kaye. Smith drifts about playing a guitar, like a wandering troubadour of old (the other passengers on the boat nervously give her a wide berth).

many later Godard works. Sometimes, Godard's films have struggled to make up the running time, and the padding has been glaringly obvious (repeated takes and captions, black leader, other repetitions, etc. The padding goes beyond being obvious and attains new levels of tedium in the second half of *Socialism*).

Yes, a ship; yes, the inevitable 'Ship of Fools' mediæval motif; yes, a cruise around some of the great cities of the past 3,000 years: Alexandria, Athens, Barcelona, and Napoli (which came first, do you think, the free tickets for the Mediterranean cruise, or the idea of making a movie on a cruise?). Some of the imagery is simply too easy for J.-L. Godard, but he films it anyway: people playing slot machines, people swimming in a pool (including a girl in a bikini), children dancing, adults dancing in a disco, punters following an exercise class, diners dining in restaurants, a cleaner cleaning, a waiter waiting, a waitress waitressing, etc. A cruise and its vacationing punters is a space of pure capitalism, and so obvious and pat it's a wonder why Godard bothered to film anything on the ship at all (having done it all 45 years earlier, in the mid-1960s).

Film Socialisme is Godard's *Titanic*[15] (!). *Film Socialisme* is what *Titanic* should have been, if Uncle Jean-Luc had got hold of it: instead of the dreadful romance between wimpy Leonardo di Caprio and drippy Kate Winslett, it would've been a documentary about passengers on an Atlantic Ocean voyage – gambling, drinking, eating, dancing, etc. And, in a *Titanic* moment, the ship *Costa Concordia* later ran aground for real in January, 2012.

※

For those viewers hungry for stories, *Film Socialisme does* have a 'story' of sorts (in the first half), which concerns a former WWII collaborator or spy Otto Goldberg (Jean-Marc Stehlé) who's travelling incognito (and of course he's journeying with an attractive, young woman (Alissa) – that's what Jean-Luc Godard would do, isn't it, if he were an ageing tycoon? – it's Godard's nostalgic fantasy of being old but notorious, old and crabby but with a cutie on your arm. And the oldie has the all-important link to the Second World War).

There's also some discussion of gold/ money that went missing WWII, and ended up in Russia (the Sins of the Fathers, the guilt over the past, looms large over *Film Socialisme*, as it does any time anybody brings up the topic of WWII ins Godard's later work). A

---

15 *Titanic* had been referenced in *In Praise of Love*.

Russian secret agent (Olga Riazanova) asks questions,[16] and other characters (played by Quentin Grosset, Mathias Domahidy, Maurice Sarfati, Bernard Maris, Marie-Christine Bergier *et al*) prod and pry.

The feeling of *déja vu* stalks throughout *Socialism Film,* as you watch it (especially if you've recently been watching other Godard films, as I have). The filmmakers are working thru themes, issues, motifs, elements, camera angles, voiceovers, sound effects, and bits of actorly business that have not only all been done before by the Swiss-French Maestro – and better too – they have also been drained of much of their value or significance. *Socialism* is thus a ghost of a movie, a movie not in search of a story or a character or a 'meaning' or something to say, and not an 'attempt' at a movie (like *Pierrot le Fou*), but a movie that's haunting itself into oblivion. (There isn't the energy in *Socialism* for anything as strenuous as a 'search'. It takes enough energy just getting from your cabin to the bar).

In the end, *Film Socialisme* is cinema at its most fundamental: *Film Socialisme* literally *is* simply sounds and images, simply a series of shots strung together.

And yet, J.-L. G. cannot pick up a camera and not do something exceptional. Godard is a natural filmmaker as very few filmmakers *genuinely* are. Godard really is a filmmaker who will be filming whatever happens,[17] and yet also a filmmaker who will send the crew home time after time because he can't think of what to film, or isn't happy with what's already in the can. In this view, maybe being on a cruise ship on a voyage around the Mediterranean is a perfect setting for a filmmaker such as Godard: because he always has something to film, because he can walk out of his cabin and start shooting, because he hasn't got to travel to a sound stage or a location, because it's all right there, and it's a hotel, too, with restaurants as well, all handy for film crews and actors (and a ship on the Med makes a change for the Ciné-Guru from the banks of Lake Geneva).

And yet, and yet… there's no doubting J.-L. G.'s extraordinary ability to conjure incredible images.[18] In *Socialism:* a lone jogger on a rain-swept deck. An exquisite close-up of a young woman reminiscent of Sandro Botticelli or Fra Angelico. And the ocean as a shimmering, molten silver (at night, by day, at sun-down). The framing and compositions (by DPs Grivas and Aragno) are beautiful. The scenes

---

16 The Russian spy evokes Russian culture, but she speaks in French and doesn't appear particularly Russian (even with Russian props placed prominently in the foreground of a shot).
17 When a recording studio is on fire (as in *One Plus One*), he'll film it.
18 Sometimes it seems as if Godard's quirky, radical, polemical kind of film essay would work well on a stage, in an off-off Broadway or fringe show.

invoking Ancient Egypt (and modern-day Alexandria) are marvellous (the haunting music helps enormously). In sections like this, *Film Socialisme* becomes very poetic and resonant.

※

One of the very striking aspects of *Film Socialisme* is that *every single shot* is a one-off, and not part of continuity editing *at all*. In almost every other movie you've seen, shots will be constructed to form scenes, or mini-scenes of, say, four shots, even in documentaries or abstract or *avant garde* movies. In *Film Socialisme,* no. Not only is there no shot-reverse-shot editing pattern, the entire movie comprises single shots. Thus, there will be:

(1) a shot of the sea, with the camera tilted down to the water, by day;

(2) a shot of some dancers on a nightclub floor, at night;

(3) some diners eating in a restaurant (day again);

(4) a long shot of a rainy, empty deck at night. And so on.

Film Socialisme does not include two successive images of the same scene (except in very rare instances, and more in the Martin gas station sequence in the 2nd half). So that when shot-reverse-shot occurs (i.e., two shots of the same scene, cut in continuity), it's surprising.

Also, the camera in *Socialism Film* is placed on the tripod and films from a fixed position, seldom even tilting or panning, as if Godard is going back to the cinema of D.W. Griffith and Géorges Méliès. (If a mobile camera shot occurs, it will be one of the many film clips cut into *Socialism*).

Not only that, but all of the sound is fragmented too, to a striking degree: sounds that don't match the images; voices that aren't identified, quoting extracts and authors that aren't identified (offscreen voices are everywhere in *Socialism*); music that starts and stops without logic; and sound that isn't recorded properly (or mixed properly). The wilful, aggressive eccentricity of *Film Socialisme* is impossible to miss: this is a movie which will grate against the sensibilities of most of the global media audience.

But there *is* a kind of poetic continuity, which's embodied in the ship itself, or unified by the single location of the ship (yet a giant luxury vessel like this is really a whole series of spaces – part-shopping mall, part-restaurant, part-theatre/ disco, part-bedroom, part-corridor, part-deck, part-swimming pool, etc).[19] And there's also the

---

[19] Yet Godard and his crew don't film everything on the ship: they don't go into the bridge, the captain's office, the communications room, the engine room, the crew's quarters, etc (which Godard would've done in the 1960s).

continuity of the background story of treasure from World War Two (tho' you have to work hard to pick it up and follow it). There are continuities of theme, of course, and issues. And the simple continuity of a succession of images.

❊

As *Film Socialisme* is so unusual, it makes more sense to draw attention to some of the elements, in list form, instead of a more conventional analysis:

>>> STORY. By now you will've realized that J.-L.G. doesn't deliver stories in the conventional manner. He's tried, but he says he can't do it. Or doesn't want to do it. So don't force him to! And don't expect anything resembling a 'story' or 'characters' in this 2010 picture. (Godard might start out trying to portray a story, but very soon that notion is abandoned for the usual Godardian Box of Tricks).

>>> CHARACTERS. None. See above.

Oh, OK: yes, there *are* characters in *Film Socialisme* if one demands them to be there. And there *is* something of a story. Or, rather, fragments of scenes which might constitute a story (about WWII, about missing gold/ money,[20] about the French Resistance (yet again), and collaborators, etc). But, as with an opera which you haven't seen for years, you might need to prepare for watching *Socialism* by reading a synopsis.

>>> GODARD'S MOTIFS. *Socialism* is something of a summary of J.-L. Godard's cinema to date. *Socialism* contained the whole panoply of Godard's familiar motifs: sound that dipped out • Music that stops abruptly • Distorted sound • Quotations (audio, video, captions and voiceover) from cinema, TV, newsreels, photography and books • Multiple images and superimpositions (quite a bit of *Film Socialisme* looks like *Histoire(s) du Cinéma*, as with many of Godard's late works – once he'd developed that approach of *Histoire(s) du Cinéma*, he used it everywhere) • Freeze frames • Step-motion • Slow motion • Re-filmed video footage[21] • Filming people at work • TV screens • Cameras • Numerous intertitles and word games in the captions (in different colours) • Gas stations. (No cameo from the Maestro, tho').

---

20 If you want a more conventional movie about missing Nazi gold, try the entertaining Jackie Chan picture *Operation Condor: Armor of God 2* (1992), a delightfully ridiculous treasure hunt plot for buried Nazi gold in the *Indiana Jones* mold. It's also a regular motif in Japanese animation (in the *Lupin III* movies).
Jackie Chan and Jean-Luc Godard – what a meeting that might be!
21 There's a huge amount of this, some of it taken to very degraded extremes, like pointillism in French (Post-)Impressionism – Godard in his Georges Seurat phase. In the gas station sequence, the boy is painting by numbers a Pierre Renoir landscape (one of Godard's favourite artists): to emphasize that, the video footage is treated with colour balancing, so it becomes as colourful as an Impressionist painting.

>>> GODARDISMS. Godardisms are peppered throughout *Film Socialism*, though it's not always certain whether they are direct quotes, or Godard re-phrasing other authors, or Godard's own Godardisms (note that the movie listed a host of references in the opening credits):

• money was invented so people wouldn't have to look in each other's eyes

• don't talk about the invisible, show it

• AIDS is a tool for killing all the black people in Africa

>>> QUOTATIONS. Quotations from authors, philosophers, poets, movies, filmmakers and politicians are everywhere in *Film Socialism*.

Who's here? Oh, all the usual contributors to a Godardfest, all your favourites: Stalin, Hitler, Heidegger, Weil, Sartre, Nietzsche, Sophocles, Balzac, Shakespeare, Husserl, Griffith, Beckett, Chaplin, Rossellini, Pasolini, Eisenstein, Hitchcock, Arendt, Bismarck, Giraudoux, Tardieu, Derrida, Benjamin, Alexander the Great *et al* (a list of the quotations – from movies, from literature/ philosophy, and from music – is included in the opening credits. It's a huge and impressive list, yet it only cites some of the prominent credits, because there're many more quotations). Needless to say, the references are seldom identified.)

>>> MOVIES. Among the numerous movies and TV material that *Film Socialisme* cannibalizes (I mean, respectfully quotes from) are: *Battleship Potemkin, Alexander the Great, Medea* (1969), Westerns, Biblical extravaganzas, bullfights, the Spanish Civil War, newsreel footage from WWII, and Jean-Luc Godard's own movies (such as one of his favourites, *Weekend*).

>>> ISSUES. The issues and themes of *Socialism Film* are very familiar from Jean-Luc Godard's cinema: the Holocaust, World War Two, spies, collaborators, betrayal, the French Resistance, the Spanish Civil War, Russia, the Cold War, television, Amerika, bullfighting, Christianity, Jesus, post-colonialism, death, Italy, France, Germany – the list goes on and on (give Godard a topic, and he'll talk about it. That is a *lot* of issues to explore in a single movie – and way beyond what most movies attempt. Of course, some of those issues are simply raised in brief exchanges of dialogue, not 'explored' in any depth).

Egypt was an intriguing addition to the Godardania on display in *Socialism*, with the Maestro evoking Ancient Egyptian culture (via statuary, architecture, paintings and someone (probably Alissa) tracing hieroglyphs with a pen on a piece of paper).

>>> CAMERAS. Yes, many characters have cameras and are constantly taking pictures, or filming other people. (A recurring motif

in Godard's cinema, but in amongst thousands of tourists, it's even more prominent. Now everyone's a photographer – but not everyone can be Ansel Adams or Robert Doisneau).

>>> WOMEN. *Film Socialisme* still exhibits the inclination that Jean-Luc Godard has for beautiful young women who might've stepped out of an Early Renaissance painting by Fra Filippo Lippi or Rogier van der Weyden (Alissa (Agatha Couture) on the *Costa Concordia* ship, or Flo (Marine Battaggia) in the gas station episode). But there is no love, no romance, and no sexuality in *Film Socialisme* (well, not as a major ingredient, as in so many of Godard's previous movies). Indeed, this is a movie which for once doesn't feature the usual bickering romantic/ anti-romantic couple.

>>> WAR, WORLD WAR TWO, THE HOLOCAUST. This is one of the key themes of Jean-Luc Godard's later works: *Socialism* is completely saturated in World War Two – the crimes, the betrayals, the (French) Resistance, the espionage, and of course the Shoah (with its horrific newsreel footage).

It's the Sins of the Fathers again. It's guilt and regret. It's the feeling of hopelessness in the face of immense suffering. It's another swansong for the Death of Europe[22] (which's aligned with the Death of Cinema). The Amerika-bashing is kept at a distance, however (unusually – maybe Jean-Luc Godard feels that he has said all he wants to say or needs to say on that subject. It's still present, tho' – let's face it, that love-hate (hate-hate) relationship that Godard has with North Amerika has fuelled his art for 50-plus years! Hell, Godard has squeezed every ounce of juice out of his attacks on the U.S.A.).

>>> ACTING. The bits of actorly business that Jean-Luc Godard has made his own are included in *Socialism* too: a scene where a young boy (in the first part) nearly puts his hand on the shoulder of a pretty girl (Alissa) then refrains (very Jean-Pierre Léaud); another young boy (in the second part) conducts an imaginary orchestra; looking at an actor while hearing other actors off-screen (for a long time); characters pick up books and read aloud from them (an act that Godard has made own – no one in the history of cinema has included so many scenes of literary and philosophical quotation, no one has filmed so many people picking up books); people declaim into the dark night, standing at a ship's handrail; actors are blocked in static situations; actors chase each other.

The young woman (Alissa), bored, lying on the bed in her cabin,

---

[22] 'Poor Europe', says a character, looking out into the black night from the ship.

watches a documentary on a DVD player featuring some kittens miaowing.23 The clip goes on and on. Then she mimics the animals silently (after she's been told by her guardians to keep it down).

Well, that's mildly interesting: but how about the scene in the gas station sequence where the boy sits on the stairs not doing much of anything, while a voice is heard muttering about something offscreen? The camera holds and holds on this kid, and you think to yourself: the Most Important Film Director of the past 50 years is making me look at this child for a very long time. Why? (*Socialism* is very indulgent to this kid, allowing him to perform several bits of business (pretending to be blind and exploring his mom while she washes up in a kitchen). Now, in films such as *Two or Three Things I Know About Her* and *A Married Woman*, Godard proved to be a gifted director of children – particularly when he had Christopher Bourseiller to work with. But here in *Socialism*, it seems indulgent and a dead-end).

>>> VOICEOVER. *Socialism* is filled with voices, many of them off-screen and not identified. There are voices all over the place (and all over the stereo spectrum, and the 5.1 surround sound spectrum). Some are actors reciting lines in post-production, some are lifted from scenes, and many voices are from TV and cinema.24

>>> SOUND. *Socialism Film* employs a 5.1 surround sound mix, which inevitably J.-L. Godard and his sound crew (Gabriel Hafner and François Mussy) do *not* treat in the regular manner. As usual in Godard's cinema, sounds are placed on either side of the stereo spectrum (often it's voices – there'll be a wind noise sound effect on the left channel, and voices on the right).

Some people in the sound team must really dislike the way that *Socialism* makes them look like idiots: there are many scenes filmed outside on the deck of the ship on the Mediterranean Sea, where the wind is creating a wall of white noise over the microphone (as if the Maestro had insisted that they didn't use the usual wind shield or microphone baffle). There are also clicks and fudges in the soundtrack, which any professional sound editor would automatically edit out. And the white noise/ wind noise is included in many scenes, not just one or two, where the audience would get the point.

There are also the crackly, buzzing sounds of a mic not plugged in properly, or a mic with a loose wire: these recur many times. Safe to say these are sounds you have never heard in any movie ever – not

---
23 Cats, and their links to Ancient Egypt, are one of the minor motifs in *Film Socialisme*.
24 The list of names at the top of the movie gives you a clue to some of the quotations, but none of them are identified.

like this, not used repeatedly, not from a veteran filmmaker, and not as part of a scene which wouldn't normally have a buzzy, crackly sound effect (we're not in a spacecraft about to blow up in an electrical storm, in a *Star Wars* or superhero movie, for instance, where communications become disjointed).

There are scenes in the disco on the ship in *Socialism* where the sound is one ugly mass of distorted noise: who else would feature a scene in a nightclub and include the high volume distortions of the music, as if recorded on an amateur video camera? So it's not music anymore but a horrible mess? And without replacing the direct sound with some innocuous Euro-pop? Only Jean-Luc Godard! Outside of amateur videos, no professional movie would include a scene like that (or is it an ironic comment on how nightclub scenes are often filmed, where characters can happily talk to each other, instead of yelling, and where even the footsteps of the characters can be heard as they dance? The director of *Saturday Night Fever* (1977), John Badham, recalled that the sound team wanted to include the sound of footsteps, which are added everywhere in movies, until he reminded them they you wouldn't hear them in a disco).

>>> MUSIC. Once again, there is plenty of Edition of Contemporary Music record label-style music, all deep, low, sombre, sustained tones (which Jean-Luc Godard and his sound crew have probably plucked right off the shelf in the editing suite in Switzerland and cut into the show – Beethoven, Pärt, Busch, etc). But the way that Godard and his sound team (Hafner and Mussy) deploy music is so extraordinary, the way they can make the audience hear music as if for the first time. And there's lots of found music and direct sound.

>>> GAS STATIONS. Nobody in the whole history of cinema has employed gas stations like Jean-Luc Godard (what is it with Godard and gas stations?!), and in *Socialism* they crop up again as a key motif and location. And, yes, there's a pretty girl (Florine – played by Marine Battaggia) standing next to the gas pump reading a book, with a lama nearby! (the book is by Honoré de Balzac).[25] And, yes, when some German tourists ask for directions, Flo tells them to go invade another country. Flo criticizes the television crew that've turned up to film there in a classic, Godardian manner – about using the verb 'to be'[26] (what other filmmaker features characters so often criticizing strangers on their use of grammar?!).

The J.J. Martin gas station sequence (set in France), entitled *Quo*

---
25 If you diss Balzac, Flo tells the TV crew, I'll kill you!
26 Charlotte in *A Married Woman* wakes up and murmurs the verb *être*.

Vadis Europa?, is the most conventional segment of *Film Socialisme*, but that means 'conventional' within the context of a J.-L. Godard movie! Which is to say, not 'conventional' at all. There're half-formed personalities, there're some mildly intriguing action, there're scenes which have some kind of dramatic unity of time and space. But what it all amounts to, unless you're paying *very* close attention, would be beyond many cinema viewers. I don't mean that in a patronizing way, to say that most audiences wouldn't understand it, I mean that the filmmaking is wilfully obscure, unconventional, and often downright perplexing or irritating. (Hollywood producers note that contemporary audiences are more technically savvy nowadays, so they have to up their game in terms of delivering convincing visual effects and detail and 'realism'. Yes, but a Godard movie demands *much* more from an audience!).

Yet, the Martin gas station sequence in *Film Socialisme is* in focus, it *is* well-lit, it *is* recorded for sound properly (none of that hellish wind noise!),[27] and you can see recognizably movie-ish things like people speaking and even interacting (occasionally, tho' not much). But don't expect a 'story', 'characters', or even 'themes' or 'issues'. (And the snippy, surly, bickery interaction between people will further bemuse viewers unused to Godardian modes of cinema: just *what* are these people arguing about in this sunny roadside garage?).

(There's a 'story' of sorts in the gas station sequence in *Socialism* – it's about selling up, about moving to (North) Amerika (echoes of *Passion* and other Godard movies), about the anxious relationship between parents and their children (wondering why their children don't love them), and about a film crew from TV channel F.R. 3 visiting the garage for filming.)

Yet parts of the Martin gas station sequence are boring. It seems incredible, but it's true: there are some lengthy takes in this section of *Socialism* where not only is nothing much happening (as in Andy Warhol's films), the nothingness is dull (*viz.*, a shot of the France 3 TV presenter (Élisabeth Vitali) against a wall, while she talks, but isn't heard; instead, we hear other voices; *viz.*, the young, black camerawoman (Eye Haidara)[28] from the TV crew filming Flo outside... It's half-baked. No, quarter-baked. No, it isn't much of anything).

✱

The final section of *Film Socialisme* enters *Histoire(s) du Cinéma*

---

27 Though the sound of the cars on the highway next to the gas station are not mixed out, as any regular movie sound crew would do, but kept high on the track.
28 When the camerawoman (clad in a bikini top, baseball cap and jeans) asks the kid what he's thinking about, he replies her ass.

territory, a film essay in the form of a Godardian collage, with numerous quotations, including from earlier scenes in the movie (such as the *Costa Concordia* cruise ship), plus the usual battery of photographs, video clips, movie quotations, treated video, slow motion, etc. A pair of hands (probably Jean-Luc Godard's) operate an old Box Brownie camera. Voices are heard declaiming off-screen, in the usual Godardian, polemical manner (though mainly in French now),[29] and the intertitles become more and more rapid, winding up the movie not with an 'ending' of any conventional kind,[30] but a series of philosophical and political statements about modern history.

The 2010 movie recapitulates the cities of the past visited earlier on the cruise ship: Barcelona (footage of bull-fighting), Alexandria (more Egyptian imagery), Greece (scenes from *Alexander the Great*, the Greek theatres of old), Odessa (yes, there are scenes from *Battleship Potemkin* yet again), and so on.

Some of this looks again like padding (not least because the same material was already used in the section on the Mediterranean cruise), and some of it rehashes music, sound effects and images already employed in many previous Godard movies, including his mammoth history of cinema documentary. *Viz.*: more images of the Holocaust, more photos of Simone Weil, more flashcuts of Adolf Hitler, Josef Stalin, etc. A movie haunted by other movies, a ghost of a ghost of a ghost. (If you watch a lot of Godard movies, you find that not only does Godard repeat material from earlier in a movie, he also cannibalizes his own movies).

Is anybody still sitting in the theatre during this section of *Film Socialisme*? Has anyone lasted thru the playback of the DVD or video to this point? You can bet your *ss that quite a few viewers will've abandoned *Socialism way* before this point here, at one hour 20 minutes into the movie! And parts of *Socialism* will try the patience of even diehard, dedicated and determined Godard fans. (Critics such as Rogert Ebert and Mark Kermode, who saw it at Cannes, loathed it).

And, yet again, *Film Socialisme* is a movie that's really a film essay (but not even that this time); which is to say, a movie that might more appropriately be a written piece filled with photographs and captions (Jean-Luc Godard could have had a secondary career in advertizing, or political propaganda, churning out slogans, captions, texts and images. Actually, he did work for 20th Century Fox in the

---

[29] Though there is a sequence in multiple languages.
[30] The story of the Martin gas station is told in retrospect using captions (which this time feels more laborious than a voiceover).

publicity department). Godard never left his first calling as a film critic behind, and he has never renounced cinema as a primary cultural force in the world.

Ultimately, the value of *Socialism* may be simply to send viewers to other, much finer Godard products (but on the basis of this film, would they?). Everything here has been achieved to a much greater depth in, for ex, *Histoire(s) du Cinéma*, or *In Praise of Love*, or *Passion*.

37

ADIEU AU LANGAGE

GOODBYE TO LANGUAGE

My thought is *me*; that is why I can't stop. I exist by what I think.

Jean-Paul Sartre, *Nausea*

INTRO.

There is no stopping Jean-Luc Godard.

Godard is a force of nature in cinema.

This remarkable, abundantly talented, wilfully eccentric and explosive filmmaker delivered *Goodbye To Language* (*Adieu au Langage*) in his 84th year (this time in 3D!).

2014!

– I simply can't believe that we are discussing a New Godard Movie in 2014! It is simply astounding. (I mean, *come on*, Godard was making movies *50 years ago*! By 1964, he had *already* directed 8 features and 8 shorts, and *four* of those films were masterpieces: *Contempt, Band of Outsiders, Breathless* and *Vivre Sa Vie*!).

This is one of the most sensational artists in the history of the world.

PRODUCTION.

Goodbye To Language is shorter (at 69 minutes) than some of Jean-Luc Godard's later pieces, but in pretty much every respect it is the same sort of material as the later feature films like *Notre Musique, Film Socialism* and *In Praise of Love*. *Goodbye To Language* had a hugely successful screening at the Cannes Film Festival: 'a thrilling cinematic experience that nearly levitated the packed 2,300-seat Lumière theater here, turning just another screening into a real happening', gushed the *New York Times*.

Goodbye To Language was celebrated by many, many critics for its use of 3-D filmmaking, with some critics comparing the innovations that *Goodbye To Language* displayed to Orson Welles and *Citizen Kane* (*Kane* being regarded by many critics as the highpoint of North American cinema). David Bordwell, Jane Campion, Amy Taubin, Jonathan Romney, Richard Brody, Manohla Dargis and A.O. Scott were among those who raved about the movie.

This movie is also Dog-Walking with Uncle Jean-Luc – yes, we are taking the director's dog Roxy for a walk in numerous scenes in *Goodbye To Language* (Godard once recalled that Roberto Rossellini asked him to walk his dog when he visited Roma).

And a key Godardian motif was back – did you miss it? – the bickering romantic couple, which had been absent from the previous few outings from the Maître. And we get a double helping! Not one romantic couple arguing, but two!

❖

Goodbye To Language was produced by Brahim Chioua, Vincent Maraval and Alain Sarde for Centre national de la cinématographie and Canal Plus, dis. by Wild Bunch; Fabrice Aragno was DP; Oriane Cattiaux was makeup artist; Jean-Paul Battaggia was assistant director; Maria Muscalu was stylist and Phill Zagajewski was the playback singer. In the cast were: Héloïse Godet, Kamel Abdeli, Richard Chevallier, Jessica Erickson, Alexandre Païta, Christian Gregori, Marie Ruchat, Jeremy Zampatti, Bruno Allaigre and Zoé Bruneau (you likely won't recognize a single face, unless you watch French TV). Released: May 21, 2014. 69 mins.

Fabrice Aragno was a key collaborator[31] in making *Goodbye To Language:* it was Aragno who ran some tests with 3-D technology for Jean-Luc Godard, to show him how it might work. Aragno was the DP, also recording the sound at the same time (a very challenging task). Aragno helped with the sound mix of *Goodbye To Language,* as well as assisting with the 3-D edit (Godard edited the 2014 movie in 2-D himself – this cut was used as the basis for the 3-D version.[32]

The script for *Goodbye To Language* was a large document with the text on one page and collages of images on the other page (including pictures of the actors, before they had been cast). As if the whole movie was already present, and already edited (so it was an unusual approach for Godard). Actress Héloïse Godet remarked that the final movie stuck to the script exactly. There was *no* improvization, and Uncle Jean-Luc's direction was very precise ('he was so detailed in his direction about the movements, the way of talking'). The actors stuck to the script (altho' Godard sometimes rewrote scenes the night before). There were no rehearsals before shooting (but there never is with a Godard movie!).[33] There was very little discussion about psychology or motivation or all of the other stuff that some actors (and not only Method actors) like to have (again, as expected – Method acting and the psychological analysis of characters is completely anathema to Godard). Rumours of multiple takes were unfounded, as anybody who knows anything about Godard and his shooting style would realize (tho' there were re-takes for technical issues).

Jean-Luc Godard and Anne-Marie Miéville seem to appear in brief cameos in *Goodbye To Language* – in the scene (aptly enough) of a painter painting (the face's obscured). Certainly that croaky off-screen

---

31 Aragno has explained in interviews how the movie was made, with many tests, new camera rigs, and a variety of cameras, including HD, Panasonic and Canon cameras.
32 As well as 3-D cameras, the production also used other cameras, including domestic video cameras (the cameras pop up in the end credits).
33 Tho' Godard did meet the actors in a café in Paris.

voice is unmistakably Godard (the voice is the first thing a comedian does if they're doing an impression of God-Art).

Héloise Godet recalled that her 45-minute audition was filmed by an assistant of the Maestro's, so he could see it back at Godard Central HQ in Rolle. This was back in 2011. Godet then had to wait a considerable period (not taking up other acting offers in the meantime – an anxious time for an actor), until the call came from the Master to travel to Switzerland, and filming was about to begin.

Jean-Luc Godard preferred actors, especially in his later works, who could deliver what he was after without being a pain in the *cul* and without asking too many questions (or any questions at all!), without being demanding, or touchy, or prima donna-ish. For some actors, the requirements were too much, and quite a few actors walked or were replaced (again, especially in Godard's later career).

However, Jean-Luc Godard was also very famous (in France, at least), and plenty of actors were keen to work with him. Godard is a living legend with few equals in all cinema, and everybody knew his work (again, in France, at least).

Goodbye To Language was thus similar to other recent Godardian projects in having a lengthy gestation and shooting period. Filming for *Goodbye To Language,* for example, had begun some four years b4 the movie was released. There were also re-shoots of some scenes (in November, 2013), as well as additional dialogue sessions. (For those who disliked *Goodbye To Language,* the additional days of shooting and recording probably didn't help to clarify the movie. These were not typical reshoots, to fill in plot holes, or to film a happy ending at the behest of a film studio and executives).

An unusual device for Jean-Luc Godard is employed in *Goodbye To Language*: foreshadowing. Such temporal conventions of traditional film narrative are rarely used by the Master. But here, we have the Mary Shelley/ *Frankenstein* scene being noted way before we see it, and the scene of close-ups of paint and brushes is seen several times before the scene is explained/ revealed.

Much of *Goodbye To Language* was filmed by the Master himself, using off-the-shelf video cameras. You can spot a Godardian shot a mile away – shaky, handheld, unusual, and happy to move the camera in any direction, on any axis, at any speed. The lengthy sections involving Roxy the dog, for instance, were mostly filmed by the Maestro (in every season). The camera turns upside-down, it spins, it shoots very off-kilter shots.[34]

Much of *Goodbye To Language* looks as if Jean-Luc Godard and his team filmed it in and around his home in Nyon and Rolle – as if they simply stepped out onto the street and started filming... as if they wandered over the road to Lake Geneva to get yet more shots of that body of water which crops up in so many of Godard's movies (from *Passion* in 1982 onwards). Or they simply got in the car and drove and drove, while the DP (or Godard as a passenger) filmed the dashboard, the wing mirror, the windshield, the snow, the rain, the roadworks, the approaching headlamps. Some scenes were filmed in Godard's own home. Some shots look as if the camera was simply pointed out of the windows at Castle Godard to film the street outside[35] (in snow, in rain, in more snow).

Another noticeable departure from previous works was the high proportion of unusual camera angles – the camera is down on the ground, for example, or it's rotating, or it's upside-down.

The setting for much of the first half of the 2014 movie is a sort of in-between zone, somewhere outdoors, that might be a car lot, a road, a park, a waterfront, a city street, who knows what it is, or where it is (a gas station perhaps). Actors sit about or perform rather pointless actions, and deliver pithy, poignant pieces of philosophizing from the Trickster Prince of Cinema.

More than even films like *In Praise of Love* or *Our Music*, *Goodbye To Language* looks as if most of it was created in the editing suite. That is, the movie simply doesn't have the footage required, so that long sections wing by which're patched up with voiceovers of several types: (1) the characters/ actors, (2) other voices, philosophizing, and (3) the found sounds, the newsreel sounds, and the quotes from movies and television. (It seems that maybe a fifth of *Goodbye To Language* actually comprises other films).

Considering the first type of voiceover or voice-off in *Goodbye To Language*: we know that some of the actors came back (in 2013) to record new material, and for re-shoots (in Nov, 2013). Part of *Goodbye To Language* thus sounds like a radio play, in which new scripts were written to stitch together the existing footage (with the augmentations of the re-shoots). Indeed, Godard had been passing off radio plays as cinema since the days of the Dziga Vertov Group – voices and sounds are heard over a black screen.

---

34 In the middle of a dialogue scene in a room, the film cuts to a shot of the clouds, for no obvious reason.
35 As also in *JLG/ JLG*.

Thus, in *Goodbye To Language* we are often looking at images which have nothing to do with what we're hearing. There are shots from the interior of a car, for instance, as it drives along: we hear the sounds of a man and a woman arguing (one of the two couples in *Goodbye To Language*). Well, we don't see them in the car, so it could be anyone. (By this time, you either accept it or you don't: there are no clarifying shots of who's in the car, for example. Thus, the images of the car journeys could be exchanged for any other kind of neutral image: a shot of some clouds, a shot of waves on a shore, etc).

It's a sort of Do-It-Yourself, Make-A-Godard-Movie-Kit:

Step 1: You collect images on cheapo video cameras (swing that lens up a tree! film your dawg! shoot the sunset! now film Lake Geneva *again*! Go camera!).

Step 2: You hire some actors and do the franxious, domestic Godardian lovers bit (the 'At Home With Jean-Luc' scenes).

Step 3: You edit it all together.

Step 4: You realize you don't have enough to make a full-length (80-minute-plus) movie, so you write a new script to patch it together.

Step 5: You record new lines of dialogue and cut them into the piece.

Step 6. You pad out scenes with black leader, you add black leader in between the film quotations, and pack it into the corners of the film wherever you can.

Voilà! It's another 'Film de Jean-Luc Godard'.

Extraordinarily, around a third of *Adieu* is what many would class as 'home movies': it's Jean-Luc Godard and/ or Anne-Marie Miéville *avec* some low-cost video cameras collecting images. Then you add some philosophizin', and some music from the Minimalist Edition of Contemporary Music Records composers, and – *bingo!* – you got yourself a movie that can be shown at the Cannes Film Festival to two thousand ecstatic *cinéastes*!

SAME OLD STUFF.

Goodbye To Language contains all of the usual ingredients of a late Godardian piece: countless cinematic allusions (to classic Hollywood and European movies, to television, to porn); newsreel (WWII, bombers); sudden violence; scenes in cars; actors declaiming solemnly and spouting philosophical nuggets;[36] painting; nudity;[37] smoking; television sets;[38] cel phones; the Holocaust; Adolf Hitler; coloured captions (in white and red over black); off-screen voices (often unexplained/ unidentified); endless quotes from literature; people picking up books; people leafing thru books;[39] re-filmed and electronically treated video imagery; classical music; abrupt off-screen sounds (rain, waves, TV sets, cars – and birds cawing, of course); mysterious off-screens sounds;[40] and a movie divided into sections (1: Nature, 2: Metaphor. etc).

Indeed. *Goodbye To Language* seems like a farewell to cinema in that it reprises motifs and echoes of 100s of Godardisms, such as:

- a partially-clad couple bickering in an apartment (*Contempt*);
- couples driving in cars (*Pierrot le Fou*);
- Lake Geneva (from *Passion* onwards);
- waves on the Lakeshore (*JLG/ JLG*);
- the tourist boat on the Lake (from *Nouvelle Vague*);
- sex in the shower (from *Carmen*);
- references to terrorism (from *The Little Soldier*);
- film quotations (from *Histoire(s) du Cinéma*);
- gas stations (any movie);
- smoking (any movie);
- and the ruminations on WWII (any movie).

There are shots in *Goodbye To Language* (and sounds, too) that no professional filmmaker would allow to be included in the final cut of their movie. There are moments in *Goodbye To Language* when you do wonder whether we'd even be talking about this movie, let alone watching it, if it hadn't been directed by a Cinema Genius, our Lord and Master, Herr Godard. If you isolated sections of *Goodbye To Language,* and contemplated them on their own, you'd have incompetently filmed video that nobody would look at. Like jerky, handheld shots of a paperback book.

Pourquoi? Why? Why is *Goodbye To Language* revered?

Because it's Jean-Luc Godard.

*

---

[36] By this time, every new actor in a Godard production has watched how all of the other actors performed in previous Godard movies, and they've aped the style: solemn line readings where people don't converse, they speak philosophy aloud.
[37] Godard has actresses (Héloïse Godet and Jessica Erickson) who're happy to disrobe this time – so *Goodbye To Language* makes full use of that.
[38] There're scenes where classic European and Hollywood movies play on a big, flat-screen television behind the actors. Characters look at famous people on their cel phones.
[39] Such as Nicolas de Staël – one of Godard's favourites.
[40] Over a black screen, there's the sound of something crashing to the ground – a lamp, perhaps? With no relation to what happens before or after the screen went black.

Among the numerous citations and allusions in *Goodbye To Language* are: Mary Shelley; Lord Byron; Rainer Maria Rilke; Fyodor Dostoievsky; Nicolas de Staël; Auguste Rodin; Claude Monet; Alexander Solzhenitsyn; Jean-Paul Sartre; Jean Anouillh; Jorge Borges; Ludwig Wittgenstien; Jacques Derrida; Gustave Flaubert; Victor Hugo; Sigmund Freud; Ezra Pound; V.S. Naipaul; Marcel Proust; Jean-Pierre Melville; Plato; Charles Darwin; and Mao Zedong (the credits list some of the authors cited or alluded to – apart from those mentioned above, there are Samuel Beckett, Paul Valéry, Jack London, William Faulkner and A.E. van Vogt).

Movie quotations include *Les Enfants Terribles, Dr Jekyll and Mr Hyde, Only Angels Have Wings, Pirahna, People On Sunday, Les Enfants Terribles, The Snows of Kilimanjaro, Beauty and the Beast* (Jean Cocteau, *d'accord – pas* Disney), *Metropolis* and porn (some of the quotes are flashcuts out of black – where you just see a glimpse of a Hollywood picture from way back flashing out of darkness, imprinting itself on the retina).

Some of the cinematic quotations heighten the differences in form and style: for example, late in *Goodbye To Language,* the extraordinary, German epic *Metropolis* plays on a flat screen TV: we see the famous characters emoting in high drama, lit by the famous Expressionist lighting. But in the room, in the foreground of *Goodbye To Language,* Ivitch wanders into frame, pulls on a dress (after flashing her ass), then sits there grumpily groaning gloomy Godardisms like, 'I hate characters', as she stares at the movie. (Why is Godard showing a scene of a character dissing *Metropolis*? He revered director Fritz Lang. It should be *Schindler's List* and Steven Spielberg!).

The performance style in Jean-Luc Godard's work does seem a little uninspired and samey at times, as if every actor who is auditioned and cast for a Godard movie thinks they have to deliver their lines in too-serious, or mock-serious tones (actors in *Goodbye To Language* have recalled that the Maître asked for slow and quiet line readings). The couple in the second half of *Goodbye To Language* are particularly po-faced and artificial (and completely unconvincing).[41] Hell, where is the comedy? where is the irony? where is the playfulness of actors like Jean-Pierre Léaud or Anna Karina?! Why does a Godard-written piece of dialogue (about World War Two or contemporary culture, say), have to be delivered in such quiet, pompous,

---

[41] They are also humourless and perpetually grumpy: we'll have children, the man says. Not now, the woman says; maybe you can have a dog. Is this a parody of the relationship of Miéville and Godard?!

studied tones? Are they secretly apeing the Master himself? Or just copying what every other actor before them has done in a Godard-directed piece? (There's no doubting that long stretches of Godard's later works discard humour – as if the Maestro has forgotten that there are other ways of making statements, delivering messages, or providing insights about being alive in the 21st century than speaking in brooding, enigmatic tones). And yet quite a few critics found *Goodbye To Language* funny.

3-D.

Goodbye To Language is another pioneering movie technically, with the Master this time taking on 3-D filmmaking technology (which had seen a huge resurgence in the 2000s and 2010s). While the Hollywood movie industry took up 3-D as another marketing tool for blockbuster flicks such as *Avatar, Alice In Wonderland* and *The Hobbit* (and using it in the same gimmicky way as it had been deployed in the 1950s, along with widescreen), the use of 3-D technology by the French Genius and his team was typically innovative (and quirky).

Jean-Luc Godard has long been fascinated by visual perception and the psychology (and philosophy) of seeing. From his earliest movies, Godard has been exploring modes of perception and comprehension (remember how Godard speaks of the camera as a microscope, or a scientific instrument for examining life). So taking up 3-D cinematic technology was as inevitable as Godard's interest in video, or high definition television, or surround sound, or using lightweight, handheld cameras. Indeed, Godard's passion for all things technological and mechanical is one of the lesser-known aspects of his enormous talent (Godard is a *true* innovator – a word like 'pioneer' is thrown around a lot, but very few filmmakers are genuine innovators).[42]

In *Goodbye To Language*, 3-D was deployed as another way of creating superimpositions, one of the key visual devices of Jean-Luc Godard's later cinema and television work. Thus, an image on the right would be superimposed over an image on the left (in one instance, a penis of an actor and the pudenda of another actor – very typical of Godard!). (But the effect when viewed in normal, 2-D conditions, where superimpositions are used, isn't as effective).

---

[42] There simply isn't *time*, for a start, with commercial movie productions.

THE 'STORY'.

In concocting characters and stories in *Goodbye To Language*, vaguely achieved and indistinct and ambiguous tho' they are, Jean-Luc Godard is still clinging onto traditional, Western forms of art and cinema. While *Goodbye To Language* might be really interested in exploring new cinematic technologies (such as high definition and 3-D), or spouting philosophical maxims, or contemplating Big Issues like nature, animals, children, war, death and love, there are still attempts at evoking characters, situations and stories.

The narrative elements in *Goodbye To Language,* as in the other later works of Jean-Luc Godard as director, are fragmentary and potentially unsatisfying, and nothing like the carefully plotted and scripted stories in *Contempt,* say, or *Weekend.*

Dissatisfying, that is, if you are looking for things like regular characters and storytelling. Because *Goodbye To Language* is a movie or a work which questions what a movie is, what storytelling is, and even what looking is, or what language is. ('I hate characters', gripes Ivitch. But even actors cast as 'non-characters' are still characters, due to the mechanisms of the medium of cinema, or even of one shot following another shot – or, anyway, at least because of the super-cargo of cinema, a vast machine or cyber-network that churns out characters and stories and themes by the million).

With *Goodbye To Language,* we are in a whole other world of art and cinema, in a realm where fundamentals are being questioned. Not only fundamental issues such as life, death, love, language and politics, but also the foundations of art and cinema themselves.

For a filmmaker in his eighties to be so inquisitive, to have admitted that he is still searching and exploring cinema and art and technology, at this level, and in this depth, is quite remarkable.

❖

There are shots, images, sounds, music, etc, in *Goodbye To Language,* but for some viewers and critics they don't have meaning, or add up to anything, or tell a story. Humans are continually looking for patterns, ideas, structures, as if the human brain can't help trying to make sense out of reality, or what is put in front of them.

Thus, some critics complained that while the 3-D filmmaking and the image-making in *Goodbye To Language* is extraordinary, the images seem emptied of 'meaning'. But *Goodbye To Language* is clearly exploring questions like, 'what is cinema?', 'what is language?', 'what is the value or worth of communication?' In which case, a 'story', or 'characters', or 'ideas', or 'themes', or conventional 'dramaturgy' isn't essential, or even wanted.

And yet, of course, *Goodbye To Language does* contain 'characters' (of a kind), and it *does* foreground one of Jean-Luc Godard's chief themes: *love*. Yes, *Goodbye To Language,* released in the 84th year of the Maestro, is another film about love. And, specifically, love between men and women, and love that's romantic and erotic (both couples're depicted in intimate scenes, nude, and having the conversations (arguments) of lovers in conventional drama).

There are two couples in *Goodbye To Language,* who inevitably mirror each other (to add to the confusion/ mirroring, the actors are cast to look like each other). They are not differentiated much, either. The guy who stalks about with a handgun with a Hitler moustache (Daniel Ludwig) is an irate ex-husband.

The two couples are:

First couple:	Héloise Godet as Josette
	Kamel Abdeli as Gédéon
Second couple:	Zoé Bruneau as Ivitch
	Richard Chevallier as Marcus

Jean-Luc Godard's love of oppositions and dualities extends throughout his cinema – from stories (two women, two couples, two cities, etc) and ideologies (West/ East, capitalism/ Communism, etc), to technical aspects (left and right channels in stereo). When he's mixing sound, for example, it's typical for the Master to have one sound on the left channel, and a different one on the right channel (and he continued to use this approach even in the age of surround sound and multi-channel sound, as if he's still living in the early days of stereo as recorded on two-track tape machines in the 1960s). And when Godard came to use 3-D technology, he'd have an image on the left and a different image on the right which, with 3-D goggles, could be combined.

In one scene, Héloise Godet takes off her clothes and puts them in the washing machine, then sits in the nude in the kitchen. Eh? Doesn't she have other clothes?! (Oh, these non-characters are so cool, so French: they sit about nude, pulling on a jacket, and then lighting a cigarette. Of course! Well, it worked fifty years ago, in *Contempt,* but Kamel Abdeli is no Michel Simon, and Héloise Godet is no Brigitte Bardot).

Héloise Godet washes her hands in a local park basin sprinkled with Fall leaves. She (or her twin) stands by some railings with Geneva Lake behind her. She chats to Gédéon in the bathroom (again with the bathroom scenes in Godardania, and again with the nudity).

*

In the second half of *Goodbye To Language,* the second version of the Eternal Godardian Couple replay many of the same scenes from the first half, with the first couple. With variations, of course. For instance, Ivitch is angrier and more dissatisfied, coming across like the familiar grumpy, old Godardian Ranter (laying into numerous pet hates of Godard's – like the price of gas, and why she wasn't born on a planet of fervent *cinéastes* instead of boring, old Earth. Just kidding). Ivitch hates other people's happiness (in true, Existential, outsider, Sartre-Camus-style), and announces, like an Anti-Christ Alien landing on Planet Earth: 'I have come here to say 'no". (Or maybe it's the lame, blank way that Zoé Bruneau plays Ivitch – she's just ridiculous and completely unconvincing).

There's an ugly sexual encounter in the shower, with the man forcing himself upon the woman, which's a nod to the (better) scene in *Prénom: Carmen* in 1983 (featuring Maruschka Detmers and Jacques Bonaffé).

The problem with the second couple in *Goodbye To All That* is they are superfluous, and what they do and say is redundant, merely repeating what we've already seen in the first half. They are much crankier, and their verbal snarking doesn't mask their alarming hostility towards each other.

*

Mary Shelley (author of *Frankenstein*) appears towards the end of *Goodbye To Language,* writing in a book. The voiceover explains about her and Lord Byron and Percy Bysshe Shelley, and the famous, fateful night in 1816 at Lord Byron's Swiss Villa Diodati at Lake Geneva when Mary Shelley's *Frankenstein* and Dr John Polidori's *The Vampyre* were conjured up. Other films which explored the creation of Shelley's landmark novel include *Gothic* (Ken Russell, 1987), *Haunted Summer* (Ivan Passer, 1988), *Frankenstein Unbound* (Roger Corman, 1990), and one of the most famous horror films ever made, *The Bride of Frankenstein* (James Whale, 1935).

In *Adieu au Langage,* the Shelley-Shelley-Byron sequence is staged in the casual, throwaway manner of the scenes in *Weekend* (where Jean-Paul Léaud played Louis Antoine Léon de St Just, a figure from the French Revolution, Blandine Jeanson was Emily Brontë dressed as

Alice in Wonderland and Yves Afonso was Tom Thumb). Even so, it was highly unusual for Godard to be staging scenes from so far into the past in his recent cinema (where he seemed to have jettisoned dramatizations of this kind decades ago).

BLACK LEADER.

There are many sections of black leader in *Goodbye To Language* – sometimes it seems as if Jean-Luc Godard (and his team) just don't have the images to illustrate his themes and concerns. One notes the shortness of *Goodbye To Language* (69 minutes), the repetitions, and the extensive use of black: a film in search of a film, once again, then, a film trying to become a film, a film in the form of notes for a film essay... (Will the black leader build up in the cutting room, growing overnight like a Monster of the Id in a 1950s B-movie, so that Godard's very last film will be nothing but black?).

Because Jean-Luc Godard has by this time, in twenty-fourteen, aged 84, filmed *everything* – and *then some*. He's *done it all*, in terms of a film career. Everything. *Tout. Toto.* Yet he still has things he wants to say, and he still wants to say them with sounds and images. But there are times in *Goodbye To Language* when it seems as if the filmmaker can't quite find the images to go with the voiceover or the dialogue, or to embody his themes and passions. (Or it may be that the sounds and the dialogues don't require images, hence they play over black).

SOUND AND MUSIC.

There is far less music in many sections of *Goodbye To Language* than other recent Godard movies. But the music is also used to astonishing effect, from sudden stabs of strings, to very low, bassy drones, to plangent choirs (all of the usual suspects were featured – Peter Tchaikovsky, Jean Sibelius, Arnold Schoenberg, Giya Kancheli. Emmanuel Ferrier was music consultant). And, once again, Godard uses music in repetitive surges, something he has been doing from his early works (the same intros are repeated, as if constantly re-setting the movie, or acting as refrains/ reprises in poetry).

Sound-wise, *Goodbye To Language* is stuffed with the outrageous and intricate/ poetic idiosyncrasies of Godardian sound: sounds with extraordinary crispness and closeness, sounds deliberately muffled, sounds with wind noise on the mic, sounds recorded crudely, sounds where voices're allowed to distort, and sounds mixed with elaborate intricacy.

Godard has established his own sub-genre of sound in television and cinema. Reminding us that: to carve out your own niche in sound is a major accomplishment.

POST-PRODUCTION.

Goodbye To Language is another of the many Godard works to have been extensively worked-over in post-production. I would imagine that Godard is at his happiest when he is in his editing suite, cutting the footage, mixing the sound, orchestrating the start and stop points for the music, and juggling voiceovers and dialogue.

In his editing studio he can sift thru hours of classic movies, Hollywood movies, *avant garde* movies, good movies and terrible movies, and newsreel from WWII (and other faves, like the Spanish Civil War, the Vietnam War, etc). He can mess around with the colour, contrast, brightness of the video footage (turning an everyday field of grass or poppies or Fall leaves into a Post-Impressionist canvas worthy of Paul Gauguin or Claude Monet). He can pick CDs from the vast array on the shelves of Edition of Contemporary Music artists, classical composers, and the odd French folk song, and cut them into the movie. He can merrily mix dialogue, sound effects and music on the console. And he can puff away on the endless supply of cigars (there are no 'NO SMOKING' signs any place that Godard works!).

NATURE.

Many images of trees and leaves in the Fall. Snow. More snow. Melting snow. Drifting snow. Snow-laden trees beside Lake Geneva. Cars in snow. Images from inside a car – by day, by night, in heavy rain, in snow. Rivers in spate. (The 2014 film haunts a river like a ghost – a ghost with a dog – a ghost armed with a camera and a dog).

We see one of Godard's favourite spots beside Lake Geneva several times – in Fall, Winter, Summer, etc (this patch of land and water crops up in works like *J.L.G.* and *Our Music*).

Many images of trees, often looking up thru the branches and leaves at the sky (filmed by Jean-Luc Godard in his trademark handheld style). Some of the images, backed by slow, moody and minimalist strings, are extremely beautiful – with a casual, throwaway beauty, reminding us that the natural world is beautiful *all the time*, but humans *don't see it*.[43]

Goodbye To Language is full of 10-second scenes, or mini-scenes

---

43 Don't – won't – can't.

lasting 17.42 seconds, of music + sounds + images, which are breathtakingly lyrical – very much the cinematic equivalent of a line of poetry, or the simple, poetic and mystical form of Japanese *haiku* (like a Matsuo Basho *haiku* poem filmed in video: 'an Autumn tree'... 'a lake in snow').

> The old pond
> A frog leaps in.
> Sound of the water (M. Basho)

And often that lyricism is simply cut dead: the music stops with the shift to a different scene.

There are images of trees in Fall worthy of Vincent van Gogh or Pierre Renoir, of branches against a clear, blue sky, and of snowy trees reminiscent of Casper David Friedrich or Camille Pissaro. At times, *Goodbye To Language* looks as if Jean-Luc Godard and his team were somehow channelling the spirits of the great Impressionist and Post-Impressionist painters.

IMAGES.

A close-up of a painter painting. Extreme close-ups of paintbrushes on canvas (in a sea of black, of course). Two people working at a table, with sketchpads and paints. (The offscreen voices identify one of them as Jean-Luc Godard; the other is presumably Anne-Marie Miéville).

A partially-nude woman holding a bunch of flowers. A woman getting dressed beside a television set, in front of a lamp. A woman posing as an artist's model. Blood in a bath, suggestive of suicide (no – there's purple in there, too; is it pigment? Or a joke on what Godard used to say about blood in films in the 1960s: it's not blood, it's red).

Many of the images in *Goodbye To Language* are simply breathtaking in their beauty, as if one of the goals of the 2014 movie was to be even more painterly and sensual than ever before. Aided by sophisticated post-production techniques, *Goodbye To Language* conjures treated video images as paintings. With its flame-hot oranges (of Fall leaves), its brilliant, juicy greens (of Summer grass),[44] and its vibrant reds (of roadside poppies), *Goodbye To Language* references many of Godard's favourite artists, such as Claude Monet, Pierre Renoir, Edgar Degas, and Eugène Delacroix (in another life, Godard might've been a painter. Not a technical genius, nor an oil painter (not

---

44 Switzerland is super-green in Summer.

enough patience!), but an earthy Expressionist, like Géorges Rouault or James Ensor, with a loose, rapid style. He had an exhibition of his paintings in his teens).

Parts of *Goodbye To Language* come across as contemporary art, the sort of *avant garde* video footage that's included in many an art installation around the world (those exhibits which feature video monitors, which in art installations are mandatory). In this respect, cinema certainly lags behind contemporary art, which has explored the sensual, plastic qualities of video extensively.

HISTORY.

Very soon in *Goodbye To Language,* Jean-Luc Godard is once again going over modern history, honing in on his obsessions with World War Two, with fascism, with Adolf Hitler, with the Holocaust – for J.-L. G., something happened in WWII that altered forever life in the West. I mean, beyond the obvious ways – like the deaths of millions, the re-organization of political power in the world, the changes in society, culture, technology and ideology, etc.

For Jean-Luc Godard, World War Two was the Grand Catastrophe that changed everything. Godard isn't interested in how or why it happened, or how or why Adolf Hitler could be democratically elected (the event is referenced in *Goodbye To Language*), or how or why so much changed after the war. He doesn't psychoanalyze the war, or rationalize its morality; he's not debating the war on a po-faced TV show. He's interested in the ways in which WWII continues to shape the world today, how the world in the West (as well as many other regions)[45] has been completely defined by WWII (and how few people seem to be aware of that, or even discuss it anymore). [46]

Sometimes one wonders if one of the secret subtexts of the cinema of Jean-Luc Godard is that he wishes more than anything that he had been in his twenties during WWII (instead of being 15 when the war ended in 1945). So that he could've filmed it. He would've been a determined youth armed with a 16mm wind-up Bolex camera, say, sent by the Allies to film the front lines in Europe and Africa. And he would've joined the teams visiting the concentration camps for the first time. Or he would've played an active role in the French Resistance.

Jean-Luc Godard is in short a filmmaker haunted by World War

---

45 But what about Africa? a character asks in *Goodbye To Language*. Africa is one of the political undercurrents, the hidden guilts, the sins that lurk beneath Godard's cinema.
46 In 2013, Hayao Miyazaki commented: 'Including myself, a generation of Japanese men who grew up during a certain period have very complex feelings about World War II'. This certainly is true of J.-L. G., whose views on everything seem to be complex – but about WWII, *very* mixed and *very* complicated.

Two as few filmmakers have ever been (and by the guilt that he didn't actively participate). The war and the Shoah provide Godard with so much to discuss, to love, to hate, to fear. WWII is an event that Godard has contemplated at length – it is the Grand Event that looms behind all of his later work (certainly from the late 1980s to the present day).

A boy entering the gas chambers asks his mother, 'why?', and an SS officer snaps, 'there is no 'why'.' (The anecdote is related in the film).

GODARD DOES *LASSIE*.

The real star of *Goodbye To Language* is of course Roxy the dog.

There's no doubting the astonishing facility of the Master's for seeking out arresting images, for sneaking his camera into parts of the landscape or the urbanscape which nobody else has ever filmed (or so it seems). On a purely visual level, *Goodbye To Language* features a remarkably wide variety of styles and approaches to image-making: there is black-and-white, step-motion, freeze frames, altered video with colours like Fauvist art, pin-sharp, high definition images, scratchy, grainy, low res images, lots of found footage (much of it re-filmed off video monitors), and every form of camera movement. Plus of course 3-D.

We are bombarded with images. If you are a fan of cinema, or someone who lives/ has lived in the Westernized world, you will probably have seen thousands and thousands of images. To create a work which contains images that appear new (or seem to, anyway), is truly remarkable.

There are also many sections of *Goodbye To Language* which look like home videos – especially of that dog! (Ah, bless our animals!). The dog (Godard's own pet, Roxy) is filmed everywhere. A dog in the snow. A dog by Lake Geneva. A dog in long grass. A dog asleep. A dog swimming in a river (the Maestro himself filmed the hound, using several domestic video cameras).

Nobody would've guessed that late in his career the world-famous genius filmmaker Jean-Luc Godard would make a movie starring a dog! And include so many shots from the point-of-view of a pooch! Yes, *Goodbye To Language* is Godard's *Lassie*! Now it's not 'a girl and a gun' for Godard, but 'a camera and a dog'!

Oh, yes, sure, there is a thematic/ philosophical reason for the dog appearing so much in *Adieu*. An animal is *in* the world, *in* life, in a fuller, realer way than humans are, perhaps – the dog doesn't have the layers or barriers or constructs of language/ art/ culture between themselves and life. A dog just *is* - it has Rilkean beingness,47 you might say (or in the terms of theories of liberation and non-duality, an increasingly popular way of looking at existence, there is no separation for a dog: all is one: it's *there*, and that's all there is).

GODARDISMS.
- The two great inventions are infinity and zero remarks Gédéon; no, Josette retorts, sex and death. 48
  - There's no Noble Prize for music or painting.
  - A woman can annoy you, or kill you, but is harmless.
  - 'I have come here to say no'

CINEMA AS EXPLORATION.
Incredibly, *Goodbye To Language* has a filmmaker in his eighties, a filmmaker who has done everything in cinema and television, going back to fundamental questions, such as: 'what is an image'? 'What is a sound'? To be so curious - so child-like, in a way - is pretty darn extraordinary, in a world (of mass media/ cinema/ television, etc) which's so cynical, so weary, so seen-it-all-before.

For Jean-Luc Godard, the camera is the tool, the weapon, the scientific instrument, the means, the way-in, the vehicle and the laboratory for this continuing exploration of the world using images and sounds. And not only the camera, but also the microphone, the sound mixing desk, the vision mixer, the editing machine, the computer. Godard's cinema somehow makes the audience aware of every piece of technology it took to get those images and sounds onto the screen. Few other filmmakers have sought to expose every single machine and mechanism in the manufacture of cinema and television. While many filmmakers have foregrounded aspects of cinema, few other filmmakers seem so dedicated to revealing everything - not the usual movies-about-movie elements, such as cameras, lamps, tripods, microphones and the backs of sets - but *everything*.

Jean-Luc Godard is himself a living television studio, a film soundstage, a recording studio - and he's the factories that manufactured the cameras and the digital recording machines... and the TV sets and monitors and screens and every media outlet... and

---

47 A quote on the soundtrack over images of the dawg is from Rainer Maria Rilke, about Rilke's notion of being 'outside' and innerness (*innigkeit*), where inside becomes all outside (and vice versa).
  'What is outside me, is really within me, is mind - and vice versa' (*Novalis Schriften, Die Werke Friedrichs von Hardenberg*, eds. R. Samuel, *et al*, Kohlhammer, Stuttgart, 1960-88, 3, 429).
48 Eh? Since when was death 'invented'? 'Invented' by humans? Err, right!

Godard is a city, a country, and the whole history of cinema.

THE CRITICS.

You can predict, without bothering to check, that the same people will love *Goodbye To Language* and the same people will hate it – as have loved or hated everything that Godard has produced as a director since the 1980s. The same film critics will attack *Goodbye To Language*, and the same critics (tho' far fewer of them!) will applaud it. The audience for *Goodbye To Language* will be tiny. And anyone straying into it without knowing anything about Godard or this kind of Euro-art-film-essay will likely drift away after 5 minutes, confused, bemused, or bored.

I have checked the critics' response to most of Jean-Luc Godard's movies, including his latest works. But there's no need with *Goodbye To Language* – we know what the critics are going to say.

Like most of Jean-Luc Godard's later works, *Goodbye To Language* doesn't make itself easy to enjoy or like, doesn't go out of its way to embrace the viewer, and doesn't offer anything approaching 'entertainment' (no dancing! No jokes! No car chases!).[49] Or a 'story'. Or 'characters' (and even the 'themes' change every minute, or with every shot).

However, *Goodbye To Language*, enjoyed a stronger positive response than recent works such as *Film Socialisme* (admirers included Haskell, Brody, Bordwell, Taubin, Corliss, Romney, Rosenbaum, White, Phillips, de Baecque and Hoberman)– many critics placed *Goodbye To Language* in their top three films of the year, and it received many awards.

And yet there is too much repetition and redundancy in *Goodbye To Language* – the same sorts of images are repeated so many times they lose their impact: a dog by a river; cars on a boring suburban road; moving cars viewed from inside; and yet another woodland. The film can take empty shots like this and cut them together ingeniously, and add philosophical voiceover, a bit of music and – *voilà*! – you've got yourself a Godard movie. Those three elements Save The Day so many times in Godard's late work: clever editing, fancy dialogue and music.

---

[49] Yet there are numerous shots of cars from the outside and from the inside, driving.

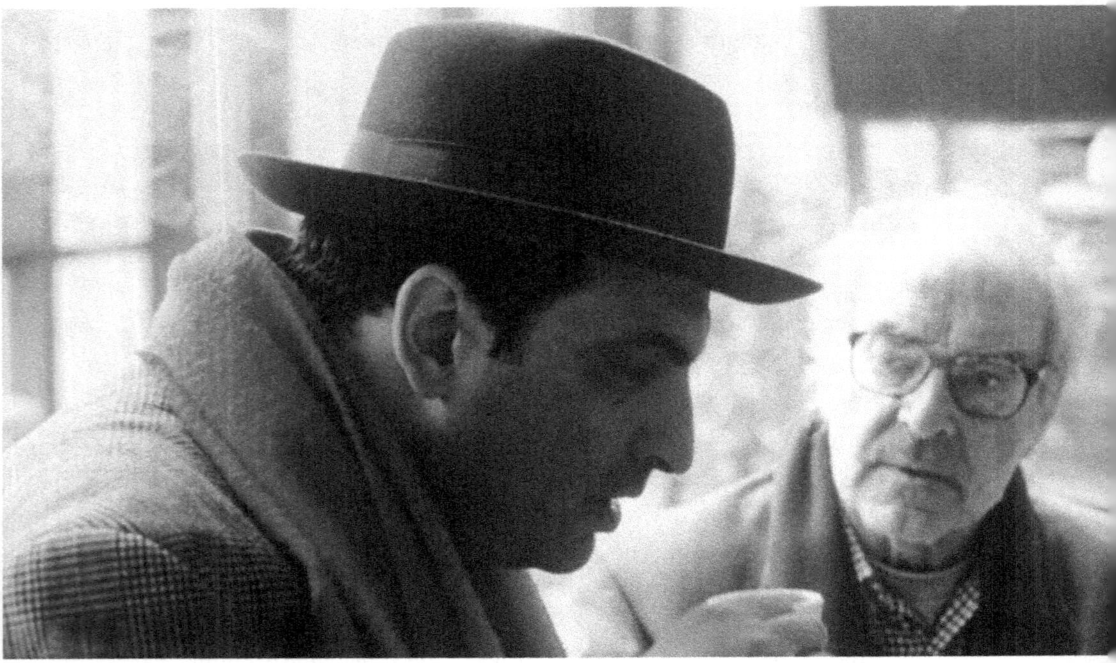

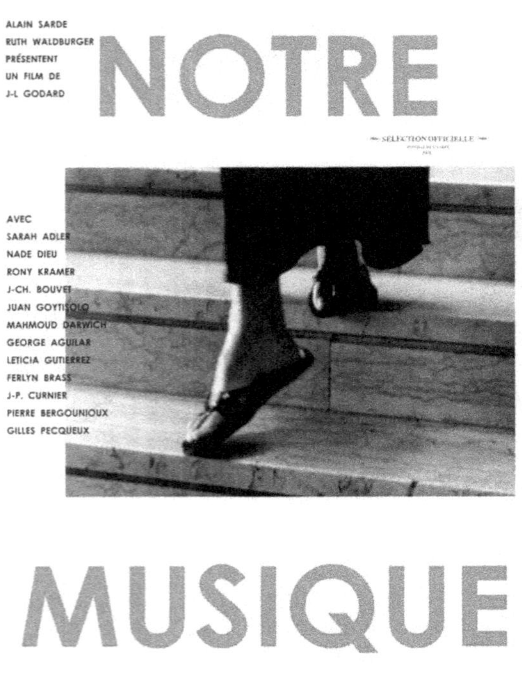
ALAIN SARDE
RUTH WALDBURGER
PRÉSENTENT
UN FILM DE
J-L GODARD
NOTRE
SÉLECTION OFFICIELLE
AVEC
SARAH ADLER
NADE DIEU
RONY KRAMER
J-CH. BOUVET
JUAN GOYTISOLO
MAHMOUD DARWICH
GEORGE AGUILAR
LETICIA GUTIERREZ
FERLYN BRASS
J-P. CURNIER
PIERRE BERGOUNIOUX
GILLES PECQUEUX
MUSIQUE
PRODUCTION AVVENTURA FILMS · PERIPHERIA · FRANCE 3 CINÉMA · CANAL PLUS · VEGA FILM · TSR · REGIO · DFI
DIRECTION ARTISTIQUE A-M MIÉVILLE · MÉMOIRE ELIAS SANBAR · CENTRE ANDRÉ MALRAUX SARAJEVO
VEGA

"A SUPREME MASTERPIECE!"
–Nathan Lee, THE NEW YORK SUN
"One of Godard's BEST-EVER
–John Anderson, NEWSDAY
JEAN-LUC GODARD
NOTRE MUSIQUE
official selection
CANNES · TORONTO · NEW YORK · CHICAGO
winner
BEST FILM OF THE YEAR ·
FIPRESCI INTERNATIONAL CRITICS PRIZE

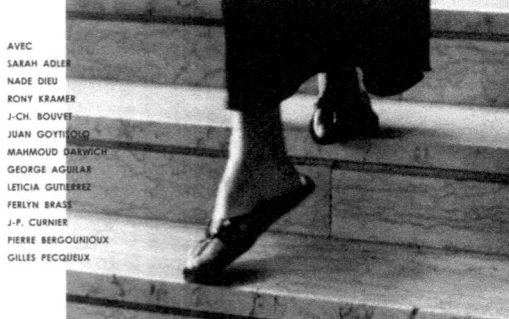

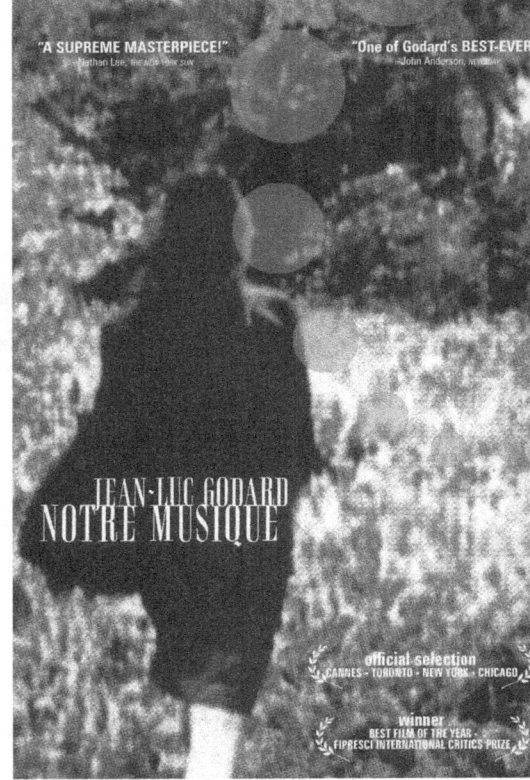

Film Socialisme (2010)

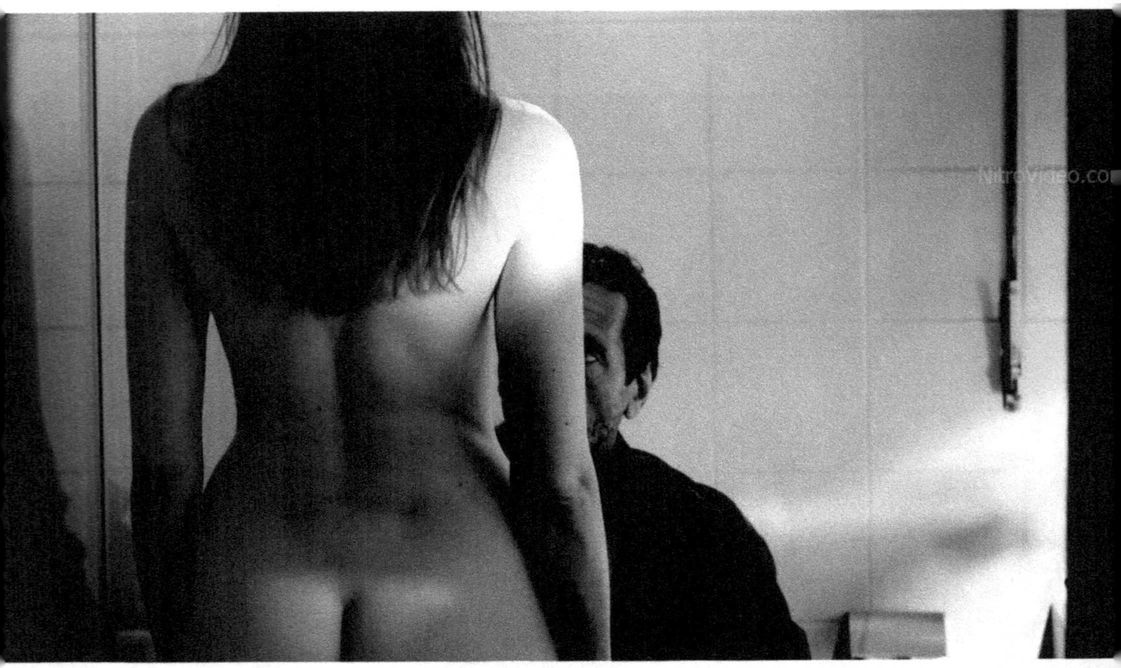

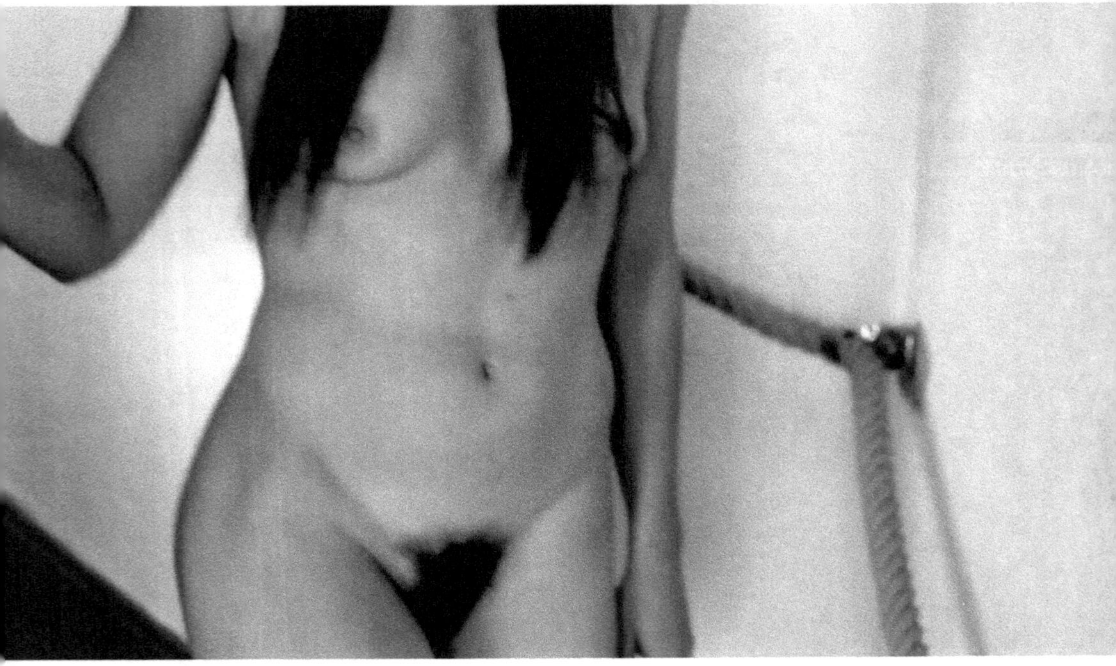

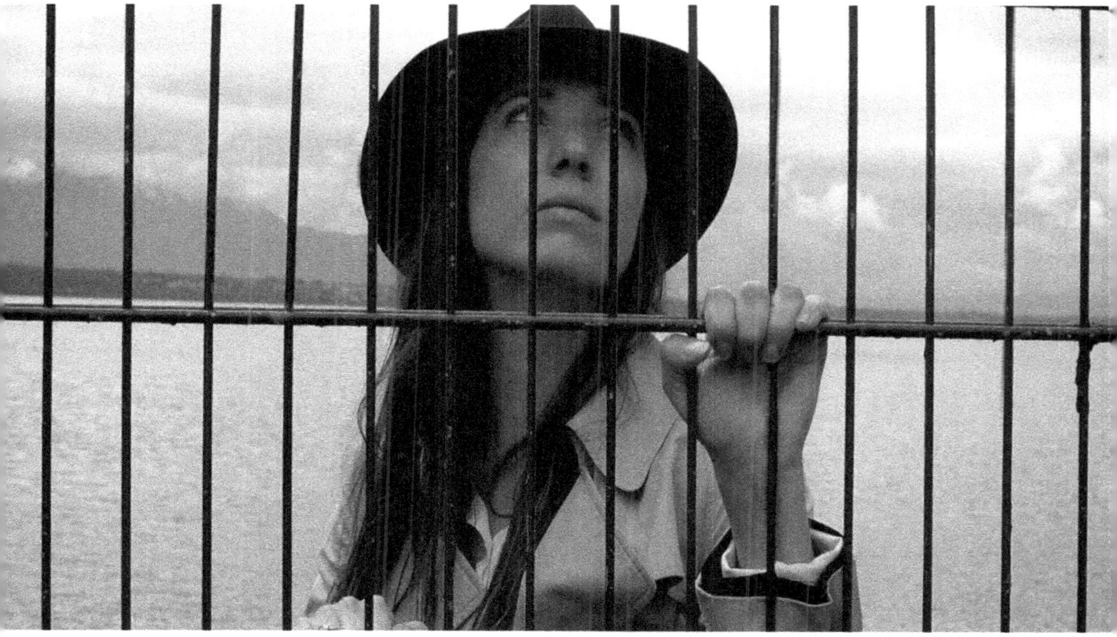

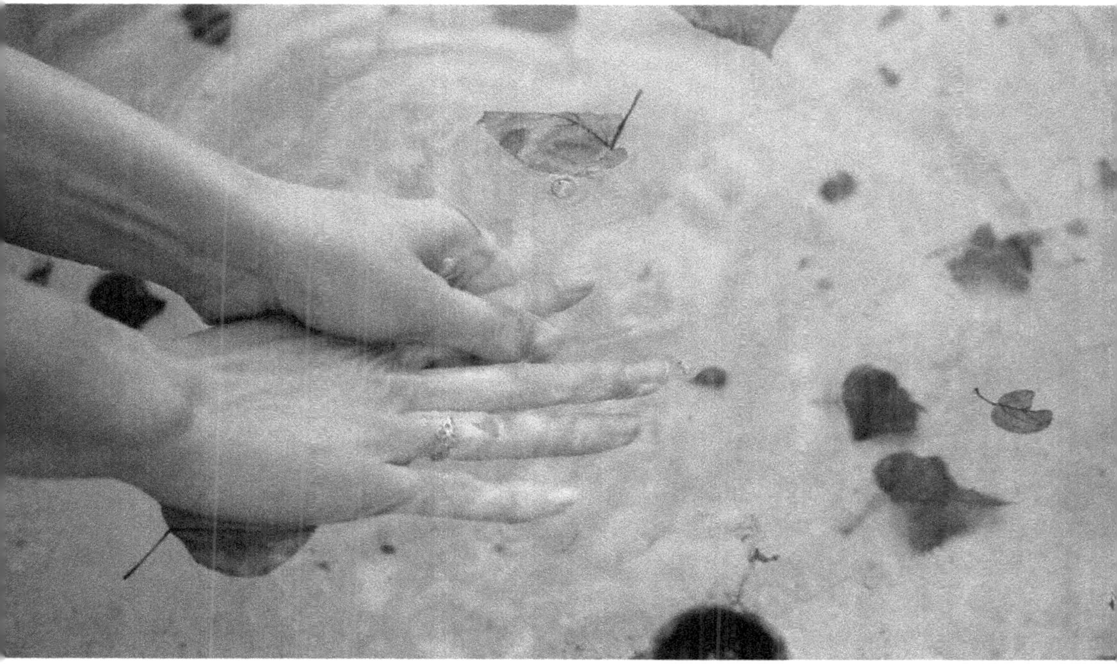

38

OTHER FILMS DIRECTED BY JEAN-LUC GODARD

LE NOUVEAU MONDE/ THE NEW WORLD

Anthology/ episode/ multi-part movies were popular in the 1950s and 1960s (J.-L. Godard contributed to a few). They were, obviously, producer-led pictures: a film producer would come up with an idea for a movie, go to Ingmar Bergman, telling him that Federico Fellini and Jean Renoir had already signed up to do it (they hadn't). When Bergman agreed, the producer'd go to Fellini and Renoir, and so on. For *RoGoPaG*, it was producer Alfredo Bini (who produced Pier Paolo Pasolini's movies) who put together the episode film of 1963. Alberto Barsanti and Angelo Rizzoli co-produced. Released: Feb 19, 1963. 122 mins.

RoGoPaG is a curious movie, with the *La Riccotta* (*Curd Cheese*) episode (directed by Pier Paolo Pasolini), being regarded by most critics as the most successful (and the most fun) installment: *La Ricotta* features Orson Welles as a film director shooting a Technicolour, religious movie in the countryside outside Rome. *Curd Cheese* is a wicked satire on Christian/ Catholic beliefs, how religion operates in the real, secular world (and among the working class), and a comical swipe at organized/ institutionalized religion which some found questionable (for instance, the film was seized by the authorities on March 1, 1963, on the grounds of insulting the State, with a writ signed by the public prosecutor, and Pasolini received a four month suspended sentence in prison (in Rome, the Appeals Court on May 6, 1964 revoked the charge, 'because the act does not constitute a crime'). That might've put off some filmmakers from going ahead with a feature-length portrayal of Jesus – but not Pasolini and Alfredo Bini! They steamed ahead with *The Gospel According To Matthew!*).

For Godard's segment in *RoGoPaG*, entitled *The New World* (a.k.a. *Le Nouveau Monde/ Il Nuovo Mondo*), many regular Godardians joined the crew (Bitsch, Guillemot, etc). Jean Rabier was DP. The cast included: Jean-Marc Bory, Alexandra Stewart, Michel Delahaye and Jean-André Fieschi. It was filmed in b/w and ran for about 20 minutes.

The New World is typical Godard: a man (Jean-Marc Bory), a woman (Alexandra Stewart), a neurotic relationship, and Paris... all very Godardian (but made in Italian), tho' not his most satisfying work by any means. It's *Breathless Revisited* for the n-th time. It must have been a kick for Godard to be included alongside heroes like Roberto Rossellini and Orson Welles in the same movie.

So the background story for *The New World* has an atomic bomb exploding over Paris (but 80 miles up),[1] which changes the city, but subtly, psychologically, socially: *The New World* looks forward to *Alphaville* (1965) with its evocations of the strange city of the present/ near future, where the inhabitants act oddly (here they take pills)[2] and regular logic is disrupted. (This was how Godard described the sketch, in a *Cahiers du Cinéma* interview: 'things are the same, but different' – just like all films are the same but different, or seemingly different but actually the same). The nuclear bomb and futuristic elements are delivered in the familiar cheapo manner of low budget filmmaking: with sound effects, with newspaper photos, and with a *lot* of voiceover explaining what's happened.

Anyhoo, the atom bomb and sci-fi elements in *The New World* are simply a pretext for something else (as in *Alphaville*), because the 1963 short evokes yet another romantic couple in the Godardverse, yet another relationship on the skids, yet another story where the man is perplexed/ confused/ irritated by the woman (50 years later, in *Goodbye To Language*, Godard was trotting out the same gender baloney: 'a woman can annoy you, or kill you, but is harmless').

Yes, it's the *Godard Soap Opera Show* once again: he loves her, she 'ex loves' him; he makes a date with her, she doesn't appear; he follows her to a swimming pool[3] (more stalking from the Godard Male), and observes her kissing a guy; quizzed about it later, the woman doesn't know what he's talking about (fed up, he pushes her roughly).

We've seen this soap opera *à la* God-Art many times before and since *The New World* (again, fifty thousand years later in *Goodbye To Language*, it's the same *shtick*).

The atom bomb going off is used as an explanation for people acting weirdly, and Alessandra not showing up for their rendezvous is explained by her living with a different logic to the husband (that's what he reasons to himself). But in a Godard movie, women always perplex men! They always live to/ in/ with a different logic or poetry from men!

For the rest, *The New World* is Godard operating on auto-pilot: he could send out a second unit team to get: (1) a shot of a woman standing by a window (the first shot of the movie – of course, she's smoking a cigarette); (2) shots of a man and woman sitting opp. each other at a table (talking, smoking); (3) shots of a man driving a car

---

1 Don't ask why (or how) a bomb was detonated 80 miles above the planet – this is Godard! An air-burst detonation needs to be exploded much closer to the target.
2 One of the few instances of drug-taking in a Godard movie – outside of the industrial consumption of tobacco and alcohol.
3 Cue gratuitous images of women in bikinis.

seen from inside; (4) shots of Paris by day; and (5) shots of women in bikinis.[4]

GODARD IN AMERICA

Godard In America (1970) is a documentary following the Master's tour of the U.S.A., aided by his faithful sidekick, Jean-Pierre Gorin. It was directed by Ralph Thanhauser. Critic Andrew Sarris also appeared. Released: Spring, 1970. 45 mins.

Godard In America is another shoddy piece of filmmaking typical of the era: shaky, black-and-white photography includes pointless shots of ceilings and empty rooms, while the core of the piece is a sit-down, round-table talk with a bunch of critics armed with notebooks and tape recorders (later it's a patch of grass, and then a lecture hall jammed with bemused students), while Godard waxes lyrical, as only he can. Speaking in Frenglish, with his lisp firmly in place, and chain-smoking (*d'accord*), Godard holds forth on topics such as 'Ollywoood, politics, Maoism, images and sounds, and other pet loves and hates. Gorin, sitting beside him, interjects occasionally. (The documentary is only really interested in the Maestro – several times, when Gorin is speaking, the camera pointedly stays on Godard).

The spiel that the Godard-Gorin Double Act trots out is the same ideological shtick they featured in the Dziga Vertov Group films: you know it off by heart by now: Marxism and Maoism heap good, Amerika and Capitalism heap bad. Don't be a dirty, money-grabbing Boss! Don't buy into the Amerikan Dream! Don't run out of cigarettes!

The Two G.s encourage their listeners (students and the press) to take up the political struggle against the social system. They quote Chairman Mao and Karl Marx. They explain (at length) how their next documentary will be filmed (with the aid of storyboards scribbled in a notebook by Uncle Jean).

Not once are Godard and Gorin seriously challenged in the documentary; meanwhile, the contributions from the journos and the students are kept to a minimum. It's a shame: here in the United States of America – which Godard had attacked numerous times (in every

---
4 Yes, Jean-Luc, we know that the name 'bikini' comes from Bikin Atoll, an atomic bomb connection.

single film!) – there was an opportunity to question the Maestro about his love-hate relationship with it all.

ANTICIPATION OR LOVE IN THE YEAR 2000

Anticipation ou L'Amour en L'An 2000 (Anticipation or Love In the Year 2000) was an episode in the anthology movie *The Oldest Profession (Le Plus Vieux Métier du Monde*, 1967). Produced by Joseph Bercholz and Horst Wendlandt, *The Oldest Profession* featured film directors Mauro Bolognini, Michael Pfleghar, Franco Indovina, Philippe de Broca and Claude Autant-Lara. Released April 21, 1967. 119 mins.

Some well-known stars appeared in *The Oldest Profession*, including Raquel Welch, Jean-Claude Brialy, Jeanne Moreau, Enrico Salerno, Elsa Martinelli, and in Godard's episode, Anna Karina (this was about the last time they collaborated on a movie).

The concept of *The Oldest Profession* was a history of prostitution. Thus, each director took on the oldest job in a different era, from prehistory thru Ancient Rome to the present day and finally the future (this was Godard's segment). The Maestro had of course explored the subject several times by 1967 (and he would in later movies, such as *Slow Motion*).

Filmed in black-and-white, *Anticipation or Love In the Year 2000* was a minor addition to the Godard Laffathon. Anna Karina, Jacques Charrier, Jean-Pierre Léaud, Daniel Bart, Jean-Patrick Lebel, and Marilu Tolo appeared in a story of a visitor to Earth who's offered two women: the first one (Marlene – Miss Physical Love, played by Marilu Tolo) is replaced by the second one, Hostess 703 (a.k.a. Natasha a.k.a. Eleanor Romeovich – Karina).

So it's a kind of companion piece to *Alphaville*. The setting is another bland apartment somewhere on Earth (but probably Paris), and the main sequence is once again the Godardian Soap Opera: a Man, a Woman, and Lerrrve. Or, rather, talking about love, as the two characters circle around each other warily in the time-honoured manner of the Godardian Romantic Couple.

Aside from some Godardian oddities – such as a character

speaking in a self-conscious, halting fashion – *Anticipation or Love In the Year 2000* presents the same concerns of Jean-Luc Godard's that had been explored so much wittier in *Two or Three Things I Know About Her* or *Pierror le Fou*. Anna Karina plays her usual sweet, naïve, semi-innocent soul, who fascinates and perplexes the man, Nick (played by Jacques Charrier). A memorable scene has Karina and Charrier spraying each other with water, an early Godardian version of a come-shot.

ONE P.M.

D.A. Pennebaker (1925-2019) is the director of some well-known music documentaries, including biographies of Bob Dylan (*Dont Look Back, Something Is Happening* and *Eat the Document*), a fantastic David Bowie concert (*Ziggy Stardust*), and the Monterey Pop Festival (*Monterey Pop*). Pennebaker filmed other music-related documentaries – with Little Richard, John Lennon, Alice Cooper, Depeche Mode, Jerry Lee Lewis, Chuck Berry and Stephen Sondheim.

D.A. Pennebaker was an advocate of direct cinema. Pennebaker often worked with Al Maysles, who had collaborated with Godard on the *Six In Paris* film. Pennebaker's approach to documentary production drew on the example of Robert Flaherty. Pennebaker liked to use long takes to capture whatever was happening, without staging events, and without commenting upon them with voiceovers. (By contrast, Godard also deployed lengthy takes, but seldom resisted the urge to add a voiceover, to create his own interpretation of what was happening. Godard exhibited one of the most powerful ideological projects in contemporary cinema – everything he did was Godardized, and never 'objective' or 'distanced'. Godard's documentaries were not really documentaries in the traditional 'objective' sense of recording a situation, they were full of staged and contrived events. They were fiction, and self-consciously acknowledged that. And after shooting was complete, the editing and the sound would further shape the material into a Godardified outcome).

D.A. Pennebaker pioneered the combination of lightweight cameras (which he liked to wield handheld), along with synchronized sound. Godard was fond of handheld camerawork, and of sync sound. Pennebaker had special cameras developed for his documentary work, and Godard also commissioned lightweight cameras (and fast lenses) from manufacturers.

Filmed in July, 1973 at the Hammersmith Odeon in London Town by director D.A Pennebaker and his crew, *Ziggy Stardust and the Spiders From Mars* (1973) was a record of the famous last show of David Bowie in his Ziggy Stardust persona and the Spiders From Mars. It is a marvellous rock movie for a number of reasons: first, (1) it captures David Bowie at the height of his powers as a performer, musician and vocalist, and (2) it's got the flamboyant glitter-era costumes and the theatricality, and (3) it's got the camp personas to a 'T' (including some mime!), and (4) it's got the attitude and the cool, and (5) it's got the audience going nuts.

Despite the technical flaws (there're numerous instances of dreadful photography – out of focus, badly-lit, an over-use of zooms, and generally unprofessional – like nearly all filmed records of pop concerts of the period – and much of the Dziga Vertov Group material), and a couple of scenes where the guitar solos are a tad too long – *Ziggy Stardust and the Spiders From Mars* comes over as a thrilling, in-your-face rock show. The energy and magic of David Bowie and the band is undeniable, yet this is the one thing – the total exhilaration of *being there* – that so many rock movies can't capture. *Being there* and watching a movie of it are utterly different experiences, as we all know!

In the early 1960s, D.A. Pennebaker had met Godard and talked about making a movie together (Godard had admired *Primary*, 1960, a documentary about J.F. Kennedy on the campaign trail). In 1968, Godard and Pennebaker began filming a documentary about the political movements in the U.S.A., entitled *One A.M.* (= *1 A.M.* = *One American Movie*). Godard had imagined (or hoped) that America would explode. It did, but not in the way that Godard thought.

Richard Leacock helped with the shooting, and figures such as Rip Torn, Tom Hayden, Anne Wiazemsky, Carol Bellamy, and Tom Luddy appeared (as themselves), along with the Jefferson Airplane band (including Grace Slick and Marty Balin).

However, the production was abandoned by Jean-Luc Godard, who left the U.S.A. to form a Marxist-Leninist Ciné-Utopia somewhere between Paris and Rolle. Later, D.A. Pennebaker pieced together the footage filmed by Godard and company, adding some of his own material. This became *1 P.M.* (= *One P.M.* or *One Parallel Movie*, or *One Perfect Movie* or *One Pennebaker Movie*, as Godard dubbed it).

D.A. Pennebaker acknowledged that *One P.M.* wasn't the movie that Godard likely intended. Indeed, it can't be regarded as a true Godard piece, because the Maestro abandoned it, and it was put together by others.

∗

Some of the bits of business in *One P.M.* are typical Godard: Rip Torn wearing a Native American headdress (Native Americans crop up in several Godard flicks), the manipulation of a tape recorder (with Torn repeating the dialogue, relates Godard's form of revolutionary politics), the militant rants, the handheld camerawork, the lengthy takes, the low lighting, etc. Some scenes, however, are clearly from D.A. Pennebaker, not Godard.

Several figures express their ideological views in speeches or interviews (in the manner of the Dziga Vertov Group pieces). Some of the speeches and interviews cover familiar issues of the late 1960s period, which Godard explored in his films: the military-industrial complex, student/ youth movements, labour and unions, race/ ethnicity, militant politics, etc. There's a rambling musical performance by some guys on a city street, and Jefferson Airplane perform on a Gotham rooftop.

One P.M. is also a portrait of the Director At Work, another 'making of' documentary: Jean-Luc Godard is seen rehearsing Rip Torn with the playback of the tape machine, listening to political speeches (sometimes interjecting), watching the street performance (and, as often in a Godard movie, he can be heard asking questions off-camera). Godard is often the focus of any gathering – the camera can't help wandering over to the Maestro as he stands and listens, sucking on his tobacco baby pacifier.[5]

---

5 *One P.M.* is another movie where everybody smokes. If anybody asks the question, 'can I smoke?', the answer is always 'Oui, oui, oui!'

HERE AND ELSEWHERE

Here and Elsewhere (1976) was in part a look back at the politicized period of filmmaking of 1968 to 1973. *Here and Elsewhere* featured scenes from the unfinished film about Palestine, produced during 1970. Unfortunately, some of the flaws of the 1968-1973 films persisted in *Here and Elsewhere* – such as the dogged insistence on repetition (on repetition... on repetition). Another irritating approach was to layer voiceovers from the filmmakers on top of footage of people speaking (which seems patronizing, as their voices are taken away and replaced by the filmmakers. It can seem a form of the Imperialism that Godard and Gorin fought against). A man addressing a large political gathering, for example, doesn't have his words translated (either as dubbing or subtitling). Instead, the voiceovers move in once again. Sometimes they summarize what the speaker is saying (tho' only briefly), but at other times they have their own agenda.

We also see some dramatizations of the war in the Middle East, but clumsily staged, in the manner of the other Dziga Vertov Group works. A youth firing a rifle. Some men sitting on the ground and debating, like the scenes in the other D.V.G. movies. Thus, Godard and company continued to apply the approach to politicized dramaturgy that they had developed over the years in the Dziga Vertov Group projects to the people of Palestine. Unfortunately, what might've worked in Prague or Paris among students seems out of place and awkward in the Middle East. The incredibly intense and centuries-old turmoil in the region seems just too big for Godard and the filmmakers to circumscribe (at least when employing their usual methods). There is no attempt to situate their project within a historical context.

Palestine Will Win pitted the working class and the militants of the Middle East against the Imperial machine of Israel, backed by the U.S.A. The political critique is the same as the rest of the Dziga Vertov Group films: the little man versus the big man, the minority versus the majority, the rebels versus Uncle Sam.

Here and Elsewhere features archetypal bits of Godardian business: there's a desk calculator with Godard punching in numbers: 1789, 1917, 1936, 1968 (you know what these refer to, of course – Godard's wine list of vintage years. 1917 is significant not because of the Russian Revolution but for its rather yummy Burgundy).

A sequence includes handheld viewers for photographic slides with the pictures being changed by hand in darkness (i.e., it's another way of collating a group of images in a single screen, but adding a bit of performance). A variation on this has some slide projectors showing images on a wall which are changed, so the screen is divided into several smaller screens (a typical device in audio-visual presentations of the period). And we have the classic configuration of multiple video monitors playing different clips: a football match, captions, and flashes of stills and footage.

Here and Elsewhere also includes some pornography (in the form of images from *Playboy* and similar magazines, with, once again in Godard's cinema, an emphasis of women's behinds).

It's crudely achieved – compared to video installation art, such as that of Nam June Paik, for instance. Korean Paik (1932-2006) is one of the great video artists. Standing in front of one of Paik's giant installations, with TV monitors playing different material all over the place, is quite an experience.

Another skit in *Here and Elsewhere* features a big close-up of V.U. meters on a tape machine responding to a speech by – who else? – Adolf Hitler. Another one has the faders on an amplifier being turned up and down. It's variation on Godard's foregrounding of the mechanisms of the video age in the Brechtian manner, this time focussing on sound.

In the present-tense of *Here and Elsewhere* we have a family out of media cliché: mom, dad and cute kids. They are shown watching TV (for a long time, in many repeated scenes). They pin photos to a wall. A bunch of people (including the father) queue up to utter a line or two in front of a video camera and hold up a photograph (it's another example of Godardian anarcho-politico dramaturgy in the Brechtian manner, that appears rather laboured).

GRANDEUR AND DECADENCE

Commissioned by T.F. 1 as part of the *Série Noir* series, *Grandeur and Decadence* (*Grandeur et Décadence d'un Petit Commerce de Cinéma*, a.k.a. *The Grandeur and Decadence of a Small-Time Filmmaker,* 1986), was yet another movie about cinema written and directed by Jean-Luc Godard (it was based on a novel by James Hadley Chase – another low-brow novel, then, and another thriller). Handed a commission from a television company, Godard is *not* going to deliver something neat and tidy and formulaic and easy to follow! No – he's going to do his idiosyncratic fiction-film-as-essay-as-poem-as-lecture-as-rant thing again.

Some critics have enthused madly about *Grandeur and Decadence*, calling it (A) Godard's finest movie of the Eighties,[6] and (B) one of his funniest satires on movie-making, and even (C) his greatest movie ever.

It's not.

In the 1980s, for ex, *Passion* and *Hail Mary* are *infinitely* superior.

The only name actor in *Grandeur and Decadence* is Jean-Pierre Léaud – playing his usual highly-strung, neurotic, French, intellectual persona (now sporting a moustache). Léaud can light up even the dullest scenes – which he has to do here. Because *Grandeur and Decadence* isn't as funny as it would like to be, and many of the jokes are in-jokes for those in the know.[7] Godardians will enjoy *Grandeur and Decadence*, but those coming to this sort of TV film for the first time will see:

(1) Scenes of people in under-lit/ half-lit restaurants/ hotels/ wherever, talking about Lordy knows what;

(2) Drifting dissolves and video superimpositions which seem to amount to... nothing much;

(3) Actors picking up books, quoting from them, then tossing them angrily aside (it's always the book's fault! for being a darn book! how *dare* that book be a book! and not a woman in a bikini!);

(4) Actors queuing up for auditions (where they're treated like cattle by the Gestapo);

(5) Inter-titles and captions (which don't explain much); and

(6) Bewildering allusions to some of Godard's favourite targets and topics (cinema, WWII, the Holocaust, Judaism, money, etc).

Style-wise, *Grandeur and Decadence* has a grubby, cheap video look which fits the material but offers nary a slice of romance or glamour or poetry. Everything seems to have been filmed in one building, with occasional glimpses out of the ground floor windows onto the street outside (as if the movie never got out of the production office, and decided to set every scene there. And after a while, you too are longing to get outside).

---

6 'To me, the film seems to be one of Godard's key works of his later period' (W. Dixon, 166).
7 Take the list of film producers cited by one of the characters – Georges de Beauregard, etc – no one will've heard of them except truly dedicated *cinéastes*.

And there are repetitions which try the patience of even diehard Godardians like us. In one sequence, the extras plod into a room to recite one line of Summat Meaningful when they're in frame, then they walk on. The sequence goes on and on – but not in a nice way. 8

There *are* amusing scenes in *Grandeur and Decadence*: in one, the director and the producer sit down and watch TV which's broadcasting a roaring fire: is this a nod to François Truffaut? (Truffaut died a couple of years b4 this TV film). In *Day For Night* (1973), which Jean-Luc Godard detested (he thought that Truffaut had sold out), Truffaut remarked that the television set replaces the hearth/ fireplace at the heart of the home.

There are classic Godardisms in *Grandeur and Decadence* – like the insistence on not looking back (*à la* Orpheus and Eurydice),9 like the sudden explosions of anger (Godard seemed even angrier in the '80s than the '60s), like the numerous unidentified voices-off, and of course the many asides about cinema.

By far the most compelling aspect of *Grandeur and Decadence* is the music on the soundtrack. Arvo Pärt's incredible, truly awe-inspiring *Cantus For Benjamin Britten* is used, as well as the soft rock of Janis Joplin. (Pärt's *Cantus* is played under, of all things, the audition scene where actors queue up to say a single line, while Léaud yells at them off-screen – 'again!' or 'louder'. It's an obscene mis-use of a transcendent piece of music).

The Maestro has a brief cameo, towards the end of *Grandeur and Decadence*. Thankfully, Jean-Luc Godard isn't doing one of his ridiculous, affected bits of business (as in *King Lear*). Unfortunately, it's a very short cameo, and soon we're back with static, boring shots of people leafing thru books in long shot, extras trotting up to the camera to utter a line or two, and the camera shooting out of the window to the street with actors in dark silhouette in the foreground.

Nothing is happening in *Grandeur and Decadence*, no one is saying anything remotely interesting (a cardinal sin for a Godard movie), and the lighting is so bad you can barely make out anyone's face. In *Grandeur and Decadence*, the filmmaking genius of J.-L. G. seeps away in a series of dull and pointless scenes and shots. Godard has sometimes made films (particularly in his later career), by waiting and waiting for just the right moment to shoot: crews have told stories of how the Genius Film Director seems to be waiting for some

---

8 Casting a movie can be a little like that.
9 Cited in *Alphaville*.

miraculous event or moment.[10] Well, he'll have to keep waiting in *Grandeur and Decadence*, because there are no miracles and no poetry waiting in the shadders to spring out and miraculize the movie into trembling transcendence.

THE POWER OF SPEECH

Puissance de la Parole (*The Power of Speech*, 1988) was a short, 25-minute video piece directed by the Master. It was part-inspired by two North American writers: James M. Cain (*The Postman Always Rings Twice*) and Edgar Allan Poe[11] ("The Power of Words").

The Power of Speech is mounted in Godard's later viddy/ telly manner: contemporary-set scenes of a mainly domestic kind intercut with found footage and edited with a self-conscious fretfulness on a vision mixer. Clouds, the Earth from space, the moon, stars, skies and other 'cosmic' material is whip-creamed into the rather familiar narrative of two lovers who're separated and bickering (and, yes, one of them works in a gas station!).

Oui, we're back with two lovers *yet again* in the cinema of Jean-Luc Godard – they are connected by a phone call: one lover yells and berates the other, while the other lover refuses to speak/ keeps silent/ utters disconnected phrases ('yes, yes, yes'). Guess which gender the shouty, angry lover is? and guess which lover the quieter one is? And guess which gender the lover is who disrobes and washes their body?

The Power of Speech has plenty of hi-falutin', philosophical/ political material jimmied into its sort-of narrative of Love Falling Apart, and the imagery is cut with a beguiling pace and spontaneity. But it does seem like a mere footnote to earlier Godard-helmed outings, such as *Hail Mary, Passion* and *First Name: Carmen*. And one of the guys (it's either Bouise or Irribaren, I forget which) is a horrible, spoilt brat presence – one of those actors who make the mistake of thinking that acting in Jean-Luc Godard movie means yelling their lines. (When actors go wrong in a Godard movie, they sometimes go *very* wrong).

---

10 Some film crews, like those on *Heaven's Gate* or *Ryan's Daughter*, ache to shoot the director (Michael Cimino and David Lean) who keeps them waiting around for 'just the right light' or whatever the •••• they are searching for.
11 Godard had already used Poe's work in films such as *Vivre Sa Vie*.

2 X 50 YEARS OF FRENCH CINEMA

2 x 50 Ans de Cinéma Français[12] (= *2 x 50 Years of French Cinema*, 1995) was a commission to celebrate the hundreth anniversary of cinema in 1895. Aided by Michel Piccoli and regular partner-in-crime Anne-Marie Miéville, Jean-Luc Godard appeared (as himself) in a documentary/ celebration/ discussion of French cinema. (The credits: producers: Bob Last and Colin MacCabe, direction and editing: Godard and Miéville, A.D.: Gilbert Guichardière, sound: Stéphane Thiébaut, cast: Godard, Piccoli, Patrick Gillieron, Fabrice Bénard, Estelle Grynszpan and Dominique Jacquet).

2 x 50 Years of French Cinema was mounted in Godard's familiar video essay style, which was used in *Histor(ies) of Cinema* from the same era: sorrowful classical music ~ intertitles in coloured, Helvetica font ~ sombre voiceover ~ video mixer superimpositions ~ found footage ~ historical material (photographs and movies) ~ and low-key scenes featuring the Maestro.

If you commission the Great God-Art for a documentary, you'd better be prepared for something unusual/ eccentric/ wilful/ different – Godard never spends other people's money the way they think it ought to be spent, and he does the same in *2 x 50 Years of French Cinema*. Instead of what you might ask for – a chatty, informal survey of French film introduced by Uncle Jean-Luc (sitting in an armchair next to a cosy fire in one of those kitschy television versions of an olde worlde living room), expect something else! [13]

For ex, a large amount of time in *2 x 50 Years of French Cinema* is given over to a discussion between Messrs. Piccoli and Godard at a table in a hotel restaurant – and guess who does most of the talking! Yes, when Godard is switched on (and when he's got his cigar and lighter and ashtray), there are few filmmakers who can match him for philosophical-political-metaphysical-cinematic spiel, few who know as much about cinema, and few who are as passionate about cinema. Even if he's talking utter rubbish, there aren't many (or any) minds in the movie business as formidable as Godard.

So Godard talks – and everyone listens.

It's typical, for instance, that Godard spends a lot of time debating the true origin of cinema, and what the Lumiére Brothers had to do with it in 1895 (a cultural/ political organization deciding that the

---

[12] The title is typically Godardian – and we know which 50 years he prefers of French cinema (and of all cinema): the first. (For ex, in *Histor(ies) of Cinema*, far more is quoted from cinema up to the 1950s than afterwards).
[13] Godard doesn't do 'cosy' or 'safe'.

'birth of cinema' took place in 1895 is bound to irk Godard!).

Did Michel Piccoli think he'd been had? – here he was on camera, but it was the Master who did all the talking! (and the reverse angles were refused, so the camera is always on Piccoli). But in the second half of *2 x 50 Years of French Cinema*, Piccoli gets to have the screen to himself, as he hangs around in his hotel room.

Yes, *2 x 50 Years of French Cinema* is more like an appendix to *Histoire(s) du Cinéma* (which had already covered French film in detail). *2 x 50 Years of French Cinema* is one of those Godard documentaries/ essays where the actors/ characters/ people within the piece discuss the piece you're watching, make phone calls about it, etc. *Mise-en âbyme, oui*. Self-reflexivity brought to a quivering peak of self-self-self-reflexiveness.

So we have Michel Piccoli as Michel Piccoli asking the hotel staff if they've heard of this or that classic French movie, or this or that famous French *ciné*-celeb. Jean Gabin? *Non*. Jean Renoir? *Non*. Jean Cocteau? *Non. La Règle de Jeu? Non. Journal d'un Curé de Campagne? Mais non*. Well, the waiters/ chefs/ maids are in their twenties, and they *have* heard of Madonna, but not Eddie Constantine.

At the end of *2 x 50 Years of French Cinema*, there's a series of quotes from and *hommages* to many famous names in French cinema, such as: André Bazin, Henri Langlois, François Truffaut, Jean Renoir, Eric Rohmer, Robert Bresson, etc.

If you know Godard's work, and have seen *Histor(ies) of Cinema* and other documentaries/ essays, *2 x 50 Years of French Cinema* comes across as a low-to-middling affair, the sort of trifle that Godard could conjure in two or three days (a day for planning, a day for filming, a day for editing/ dubbing/ mixing/ grading). Well, OK, a little longer for post-production (someone's got to type out all of those captions!).

But this is a kind of Instant Cinema, or Instant TV: shoot on video... include a *long* interview (where the participants rattle on and on about stuff they know in depth)... add a couple of bits featuring non-professional (i.e. cheap) actors... and – this is the best bit! – shoot the entire thing in your hotel! (Yes, Godard is the only filmmaker with the balls to wander downstairs from his hotel room with a two-person camera crew and make a movie in the hotel restaurant! At least Roger Corman, another genius of cheapo movie-making, might include a guy in a monster suit and some pretty girls in bikinis to terrorize!).

LIBERTY AND HOMELAND

Liberté et Patrie (*Liberty and Homeland,* 2002) was another entry from the laugh riot team of Godard & Miéville.

By this time – 2002 – Godard and Miéville could probably have made any film about any subject simply by raiding their back catalogue. Like a super-skilled DJ or re-mixer, they could paste together a movie from all sorts of bits they'd shot over – what? – 40 years. Thus, *Liberty and Homeland* contains segments from *Weekend* (Jean-Pierre Léaud in costume), some porn from *Histoire(s) du Cinéma*, and much more.

No need to go outside the building in Switzerland to shoot, either – the 2002 short film is entirely produced in-house (literally *in-the-house*, moving no further than a flatbed editing table or Avid editing system (indeed, some shots in *Liberty and Homeland* look just like the filmmakers have pointed a camera towards Lake Geneva from the kitchen window. *Uh-huh*, if you're as good as Godard, you make a movie while you wait for your coffee to boil. *Bien sûr, mon ami*).

OTHER FILMS

Les Carabiniers (a.k.a. *The Soldiers/ The Riflemen,* 1963), was produced by Carlo Ponti and Georges de Beauregard, photography by Raoul Coutard, music by Philippe Arthuys, and cut by Lila Lakshmanan and Agnès Guillemot. It was adapted by Godard, Roberto Rossellini and Jean Gruault from a play by Beniamino Joppolo. The cast included: Marino Masé, Albert Juross, Patrice Moullet, Geneviève Galéa, Catherine Ribeiro, Jean-Louis Comolli, Gérard Poirot and Jean Brassat (future film director Barbet Schroeder has a cameo as a car salesman).

❉

Allemagne année 90 neuf zéro (*Germany Year 90 Nine Zero,* 1991), was prod. by Nicole Ruellé, with photography by Stepan Benda, Andreas Erben and Christophe Pollock. It starred Eddie Constantine, Hanns Zischler, Claudia Michelsen, Nathalie Kadem, André S. Labarthe, Robert Wittmers and Kim Kashkashian. The title references a 1948 film directed by one of Godard's gurus, Roberto Rossellini (*Germany, Year*

Zero, scripted by Max Kolpé, Carlo Lizzani and Rossellini). The film explored German issues, with Constantine reprising the character of Lemmy Caution for the last time. Released: Nov 8, 1991. 62 mins.

Making *Germany Year 90 Nine Zero* involved typical Godardian tactics of searching and testing and pondering – right in the middle of shooting. As assistant Romain Goupil recalled:

> We go to a place that has been reserved, we look around, he searches, we look around, then when nobody expects it, he says, 'Let's shoot.' It's very hard. There was a great deal of tension. (B, 535)

Godard and his crew filmed Eddie Constantine reading in *Germany Year 90* but Godard wasn't happy with the shot: 'he looks at the shot and says, "It's empty." But there's a moment when Constantine gets up, and he says, "Violà" – and we went back to the same place and re-did it' (B, 535).

※

For Ever Mozart (1997), wr., dir. and ed. by J.L.G., was prod. by Alain Sarde and Ruth Waldburger, and starred Vicky Messica, Madeleine Assas, Frédéric Pierrot, Ghalia Lacroix, Bérangère Allaux and Michel Francini. It explored familiar Godardian issues such as the war in Bosnia and Serbia, making a film, putting on a play, literature and classical music. Released July 4, 1997. 94 minutes.

COLOPHON

☆

Jean-Luc Godard is a fantastically inspiring filmmaker on so many levels. He is the one who says, no, you don't have to do that in a movie, you don't need that, you can do this instead, you can try this, and this, and *this*. Who says films must have stories, characters, beginnings and endings, themes, and all the rest? There are no rules, and if there are, break them. Be fearless. If you have something to say, *say it*.

There is no stopping Jean-Luc Godard, and his invention is boundless. Godard can do *anything*, and he has done *everything*. Utterly remarkable, Godard is the best there is. So inventive and radical, no one else can catch up with him.

Je vous salue, Jean-Luc.

APPENDICES

FILM AVAILABILITY

Many of the key films directed by Jean-Luc Godard – *Breathless, Weekend, Passion, Pierrot Le Fou,* etc – are available on video and DVD (with some more recently coming out on Blu-ray). But a large number of television and video projects are not available in any of the usual places. Much of Godard's work in TV and video in the 1970s remains largely unknown (and there is a *lot* of it).

There are of course many differences in the editions, in key areas such as dubbing and subtitles. In general, the original language versions are always the ones to go for, or any dub which Godard oversaw. (For instance, the *Contempt* DVD contains a terrible English language dub).

I would recommend always watching a movie in the original language, if possible. Some critics have noted that subtitles don't do justice to works like *Histoire(s) du Cinéma.* You just have to accept that. It doesn't matter if you don't speak French, either: sit back and enjoy a genius at the height of his powers creating a work unlike anything else in the history of anything.

The following are the main distributors to try first:

In the U.S.A.: Criterion. Lionsgate. Wellspring Media.

In Britain and Europe: Studio Canal. Artificial Eye. Optimum Home Entertainment. Nouveaux Pictures. Umbrella Entertainment.

GODARDISMS

- 'This life is either nothing, or it has to be everything'.
- 'It's necessary to struggle on two fronts at the same time'.
- 'You can only think of something if you think of something else'.
- 'Partout c'est beau' ('everywhere is beautiful').
- 'We're jesters. We out-live our problems'.
- 'Everyday you live moments that seem exceptional.'
- 'When one of my character says 'I love you', the 'I' is taken from one context, the 'love' from another and the 'you' from a third'.
- 'To show and to show myself showing'.
- 'I have no ideas'.
- 'There is nothing invented in the cinema. All one can do in the cinema is observe and put in order that which one has seen *if* one has been able to see well'.
- 'Cinema is life'.
- 'Instead of making films, we'll make cinema'.
- 'Everything can be put into a film. Everything should be put into a film'.
- 'No matter where or when, the classics always work'.
- 'We're in an old part of the universe, where nothing happens'.
- 'Every desire must meet its lassitude, its truth'.
- 'Orgasm is the only moment when you can't cheat life'.
- 'Everyone is searching. Everyone is in between'.
- 'Advertizing is a form of fascism'.
- 'Things are right in front of us. Why make them up?'
- 'If I speak of time, it has gone already'.

THE BEST OF GODARD

Jean-Luc Godard produced his top ten lists in his film criticism for each year (i.e., the best of 1963: *Le Procès de Jeanne d'Arc*, *The Exterminating Angel*, *The Birds*, *The Nutty Professor*, etc), so here's two Godard lists:

SOME OF THE BEST GODARD MOMENTS

(20 best moments – in no particular order)

1. Joseph touching Mary's belly in *Hail Mary*.
2. Marianne and Ferdinand on the beach in *Pierrot le Fou*.
3. Marianne and Ferdinand dancing and singing in *Pierrot le Fou*.
4. The night of love poetry in *Alphaville*.
5. The Madison dance in *Bande à Part*.
6. The traffic jam in *Weekend*.
7. Nana in the cinema in *Vivre Sa Vie*.
8. Angéla and Emile communicating with book covers in *A Woman Is a Woman*.
9. Paul in the shopping mall in *Masculin Féminin*.
10. Michel and Patricia on the Champs-Élysées in *Breathless*.
11. The *tableaux* of paintings in *Passion*.
12. The cosmic coffee cup in *Two or Three Things I Know About Her*.
13. The quoting from books scene in *Two or Three Things I Know About Her*.
14. The supermarket scene in *Tout Va Bien*.

15. The Italian cinema montage in *Histoire(s) du Cinéma*.
16. The war montage in *Notre Musique*.
17. The porn and paperback bookstore scene in *One Plus One*.
18. The dance of hands in *A Married Woman*.
19. The projection room scene in *Contempt*.
20. Worshipping Brigitte Bardot in *Contempt*.

TEN BEST GODARD FILMS

(In no particular order)

1. *Hail Mary*
2. *Pierrot le Fou*
3. *Bande à Part*
4. *Weekend*
5. *Two or Three Things I Know About Her*
6. *Passion*
7. *Vivre Sa Vie*
8. *Contempt*
9. *Masculin Féminin*
10. *La Chinoise*

INGREDIENTS FOR A GODARD MOVIE

To make a Jean-Luc Godard movie, you will need:

- scenes in cinemas, nightclubs, bars, cafés and hotels
- characters undressing;
- nude women[1]
- characters discussing sex and love
- sudden alterations in sound, from local sound to silence
- very loud sounds
- music fading in abruptly then disappearing
- classical music; contemporary new music; cheesy pop songs
- poetic dialogue, including quotes from classic poets
- characters reading aloud from books
- attacks on North Amerika, capitalism, war, the Vietnam War, politics
- the background sound, in cafés for example, almost drowning out dialogue
- off-screen gunshots
- guns
- cars (big Yank cars, Alfa Romeos, 2CVs, a Mercedes)
- cameras (characters carrying cameras)
- tape recorders
- tins of red, blue and yellow paint
- coloured filters for the camera
- characters quoting from Hollywood movies
- snatches of pop songs (don't worry about copyright: go ahead!)
- quotations from movies (again, don't let rights issues stop you!)
- characters suddenly looking into the camera
- characters breaking out into dances
- characters hunched over pinball machines or jukeboxes
- characters eternally smoking, lighting up cigarettes, asking people for cigarettes

---
[1] Tell the actors that nudity is required *before* you ask them to undress on set.

- characters in bathrooms, looking in mirrors
- characters fiddling with their hair
- jump cuts
- tracking shots along walls, cafes or traffic jams
- the camera dollying in and out unmotivated, or panning slowly around a room
- actors being interviewed
- close-ups of money changing hands
- the camera panning over posters, billboards, postcards, book covers, magazine covers
- philosophical, humorous and graphic intertitles, often edited musically
- shots of workers and factories
- a Métro scene
- tracking shots from the windows of cars around Paris
- handheld shots of characters walking Paris's streets.
- a variety of voiceovers, including by the director
- silly accents
- characters dressing up as figures from history and literature

FANS ON THE FILMS OF JEAN-LUC GODARD

Extracts from online reviews of Jean-Luc Godard's movies.

GODARD PAGE ON FACEBOOK

He is a poetic genius, I love all his work but esp his collabs w/ Anna Karina!
•
Said what I said.... JLG ...great influence on my thoughts & intellectual life...
•
All my admiration, appreciation, let's say LOVE, for your creative life, films, courage and perseverance... Long Live Godard
•
Sartre du Cinéma
•
GODARD... LE CINEMA!
•
Je vous salue Godardiens....

AMAZON.COM

Regardless of how the mystique is generated, *Breathless* provides a wonderful cinematic experience, as it is full of surprises and leaves the audience in a breathtaking, yet quirky visual journey.
•
My Life to Live is a truly remarkable film: a synthesis of artistic vision and moral tale, suffused with haunting melody, the ballad of a contemporary tragedy.
•
Band of Outsiders is playful, wondrous, hilarious, breezy, but at the same time melancholic, dark in its undertones.
•
Band of Outsiders is a really, really great movie. Simple, minimalist, and very expressive.

ON *PIERROT LE FOU*

PIERROT is one of the few examples of true mystical cinema that we have.
•
Pierrot le Fou is the most beautiful movie I have ever seen.

- What I love about the two Godard/ Belmondo films (*Breathless* and *Pierrot le Fou*) is the marriage of the sacred and profane, the comic and the tragic, the high and the low. Only true masters achieve a world view that encompasses so much of life... It's a very funny film in parts and a very sad film in other parts and even a bit mystical toward the end. It's a poignant elegy for the brevity of all things.
- As for Belmondo, the screen has never been visited by a cooler presence since the days of Bogart. Anna Karina, on the other hand, seems to have the ability to swallow the earth and all it contains through her magnificently large eyes.
- Give *Pierrot le Fou* a shot, it defied everything I thought it would be. I don't think I'll ever see anything else like it.
- Godard is wonderfully inventive in his use of language, situations, visuals, images. He inspires me. One of my favorite parts of *Pierrot le Fou* is the scene in which Jean-Paul and Anna romp through a forest, hand-in-hand, improvising lyrics (my own romantic fantasy).
- It is fresh, it is exciting, it is dangerous, it is meaningful, and it is loud, abrasive and epic in every sense of the word. It is cinema; cut, paste and send.
- Godard's *Pierrot le Fou* is one the most successful comedy/ tragedy/ political/ crime-thriller/ musicals he ever made. It breaks all the rules, as all his movies do, but plays with such gusto and joie de vivre to keep any audience in their seat until the end.

ON *CONTEMPT*

- *Contempt* is Jean-Luc Godard's masterpiece, and quite possibly the best film of the 60s. The film has so many layers and meanings, one viewing is not enough.
- This is a superior film to *Breathless*, IMHO... the film is total eye candy, if not due to the awesome BB, then by the gorgeous locations...
- A truly haunting movie. A must-see Godard classic.
- What a great movie this is and I saw it 20 times.

ON *HAIL MARY*

- *Hail Mary* is perhaps Godard's most spiritual film and it can be quite lyrical as it attempts to tell the story of the Annunciation in a modern setting... Godard uses the film to contrast pure love with love of the flesh and does quite a good job. So why only three stars? Godard's film moves at a glacial pace and his difficult philosophy is on display in its most brutal form. There are moments of complete confusion for the viewer as one tries to sort it all out.
- To see this movie when it screened in Boston, I had to cross a picket line set up by the SLAVES OF THE IMMACULATE HEART OF MARY, the vestiges of a rabid right wing anti-semitic movement headed by the radio personality

Father Coughlin (father of hate radio) in the 1930s.

It was worth it to see what was arguably Godard's most beautiful film. Like most really smart people, Godard is only about 20% right, but that beats the 2% average for the rest of us. Godard's musings on the Rubik cube as an argument for intelligent design are crap, but the tension between Mary's conflicted maternal sexuality and Joseph's subjugated male sexuality are as primordial as the blues and every bit as poetic. The gynecological exam (much more humane in France than the US) that validates her prepartum virginity throws arguments about physical purity into the pit of absurdity where they belong.

•

'Hail Mary' released in 1985 is quite likely the most controversial film of the 20th century. Banned by the Catholic Church for its raw and sometimes scathing modern day depiction of the Virgin Mary, I believe this is a movie whose time has finally come and will soon be recognized as the classic it truly is. After listening to all the ranting and raving condemning this film you will surely be surprised, and I hope delighted, by what you experience when you finally watch it.

AT THE INTERNET MOVIE DATABASE

ON *PASSION*

I found the film compelling and intriguing; I wanted to know more about the people and the universe that they populated. The lack of narrative structure was not a negative factor in my enjoyment of the film, for the anarchic content was, of itself, enough to keep my mind from wandering away from it. Godard's reflexive jibes at cinema convention were acerbic and witty, carrying with them a tremendous knowledge of the mechanics of filmmaking. The story of *Passion* what story there is, is subservient to the process of filmmaking and Godard's desire to subvert it. For me, that is what makes this film so entertaining.

•

The characters' aggressive tussling, either through physical pulling and pushing or through their cars (reminiscent of Godard's masterpiece *Weekend*), also signify the difficulty and pain inherent in any kind of birth. The quiet moments call out to be examined and celebrated as much as the grand statements while others jostle for their money, their moment, or even a simple explanation as to what it all means.

•

Like most of Godard's late work, this mosaic approach will not appeal to all who cross its path (what film ever does?) but, even if it does ultimately fall short of answering any of the questions it asks, adherents will find much to ruminate on.

•

Godard's *Passion* is a puzzle, and Delacroix's The Entry of the Crusaders into Constantinople is a puzzle with historical information behind it. I'd have to say that watching Godard's *Passion* was like being spoon-fed personal beliefs; not a work, but his philosophy. But, I liked it.

•

Jean-Luc Godard makes me think clearer. After having read the other comments accusing *Passion* of being boring and pretentious crap, I can only say that I strongly disagree. Comments like those just make me angry. JLG's films are definitely not boring; unless you are completely unintellectual and don't have a clue of what is going on. *Passion* and JLG's other films are fresh and intellectual and philosophic. Godard is unique.

ON *HAIL MARY*

This is a fascinating film. The story of a modern day Virgin Mary dealing with issues like human sexuality and the divinity as well as themes of intelligent design/ creationism are challenging for the viewer to say the least.

•

Roussel is terrific in the role of Mary and really captures the confused teenage nature of the role. I thought she was very good in the way she handles her character's thoughts, feelings and emotions.

•

There is something about Godard that I find hypnotic. Even when you know it's not right, it still seems like it is perfect for the cinema! The way he moves his characters about within a frame. The mannerisms and political diatribe he allows his actors to divulge in, and sometimes the crude visual beauty makes for some mind-stimulating cinema. And for this one, he pushes it that little bit further, as he does with all his work. The older he gets, the more eccentric he has become, and the more fascinating he is. To me, this is his last real masterpiece before he became the mad professor of the Wacky Cinema According To Godard!

AT I.G.N. BOARDS

He made me love movies.

•

Pierret Le Fou and *Contempt* are my two favorites by a long shot.

•

Definitely, definitely give all his 60's films a shot. He had one of the most indisputably great directorial runs ever.

AT METACRITIC.COM

ON *NOTRE MUSIQUE*

No review necessary. He is the greatest French filmmaker since Bresson, and certainly the most profound and influential of the past 50 years. See this movie at all costs if it is playing anywhere within 50 miles of you.

•

Sublime, dense and illuminating. Godard's creates a symphonic fugue of parallels and associations, dualities and ironies, struggling towards the light.

•

I give Maestro Godard a 10-infinity for this masterpiece. Forever the experimentalist, he creates a symphonic fragment that also seems like a visual jaunt through Faulkner's *Sound and Fury*. It is a provocative examination of reality and something else.

•

Spectacular!! GODard is GOD of cinema!!

FILMOGRAPHY

The chief works of Jean-Luc Godard as film and TV director.

Operation Concrete (1954), a.k.a. *Opération Béton*
Une femme coquette (1955), a.k.a. *A Flirtatious Woman*
All the Boys Are Called Patrick (1959), a.k.a. *Charlotte et Véronique, ou Tous les garçons s'appellent Patrick*
Charlotte et son Jules (1960), a.k.a. *Charlotte and Her Boyfriend*
Breathless (1960), a.k.a. *À Bout de souffle*
The Little Soldier (1960/63), a.k.a. *Le Petit Soldat*
Une histoire d'eau (1961), a.k.a. *A Story of Water*
A Woman Is a Woman (1961), a.k.a. *Une femme est une femme*
Vivre sa Vie (1962), a.k.a. *My Life to Live*
The Seven Deadly Sins (1962) (episode: *La Paresse*)
Contempt (1963), a.k.a. *Le Mépris*
The Soldiers (1963), a.k.a. *Les Carabiniers*
RoGoPaG (1963) (episode: *Il Nuovo mondo*)
Band of Outsiders (1964), a.k.a. *Bande à part*
Reportage sur Orly (1964), a.k.a. *Reporting On Orly*
A Married Woman (1964), a.k.a. *Une femme mariée*
Les plus belles escroqueries du monde (1964) (episode: *Le Grand escroc*)
Pierrot le Fou (1965), a.k.a. *Crazy Pete*
Paris vu par (1965) (episode: *Montparnasse-Levallois*)
Alphaville, une étrange aventure de Lemmy Caution (1965), a.k.a. *Alphaville: A Strange Adventure of Lemmy Caution*
Made in U.S.A. (1966)
Masculin féminin: 15 faits précis (1966), a.k.a. *Masculine, Feminine*
The Oldest Profession (1967) (episode: *Anticipation, ou l'amour en l'an 2000*)
2 ou 3 choses que je sais d'elle (1967), a.k.a. *Two of Three Things I Know About Her*
Weekend (1967), a.k.a. *Le Week-end*
Far from Vietnam (1967), a.k.a. *Loin du Vietnam*
La Chinoise, ou Plutôt à la Chinoise (1967), a.k.a. *La Chinoise Or, More Actually, After the Fashion of the Chinese*
One Plus One (1968), a.k.a. *Sympathy For the Devil*
Cinétracts (1968) (segments: 1, 4, 7, 9, 16, 18, 19, 23)
Un film comme les autres (1968), a.k.a. *A Film Like Any Other*
Joy of Learning (1969), a.k.a. *Le gai savoir*
Amore e rabbia (1969) (episode: *L'Amore* in *Love and Anger*)
Le vent d'est (1970), a.k.a. *The Wind From the East*
British Sounds (1970), a.k.a. *See You at Mao*
Pravda (1970)
Vladimir et Rosa (1970), a.k.a. *Vladimir and Rosa*
Struggle in Italy (1971), a.k.a. *Lotte in Italia*
Tout va bien (1972), a.k.a. *All's Well*
Letter to Jane: An Investigation About a Still (1972), a.k.a. *Lettre à Jane*
1 P.M. (1972), a.k.a. *One P.M./ One Pennebaker Movie*
Numéro deux (1975), a.k.a. *Number Two*
Ici et ailleurs (1976), a.k.a. *Here and Elsewhere*
Six fois deux/ Sur et sous la communication (2 episodes, 1976)

France/ tour/ detour/ deux/ enfants (1977), a.k.a. *France/ Tour/ Detour/ Two Children*
Comment ça va? (1978), a.k.a. *How's It Going?*
Scénario de 'Sauve qui peut la vie' (1980), a.k.a. *Scenario For Sauve Qui Peut La Vie*
Slow Motion (1980), a.k.a. *Sauve qui peut (la vie)*
A Letter to Freddy Buache (1982)
Passion (1982)
Scénario du film 'Passion' (1982)
First Name: Carmen (1983), a.k.a. *Prénom Carmen*
Petites notes à propos du film Je vous salue, Marie (1983)
Détective (1985), a.k.a. *Detective*
Hail Mary (1985), a.k.a. *Je vous salue, Marie*
Soft and Hard (1986), a.k.a. *A Soft Conversation Between Two Friends On a Hard Subject*
Meeting Woody Allen (1986)
Grandeur et décadence d'un petit commerce de cinéma (1986), a.k.a. *Grandeur and Decadence* (part of *Série noire* TV series)
Keep Your Right Up (1987), a.k.a. *Soigne ta droite*
King Lear (1987)
Puissance de la parole (1988), a.k.a. *The Power of Speech*
Les Français vus par (1988), a.k.a. *The Cowboy and the Frenchman*
On s'est tous défilé (1988)
Le rapport Darty (1989), a.k.a. *The Darty Report*
Nouvelle vague (1990), a.k.a. *New Wave*
Germany Year 90 Nine Zero (1991), a.k.a. *Allemagne 90 neuf zéro*
Contre l'oubli (1991) (episode: *Pour Thomas Wainggai*)
How Are the Kids? (1993) (a part of *L'enfance de l'art*)
Hélas pour moi (1993), a.k.a. *Woe Is Me*
Les enfants jouent à la Russie (1993), a.k.a. *The Children Plan Russian*
Je vous salue, Sarajevo (1993), a.k.a. *Hail, Sarajevo*
JLG/ JLG - autoportrait de décembre (1995), a.k.a. *JLG By JLG*
2 x 50 Years of French Cinema (1995), a.k.a. *2 x 50 Ans de Cinéma Francais*
For Ever Mozart (1996)
Histoire(s) du cinéma (1998), a.k.a. *Histor(ies) of Cinema*
The Old Place (1999)
De l'origine du XXIe siècle (2000), a.k.a. *Origins of the 21st Century*
In Praise of Love (2001), a.k.a. *Éloge de l'amour*
Liberty and Homeland (2002), a.k.a. *Liberté et patrie*
Ten Minutes Older: The Cello (2002)
Moments choisis des histoire(s) du cinéma (2004), a.k.a. *Chosen Moments of Histoire(s) of Cinema*
Notre musique (2004), a.k.a. *Our Music*
Vrai faux passeport (2006), a.k.a. *The True False Passport*
Une catastrophe (2008), a.k.a. *A Catastrophe*
Socialism (2010), a.k.a. *Film socialisme*
Adieu au Langage (2014), a.k.a. *Goodbye To Language*
Bridges of Sarajevo (2014), a.k.a. *Les Ponts de Sarajevo*
The Image Book (2018), a.k.a. *Le Livre d'Image*

BIBLIOGRAPHY

BY JEAN-LUC GODARD

Vivre Sa Vie, in *L'Avant-Scène Cinéma*, 19, Oct, 1962
Alphaville, tr. P. Whitehead, Lorrimer, London, 1969
Jean-Luc Godard, ed. T. Mussman, Dutton, New York, NY, 1968
Introduction à une véritable histoire du cinéma, Editions Albatros, Paris, 1977
Godard On Godard, ed. A. Bergala, Cahiers du Cinéma, Paris, 1985
Revolution, 1, February, 1985
Godard On Godard, eds. J. Narobi & T. Milne, Da Capo, New York, NY, 1986
Interview, in R. Bellour, 1992
Interview, "Godard in His 'Fifth Period'", by K. Dieckmann, in M. Locke, 1993
Interview, Montréal Film Festival, 1995
Interviews, ed. D. Sterritt, University of Mississippi Press, Jackson, 1998
Godard On Godard 2, ed. A. Bergala, Cahiers du Cinéma, Paris, 1998
Histoire(s) du cinéma, Galimard-Gaumont, Paris, 1998
"An Audience With Uncle Jean-Luc", *The Guardian*, Feb 11, 2000
"The Godard Interview: I, A Man Of The Image", with M. Witt, 2005

OTHERS

R. Alder. *New York Times*, January 9, 1969
R. Altman, ed. *Sound Theory, Sound Practice*, Routledge, London, 1992
—. *Film/ Genre*, British Film Institute, London, 1999
D. Andrew. *The Major Film Theories*, Oxford University Press, Oxford, 1976
—. *Concepts In Film Theory*, Oxford University Press, Oxford, 1984
—. ed. *Breathless*, Rutgers University Press, New Brunswick, NJ, 1987
G. Andrew. *The Film Handbook*, Longman, London, 1989
R. Armes. *French Cinema*, Oxford University Press, Oxford, 1985
J. Aumont. "The Fall of the Gods: Jean-Luc Godard's *Le Mépris*", in S. Hayward, 1990
—. *Amnésies: fictions de cinéma d'après Jean-Luc Godard*, P.O.L., Paris, 1999
G. Austin. *Contemporary French Cinema*, Manchester University Press, Manchester, 1996
M. Barker, ed. *The Video Nasties: Freedom and Censorship In the Media*, Pluto Press, London, 1984
—. & J. Petley, eds. *Ill Effects: The Media/ Violence Debate*, Routledge, London, 1997
S. Barrowclough. "Godard's Marie", *Sight & Sound*, 52, 2, Spring, 1985
R. Barthes. *The Pleasure of the Text*, Hill and Wang, New York, NY, 1975
—. *S/Z*, Hill and Wang, New York, NY, 1974
—. *Image, Music, Text*, tr. S. Heath, Fontana, London, 1984
G. Bataille. *Literature and Evil*, Calder & Boyars, London, 1973
—. *The Story of the Eye*, Penguin, London, 1982
L. Bawden, ed. *The Oxford Companion To Film*, Oxford University Press, Oxford, 1976
A. Bazin. *What Is Cinema?*, University of California Press, Berkeley, CA, 1960, 2 vols
—. "Cinema and Theology", *South Atlantic Quarterly*, 91, 2, 1992
M. Beja. *Film and Literature: An Introduction*, Longman, London, 1979
R. Bellour & M. Bandy, eds. *Jean-Luc Godard*, M.O.M.A., N.Y., 1992
A. Bergala. *Nul mieux que Godard*, Cahiers du Cinéma, Paris, 1999
R. Bergan & R. Karney *Bloomsbury Foreign Film Guide*, Bloomsbury, London, 1988
I. Bergman. *Bergman On Bergman, Interviews With Ingmar Bergman*, eds. S.

Björkman, *et al*, tr. P. B. Austin, Touchstone, New York, NY, 1986
—. *The Magic Lantern: An Autobiography*, London, 1988
—. *Images: My Life In Film*, Faber, London, 1994
P. Biskind. *Easy Riders, Raging Bulls: How the Sex 'n' Drugs 'n' Rock 'n' Roll Generation Saved Hollywood*, Bloomsbury, London, 1998
P. Bogdanovitch. *This Is Orson Welles*, Da Capo, New York, 1998
D. Bordwell & K. Thompson. *Film Art: An Introduction*, McGraw-Hill Publishing Company, New York, NY, 1979
—. *The Films of Carl-Theodor Dreyer*, University of California, Berkeley, 1981
—. et al. *The Classical Hollywood Cinema: Film Style and Mode of Production To 1960*, Routledge, London, 1985
—. *Narration In the Fiction Film*, Routledge, London, 1988
—. *Ozu and the Poetics of Cinema*, British Film Institute, London, 1988
—. *Making Meaning*, Harvard University Press, Cambridge, MA, 1989
—. & N. Caroll, eds. *Post-Theory: Reconstructing Film Studies*, University of Wisconsin Press, Madison, WI, 1996
—. *The Way Hollywood Tells It*, University of California Press, Berkeley, CA, 2006
F. Brady. *Citizen Welles*, Scribner's, New York, 1989
P. Braunberger. *Pierre Braunberger*, Centre National de la Cinématographie, Paris, 1987
D. Breskin. *Inner Voices: Filmmakers In Conversation*, Da Capo, New York, 1997
R. Bresson. *Notes On the Cinematographer*, Quartet, London, 1986
R. Brody. *Everything Is Cinema: The Working Life of Jean-Luc Godard*, Faber, London, 2008
R. Brown, ed. *Focus On Godard*, Prentice-Hall, N.J., 1972
Z. Bruneau. *En Attendant Godard*, Maurice Nadeau, Paris, 2014
S. Bukatman. *Terminal Identity: The Virtual Subject In Postmordern Science Fiction*, Duke University Press, Durham, NC, 1993
P.J. Burgard, ed. *Nietzsche and the Feminine*, University Press of Virginia, Charlottesville, 1994
I. Butler. *Religion In the Cinema*, A.S. Barnes, New York, NY, 1969
J. Butler. *Gender Trouble: Feminism and the Subversion of Identity*, Routledge, London, 1990
M. Caen,. "Eye of the Cyclone", *Cahiers du Cinéma*, 2, British Film Institute, London, 1966
I. Cameron, ed. *The Films of Jean-Luc Godard*, Praeger, N.Y., 1969
V. Canby. "*Vladimir and Rosa*", *New York Times*, April 30, 1971
N. Carroll. *Mystifying Movies: Fads and Fallacies of Contemporary Film Theory*, Columbia University Press, New York, NY, 1988
J. Caughie, ed. *Theories of Authorship: A Reader*, Routledge, London, 1988
—. & A. Kuhn, eds. *The Sexual Subject: A Screen Reader In Sexuality*, Routledge, London, 1992
M. Cerisuelo. *Jean-Luc Godard*, Lherminier, Paris, 1989
G. Chester & J. Dickey, eds. *Feminism and Censorship: The Current Debate*, Prism Press, Bridport, Dorset, 1988
J. Chown. *Hollywood Auteur: Francis Coppola*, Praeger, New York, NY, 1988
M. Ciment. *Projections 9: French Filmmakers On Filmmaking*, Faber, London, 1999
H. Cixous. *The Newly Born Woman*, tr. B. Wing, Minnesota University Press, Minneapolis, 1986
—. *The Hélène Cixous Reader*, ed. Susan Sellers, Blackwell, Oxford, 1994
J. Collet: *Jean-Luc Godard*, Crown, 1968
T. Conley. "Language Gone Mad", in D. Wills, 2000
D.A. Cook. *A History of Narrative Film*, W.W. Norton, New York, NY, 1981,

1990, 1996
—. *Lost Illusions: American Cinema In the Shadow of Watergate and Vietnam*, Scribners, New York, NY, 2000
P. Cook, ed. *The Cinema Book*, British Film Institute, London, 1985
—. & M. Bernink, eds. *The Cinema Book*, 2nd ed., British Film Institute, London, 1999
T. Corrigan. *A Cinema Without Walls: Movies and Culture After Vietnam*, Rutgers University Press, NJ, 1991
—. *New German Cinema*, Indiana University Press, Bloomington, IN, 1994
J. Cott. *Rolling Stone*, June, 1969.
P. Cowie. *The Cinema of Orson Welles*, Da Capo, New York, NY, 1973
—. *Ingmar Bergman*, Secker & Warburg, London, 1982
—. *Coppola: A Biography*, Da Capo Press, 1994
A. Croce. "*Breathless*", *Film Quarterly*, 14, Spring, 1961, in D. Andrew, 1987
S. Cunningham & R. Harley. "The Logic of the Virgin Mother: A Discussion of *Hail Mary*", *Screen*, 28, 1, Winter, 1987
C. Desbarats & J.P. Gorce, eds. *L'Effet-Godard*, Milan, Toulouse, 1989
G. Day & C. Bloch, eds. *Perspectives On Pornography: Sexuality In Film and Literature*, Macmillan, London, 1988
J. de Baroncelli. *Le Monde*, Nov 9, 1965
M. Deeley. *Blade Runners, Deer Hunters and Blowing the Bloody Doors Off*, Faber, London, 2008
T. de Lauretis & S. Heath, eds. *The Cinematic Apparatus*, St Martin's Press, New York, NY, 1980
—. *Alice Doesn't: Feminism, Semiotics, Cinema*, Indiana University Press, Bloomington, IN, 1984
—. *Technologies of Gender*, Macmillan, London, 1987
G. Deleuze & F. Guattari. *Cinema 1: The Movement Image*, Athlone Press, London, 1989
—. *Cinema 2: The Time Image*, Athlone Press, London, 1989
—. *What Is Philosophy?*, Verso, London, 1994
J. Derrida. *Of Grammatology*, Johns Hopkins University Press, Baltimore, MD, 1976
—. *Spurs: Nietzsche's Styles*, University of Chicago Press, Chicago, IL, 1979
—. *Writing and Difference*, University of Chicago Press, Chicago, IL, 1987
—. *Archive Fever*, University of Chicago Press, Chicago, IL, 1999
R. Dienst. "The Imaginary Element", in D. Willis, 2000
W.W. Dixon. *The Films of Jean-Luc Godard*, State University of New York Press, Albany, NY, 1997
L. Doan, ed. *The Lesbian Postmodern*, Columbia University Press, New York, NY, 1994
M. Doane *et al*, eds. *Re-Visions: Essays In Feminist Film Criticism*, University Publications of America, Frederick, MD, 1983
—. *The Desire To Desire: The Woman's Film of the 1940's*, Macmillan, London, 1988
—. *Femmes Fatales: Feminism, Film Theory*, Routledge, London, 1991
J. Douin. *Jean-Luc Godard*, Rivages, Paris, 1994
Steven C. Dubin. *Arresting Images: Impolitic Art and Uncivil Actions*, Routledge, London, 1992
R. Durgnat. *Films and Feelings*, Faber, London, 1967
—. *A Mirror For England: British Movies From Austerity To Affluence*, Faber, London, 1970
A. Dworkin. *Pornography: Men Possessing Women*, Women's Press, London, 1984
—. *Intercourse*, Arrow, London, 1988
—. *Letters From a War Zone: Writings, 1976-1987*, Secker & Warburg,

London, 1988
A. Easthope, ed. *Contemporary Film Theory*, Longman, London, 1993
M. Eliade. *Ordeal By Labyrinth*, University of Chicago Press, Chicago, IL, 1984
—. *Symbolism, the Sacred and the Arts*, Crossroad, New York, NY, 1985
T. Elsaesser. *New German Cinema: A History*, Macmillan, London, 1989
—. *The B.F.I. Companion To German Cinema*, British Film Institute, London, 1999
—. *European CInema*, Amsterdam University Press, Amsterdam, 2005
R. Evans. *The Kid Stays In the Picture*, New York, NY, 1994
D. Fairservice. *Film Editing*, Manchester University Press, Manchester, 2001
M. Farber. *Negative Space*, Studio Vista, London, 1971
A. Farassino. *Jean-Luc Godard*, Il Castoro, Milan, 1996
J.L. Fell, ed. *Film Before Griffith*, University of California Press, Berkeley, CA, 1983
F. Fellini. *Fellini On Fellini*, Delacorte, New York, NY, 1976
J. Finler. *The Movie Directors Story*, Octopus Books, London, 1985
—. *The Hollywood Story*, Wallflower Press, London, 2003
C. Fleming. *High Concept: Don Simpson and the Hollywood Culture of Excess*, Bloomsbury, London, 1998
G.E. Forshey. *American Religious and Biblical Spectaculars*, Praeger, Westport, CT, 1992
M. Foucault. *The History of Sexuality*, Penguin, London, 1981
—. *The Use of Pleasure: The History of Sexuality*, vol. 2, Penguin, London, 1987
—. *Politics, Philosophy, Culture: Interviews and Other Writings, 1977-1984*, ed. L.D. Kritzmon, Routledge, New York, NY, 1990
J. Franklin. *New German Cinema*, Columbus Books, 1986
K. French, ed. *Screen Violence*, Bloomsbury, London, 1996
P. French et al. *The Films of Jean-Luc Godard*, Blue Star House, 1967
F. Gado. *The Passion of Ingmar Bergman*, Durham, NC, 1986
J. Gallagher. *Film Directors On Directing*, Praeger, New York, NY, 1989
H. Geduld, ed. *Filmmakers On Filmmaking*, Indiana University Press, Bloomington, IN, 1967
J. Geiger & R. Rutsky, eds. *Film Analysis*, Norton & Company, New York, NY, 2005
J. Gelmis. *The Film Director As Superstar*, Penguin, London, 1974
D. Georgakas & L. Rubenstein, eds. *Art, Politics, Cinema: The Cineaste Interviews*, Pluto Press, London, 1985
J. Gerber. *Anatole Dauman: Pictures of a Producer*, British Film Institute, London, 1992
L. Gianetti: *Godard and Others*, Tantivy, 1975
—. *Understanding Movies*, Prentice-Hall, NJ, 1982
P.C. Gibson & R. Gibson, eds. *Dirty Looks: Women, Pornography, Power*, British Film Institute, London, 1993
J. Gomez. *Ken Russell*, Muller, 1976
M. Goodwin & G. Marcus. *Double Feature,* Outerbridge & Lazard, New York, 1972
R. Gottesman, ed. *Focus On Citizen Kane,* Prentice-Hall, Englewood Cliffs, NJ, 1971
— ed. *Focus On Orson Welles,* Prentice-Hall, Englewood Cliffs, NJ, 1976
P. Grace. *The Religious Film: Christianity and the Hagiopic*, Wiley-Blackwell, Sussex, 2009
D. Graham, ed. *Film and Religion*, St Mungo Press, 1997
B.K. Grant, ed. *Film Genre*, Scarecrow Press, Metuchen, NJ, 1977
—. ed. *Crisis Cinema: The Apocalyptic Idea In Postmodern Narrative Film*, Maisonneuve Press, 1993

—. *Film Genre Reader II*, University of Texas Press, Austin, TX, 1995
J. Green. *The Encyclopedia of Censorship*, Facts on File, New York, NY, 1990
N. Greene. *Pier Paolo Pasolini*, Princeton University Press, Princeton, NJ, 1990
N. Griffin & K. Masters. *Hit & Run: How Jon Peters and Peter Guber Took Sony For a Ride In Hollywood*, Simon & Schuster, New York, NY, 1996
E. Grosz. *Sexual Subversions*, Allen & Unwin, London, 1989
—. *Volatile Bodies,* Indiana University Press, Bloomington, IN, 1994
—. *Space, Time and Perversion*, Routledge, London, 1995
I. Halberstadt, *Pix*, 2, B.F.I., 1997
L. Hanlon. *Fragments: Bresson's Film Style*, Farleigh Dickinson University Press, Rutherford, 1986
S. Harwood. *French National Cinema,* Routledge, London, 1993
M. Haskell. "Immaculate Deception", *Vogue*, Oct, 1985
S. Hayward & G. Vincendeau, eds. *French Film*, Routledge, London, 1990
S. Heath. *Questions of Cinema*, Macmillan, London, 1981
—. *Cinema and Language*, University Presses of America, 1983
J. Hellmann. *American Myth and the Legacy of Vietnam*, Columbia, 1986
W. Herzog. *Herzog On Herzog*, ed. P. Cronin, Faber & Faber, London, 2002
G. Hickenlooper. *Reel Conversations: Candid Interviews With Film's Foremost Direcors and Critics*, Citadel, New York, NY, 1991
C. Higham. *Orson Welles*, St Martin's Press, New York, NY, 1985
J. Hill & P.C. Gibson, eds. *The Oxford Guide To Film Studies*, Oxford University Press, Oxford, 1998
J. Hillier, ed. *Cahiers du Cinéma: The 1950s, New-Realism, Hollywood, New Wave*, Harvard University Press, Cambridge, MA, 1985
—. ed. *Cahiers du Cinéma: The 1960s*, Harvard University Press, Cambridge, MA, 1986
—. *The New Hollywood*, Studio Vista, London, 1992
—. *American Independent Cinema: A Sight & Sound Reader*, British Film Institute, London, 2001
L.C. Hillstrom, ed. *International Dictionary of Films and Filmmakers: Directors*, St James Press, London, 1997
F. Hölderlin. *Poems and Fragments*, tr. M. Hamburger, Anvil, London, 1994
D. Holmes & A. Smith, eds. *100 Years of European Cinema*, Manchester University Press, Manchester, 2000
A. Horton & J. Maretta, eds. *Modern European Filmmakers*, Ungar, New York, NY, 1981
A. Insdorf. *Indelible Shadows: Film and the Holocaust*, Cambridge University Press, Cambridge, 1989
L. Irigaray. *The Irigaray Reader,* ed. M. Whitford, Blackwell, Oxford, 1991
H. Jacobson. "Hail Mary", *Film Comment*, 21, Nov, 1985
F. Jameson. *Signatures of the Visible*, Routledge, New York, NY, 1990
—. *Postmodernism, or the Cultural Logic of Late Capitalism*, Verso, London, 1991
P. Kael. *Kiss Kiss Bang Bang,* Bantam, New York, NY, 1969
—. *Going Steady*, Bantam, New York, 1971
—. *Taking It All In*, Marion Boyars, 1986
—. *State of the Art*, Marion Boyars, London, 1987
—. *Movie Love*, Marion Boyars, London, 1992
A. Kaes. *From Hitler To Heimat: The Return of History As Film*, Harvard University Press, Cambridge, MA, 1989
N. Kagan. *The Cinema of Oliver Stone*, Roundhouse, 1995
E. Ann Kaplan, ed. *Psychoanalysis and Cinema*, Routledge, London, 1990
—. ed. *Women In Film Noir*, British Film Institute, London, 1998
B.F. Kawin. *Mindscreen: Bergman, Godard and First-Person Film*, Princeton University Press, Princeton, NJ, 1978

—. *How Movies Work*, Macmillan, New York, NY, 1987
P. Keough, ed. *Flesh and Blood: The National Society of Film Critics On Sex, Violence, and Censorship*, Mercury House, San Francisco, CA, 1995
M. Kermode. *Hatchet Job*, Picador, London, 2013
M. Kinder. "A Thrice-Told Tale: Godard's *Le Mépris*", in A. Horton, 1981
G. Kindem. *The International Movie Industry*, Southern Illinois University Press, Carbondale, IL, 2000
R. Kinnard & T. Davis. *Divine Images: A History of Jesus On the Screen*, Citadel Press, New York, NY, 1992
M. Klein. *Film Quarterly*, 19, 3, 1966
T. Jefferson Kline. *Bertolucci's Dream Loom: A Psychoanalytic Study of Cinema*, University of Massachusetts Press, Amherst, 1987
P. Kolker. *The Altering Eye: Contemporary International Cinema*, Oxford University Press, New York, NY, 1983
—. *Bernardo Bertolucci*, British Film Institute, London, 1985
—. *A Cinema of Loneliness: Penn, Kubrick, Coppola, Scorsese, Altman*, Oxford University Press, New York, NY, 1988
—. *A Cinema of Loneliness: Penn, Stone, Kubrick, Scorsese, Spielberg, Altman*, Oxford University Press, New York, NY, 2000
S. Kracauer. *Theory of Film*, Princeton University Press, Princeton, NJ, 1997
J. Kreidl: *Jean-Luc Godard*, Twayne, Boston, 1980
L. Kreitzer. *The New Testament In Fiction and Film*, J.S.O.T., 1993
—. *The Old Testament In Fiction and Film*, Sheffield Academic Press, Sheffield, 1994
J. Kristeva. article in *Art Press*, 4, 1984-85
—. *Powers of Horror: An Essay On Abjection*, tr. Leon S. Roudiez, Columbia University Press, New York, 1982
—. *The Kristeva Reader*, ed. T. Moi, Blackwell, Oxford, 1986
—. *Tales of Love*, tr. Leon S. Roudiez, Columbia University Press, New York, 1987
—. *Black Sun: Depression and Melancholy*, tr. L.S. Roudiez, Columbia University Press, New York, NY, 1989
—. *Strangers To Ourselves*, tr. L. Roudiez, Harvester Wheatsheaf, Hemel Hempstead, 1991
B. Krohn. *Hitchcock At Work*, Phaidon, London, 2000
A. Kuhn. *Women's Pictures: Feminism and the Cinema*, Routledge & Kegan Paul, London, 1982
J. Lacan. *Écrits: A Selection*, tr. Alan Sheridan, Tavistock, 1977
—. and the École Freudienne. *Feminine Sexuality*, ed. J. Mitchell and J. Rose, Macmillan, London, 1988
M. Landy. "Godard: Thinking Media", *Film-Philosophy*, 6, 30, Sept, 2002
M. Lanning. *Vietnam At the Movies*, Fawcett Columbine, New York, NY, 1994
R. Lapsley & M. Westlake, eds. *Film Theory: An Introduction*, Manchester University Press, Manchester, 1988
A. Lawton. *Kinoglasnost: Soviet Cinema In Our Time*, Cambridge University Press, Cambridge, 1992
—. *The Red Screen: Politics, Society, Art In Soviet Cinema*, Routledge, London, 1992
J. Leach. *A Possible Cinema: The Films of Alain Tanner*, Scarecrow Press, Metuchen, NJ, 1984
B. Leaming. *Orson Welles*, Viking, New York, 1985
V. Lebeau. *Psychoanalysis and Cinema*, Wallflower, London, 2001
R. Lefèvre. *Ingmar Bergman*, Paris, 1983
P. Leprohan. *The Italian Cinema*, tr. R. Greaves & O. Stallybrass, Secker & Warburg, London, 1972
Julia Lesage. "Godard-Gorin's *Wind From the East*: Looking at a film

politically," *Jump Cut*, no. 4, 1974
—. *Jean-Luc Godard: A Guide To References and Resources*, G.K. Hall, Boston, 1979
J. Leutrat. *Des traces qui nous ressemblent: Passion de Jean-Luc Godard*, Comp' Act, Seyssel, 1990
—. *Jean-Luc Godard*, Schena-Didier, Paris, 1998
—. "Godard's Tricolor", in D. Wills, 2000
P. Lev. *The Euro-American Cinema*, University of Texas Press, Austin, 1993
E. Levy. *Cinema of Outsiders: The Rise of American Independent Film*, New York University Press, New York, NY, 1999
J. Lewis. *The Road To Romance and Ruin: Teen Films and Youth Culture*, Routledge, London, 1992
—. *Whom God Wishes To Destroy: Francis Coppola and the New Hollywood*, Duke University Press, Durham, NC, 1995
—. ed. *New American Cinema*, Duke University Press, Durham, NC, 1998
—. *Hollywood v. Hard Core: How the Struggle Over Censorship Created the Modern Film Industry*, New York University Press, New York, NY, 2000
—. ed. *The End of Cinema As We Know It: American Film In the Nineties*, New York University Press, New York, NY, 2002
J. Leyda, ed *Filmmakers Speak*, Da Capo, New York, 1977/ 84
—. *Kino: A History of the Russian and Soviet Cinema*, 3rd edition, Allen & Unwin, London, 1983
M. Litch. *Philosophy Through Film*, Routledge, London, 2002
P. Livington. *Ingmar Bergman and the Rituals of Art*, Cornell University Press, Ithaca, NY, 1982
V. LoBrutto. *Sound-On-Film*, Praeger, New York, NY, 1994
M. Locke & C. Warren, eds. *Hail Mary: Women and the Sacred In Film*, Southern Illinois University Press, Carbondale, 1993
R. Long. *Ingmar Bergman*, Abrams, New York, NY, 1994
Y. Loshitzky. *The Radical Faces of Godard and Bertolucci*, Wayne State University Press, Detroit, MI, 1995
—. ed. *Spielberg's Holocaust: Critical Interpretation On 'Schindler's List'*, Indiana University Press, Bloomington, IN, 1997
L. Lourdeaux. *Italian and Irish Filmmakers In America: Ford, Capra, Coppola and Scorsese*, Temple University Press, Philadelphia, PA, 1990
J. MacBean: "Godard and the Dziga Vertov Group", *Film Quarterly*. 26, 1, Autumn, 1972
—. *Film and Revolution*, Indiana University Press, Bloomington, IN, 1975
C. MacCabe. "Principles of realism and pleasure", *Screen*, 17, 3, Autumn, 1976
—. *Godard, Images, Sound, Politics*, Macmillan/ British Film Institute, London, 1980
—. *Godard: A Portrait of the Artist At 70*, Faber, London, 2003
P. Malone. *Movie Christs and Antichrists*, Crossroad, 1990
R. Maltby. *Harmless Entertainment: Hollywood and the Ideology of Consensus*, Scarecrow Press, Metuchen, NJ, 1983
—. & I. Craven. *Hollywood Cinema: An Introduction*, Blackwell, Oxford, 1995
—. *Hollywood Cinema*, 2nd ed., Blackwell, Oxford, 2003
M. Mancini & G. Perella. *Pier Paolo Pasolini: corpi e luoghi*, Theorema, Bologna, 1982
Mao Tse-tung. *The Little Red Book (Quotations From Chairman Mao Tse-tung)*, Foreign Language Press, Peking, 1967
M. Marie. *The French New Wave*, Blackwell, Oxfrord, 2003
E. Marks & I. de Courtivron, eds. *New French Feminisms: an anthology*, Harvester Wheatsheaf, Hemel Hempstead, 1981
A. Martin. "Recital: Three Lyrical Interludes In Godard", in M. Temple, 2000
T. Martin. *Images and the Imageless: a Study In Religious Consciousness and*

Film, Bucknell University Press, 1981
G. Mast et al, eds. *Film Theory and Criticism: Introductory Readings*, Oxford University Press, New York, NY, 1992a
—. & B Kawin, *A Short History of the Movies*, Macmillan, New York, NY, 1992b
E. Mathijs, ed. *The Cinema of the Low Countries*, Wallflower Press, London, 2004
T.D. Matthews. *Censored*, Chatto & Windus, London, 1994
J.R. May & M. Bird, eds. *Religion In Film*, University of Tennessee Press, Knoxville, 1982
—. *Image and Likeness: Religious Vision In American Film Classics*, Paulist, 1992
—. *New Image of Religious Film*, Sheed & Ward, London, 1996
J. Mayne. *The Woman At the Keyhole: Feminism and Women's Cinema*, Indiana University Press, Bloomington, IN, 1990
L. Mazdon. *Encore Hollywood: Remaking French Cinema*, British Film Institute, London, 2000
M. Medved. *Hollywood vs. America*, HarperCollins, London, 1992
P. Mellencamp & P. Rosen, eds. *Cinema Histories, Cinema Practices*, University Publications of America, Frederick, MD, 1984
—. *A Fine Romance: Five Ages of Film Feminism*, Temple University Press, Philadelphia, PA, 1995
X. Mendik & S. Schneider, eds. *Underground U.S.A.: Filmmaking Beyond the Hollywood Canon*, Wallflower Press, London, 2002
J. Mellen. "*Vladimir and Rosa*", *Cinéaste*, 4, 3, Winter, 1971
M. Merrill. "Black Panthers In the New Wave", *Film Culture*, 53, 54, 55, Spring, 1972
C. Metz. *Film Language: A Semiotics of the Cinema*, tr. M. Taylor, Oxford University Press, New York, NY, 1974
M. Miles. *Seeing and Believing: Religion and Values In the Movies*, Beacon, Boston, MA, 1996
F. Miller. C*ensored Hollywood: Sex, Sin and Violence On Screen*, Turner Publishing, Atlanta, 1994
M.C. Miller. ed. *Seeing Through Movies*, Pantheon, New York, NY, 1990
T. Miller et al, eds. *Global Hollywood*, British Film Institute, London, 2001
T. Milne. *Sight & Sound*, 34, 1, 1966
T. Modleski, ed. *Studies In Entertainment*, Indiana University Press, Bloomington, IN, 1987
—. *The Women Who Knew Too Much: Hitchcock and Feminist Theory*, Methuen, London, 1988
—. *Feminism Without Women: Culture and Criticism In a 'Postfeminist' Age*, Routledge, London, 1991
T. Moi. *Sexual/ Textual Politics: Feminist Literary Theory*, Methuen, London, 1983
J. Monaco. *The Films of Stanley Kubrick*, New York, NY, 1974
—. *The New Wave: Truffaut, Godard, Chabrol, Rohmer, Rivette*, Oxford University Press, New York, NY, 1977a
—. *How To Read a Film*, Oxford University Press, New York, NY, 1977b
G. Moore, ed. *Conrad On Film*, Oxford University Press, Oxford, 1997
K. Moore. "Reincarnating the Radical: Godard's *Je vous salue, Marie*", *Cinema Journal*, 34, 1, Fall, 1994
P. Mosley. *Ingmar Bergman*, Marion Boyars, London, 1981
G. Mulholland. *Popcorn: Fifty Years of Rock 'n' Roll Movies*, Orion Books, London, 2011
R. Murphy. *Sixties British Cinema*, British Film Institute, London, 1992
—. ed. *British Cinema of the 90s*, British Film Institute, London, 2000

—. ed. *The British Cinema Book*, Palgrave/ Macmillan, London, 2nd edition, 2009
R. Murray. *Images In the Dark: An Encyclopedia of Gay and Lesbian Film and Video*, Titan Books, London, 1998
J. Naremore. *The Magic World of Orson Welles*, Southern Methodist University Press, Dallas, TX, 1989
—. ed. *Orson Welles's Citizen Kane: A Casebook*, Oxford University Press, New York, NY, 2004
J. Natoli. *Hauntings: Popular Film and American Culture 1990-92*, State University of New York Press, Albany, NY, 1994
—. *Speeding To the Millennium: Film and Culture 1993-1995*, State University of New York Press, Albany, NY, 1998
—. *Postmodern Journeys: Film and Culture, 1996-1998*, State University of New York Press, Albany, NY, 2001
S. Neale. *Cinema and Technology*, Macmillan, London, 1985
—. & B. Neve. *Film and Politics In America*, Routledge, London, 1992
—. & M. Smith, eds. *Contemporary Hollywood Cinema*, Routledge, London, 1998
—. *Genre and Hollywood*, Routledge, London, 2000
—. *Genre and Contemporary Hollywood*, Routledge, London, 2002
J. Nelmes, ed. *An Introduction To Film Studies*, Routledge, London, 1996
T. Nelson. *Kubrick: Inside a Film Artist's Maze*, Indiana University Press, Bloomington, IN, 1982
R. Neupert. "Je vous salue, Marie: Godard the Father", *Film Criticism*, 10, 1, Autumn, 1985
—. *The End: Narration and Closure In the Cinema*, Wayne State University Press, Detroit, MI, 1995
—. *A History of the French New Wave*, University of Wisconsin Press, Maidson, 2003
P. Norman. *The Stones*, Elm Tree, 1972
—. *Sympathy For the Devil: The Rolling Stones Story*, Linden Press, New York, NY, 1984
—. *Mick Jagger*, HarperCollins, 2012
G. Nowell-Smith. *Visconti*, British Film Institute, London, 1973
—. ed. *The Oxford History of World Cinema*, Oxford University Press, Oxford, 1996
—. & S. Ricci, eds. *Hollywood and Europe*, British Film Institute, London, 1998
Michael O'Pray. *Avant-Garde Film*, Wallflower Press, London, 2003
J. Orr & C. Nicholson, eds. *Cinema and Fiction*, Edinburgh University Press, Edinburgh, 1992
—. *Cinema and Modernity*, Polity Press, Cambridge, 1993
—. *Contemporary Cinema*, Edinburgh University Press, Edinburgh, 1998
—. & O. Taxidou, eds. *Postwar Cinema and Modernity: A Film Reader*, Edinburgh University Press, Edinburgh, 2000
C. Ostwalt. "Religion & Popular Movies", *Journal of Religion and Film*, 2, 3, 1998
R. Palmer, ed. *The Cinematic Text*, A.M.S., New York, NY, 1989
—. *Hollywood's Dark Cinema: The American Film Noir*, Twayne, New York, NY, 1994
—. ed. *Perspectives On Film Noir*, G.K. Hall, Boston, 1996
J. Park. *Learning To Dream: The New British Cinema*, Faber, London, 1984
—. *British Cinema*, B.T. Batsford, London, 1990
P.P. Pasolini. *Il Vangelo Secondo Matteo*, Garzanti, Milan, 1964
—. *Oedipus Rex*, Lorrimer Publishing, 1984
—. *Pasolini On Pasolini*, ed. O. Stack, Thames & Hudson, London, 1969
A. Pavelin. *Fifty Religious Films*, A. P. Pavelin, Chiselhurst, Kent, 1990

R. Peck, ed. "Myth, Religious Typology and Recent Cinema", *Christianity and Literature*, 42, 1993
C. Penley, ed. *Feminism and Film Theory*, Routledge, London, 1988
—. et al, eds. *Close Encounters: Film, Feminism and Science Fiction*, University of Minnesota Press, Minneapolis, 1991
—. & A. Ross, eds. *Technoculture*, University of Minnesota Press, Minneapolis, MN, 1991
V.F. Perkins. *Film As Film: Understanding and Judging Movies*, Penguin, London, 1972
D. Petrie. *Creativity and Constraint In the British Film Industry*, Macmillan, London, 1991
—. ed. *New Questions of British Cinema*, British Film Institute, London, 1992
—. *Screening Europe: Image and Identity In Contemporary European Cinema*, British Film Institute, London, 1992
—. *Inside Stories: Diaries of Filmmakers At Work*, British Film Institute, London, 1996
G. Phelps. *Film Censorship*, Gollancz, London, 1975
J. Phillips. *You'll Never Eat Lunch In This Town Again*, Heinemann, London, 1991
K. Phillips. *New German Filmmakers*, Ungar, New York, NY, 1984
Pierrot le Fou, tr. P. Whitehead, Lorrimer, London, 1969
C. Potter. *Image, Sound and Story: The Art of Telling In Film*, Secker & Warburg, London, 1990
P. Powrie, ed. *French Cinema In the 1990s*, Oxford University Press, Oxford, 1999
—. *Jean-Jacques Beineix*, Manchester University Press, Manchester, 2001
M. Praz. *The Romantic Agony*, tr. Davidson, Oxford University Press, Oxford, 1933
R. Prendergast. *Film Music*, W.W. Norton, New York, NY, 1992
S. Prince. *Savage Cinema: Sam Peckinpah and the Rise of Ultraviolent Movies*, University of Texas Press, Austin, TX, 1998
—. ed. *Screening Violence*, Athlone Press, London, 2000
—. *A New Pot of Gold: Hollywood Under the Electronic Rainbow*, Scribners, New York, NY, 2000
S. Projansky. *Watching Rape: Film and Television In Postfeminism Culture*, New York University Press, New York, NY, 2001
M. Pye & Lynda Myles. *The Movie Brats: How the Film Generation Took Over Hollywood*, Faber, London, 1979
E. Rabkin & G. Slusser, eds. *Shadows of the Magic Lamp: Fantasy and Science Fiction In Film*, Southern Illinois University Press, Carbondale, IL, 1985
T. Rayns, ed. *Fassbinder*, British Film Institute, London, 1979
K. Reader. *Robert Bresson,* Manchester University Press, Mancheser, 2000
A. Reinhartz. "Jesus in Film: Hollywood Perspectives on the Jewishness of Jesus", *Journal of Religion and Film*, 2, 2, 1998
E. Rentschler. *West German Film*, Redgrave, New York, NY, 1984
—. ed. *German Film and Literature*, Methuen, London, 1986
—. ed. *West German Filmmakers On Film: Visions and Voices*, Holmes & Meier, New York, NY, 1988
P. Rice & P. Waugh, eds. *Modern Literary Theory: A Reader*, Arnold, London, 1992
J. Richards, ed. *Films and British National Identity*, Manchester University Press, Manchester, 1997
K. Richards. *Life,* Weidenfeld & Nicholson, London, 2010
M. Richardson. *Surrealism and Cinema*, Berg, New York, NY, 2006
D. Richie. *The Films of Akira Kurosawa*, University of California Press, Berkeley, CA, 1965

S. Richmond. *The Rough Guide To Anime*, Rough Guides, 2009
A. Riding. "What's In a Name If the Name Is Godard?", *New York Times*, Oct 25, 1992
R. Rinaldi. *Pier Paolo Pasolini*, Mursia, Milan, 1982
J. Riordan. *Stone*, Aurum, London, 1996
G. Ritzer. *The McDonaldization of Society*, Sage, London, 1995
—. *The McDonaldization Thesis*, Sage, London, 1997
J. Robertson. *The British Board of Film Censors*, Croom Helm, 1985
—. *The Hidden Cinema*, Routledge, London, 1989
D. Robinson. *World Cinema*, Methuen, London, 1981
G. Rodgerson & E. Wilson, eds. *Pornography and Censorship*, Lawrence & Wishart, London, 1991
S. Rohdie. *Antonioni*, British Film Institute, London, 1990
—. *The Passion of Pier Paolo Pasolini*, British Film Institute, London, 1995
G. Roheim, ed. *Psychoanalysis and the Social Sciences*, III, International University Press, New York, NY, 1951
V. Roloff & S. Winter, eds. *Godard Intermedial*, Stauffenburg, Tübinigen, 1997
P. Rosen, ed. *Narrative, Apparatus, Ideology: A Film Theory Reader*, Columbia University Press, New York, NY, 1986
J. Rosenbaum. "Eight Obstacles To the Appreciation of Godard In the United States", in R. Bellour, 1992
—. *Placing Movies*, University of California Press, Berkeley, CA, 1995
A. Rosenstone, ed. *Revisioning History: Film and the Construction of a New Past*, Princeton University Press, Princeton, NJ, 1995
R. Roud. *Jean-Luc Godard*, Thames & Hudson, London, 1970
M. Roussel. *France-Soir*, Jan 23, 1985
M Rubenstein. *Postcards From Alphaville: Jean-Luc Godard In Contemporary Art*, Institute for Contemporary Art, Long Island City, 1992
R. Ruiz. *The Poetics of Cinema*, Dis Voir, Paris, 1995
K. Russell. *A British Picture: An Autobiography*, Heinemann, London, 1989
M. Russell & J. Young. *Film Music*, RotoVision, 2000
V. Russo. *The Celluloid Closet: Homosexuality In the Movies*, Harper & Row, New York, NY, 1981
T. Ryall. *Alfred Hitchcock and the British Cinema*, Croom Helm, 1986
C. Salewicz. *Oliver Stone*, Orion, London, 1999
J. Sanford. *The New German Cinema*, Da Capo Press, New York, NY, 1982
A. Sarris. "Jean-Luc Godard Now", *Interview*, 24, 7, July, 1994
T. Schatz. *Hollywood Genres*, Random House, New York, NY, 1981
—. *Old Hollywood/ New Hollywood*, U.M.I. Research Press, Ann Arbor, MI, 1983
—. *The Genius of the System: Hollywood Filmmaking In the Studio Era*, Pantheon, New York, NY 1988
P. Schrader. *Transcendental Style In Film: Ozu, Bresson, Dreyer*, Da Capo Press, 1972
M. Schumacher. *Francis Ford Coppola*, Bloomsbury, London, 2000
M. Scorsese. *Scorsese On Scorsese*, ed. D. Thompson & I. Christie, Faber, London, 1989, 1995
Screen Reader I: Cinema/ Ideology/ Politics, Society for Education in Film & TV, 1977
Screen Reader II: Cinema and Semiotics, British Film Institute, London, 1982
C. Sharrett, ed. *Crisis Cinema*, Maisonneuve Press, Washington, DC. 1993
T. Shaw. *British Cinema and the Cold War*, I.B. Tauris, London, 2001
D. Shipman. *The Story of Cinema*, Hodder & Stoughton, London, 1984
—. *Caught In the Act: Sex and Eroticism In the Movies*, Hamish Hamilton, London, 1986
T. Shone. *Blockbuster: How the Jaws and Jedi Generation Turned Hollywood Into a Boom-Town*, Scribner, London, 2005

E. Showalter, ed. *The New Feminist Criticism*, Virago, London, 1986

R. Shuker. *Understanding Popular Music*, Routledge, London, 1994

—. *Key Concepts In Popular Music*, Routledge, London, 1998

E. Siciliano. *Pasolini: A Biography*, Bloomsbury, London, 1987

L. Sider et al, eds. *Soundscapes: The School of Sound Lectures 1998-2001*, Wallflower Press, London, 2003

M. Silberman. *German Cinema*, Wayne State University Press, Detroit, MI, 1995

K. Silverman. *The Subject of Semiotics*, Oxford University Press, New York, NY, 1983

—. *The Acoustic Mirror: The Female Voice In Psychoanalysis and Cinema*, Indiana University Press, Bloomington, IN, 1988

—. *Male Subjectivity At the Margins*, Routledge, London, 1992

—. & H. Farocki. *Speaking About Godard*, New York University Press, New York, NY, 1998

P. Adams Sitney, ed. *The Film Culture Reader*, Praeger, New York, NY, 1970

—. ed. *The Avant-Garde Film: A Reader of Theory and Criticism*, New York University Press, New York, NY, 1978

—. *Visionary Film: The American Avant-Garde, 1943-1978*, 2nd ed., Oxford University Press, New York, NY, 1979

—. *Vital Crises In Italian Cinema*, University of Texas Press, Austin, TX, 1995

D. Smith. *American Filmmakers Today*, Blandford Press, Poole, 1984

J. Smith. *Looking Away: Hollywood and Vietnam*, Scribner's, New York, NY, 1975

M. Smith. *Engaging Characters*, Oxford University Press, 1995

V. Sobchack. *The Limits of Infinity: The American Science Fiction Film*, A.S. Barnes, New York, NY, 1980

—. *Screening Space: The American Science Fiction Film*, Ungar, New York, NY, 1987/1993

—. *The Address of the Eye: A Phenomenology of Film Experience*, Princeton University Press, Princeton, NJ, 1992

—. ed. *The Persistence of History: Cinema, Television, and the Modern Event*, Routledge, London, 1995

A. Solomon. *20th Century-Fox: A Corporate and Financial History*, Scarcrow Press, Metuchen, NJ, 1988

J. Solomon. *The Ancient World In the Cinema*, London, 1978

—. *The Ancient World In the Cinema*, Yale University Press, New Haven, CT, 2001

S. Sontag. *Styles of Radical Will*, Farrar, Straus & Giroux, New York, 1966

P. Sorlin. *The Film In History: Restaging the Past*, Blackwell, Oxford, 1980

S. Spignesi. *The Woody Allen Companion*, Plexus, London, 1994

D. Spoto. *The Life of Alfred Hitchcock*, Collins, London, 1983

J. Stacey. *Hollywood Cinema and Female Spectatorship*, Routledge, London, 1994

J. Staiger. *Interpreting Films*, Princeton University Press, Princeton, NJ, 1992

—. *Perverse Spectators: The Practices of Film Reception*, New York University Press, New York, NY, 2000

R. Stam et al. *New Vocabularies In Film Semiotics*, Routledge, London, 1992

B. Steene. *Ingmar Bergman*, Twayne, Boston, MA, 1968

—. ed. *Focus On The Seventh Seal*, Prentice-Hall, Englewood Cliffs, NJ, 1972

—. *Ingmar Bergman: A Guide To References and Resources*, Boston, MA, 1987

N. Steimatsky. "Pasolini on Terra Sancta: Towards a Theology of Film", *Yale Journal of Criticism*, 11, 1, 1998

E. Stein. "*Hail Mary*", *Film Comment*, 21, Nov, 1985

L. Stern. *The Scorsese Connection*, British Film Institute, London, 1995

D. Sterritt. *The Films of Jean-Luc Godard*, Cambridge University Press,

Cambridge, 1999
—. "Godardiana: A Reply to Marcia Landy", *Film-Philosophy*, 6, 31, Sept, 2002
P. Steven, ed. *Jump Cut: Hollywood, Politics and Counter Cinema*, Between the Lines, Toronto, 1985
G. Stewart. *Between Film and Screen: Modernism's Photo Synthesis*, University of Chicago Press, Chicago, IL, 1999
J. Still & M. Worton, eds. *Textuality and Sexuality: Reading Theories and Practices*, Manchester University Press, Manchester, 1993
S. Street. *British National Cinema*, Routledge, London, 1997/ 2009
C. Sylvester, ed. *The Penguin Book of Hollywood*, Penguin, London, 1999
Y. Tasker. *Spectacular Bodies: Gender, Genre and the Action Cinema*, Routledge, London, 1993
—. *Working Girls: Gender and Sexuality In Popular Cinema*, Routledge, London, 1998
—. ed. *Fifty Contemporary Filmmakers*, Routledge, London, 2002
R. Taylor & I. Christie, eds. *The Film Factory: Russian and Soviet Cinema In Documents*, Routledge, London, 1988
—. *Inside the Film Factory: New Approaches To Russian and Soviet Cinema*, Routledge, London, 1991
—. & D. Spring, eds. *Stalinism and Soviet Cinema*, Routledge, London, 1993
—. et al, eds. *The B.F.I. Companion To Eastern European and Russian Cinema*, British Film Institute, London, 2000
M. Temple & J. Williams, eds. *The Cinema Alone: Essays On the Work of Jean-Luc Godard, 1985-2000*, Amsterdam University Press, Amsterdam, 2000
—. et al, eds. *Godard For Ever*, Black Dog Publishing, London, 2004
S. Teo. *Hong Kong Cinema*, British Film Institute, London, 1997
D. Thomas. *Reading Hollywood: Spaces and Meanings In American Film*, Wallflower, London, 2001
N. Thomas, ed. *International Dictionary of Films and Filmmakers: Films*, St James Press, London, 1990
K. Thompson. *Exporting Entertainment: America In the World Film Market, 1907-1934*, British Film Institute, London, 1985
—. *Breaking the Glass Armor: Neoformalist Film Analysis*, Princeton University Press, Princeton, NJ, 1988
—. & D. Bordwell. *Film History: An Introduction*, McGraw-Hill, New York, NY, 1994
—. *Storytelling In the New Hollywood*, Harvard University Press, Cambridge, MA, 1999
D. Thomson. "That Breathless Moment", *Sight & Sound*, 7, 1994
—. *A Biographical Dictionary of Film*, Deutsch, London, 1995
—. *Rosebud: The Story of Orson Welles*, Little, Brown, Boston, MA, 1996
—. *The Big Screen*, Allen Lane 2012
C. Tohill & P. Tombs. *Immoral Tales: Sex and Horror Cinema In Europe 1956-1984*, Titan Books, London, 1995
C. Tonetti. *Luchino Visconti*, Columbus Books, 1985
—. *Bernardo Bertolucci*, Twayne, Boston, MA, 1994
R.B. Toplin, ed. *Oliver Stone's USA*, University of Kansas Press, Lawrence, KS, 2000
—. *Reel History: In Defense of Hollywood*, University of Kansas Press, Lawrence, KS, 2002
E. Törnqvist. *Between Stage and Screen: Ingmar Bergman Directs*, Amsterdam University Press, Amsterdam, 1995
J. Trevelyan. *What the Censor Saw*, Michael Joseph, London, 1973
H. Trosman. *Contemporary Psychoanalysis and Masterworks of Art and Film*, New York University Press, New York, NY, 2000

F. Truffaut. *The Films In My Life*, tr. L. Mayhew, Penguin, London, 1982
—. *Hitchcock*, Simon & Schuster, New York, NY, 1984
K. Turan & S.F. Zito: *Sinema: American Pornographic Films and the People Who Make Them*, Praeger, New York, NY, 1974
P. Tyler. *Sex Psyche Etcetera In the Film*, Horizon, New York, NY, 1969
—. *Screening the Sexes: Homosexuality In the Movies*, Doubleday, New York, NY, 1973
M. Valck & M. Hagener, eds. *Cinephilia: Movies, Love and Memory*, Amsterdam University Press, Amsterdam, 2005
K. Van Gunden. *Fantasy Films*, McFarland, Jefferson, NC 1989
—. *Postmodern Auteurs: Coppola, Lucas, De Palma, Spielberg and Scorsese*, McFarland, Jefferson, NC 1991
R. van Scheers. *Paul Verhoeven*, Faber, London, 1997
G. Vincendeau, ed. *Encyclopedia of European Cinema*, British Film Institute, London, 1995
—. ed. *Film/ Literature/ Heritage: A Sight & Sound Reader*, British Film Institute, London, 2001
P. Virilio & S. Lotringer. *The Aesthetics of Disappearance*, tr. P. Beitchman, Semiotext(e), New York, NY, 1991
—. *War and Cinema*, Verso, London, 1992
—. *The Vision Machine*, tr. J. Rose, Indiana University Press, Bloomington, IN, 1994
—. *The Art of the Motor*, tr. J. Rose, Minnesota University Press, Minneapolis, 1995
J. Vizzard. *See No Evil: Life Inside a Hollywood Censor*, Simon & Schuster, New York, NY, 1970
A. Vogel. *Film As a Subversive Art*, Weidenfeld & Nicolson, London, 1974
J. Vronskaya. *Young Soviet Film Makers*, Allen & Unwin, London, 1972
A. Walker. *Sex In the Movies*, Penguin, London, 1968
—. *National Heroes: British Cinema In the Seventies and Eighties*, Harrap, London, 1985
—. *Hollywood, England: The British Film Industry In the Sixties*, Harrap, London, 1986
—. et al. *Stanley Kubrick, Director*, Weidenfeld & Nicolson, London, 1999
J. Walker. *The Once and Future Film: British Cinema In the 1970s and 1980s*, Methuen, London, 1985
—. *Art and Artists On Screen*, Manchester University Press, Manchester, 1993
M. Walsh. "Godard and Me: Jean-Pierre Gorin Talks", *Take One*, 5, 1, Feb, 1976
J. Wasko. *Movies and Money*, Ablex, NJ, 1982
—. *Hollywood In the Information Age*, Polity Press, Cambridge, 1994
J. Waters. "*Hail Mary*", *American Film*, 11, Jan, 1986
P. Webb. *The Erotic Arts*, Secker & Warburg, London, 1975
A. Weiss. *Vampires and Violets: Lesbians In Film*, Penguin, London, 1993
E. Weiss. & J. Belton, eds. *Film Sound: Theory and Practice*, Columbia University Press, New York, NY, 1989
O. Welles. *This Is Orson Welles*, HarperCollins, London, 1992
—. *Orson Welles: Interviews*, ed. M. Estrin, University of Mississippi Press, Jackson, 2002
A. White. "Double Helix: Jean-Luc Godard", *Film Comment*, 32, 2, Mch, 1996
L. White. *Obsession*, T.V. Boardman, London, 1962
V. Wright Wexman. *Roman Polanski*, Columbus Books, 1987
P. Willemen, ed. *Pier Paolo Pasolini*, British Film Institute, London, 1977
J. Williams & M. Temple, eds. *The Cinema Alone: Essays On the Work of Jean-Luc Godard*, Amsterdam University Press, Amsterdam, 2000
L. Williams, ed. *Viewing Positions: Ways of Seeing Film*, Rutgers University Press, New Brunswick, NJ, 1995

L.R. Williams. *Critical Desire: Psychoanalysis and the Literary Subject*, Arnold, London, 1995
—. *Sex In the Head*, Harvester Wheatsheaf, Hemel Hempstead, 1995
D. Wills, ed. *Jean-Luc Godard's Pierrot le Fou*, Cambridge University Press, 2000
S. Willis. *High Contrast: Race and Gender In Contemporary Hollywood Film*, Duke University Press, Durham, NC, 1997
R. Wilson & W. Dissanayake, eds. *Global/Local: Cultural Production and the Transnational Imaginary*, Duke University Press, Durham, NC, 1996
E. Wistrich. *'I Don't Mind the Sex It's the Violence': Film Censorship Explored*, Marion Boyars, London, 1978
M. Wolf. *The Entertainment Economy*, Penguin, London, 1999
P. Wollen: *Signs and Meaning In the Cinema*, Secker & Warburg, London, 1972
—. *Readings and Writings: Semiotic Counter-Strategies*, Verso, London, 1982
B. Wood. *Orson Welles*, Greenwood Press, Westport, CT, 1990
M. Wood. *America In the Movies*, London, 1974
P. Wood, ed. *Scorsese: A Journey Through the American Psyche*, Plexus, London, 2005
R. Wood. *Ingmar Bergman*, Praeger, New York, NY, 1969
—. *Hollywood From Vietnam To Reagan... and Beyond*, Columbia University Press, New York, NY, 2003
T. Woods. *Beginning Postmodernism*, Manchester University Press, Manchester, 1999
J. Wyatt. *High Concept: Movies and Marketing In Hollywood*, University of Texas Press, Austin, TX, 1994
E.C.M. Yau, ed. *At Full Speed: Hong Kong Cinema In a Borderless World*, University of Minnesota Press, Minneapolis, MN, 1998
J. Young, ed. *The Art of Memory: Holocaust Memorials In History*, Prestel, New York, NY, 1994
V. Young. *Cinema Borealis: Ingmar Bergman and the Swedish Ethos*, Avon, New York, NY, 1971
J. Zipes, ed. *The Oxford Companion To Fairy Tales*, Oxford University Press, 2000
—. *The Enchanted Screen: The Unknown History of Fairy-tale Films*, Routledge, New York, NY, 2011
S. Zizek. *Looking Awry*, Verso, London, 1991
—. *Enjoy Your Symptom Jacques Lacan In Hollywood and Out*, Routledge, New York, NY, 1992
—. *The Metastases of Enjoyment*, Verso, London, 1994
—. *The Indivisible Remainder*, Verso, London, 1996
—. *The Fright of Real Tears: The Uses and Misuses of Lacan In Film Theory*, British Film Institute, London, 1999
J. Zuker. *Francis Ford Coppola: A Guide To References and Resources*, G.K. Hall, Boston, MA, 1984

JEREMY ROBINSON has published poetry, fiction, and studies of J.R.R. Tolkien, Samuel Beckett, Thomas Hardy, André Gide and D.H. Lawrence. Robinson has edited poetry books by Novalis, Ursula Le Guin, Friedrich Hölderlin, Francesco Petrarch, Dante Alighieri, Arseny Tarkovsky, and Rainer Maria Rilke.

Books on film and animation include: *The Akira Book* • *The Art of Katsuhiro Otomo* • *The Art of Masamune Shirow* • *The Ghost In the Shell Book* • *Fullmetal Alchemist* • *Cowboy Bebop: The Anime and Movie* • *The Cinema of Hayao Miyazaki* • *Hayao Miyazaki: Pocket Guide* • *Princess Mononoke: Pocket Movie Guide* • *Spirited Away: Pocket Movie Guide* • *Blade Runner and the Cinema of Philip K. Dick* • *Blade Runner: Pocket Movie Guide* • *The Cinema of Donald Cammell* • *Performance: Donald Cammell: Nic Roeg: Pocket Movie Guide* • *Pasolini: Il Cinema di Poesia/ The Cinema of Poetry* • *Salo: Pocket Movie Guide* • *The Trilogy of Life Movies: Pocket Movie Guide* • *The Gospel According To Matthew: Pocket Movie Guide* • *The Ecstatic Cinema of Tony Ching Siu-tung* • *Tsui Hark: The Dragon Master of Chinese Cinema* • *The Swordsman: Pocket Movie Guide* • *A Chinese Ghost Story: Pocket Movie Guide* • *Ken Russell: England's Great Visionary Film Director and Music Lover* • *Tommy: Ken Russell: The Who: Pocket Movie Guide* • *Women In Love: Ken Russell: D.H. Lawrence: Pocket Movie Guide* • *The Devils: Ken Russell: Pocket Movie Guide* • *Walerian Borowczyk: Cinema of Erotic Dreams* • *The Beast: Pocket Movie Guide* • *The Lord of the Rings Movies* • *The Fellowship of the Ring: Pocket Movie Guide* • *The Two Towers: Pocket Movie Guide* • *The Return of the King: Pocket Movie Guide* • *Jean-Luc Godard: The Passion of Cinema* • *The Sacred Cinema of Andrei Tarkovsky* • *Andrei Tarkovsky: Pocket Guide*.

'It's amazing for me to see my work treated with such passion and respect. There is nothing resembling it in the U.S. in relation to my work.'
(Andrea Dworkin)

'This model monograph – it is an exemplary job, and I'm very proud that he has accorded me a couple of mentions… The subject matter of his book is beautifully organised and dead on beam.'
(Lawrence Durrell, on *The Light Eternal: A Study of J.M.W. Turner*)

'Jeremy Robinson's poetry is certainly jammed with ideas, and I find it very interesting for that reason. It's certainly a strong imprint of his personality.'
(Colin Wilson)

'*Sex-Magic-Poetry-Cornwall* is a very rich essay… It is a very good piece… vastly stimulating and insightful.'
(Peter Redgrove)

MEDIA, CINEMA, FEMINISM and CULTURAL STUDIES

J.R.R. Tolkien: The Books, The Films, The Whole Cultural Phenomenon
J.R.R. Tolkien: Pocket Guide
The *Lord of the Rings* Movies: Pocket Guide
The Cinema of Hayao Miyazaki
Hayao Miyazaki: *Princess Mononoke*: Pocket Movie Guide
Hayao Miyazaki: *Spirited Away*: Pocket Movie Guide
Tim Burton : Hallowe'en For Hollywood
Ken Russell
Ken Russell: *Tommy*: Pocket Movie Guide
The Ghost Dance: The Origins of Religion
The Peyote Cult
Cixous, Irigaray, Kristeva: The *Jouissance* of French Feminism
Julia Kristeva: Art, Love, Melancholy, Philosophy, Semiotics and Psychoanalysis
Luce Irigaray: Lips, Kissing, and the Politics of Sexual Difference
Hélène Cixous I Love You: The *Jouissance* of Writing
Andrea Dworkin
'Cosmo Woman': The World of Women's Magazines
Women in Pop Music
HomeGround: The Kate Bush Anthology
Discovering the Goddess (Geoffrey Ashe)
The Poetry of Cinema
The Sacred Cinema of Andrei Tarkovsky
Andrei Tarkovsky: Pocket Guide
Andrei Tarkovsky: *Mirror*: Pocket Movie Guide
Andrei Tarkovsky: *The Sacrifice*: Pocket Movie Guide
Walerian Borowczyk: Cinema of Erotic Dreams
Jean-Luc Godard: The Passion of Cinema
Jean-Luc Godard: *Hail Mary*: Pocket Movie Guide
Jean-Luc Godard: *Contempt*: Pocket Movie Guide
Jean-Luc Godard: *Pierrot le Fou*: Pocket Movie Guide
John Hughes and Eighties Cinema
Ferris Bueller's Day Off: Pocket Movie Guide
Jean-Luc Godard: Pocket Guide
The Cinema of Richard Linklater
Liv Tyler: Star In Ascendance
Blade Runner and the Films of Philip K. Dick
Paul Bowles and Bernardo Bertolucci
Media Hell: Radio, TV and the Press
An Open Letter to the BBC
Detonation Britain: Nuclear War in the UK
Feminism and Shakespeare
Wild Zones: Pornography, Art and Feminism
Sex in Art: Pornography and Pleasure in Painting and Sculpture
Sexing Hardy: Thomas Hardy and Feminism

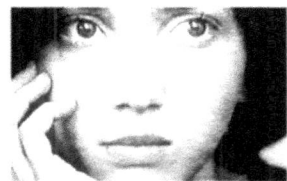
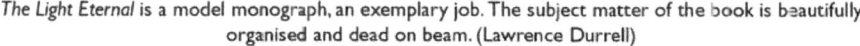

The Light Eternal is a model monograph, an exemplary job. The subject matter of the book is beautifully organised and dead on beam. (Lawrence Durrell)

It is amazing for me to see my work treated with such passion and respect. (Andrea Dworkin)

CRESCENT MOON PUBLISHING
P.O. Box 1312, Maidstone, Kent, ME14 5XU, Great Britain. www.crmoon.com

cresmopub@yahoo.co.uk   www.crescentmoon.org.uk